GARY **SNYDER** *and the Pacific Rim*

GARY SNYDER

CONTEMPORARY NORTH AMERICAN POETRY SERIES

Series Editors Alan Golding, Lynn Keller, and Adalaide Morris and the Pacific Rim   C R E A T I N G

C O U N T E R -

C U L T U R A L

by Timothy Gray   C O M M U N I T Y

U N I V E R S I T Y   O F   I O W A   P R E S S ,   I O W A   C I T Y

University of Iowa Press, Iowa City 52242

Design by Teresa W. Wingfield

The University of Iowa Press is a member of
Green Press Initiative and is committed to
preserving natural resources.

Printed on acid-free paper

Library of Congress Cataloging-in-Publication Data
Gray, Timothy, 1964-.
Gary Snyder and the Pacific Rim: creating countercultural community /
by Timothy Gray.
p.   cm.—(Contemporary North American poetry)
Includes bibliographical references and index.
ISBN 0-87745-976-2 (cloth)
1. Snyder, Gary, 1930- —Homes and haunts—Pacific Coast (North
America).   2. Snyder, Gary, 1930- —Knowledge—Pacific Coast (North
America).   3. Authors, American—Homes and haunts—Pacific Coast
(North America).   4. Snyder, Gary, 1930- —Criticism and interpretation.
5. Pacific Coast (North America)—Intellectual life.   6. California—
Intellectual life—20th century.   7. Pacific Coast (North America)—In
literature.   8. Counterculture—California.   I. Title.   II. Series.
PS3569.N88Z667 2006
811'.5409—dc22   2005052993
[B]

06 07 08 09 10 C 5 4 3 2 1

For my parents and,

especially, for Maria

CONTENTS

The Geographic Impulse

For several years now, I have been interested in the crosscultural energies that circulate in avant-garde literary communities. I have therefore found myself turning time and again to *The New American Poetry 1945–1960*, a landmark collection of early postmodern verse edited by Donald Allen and published by Grove Press in 1960. As Allen hints in the preface to this anthology, it was not just aesthetic experimentation that made the New American Poets so daring and intriguing, but also the fundamental groupishness these writers advocated during a period when individualism was the predominant focus of both cold war political discourse and literary analysis. Displaying an impulse that is communitarian and geographic by turns, Allen divides forty-four American poets into five distinct groups: those associated with Black Mountain College, those who were a part of the San Francisco Renaissance, those affiliated with the Beat Generation, those belonging to the New York School, and lastly, those with no geographical definition. Allen explains that he employs the unusual device of geographical division "in order to give the reader some sense of the history of the period and the primary alignment of the writers" as well as "some sense of milieu." While Allen admits that his divisions "are somewhat arbitrary and cannot be taken as rigid categories," these delineations continue to influence scholars in the field. By acknowledging five bohemian collectives situated on the margins of society—mysterious locations from which there arose articulate rebuttals to the geopolitical doctrines put forth by cold war ideologues and the normative cultural practices sanctioned by business leaders on Wall Street—Allen implored readers to draw a new map of America at midcentury.

Putting a slightly different spin on the geographic impulse spelled out in *The New American Poetry*, my study of Gary Snyder and the Pacific Rim regional idea operates under the assumption that *place-based* does not necessarily mean *place-bound*. The more I study avant-garde literary communities, the more I realize that they depend upon travels, traversals, and transports—both real and imagined—that take writers far beyond the physical boundaries traditionally ascribed to place. For this reason, I prefer to regard Allen's avant-garde milieus as affective sites rather than fixed spots on the map. Accordingly, my analysis of Snyder's role in the San Francisco Renaissance does not stop at the borders of that West Coast city, but pushes further westward to consider various nodal locations along the Pacific Rim where movements or spacings complicate notions of local place. As Michel de Certeau points out in *The Practice of Everyday Life*, "space is composed of intersections of mobile elements. It is in a sense actuated by the ensemble of movements deployed within it" (p. 117).

By the same token, our appreciation of postmodern localities requires an understanding of larger geographic realms, which contain increasingly mobile populations, who in turn facilitate a constant exchange of cultures and the transnational phenomenon Aiha Ong has dubbed "flexible citizenship." Such an understanding does not always come easily. Sorting through the global/local dialectics at play in the San Francisco Renaissance, though, I have come to realize that literary communities are better able to know their place in the world if they have among their ranks a mobile leader willing to trace the contours of a larger domain, make contact with a wide array of its citizens, and return home with this new knowledge in tow. Gary Snyder fulfilled this role in San Francisco during the 1950s and 1960s. Hewing to an extremely fluid exchange pattern, this adventurous poet traveled extensively around the Pacific Rim, updating an old-fashioned quest romance motif and nurturing an incipient global consciousness while committing his experiences to the page.

On the West Coast of America, Snyder's movements across vast stretches of space have inspired comment ever since Jack Kerouac cast him as Japhy

Ryder, the mountain-climbing hero of *The Dharma Bums* (1958). At midcentury, this serene yet relentlessly mobile poet made San Francisco seem like a countercultural utopia, a launching pad to a new and better world, which was often thought to be located somewhere beyond California's shores. For westward-trekking members of the Beat Generation in the 1950s, Snyder signified the calm detachment they regularly associated with Zen Buddhism. For Haight-Ashbury hippies in the 1960s, he stood forth as a tribal leader whose knowledge of Native American social structures made ecstatic dreams of communal living somewhat more practicable, though no less enjoyable. For environmental activists in the early 1970s, he emerged as an articulate spokesman for the lands, waters, and wildlife that provide the West Coast with its natural beauty and rugged character. Throughout the counterculture era, Snyder's journeys to various locations on the Pacific Rim underscored his commitment to primitive traditions and laid the foundation for an alternative lifestyle. Over time, his writings on Pacific Rim cultures became the crucial documents by which San Franciscan bohemians sought to announce their distance from mainstream America.

Some readers might find it ironic that this leader of the San Francisco counterculture was absent from the city for years at a time. In fact, Snyder lived in Asia from 1956 to 1968, during the heyday of the San Francisco Renaissance, studying Buddhism in Kyoto, traveling in India, and returning to America periodically to disseminate the new knowledge he had gained overseas. Presumably, it was Snyder's physical absence from America that caused Donald Allen to separate him from other poets in the San Francisco Renaissance and consign him instead to a group with no geographical definition. But as I hope to show throughout this book, Snyder's long sojourn along an interconnected Pacific Rim was crucial to San Francisco bohemians, insofar as his ensemble of movements provided his friends back home with the geographic spacing they needed to articulate their countercultural message. While in Asia, Snyder served as his community's offshore representative, its far-flung cultural ambassador, keeping lines of communication open across the Pacific and giving Beats and hippies at odds with cold war nationalism a set of physical coordinates with which to plot their idealistic visions of peace, love, and Buddhist mindfulness. Articulating a vision similar to the one advocated by anthropologist Victor Turner in the late 1960s, Snyder had many people in the counterculture believing that oceanic models of *communitas* might well replace hierarchical structures of *societas*, which then, as now, tended to solidify conceptions of nationhood and draw arbitrary divisions between East and West.

After tracing the semicircular route he took across the world's largest ocean—from the West Coast of America, to Northeast Asia, to South Asia, and back again—I am convinced that Snyder was among the first American writers to depict the Pacific region as a unified geometric construct: a rim. As a cultural idea, the Pacific Rim is a relatively new phenomenon, even though it is based upon a primordial arrangement of tectonic plates caused by volcanic and glacial activity. As a student of the earth, Snyder knows these geological origins well. And yet he also knows that American politicians and business leaders in the twentieth century invoked this region according to a starkly different agenda. Be that as it may, these "official" perceptions of the Pacific Rim regional structure are crucial to my study of Snyder's poetry and prose. Indeed, to follow the rise of the Rim idea is not only to be given the geopolitical context within which Snyder's literary output makes sense, but also to survey a host of motivations that shaped the cultural landscape of the American mainland during the early years of the cold war. When Snyder was embarking on his career as a writer, Americans who dared to promote partnership with Asian peoples often became the targets of anticommunist crusaders. It was not until the late 1960s, when the tide had started to turn in the Vietnam War, that political leaders in this nation finally began to invoke a form of Pacific Rim community, and then only in a security context. By the 1980s, of course, business investors were beginning to trumpet the Rim as a vibrant marketplace laying in wait, and over the next two decades the Rim became a familiar buzzword for a somewhat fantastical realm, a utopian space where cultural exchange between East and West finds sanction, a speed zone where the global economy transacts its daily business with increasing rapidity. This is the Pacific Rim that most Americans have come to know. I spend the first portion of this book chronicling the rise of this regional idea not only to enhance our understanding of postmodern globalism, but also to explain how Snyder's countercultural invocation of Asia preceded the official Pacific Rim discourse that began to make news in the 1980s and deviated from that version in fundamentally important ways.

At different junctures in this book I will be discussing the diverse range of cultural, ecological, and libidinal practices shaping Snyder's Pacific Rim consciousness. In four rather lengthy chapters and an epilogue, I supply close readings of the poetry and prose Snyder wrote during the Beat and hippie eras. At the same time, in an effort to analyze the logical frameworks governing his literary development, I focus upon the anthropological, linguistic, neotribal, and environmental models Snyder employed as he challenged the aggressive frontier mentality prevalent among cold war politicians, on the one hand, and the naive strain of Orientalist discourse that held sway in San Francisco's bohemian circles, on the other. By taking this approach, I hope to chart new routes in Snyder scholarship, even as I draw upon previous monographs authored by Tim Dean and Patrick Murphy and upon scores of articles written by other scholars over the past thirty-five years. By limiting my scope to the 1950s and 1960s, and by referring to his personal letters and journal writings in addition to his published work, I hope to provide a thick description of this itinerant poet's unique role within San Francisco's vibrant literary counterculture.

In *Asian/American: Historical Crossings of a Racial Frontier*, David Palumbo-Liu makes a wise decision to "view Asian America through the discourses of the body, the psyche, and space," asking the rhetorical question, "How have Asians been located psychically and physically in what is deemed 'American' space?" My analysis of Snyder takes inspiration and instruction from Palumbo-Liu's way of thinking, even as I reverse course and look westward from California shores. My main goal is to show how a white writer located himself psychically and physically in what cold war America usually deemed Asian space, but which the poet himself deemed part of an interconnected geographical realm, or what Pacific Rim scholar Rob Wilson refers to as a transnational imaginary. Rather than regarding Snyder as a solitary nature poet grounded firmly in the rugged landscapes of California, I prefer to view him as a hemispheric traveler, a social magnet for people seeking spiritual enlightenment, and a literary visionary whose far-flung allegiances across the Pacific region highlighted the premodern foundations of global culture. Adopting the perspective of cultural geography as a means of supplementing traditional modes of literary criticism and biography, *Gary Snyder and the Pacific Rim* not only tracks the early career of a maverick intellectual but also provides new contexts for the counterculture literature that emerged out of California a half century ago.

ACKNOWLEDGMENTS

I began this book on the shores of the Pacific Rim nearly ten years ago. Mapping out a project of this scope has been a tremendous challenge, to put it mildly. Fortunately, I have benefited from the support of many along the way. I must first thank Herb Levine, Tony Ugolnik, and Joe Voelker, who introduced me to the complexities of American poetry during my undergraduate years at Franklin and Marshall College. At the University of California, Santa Barbara, I wish to thank Julie Carlson, Aranye Fradenburg, and Christopher Newfield. Special thanks are reserved for Victoria Harrison, my kind and insightful dissertation director. I also wish to thank my student friends from those days, especially Rachel Adams, Jon Connolly, Michael Holley, and Tim Wager. Michael Davidson, of the University of California, San Diego, advised me at an early stage, and he has become a trusted mentor and friend. At the College of Staten Island, City University of New York, I have benefited from the support of my colleagues in the Department of English and from financial assistance provided by Dean Francisco Soto and Provost David Podell. I am grateful as well for fellowships funded by PSC-CUNY and the Mellon Foundation at the CUNY Graduate Center.

I am particularly indebted to friends outside academia who have influenced my thinking about literature and community: Jayne Aquilina, Jeni

Armesan, Chris and Marcy Betts, Jason Bott, Dana Brigham, Greg Campbell, Laura Cook, Stephen Druckman, Jackie Esteban, Doug Goewey, Dave Hebb, Rafael Lopez, Sue Roberts, Dava Silvia, Ann Stedronsky, Alan (Fortunate) Sun, Ann Whalen, and Kathleen Winter, as well as Brian Campolattaro, Robert Ruth, and Stephen Sikking ("like brothers"). I am also appreciative of the family support I have received from Richard Ball, the Barnetts (Don, Grace, and John), the Cummingses (Beth, Caroline, Chris, Matthew, and Milton), George Dunne, Susan Dunne-Lederhaas, Irene Gammon, the Grays (Cathy, Cherylanne, Megan, Melissa, and Scott Allen), and June and Lee Sheridan.

It is safe to say that this book would never have come into existence without the support provided by Gary Snyder. From the time I met him in 1996, Gary has been extremely patient and generous while answering my questions and granting me access to his archives. Though I was just a naive graduate student when I began this study, Gary never made me feel intimidated. I am especially grateful for his permission to quote liberally from his private journals and unpublished letters. The following persons also graciously allowed me to quote from unpublished correspondence: Cynthia Archer (for the Will Petersen Estate), Joanne Kyger, Howard McCord, Bob Rosenthal (for the Allen Ginsberg Estate), Michael Rothenberg (for the Philip Whalen Estate), and Masa Uehara. For their assistance with these archival papers, I want to thank librarians Daryl Morrison and John Skarstad at UC–Davis and Marilyn Kirstead and Gay Walker at Reed College.

I gratefully acknowledge the following, who gave me permission to quote specific material from Snyder's published writings.

"First Landfall on Turtle Island," from *Left Out in the Rain: New Poems 1947–1985.* Copyright © 1986 by Gary Snyder. Reprinted by permission of Gary Snyder and Shoemaker and Hoard, Publishers.

"Mid-August at Sourdough Mountain Lookout," "Riprap," "Nooksack Valley," "Water," "Cold Mountain Poems #1, 8, 10, 19, 24," and excerpts from "Piute Creek," "Milton by Firelight," "Migration of Birds," and "Cold Mountain Poems #6, 7" from *Riprap and Cold Mountain Poems.* Copyright © 2004 by Gary Snyder. Reprinted by permission of Gary Snyder and Shoemaker and Hoard, Publishers.

"August on Sourdough, A Visit from Dick Brewer," by Gary Snyder, from *The Back Country.* Copyright © 1966 by Gary Snyder. Reprinted by permission of New Directions Publishing Corp.

"After Work," "Beneath My Hand and Eye the Distant Hills, Your Body,"
   "For the Boy Who Was Dodger Point Lookout Fifteen Years Ago,"
   "Kyoto Footnote," "Nanao Knows," "Six Years: September," "This
   Tokyo," and "To Hell with Your Fertility Cult," by Gary Snyder, from
   The Back Country. Copyright © 1968 by Gary Snyder. Reprinted by
   permission of New Directions Publishing Corp.
"Meeting the Mountains," "Song of the Slip," "Song of the Tangle," and
   "Song of the View," by Gary Snyder, from *Regarding Wave*. Copyright ©
   1970 by Gary Snyder. Reprinted by permission of New Directions
   Publishing Corp.
"Tomorrow's Song," by Gary Snyder, from *Turtle Island*. Copyright © 1974
   by Gary Snyder. Reprinted by permission of New Directions Publishing
   Corp.
"Burning 2," "Hunting 12," "John Muir on Mt. Ritter (Burning 8),"
   "Logging 12," "The Text (Burning 17)," "This Poem Is for Birds (Hunting
   3)," and "This Poem Is for Deer (Hunting 8)," by Gary Snyder, from
   Myths & Texts. Copyright ©1978 by Gary Snyder. Reprinted by
   permission of New Directions Publishing Corp.

Portions of *Gary Snyder and the Pacific Rim* first appeared in academic
journals, in slightly different form, under the following titles:

"Semiotic Shepherds: Gary Snyder, Frank O'Hara, and the Embodiment of
   an Urban Pastoral," *Contemporary Literature* 39, no. 4 (Winter 1998):
   523–59. Copyright © 1998 by the Board of Regents of the University of
   Wisconsin System. Reprinted by permission of the University of
   Wisconsin Press.
"Explorations of Pacific Rim Community in Gary Snyder's *Myths & Texts*,"
   Sagetrieb: Poetry and Poetics after Modernism 18, no. 1 (Spring 1999):
   87–128. Copyright © 2001 by the National Poetry Foundation.
   Reprinted by permission.
"Gary Snyder: Poet-Geographer of the Pacific Rim," *Studies in the Humanities*
   26, nos. 1 and 2 (June and December 1999): 18–40. Copyright © 1999
   by Indiana University of Pennsylvania. Reprinted by permission.

I am indebted to Jack Shoemaker at Shoemaker and Hoard for accommodating special requests. I extend many thanks to the folks at the Univer-

sity of Iowa Press, especially Director Holly Carver, and series editors Alan Golding, Lynn Keller, and Dee Morris. Rob Wilson and Susan M. Schultz provided insightful readings of my manuscript, for which I am grateful, and Leslee Anderson and Charlotte Wright kindly helped me turn the manuscript into a book. Thanks also to Snyder scholars Patrick Murphy and Tony Hunt for their sage advice along the way. My young children, Alexander and Charlotte, offered inspiration and humor as I wrote between their feedings and changings. My final thanks are reserved for my parents, Harold Gray and Carolyn Gray, and for my wife, Maria Barnett, to whom this book is dedicated. More than any set of writings, they have shown me the true meaning of community and loving-kindness.

References to Gary Snyder's major volumes of poetry and prose are cited parenthetically in the text with the following abbreviations. References to all other works cited in this book, including other writings by Snyder, are cited in the notes.

AH   *Axe Handles* (San Francisco: North Point Press, 1983).

BC   *The Back Country* (New York: New Directions, 1968).

EHH   *Earth House Hold: Technical Notes & Queries to Fellow Dharma Revolutionaries* (New York: New Directions, 1969).

GSR   *The Gary Snyder Reader: Prose, Poetry, and Translations* (Washington, DC: Counterpoint, 1999).

HWHB *He Who Hunted Birds in His Father's Village: The Dimensions of a Haida Myth* (1951; Bolinas, CA: Grey Fox, 1979).

LOITR *Left Out in the Rain: New Poems 1947–1985* (New York: North Point Press, 1986).

MR   *Mountains and Rivers without End* (Washington, DC: Counterpoint, 1996).

MT   *Myths & Texts* (1960; New York: New Directions, 1978).

NN   *No Nature: New and Selected Poems* (New York: Pantheon, 1992).

OW   *The Old Ways: Six Essays* (San Francisco: City Lights, 1977).

PS   *A Place in Space: Ethics, Aesthetics, Watersheds* (Washington, DC: Counterpoint, 1995).

PTI   *Passage through India* (San Francisco: Grey Fox, 1983).

PW   *The Practice of the Wild* (1990; Washington, DC: Shoemaker and Hoard, 2004).

RRCM   *Riprap and Cold Mountain Poems* (1965, 1990; Washington, DC: Shoemaker and Hoard, 2004).

RW   *Regarding Wave* (New York: New Directions, 1970).

TI   *Turtle Island* (New York: New Directions, 1974).

TRW   *The Real Work: Interviews & Talks, 1964–1979*, ed. William Scott McLean (New York: New Directions, 1980).

G A R Y **S N Y D E R** *and the Pacific Rim*

THE PACIFIC RIM AND THE
SAN FRANCISCO RENAISSANCE
Two Communities "Taking Place" in Midcentury America

I remember thinking that it was an unusual situation for a financially strapped graduate student, but in September 1997 I was encamped on the beaches of Bali, relaxing, reading, and drinking up sunshine and bottles of Bintang beer in equal measure. The free time I owed to a university fellowship that relieved me of my teaching duties for that academic year. The opportunity to travel to Indonesia I owed to my wife's parents, who generously volunteered to defray most of the expenses, and to my sister-in-law and her husband, the latter of whom was working as an investment banker in Jakarta. In the resorts of Bali, as in the smog-filled streets of the Indonesian capital, my in-laws and I noticed, quite to our surprise, that our dollars were going a long way in the restaurants and shops. There was a reason for this, of course, though few in America had yet caught wind of it. The currency of Thailand had collapsed in July 1997, and in the course of two short months economic malaise had spread to other places in the Asia-Pacific region. Indonesia just happened to be hit rather early (just after South Korea) and extremely hard by a financial crisis that, over the course of the next few years, would continue to weaken investor confidence and shatter the daily lives of citizens in the "developing" nations of East Asia. With Japan's bubble economy already suffering through a prolonged slump, and with the ceremonial handover of Hong Kong by the British and the disclosure of Bill Clinton's Asiagate fund-raising scandal making headlines, financial prospects on the Pacific horizon seemed less than rosy. By year's end, American investors who had spent the past decade celebrating the Asian miracle began to speak of an Asian contagion instead.

Since that time, the West has hardly steered clear of East Asia. Indeed, even after the collapse of several high-profile corporations and the terrorist attacks on New York and Washington sent shock waves through its own economy in 2001, the United States continues to believe that it offers the best hope for rescuing East Asian nations from their current economic crisis. This kind of bravado marks the reversal of a trend seen in the late 1980s and early 1990s, when Californians feared that Japanese businessmen buying up prime real estate in Los Angeles and Pebble Beach might overrun their state and country. To say that Americans in the twenty-first century are "invested" in the economic stability of the Asia-Pacific region is to invite speculation on several different levels, since investment in that part of the world is not only financial, but political and psychological as well. Indeed, over the past sixty years or so, as American political leaders have announced a series of foreign policy decisions and dealt with unexpected global crises—ranging from isolationism, to world war, to containment in a time of cold war, to the energy shortage, to renewed efforts at global expansion, to overextension and widespread economic slippage, to the nuclear terrorist threat posed by North Korea—they have noticed that the tide of postmodern history seems to flow strongest in the waters of the Pacific Ocean and along the rim of nations situated on its periphery. Because America is situated on this interconnected shoreline, it cannot help thinking that the fate of East Asia is its fate, too.

Looking back at the second half of the twentieth century, historians have assigned a series of names to help explain America's rise to global prominence after World War II and its subsequent uncertainty amid unexpected economic competition from Asian nations after the Vietnam War. *The Age of Extremes*, the title of Eric Hobsbawm's magisterial chronicle of the twentieth century, is perhaps the best known.[1] The most interesting names, to my mind, are those that were uttered as the shifts were taking place. I am thinking specifically about a pair of names that delineate two separate phases of postmodern globalization. The first occurred in 1941, when Time-Life magnate Henry Luce announced the arrival of "the American Century," thereby providing geographical bearings for a new, highly centralized, world order.[2] A half century further on, however, the tables had turned. Asian economies, which had accounted for only 4 percent of the world's gross national product (GNP) wealth in 1960, accounted for 25 percent of that amount by 1991.[3] Almost on cue, pundits in the West formulated a new spatial prophecy. In 1986, economic historian Staffan Linder published *The Pacific Century*, and in 1990 Robert Elegant followed with *Pacific Destiny*.[4] During this same four-year stretch, the *Los Angeles Times* filled its Sunday editions with a "Pacific Rim Supplement."

While it is true that business leaders spearheaded this new wave of hemispheric euphoria, performing artists, particularly those on the West Coast, did not lag far behind. In 1989, Los Angeles indie rock bands Redd Kross and The Three O'Clock joined their musical compatriots in the San Francisco and Seattle scenes on *Every Band Has a Shonen Knife That Loves Them*, a tribute album dedicated to Shonen Knife, a pop-punk trio of diminutive female secretaries from Osaka who had forged a cult following in the American rock community by adopting a cutesy "Hello Kitty" persona, strumming melodic power chords, sporting matching minidresses, and singing in broken English about frivolous Western topics like ice cream, fraternity parties, and Barbie dolls.

Members of the fine arts community, too, sought to underscore the trans-Pacific exchange that was taking place. The 1990 Los Angeles Festival, whose theme for that year was "The World Is Coming to Town," placed a heavy emphasis on Pacific Rim theater and visual art, in order, festival director Peter Sellars explained, to show that Los Angeles provided Americans with "the introduction to the next century." The following year, though, David Rieff placed a far more ignominious label on this multicultural city when he referred to Los Angeles as the "capital of the Third World."[5] Meanwhile, cyberpunk science fiction writers like William Gibson and magical realists like Alejandro Morales were busy exploring dystopian aspects of the Rim, which they viewed as a place where technological advances had run amok, distorting human relationships and creating the polyglot urban nightmare that came to be known as the *Blade Runner* scenario.[6] Whether it was regarded favorably or negatively, some kind of futuristic force had apparently shifted the earth on its axis. By the 1980s, the nerve center of the world was thought to exist thousands of miles from an America that had grown accustomed to wielding authority in global matters.

Switching gears to look at the American poetry written during these decades, we can notice a similar and no less significant geographic shift. To survey the period after World War II is to witness a literary revolution, the coordinates of which stretch from the latter stages of modernism, a movement usually regarded as Eurocentric and elitist in its sentiments, to postmodernism, which by contrast stresses notions of multiplicity, heterogeneity, and periphery. Most literary and cultural theorists agree that postmodernism downplays notions of centrality, but that is not to say that it lacks its own spatial obsessions: hence John Berger's belief that it is space, rather than time, that now "hides consequences from us," and Edward Soja's call for the "reassertion of space in critical social theory."[7] In the same spirit, I want to ask why it was that the de-centered space of the Pacific Rim assumed central importance in the San Francisco Renaissance.

A preliminary answer would probably emphasize this community's physical location. Resisting the influences of New York publishing titans and Ivy League academics, the bohemian writers who gravitated to San Francisco in the late 1940s and early 1950s searched for a different model of literary citizenship. Affected by the West Coast's natural beauty as well its strikingly different social demographics, they were as apt to take a hike in the mountains as they were to spend a day in the library, to prefer Buddhist meditation over the Christian or Jewish traditions of their parents, and to look across the Pacific instead of the Atlantic for literary inspiration. But physical location only tells part of the story. In the final analysis, it was not just their perch on the shores of the Pacific, but also their utopian ideas about a Pacific Rim regional structure that helped members of San Francisco Renaissance find their voice, and their place, in the postmodern universe. Gary Snyder emerged as the leader of this community because he made this cultural geography seem attractive and surprisingly palpable. In hindsight, we should regard Snyder's advocacy of the Pacific Rim idea in the 1950s and 1960s as amazingly prescient and even somewhat daring. The significance of his travels and writings in this region will resonate more clearly if we first explore the emergence of the Pacific Rim paradigm in the early years of the cold war, a time when interest in Asian religion and literature was viewed by many Americans as offbeat and highly suspicious.[8]

The Emergence of the Pacific Rim Idea

In the 1980s and 1990s, the Pacific Rim became a popular buzzword, even if the vast majority of Americans who spoke its name did not know about its origin or understand its import. Nevertheless, during the final decades of the century the Rim was regularly summoned as the latest post-modern frontier, a speed zone where technological development and financial transaction were granted free rein, a space where distance between East and West magically collapsed. A quick glance at a world map shows the contours of the Pacific Rim stretching thousands of miles, from Australia and the Indonesian archipelago, to Singapore and Indochina, to the coast of mainland China and the Korean peninsula, to the narrow Russian beachhead at Vladivostok, to the islands of Japan, eastward across the Bering Strait and the Aleutian Islands to Alaska, and down the west coast of North America toward Mexico, before extending further southward along the coastline of Central and South America. According to the prevailing logic of Pacific Rim discourse, the curvature of this vast coastal region signifies a golden periphery of people sharing the same ocean and, by extension, the same values and geopolitical concerns.

Because they exist inside the peripheral Rim, the island nations of Oceania do not figure prominently in the official version of this discourse except as the empty void where Japanese travel agents book sex tours and nuclear nation states such as the United States, Britain, and France conduct dangerous atomic tests. Presumably, it was this prejudicial type of thinking that led famed business prophet John Naisbitt to exclude a reference to Hawaii or any other interior Pacific locality in "The Rise of the Pacific Rim," a chapter from *Megatrends 2000*, and that led the editors of the *Economist*, in a blatantly racist editorial from 1991, to argue that Pacific Islanders suffering from "fatness," "inertia," and "torpor" had better "heave themselves to their feet" if they hoped to survive in the fast-paced global marketplace. The best hope for these island nations, the editors argued in self-serving fashion, was to turn their vast stretch of sea into "a huge park, a watery wilderness" suitable for First World tourists. It did not take long for native intellectuals in the interior Pacific (including Epeli Hau'ofa of Tonga, Vilsoni Hereniko of Fiji, Albert Wendt of Somoa, and Haunani-Kay Trask of Hawaii) to expose this type of Rim discourse as neocolonial in its intent and racist in its impact, and to propose in its place a vision of a "New Oceania."[9]

Among other things, the Pacific Ocean is notable for its sheer immensity. "Merely flying over it produces a feeling of awe," the editors at the *Economist* marvel, from the comfort of their lofty capitalist perch. "You see a film, eat two meals, have a sleep, and it is still there, endlessly below." One reason the

Pacific Rim idea became so popular in the late twentieth century is that it dared people to circumscribe that vast realm and rein in its immensity. While such a call to geographic unity sounds too simple and too phenomenological, this response only seems to have hastened its arrival in postmodern consciousness. Christopher Connery, a leading scholar of the Rim idea, describes its inception as a "spatial fix," a "semiotic utopia," and a "signifying seduction."[10] Rob Wilson and Wimal Dissanayake, whose edited collection *Global/Local* stands as an important installment in Pacific Rim debates, also allude to the seductive nature of this geographic paradigm, referring to it as a "transnational imaginary," a "space of disorientation" conducive to postmodern high jinx, and a natural avenue for those tiring of the antagonistic thinking that plagued cold war rhetoric.[11] Bruce Cumings gives this frenzied articulation of euphoric spatiality an apt description when he calls it "Rimspeak."[12] The Pacific Rim, each of these scholars implies, is a region in which one finds oneself anxiously, though not altogether unpleasurably, "at sea."

As we investigate it more closely, we find that the Pacific Rim idea is exceedingly complex, with a long history that predates postmodern theories of cultural geography. Like any utopian discourse, Rimspeak has been motivated and conditioned by specific cultural and political contexts. Of the contemporary theorists just cited, Connery has provided the most explicit historical background for the emergence of the Rim idea in the "late cold war years." According to his argument, American politicians had by the early 1970s shifted from a binary and antagonistic relationship with East Asia, formulated during the early years of the cold war, to a spherical and "non-othering" discourse, which insisted on equality, even brotherhood, with peoples they had formerly viewed as their adversaries. As it came into being, the conceptual Rim linking the people of the region was regarded as a logical outgrowth of the tectonic forces that long ago shaped the physical boundaries of the Pacific Basin. Inasmuch as the unity of this new public sphere was deemed natural, the Rim idea relegated political maneuverings and cutthroat business practices to the background, and thus served as a convenient blind for more narrow agendas. Connery is astute when he calls the Pacific Rim a psychogeography, for in recent decades it has become a global fantasy space, the configurations of which are attributable less to topographical features than they are to the secret workings of ideological aesthetics.[13]

By situating Pacific Rim discourse in the late cold war years, Connery focuses on an era when the Vietnam War was winding down and Richard

Nixon was restoring communication with mainland China. It was at this juncture, when shifting geopolitical realities were forcing American political leaders to adopt new strategies for dealing with Asian nations, that Pacific partnership suddenly became a hot topic. Over the next twenty-five years, Pacific Rim discourse was used by Americans primarily to signify their appetite for overseas markets, despite the fact that Washington's China Card strategy and its paternalistic relationship with Japan became troubled or utterly transformed. Notwithstanding Connery's significant scholarly contribution, I think it important to recognize that neither the Nixon administration nor the postmodern business sector was the first to summon forth the idea of Pacific Rim community. In fact, I believe that it is possible to locate two earlier versions of twentieth-century Rimspeak. The first emerged in the late 1930s and early 1940s, primarily among the organizers of California's international expositions and the liberal idealists associated with a monthly journal called *Amerasia* (which Connery discusses briefly). The second was the countercultural invocation of Asia that took place among the bohemian writers who gathered in San Francisco in the 1950s and 1960s. The first version of Rimspeak is the subject of this section. I analyze the second version in the latter part of this introduction and throughout the rest of this book.

In some ways, the Pacific Rim discourse that emerged in the years just prior to World War II is emblematic of the genre at large, for it is sometimes difficult to differentiate a program advocating peaceful outreach efforts and community-building strategies from an agenda designed to promote imperial expansion and capitalist growth. Whatever the underlying motivations, this regional idea was popular in San Francisco, particularly at the world fair the city hosted from 1939 to 1940. Whereas San Francisco's previous world fairs (the 1915 Panama-Pacific International Exposition and the 1935–1936 California-Pacific International Exposition) emphasized Spanish mission styles and Mediterranean architecture, thereby underscoring California's ties to a Latin American frontier to its south, the 1939–1940 Golden Gate International Exposition (which, among other things, celebrated the 1937 opening of the Golden Gate and Bay Bridges) announced the city as a key player in a Pacific Rim frontier to its west. Diego Rivera murals and exhibits of southwestern Indian life were still in evidence, but so too were a number of attractions promoting trans-Pacific partnership.

A packet promoting this "Pageant of the Pacific" described the architecture of the 1939 festival as "a new 'Pacific' style . . . devised to exalt the visitor spiritually into a 'Never-Never Land' where romance is in the air." Influenced no doubt by this air of romance, the city affixed the name "Treasure Island" to a man-made landform in San Francisco Bay erected especially for the exposition. From this location, not far distant from Angel Island, the infamous way station where would-be immigrants from China were mercilessly detained, American visitors to the fair could watch the takeoff and landing of the China Clipper, a Pan American Airways plane that made weekly trips to Hong Kong. Meanwhile, at the Pacific House, fairgoers could tour exhibits showcasing the foods, housing, transportation, arts, natural resources, and customs of its Pacific "neighbors." Far more conspicuous was *Pacifica*, an eighty-foot-tall statue of an Asian woman, her arms upraised and her palms turned outward, probably in a sign of greeting but also, perhaps, in a show of astonishment or wonderment. The ambiguity of her gesture aside, the proud posture and totemic presence of Ralph Stackpole's monumental statue signaled the exposition's predominant theme: the mingling of Pacific cultures.

Indeed, it is striking to notice how different *Pacifica* was from the poster of Hercules used to promote the Panama-Pacific Exposition of 1915. On that earlier occasion, the male colossus symbolized the triumph of a nation whose great engineering feat—the Panama Canal—had recently linked two major oceans. It was hard to miss the imperial bravado behind the image of Hercules pushing apart the Panamanian cliffs. After all, Theodore Roosevelt went forward with the waterway project in large part because he and other military leaders in the Spanish-American War had grown frustrated over their inability to send battleships from Pacific ports to the Caribbean theater of war. A quarter of a century later, with *Pacifica*, the topic of military adventurism was pushed aside in favor of a more kindly version of hemispheric utopianism. In fact, it appears likely that Stackpole's sculptured embodiment of Pacific Rim community was modeled after famous statues of Liberty and Columbia, colossal women who symbolized the democratic spirit of people seeking freedom in the Atlantic sphere.[14]

Though they shared an interest in Pacific Rim culture, New Deal humanists at *Amerasia* were far more pragmatic and policy-minded than the organizers of San Francisco's world fairs. To their dismay, these liberal prognosticators saw storm clouds on the Pacific horizon throughout the 1940s, as the United States witnessed in succession the attack on Pearl Harbor, the growing might of the Soviet Union, a communist revolution in China, and the advent of a hotly contested war at the thirty-eighth parallel in Korea. Meanwhile, Yellow Peril fears were inflamed on the home front by jingoistic lawmakers, by the forced relocation and detention of Japanese-Americans under Executive Order 9066, and by popular songs such as "We're Gonna Find a Fellow Who Is Yellow and Beat Him Red, White, and Blue" and "To Be Specific, It's Our Pacific."[15] The editors at *Amerasia* were particularly disturbed when Vice President Henry Wallace was prohibited from visiting Mao Tse-tung and subsequently dumped from Franklin Delano Roosevelt's campaign ticket in 1944. Needless to say, the journal's call for Pacific Rim unity was a tough sell in such an atmosphere. The editors sought in vain to head off an incipient cold war paranoia, which with its Manichaean geopolitical vision and propensity for psychological warfare was, as Allen Ginsberg put it, "imposing a vast mental barrier on everybody." But by the end of the decade, *Amerasia* was defunct. Only rarely would a public intellectual, such as Carey McWilliams, dare to dream aloud about Pacific Rim community, and then only in elusive language.[16]

The rise and fall of *Amerasia* provides a good case study of Pacific Rim discourse and the challenges it initially faced from Americans wary of international pluralism. Proposed by the Christian-based Institute of Pacific Relations (IPR) as a liberal alternative to *China Today*, an ardently communist journal, *Amerasia* was launched in March 1937, ten years before the cold war was officially declared.[17] Over the next several years, this periodical became a forum for a unique variety of Rimspeak. In *Amerasia*'s first few issues, a large map of the Pacific region was placed opposite the table of contents. In subsequent issues, the journal's masthead portrayed (within the enlarged "A" of the title's first letter) a pictograph highlighting the spherical formation of the Pacific coastline, with a ship sailing from America toward Asia.

In the inaugural issue, the editors of the journal explained their mission, citing "an obvious need to stimulate and clarify American public opinion on the Far Eastern situation." According to the editors, "the public must be aroused to assume the responsibility for American Far Eastern affairs inherent in democratic government. Only on a basis of informed public opinion can skillful government policies avoid the dangers of the critical Oriental situation by taking advantage of every constructive opportunity for ensuring peaceful relations between nations."[18] This statement obviously ran counter to the "Fortress America" program put forth by Republican isolationists in the late 1930s. Nonetheless, *Amerasia*'s New Deal liberals held fast to their ideals during the nation's rightward turn, expressing their hope for peaceful coexistence among Pacific nations by reprinting this statement on every issue's contents page, even after the attack on Pearl Harbor.

In its second number, *Amerasia* ran an editorial that echoed this call for "peaceful relations" but edged closer to the spiritual rhetoric found in later versions of Pacific Rim discourse:

> We are united in the belief that the citizens of the United States as members of a democracy have an inalienable right to know all the pertinent and efficient causative factors involved in our Pacific and Asiatic commitments and relations, that they may actively and critically follow the methods employed by our government in carrying out its policy in that region. We are also united in striving to attain the ultimate objective of promoting among all peoples inhabiting the periphery of the Pacific Ocean a harmony of relationships which transcends the merely legalistic concepts of justice with its emphasis on property over human rights or upon specious national honor or sovereignty over the economic welfare and the spiritual needs of 700 million people who live on the islands or in the countries bordering the Pacific.[19]

According to Cyrus Peake, the editor who contributed this piece, the "peoples inhabiting the periphery of the Pacific Ocean" share a geographic cohesion that supersedes their ties to any single nation. In contradistinction to America's military leaders, who regarded the region as a theater of war, or to its business leaders, who espied a global market lying in wait, Peake and his *Amerasia* colleagues invoked the Pacific Rim as a realm of peace and human partnership, emphasizing the "spiritual needs" of its 700 million citizens. Other New Deal liberals took note of *Amerasia*'s message, including the editor of the journal *Philosophy East and West*, who convened an East-West Philosophers' Conference in 1939 to "explore the significance of eastern ways of thinking for the development of a global consciousness, a sort of 'synthesis' of ideas and ideals of East and West," and poet Charles Olson, who left the Office of War Information in 1944 to write *Call Me Ishmael* (1947), his paean to Melville's prophetic vision of the Pacific, once he detected the Roosevelt administration's rightward turn.[20]

While *Amerasia* was able to withstand isolationist and jingoistic opposition in the years leading up to World War II, the heated rhetoric of the cold war in the late 1940s proved to be a more formidable obstacle. Plagued by financial losses, lingering anti-Japanese sentiment, and threats posed by an increasingly virulent group of anticommunist agitators (who charged managing editor Philip Jaffe with espionage), *Amerasia* ceased publication in 1947, which as it happened was a watershed year in America's emergence as a global superpower. In March of that year, President Truman issued his famous doctrine calling for worldwide containment of the Soviet Union. Three months later, the editors of *Fortune*, in a two-part article entitled "Exporting Capitalism," repeated Henry Luce's "American Century" argument, championing the global agenda Truman had just marked out. Walter Lippmann followed both pronouncements with an influential book that employed Bernard Baruch's newly coined term to popularize the idea of a "cold war."[21] By this juncture, it seemed clear, America was prepared to divide and conquer the world on its own terms.

Although it faced imminent collapse in such a climate, *Amerasia* could not cease publication without issuing a prophetic warning to those in charge of foreign affairs. The entire final number consisted of Philip Jaffe's long article "America: The Uneasy Victor," which sought to make sense of the nation's confused and harmful policies in the Asia-Pacific region. The journal had always regarded isolationism as dangerous, and Jaffe reiterated this stance in his farewell piece. "During the last two years," he pointed out in the final issue's lead editorial, "despite the efforts of some to keep the world in separate compartments, it has become clear that American relations with Asia can no longer be separated either from the world as a whole or from the domestic scene."[22] Still, Jaffe knew that the present danger did not reside with the isolationists so much as it did with the new breed of cold war interventionists. He was particularly distrustful of Luce's American Century rhetoric, since it smacked of a frontier aggressiveness that ran counter to *Amerasia*'s communitarian ideals. Luce's forward thrust was especially to be avoided, Jaffe argued, since it "rejects the policy of international cooperation envisaged by President Roosevelt and given concrete form in the declarations of Yalta and in the United Nations. Its keynote is the unilateral American intervention in the image of what its members conceive to be the American pattern of society. . . . The American Century program . . . recognizes only the necessity of an expanding world market for American goods, and rejects the social and political changes that are the indispensable corollaries to the attainment of this goal. It represents the 'internationalism' of men with no sense of history; men forced to face the problem of the world market with no guide other than the traditional ideas and prejudices of their class."[23]

However prescient his warning appears in hindsight, Jaffe's heartfelt appeal for equitable international cooperation did not match the mindset of Americans in the 1950s. On the contrary, most accepted the argument that overseas locations were the proving grounds upon which the tide of communism needed to be stemmed. Although *Amerasia* dismissed it as ad hoc foreign policy, the Truman Doctrine held strong, and the Marshall Plan's directives in Europe were matched by an equally vigilant plan to democratize nations in Southeast Asia. The Korean War, fought to a stalemate, virtually guaranteed that cold war ideology would continue to map the geopolitical landscape of East Asia for years to come. In many ways, *Amerasia*'s final issue signaled the last gasp of liberal foreign policy before it was forced underground and left to hibernate for more than two decades.

To the extent that the Pacific Rim idea was invoked at all by government officials during the 1950s, it was as a defensive perimeter. In a 1950 speech defending U.S. intervention in the Korean conflict, Secretary of State Dean Acheson declared that the eminent domain of America "runs along the Aleutians to Japan and then goes to the Ryukus . . . and from the Ryukus to the Philippine Islands." In charting this course, Acheson was using the same geographic coordinates that Douglas MacArthur had used a few years earlier when he declared the Pacific an "Anglo-Saxon lake." President Eisenhower followed suit when he employed Acheson's geographic line of reasoning to promote his New Look foreign policy, which in large part consisted of psychological warfare. Those who dared to disagree with these geopolitical initiatives—Democrats like Adlai Stevenson, who pursued what became known to his critics as the Asia-last policy—were in jeopardy of being labeled soft on communism and therefore unAmerican.[24] Looking back on this era, James Clifford echoes Allen Ginsberg's sentiments, decrying the fact that "cold war politics turned [an] ancient borderland into a sealed frontier."[25]

The Pacific region's importance to America's strategy of psychological warfare led to uninterrupted military involvement in the hemisphere throughout the 1950s and 1960s. In his revisionist study of U.S. foreign policy, Thomas J. McCormick provides an interesting rationale for calling this involvement a "Rimlands War." According to McCormick's analysis, American military posturing in the Pacific after World War II was motivated more by the prospects of unbridled profit-taking than it was by the establishment of democratic institutions. American intervention in the Korean and Vietnamese conflicts, he insists, was "part of a general strategy to sustain Japanese economic recovery, ensure its participation in the world-system and keep open the possibility that China itself might someday be restored to that system and led down the capitalist road."[26] Taking McCormick's argument a step further, we might say that the Rimlands region enveloping American consciousness during the cold war years bore an uncanny resemblance to Japan's infamous Co-Prosperity Sphere. If the idea of a hegemonic sphere of influence along the western rim of the Pacific seemed dangerous to the United States in the 1930s, it nonetheless seemed to square (or perhaps circle) rather nicely with American dreams of capitalist utopia a decade or so later.

And so the cold war raged on, with American visions of military conquest and capitalist profit intact, until at last another, somewhat more desperate embrace of the Pacific Rim idea took place in the late 1960s. By 1967, doubts about the American presence in Vietnam were surfacing with increasing regularity, and even avowed anticommunists were beginning to notice that Asian nations were not falling easily into their camp. Evidently, the defensive perimeter envisioned by Acheson in 1950 was insufficient in and of itself. Of course, it is hardly a coincidence that this new version of Pacific Rim discourse arrived just as developing nations in Asia were breaking free from their colonizers and establishing their own systems of governance. As late as 1966, at an economic summit in Manila, Lyndon Johnson was referring to heads of Asian countries as "my ministers."[27] But by the time the Association of Southeast Asian Nations (ASEAN) was founded the following year, the nations of the western Pacific were proving quite capable of administering to their own needs without America's paternalistic approval or guidance. America's national security specialists acknowledged that a different language would have to be employed if they hoped to deal effectively with an Asia-Pacific region that had become self-sufficient and, in the words of William Bundy, full of "area spirit."[28]

As far as I have been able to determine, the earliest use of the word "Rim" by a government official to describe this vast region came in September 1967, when Mike Mansfield, recently returned from an overseas fact-finding mission, presented a report entitled "The Rim of Asia" to the Senate Committee on Foreign Relations. Mansfield told his colleagues that the purpose of his report was to survey the "stretch of nations which share the waters of the Western Pacific," nations whose "greater international self-assertion and diversification" in recent years necessitated new kinds of "bridge-building" strategies in what was becoming an increasingly autonomous sphere.[29] Just a month after Mansfield delivered his report, Richard Nixon, who was in the midst of launching another campaign for the presidency, outlined his own ideas about Pacific Rim community in the pages of *Foreign Affairs*. Casting his gaze over the western horizon, Nixon predicted great financial gain coming from trans-Pacific partnership, as well as an "extraordinary set of opportunities for a U.S. policy which must begin to look beyond Vietnam." According to his way of thinking, one isolated trouble spot in Southeast Asia should not overshadow the possibilities offered elsewhere in the region:

> The war in Vietnam has for so long dominated our field of vision that it has distorted our picture of Asia. A small country on the rim of the continent has filled the screen of our minds; but it does not fill the map. Sometimes dramatically, but more often quietly, the rest of Asia has been undergoing a profound, an exciting and on balance an extraordinarily promising transformation. One key to this transformation is the emergence of Asian regionalism; another is the development of a number of Asian economies; another is gathering disaffection with all the old isms that have so long imprisoned so many minds and so many governments. By and large the non-communist Asian governments are looking for solutions that work, rather than solutions that fit a preconceived set of doctrines and dogmas.[30]

This is a classic piece of Rimspeak. Like Mansfield, Nixon defines the region as a "rim," the proportions and contours of which vary according to the ongoing struggle between our psychological obsessions ("the screen of our minds") and topological facts (the full map). In an ironic twist, Asian regionalism has become the newfound weapon this renowned anticommunist wants to wield against Beijing and Moscow. To a significant extent, Nixon's call for Pacific Rim partnership signals another attempt, routinely employed by cold war ideologues, to erase all traces of political motivation. On the Rim, Nixon wants his readers to believe, ideological "isms" are subordinate to an evenhanded and pragmatic exchange among different nations sharing the same values and goals as well as the same ocean. Such was the vision, if not the reality, promoted by Pacific Rim discourse in the late cold war years.

By the end of 1967, the report by Mansfield and the article by Nixon had become the bellwethers of a new approach in the Asia-Pacific region. In January 1968, a group of fourteen political scientists, holding a roundtable discussion on U.S. foreign policy in East Asia, published a joint statement in *U.S.*

News and World Report in which they concurred with the new Pacific policy.[31] Shortly after Nixon assumed the presidency, this policy was resorting to familiar shorthand: the doctrine. The Nixon Doctrine, like the containment and New Look initiatives put forward by Truman and Eisenhower shortly after World War II, provided a rhetorical basis upon which all future foreign policy decisions were to be evaluated. Announced in July 1969, this latest doctrine extended the geographic argument its author had outlined two years earlier in his *Foreign Affairs* article. According to Tad Szulc, the Nixon Doctrine was born "almost by accident . . . in the middle of the Pacific on a quiet summer evening."[32] On a stopover in Guam en route to an eight-nation tour of Asia, the new president convened a group of reporters at the Top o' the Mar Officers' Club, a suitable place for the reshaping of a foreign policy suddenly "at sea" in the new regional order.

On this night, with the ocean looming outside the windows of the club, Nixon gave an impromptu and rather rambling account of how the United States should proceed in its relations with Asia. It was on this occasion that he put forth the idea of "Vietnamization," whereby South Vietnam would gradually assume responsibility for its own security and defense problems. "Asia for the Asians," Nixon asserted in his familiar staccato. "We should assist, but we should not dictate." This pronouncement notwithstanding, Nixon never dared to call for a decreased U.S. role in the Asia-Pacific region. "Whether we like it or not, geography makes us a Pacific power," he reminded the reporters. Accordingly, the president advocated replacing his predecessors' policy of unilateral intervention with a program of "collective security," which he hoped would advance America's global mission and at the same time pay all due respect to Asia's "new regional pride."[33] By the time Nixon left Guam, the Pacific Rim idea had become an important building block of a forward-thinking foreign policy. The Nixon Doctrine attracted additional support as the president sought rapprochement with China in the years following the Sino-Soviet split.

In 1975, Gerald Ford advanced the Pacific Rim idea with a doctrine of his own. Like his former boss, Ford announced his new regional initiative in the interior Pacific, at Pearl Harbor. While it held fast to tradition by employing geographical coordinates to announce a plan for international partnership, the Ford Doctrine was notable for summoning the oceanic region as a fantasy space in which distance was conveniently shrunk and time magically reversed. Speaking from a location he dubbed "the crossroads of the Pacific,"

Ford dedicated himself to "building across the Pacific a new bridge of under-standing between the nations of Asia and the United States," one that would "span the ageless civilization of Asia and the new civilization of America. . . . Asia is old and yet young. America is young and yet old. My mission to Asia was not to cross the Pacific in miles or in hours but to traverse the centuries and civilizations that have kept our peoples so apart and our societies so distant for so long."[34]

While Ford's bridge-building motif echoes the pragmatic strategy outlined in Mansfield's Senate report, we will notice that the spiritual language with which he couches his doctrine is not so different from the kind *Amerasia* employed a generation earlier. Then, too, Ford's Rimspeak resembles the kind that found favor in the San Francisco Renaissance, whose members likewise emphasized bridge building and time reversal in their efforts to locate a common Pacific culture. Plagued by superpower security dilemmas, an energy crisis, and economic stagflation, the members of the Ford administration were occupied with a set of challenges rather different from those faced by bohemian writers in San Francisco. And yet, at some level, both groups were seeking the same utopian realm: a fantastical place where cold war posturing might be superseded by natural and nonideological partnership among geographically linked peoples.

Predictably, the Pacific Rim idea failed to usher in the kind of end-of-ideology utopia promised by Nixon and Ford. But such failures did not stop other Americans from adopting the same optimistic tone. In the 1980s, cold war politicians who engaged in Pacific Rim discourse continued to cloak pragmatic policy concerns in futuristic language. Toward the end of his term as secretary of state in the Reagan administration, George Shultz, hardly the sort to sell American interests short, told a group of Indonesian economists that he envisioned "some kind of Pacific basic forum where like-minded countries could compare experience, discuss ideas, and prepare analyses on subjects that are of interest to most countries in the region."[35] Members of the American business sector were even more enthusiastic in their calculations (and calculating in their enthusiasm), for they regarded the Pacific Rim as a zone where free-market competition and classic laissez-faire liberalism would have no impediments. Speaking from his corporate headquarters in San Francisco in 1970, Bank of America president Rudolph Peterson redeployed the geographical coordinates used by cold warriors like Dean Acheson to zero in on new overseas markets. "When I speak of the Pacific Rim,"

Peterson explained, "I am putting the broadest possible construction on the term—the western coasts of South America, Central America, our own continent, and extending beyond Australia and the Far East to India. There is no more vast or rich area for resource development or trade in the world today than this immense region, and it is virtually our own front yard. . . . Were we California businessmen to play a more dynamic role in helping trade development in the Pacific Rim, we would have giant, hungry new markets for our products and vast new profit potentials for our firms."[36]

During this heady time of "profit potentials" across the Pacific, techno-capitalists like Alvin Toffler heralded the coming of a "Third Wave," corporate-love gurus like William Ouchi promoted "Theory Z" (based on conservative Confucian teachings about loyalty, love, and other "Asian values"), and conservative political theorists like Francis Fukuyama began forecasting "the end of history."[37] An investment guru featured in Carolyn See's apocalyptic Los Angeles novel, *Golden Days*, claimed to love the Pacific Rim for its "cheap Asian labor" and liked to imagine Hong Kong and Taipei as places where "they worked seventeen-hour days, then stayed up all night and danced."[38] By 1989, with the establishment of the Asia-Pacific Economic Cooperative (APEC), it seemed to many observers as though the Pacific Century had truly arrived. At the same time, others could not help but notice that the Pacific Rim idea was taking on a decidedly American cast. "The Pacific Rim is emerging like a dynamic young America but on a much grander scale," John Naisbitt and Patricia Aburdene crowed in the pages of *Megatrends 2000*. As recently as 2002, George W. Bush continued to talk about a "Pacific Century." But after experiencing the heavy-handed tactics of the International Monetary Fund (IMF) and the U.S. Treasury Department (both of which dodge the subject of debt relief to cash-strapped Third World economies and engage in questionable rate-fixing policies), and after witnessing the Bush administration's unrelenting push toward regime change in Iraq, citizens of poorer Pacific nations can be forgiven if they find the president's promise "to be part of Asia's future" a less-than-welcome proposition.[39]

In the 1990s, social and cultural theorists in the American academy began to examine the Pacific Rim idea with a critical eye. As this scholarship makes clear, most boosters of the regional paradigm ignore the very real conflict between those who draw the map and those who get mapped. As a result, they overlook such issues as uneven development, political repression, and labor diasporas. As Bruce Cumings puts it, "the people of the

Pacific Rim did not know that they inhabited a bustling new sector of the world system until they were told—just as the 'Indians' did not know that they were in 'West India' until Europeans informed them. 'Rim' is an American construct . . . incorporating the region's people into a new inventory of the world."[40] As previously mentioned, the spherical conception of the Pacific Rim tends to privilege the people who reside on the periphery of the ocean at the expense of the invisible people who live in the "empty" places "inside" or "off" its golden coastline: hence the prejudicial attitude of Rimspeakers at the *Economist*, whose editors warned that "little islands in the middle of nowhere are not the places for fanciful and costly bits of technology."[41] Arif Dirlik analyzes this dynamic in some detail, reminding us that "the Rim is ultimately external to the Pacific; at various locations along it are arraigned economic, political and military forces that gaze across an empty Pacific at imagined antagonists somewhere else on the Rim. The Rim in effect erases the spaces within it from which it derives its name."[42]

In their rush to celebrate a new capitalist order, Rimspeakers end up eliding the economic and personal sacrifices made by the people of the interior Pacific, many of whom (women from the Philippines, for example) are forced to migrate to global cities "on the Rim" (Hong Kong) where they can find low-level employment (as amahs) in order to send money back to needy family members in their native country. European and American investors may have helped to shore up the idea of the Rim, but as Dirlik has elsewhere explained, "the people who filled out the region with their motions and their labors have been predominantly Asian and Pacific peoples."[43] Christopher Connery speaks cogently when he says that the Pacific Rim idea betrays postmodern culture's obsession with the "suppression of distance." But as Doreen Massey and other scholars working in the field of human geography rightly point out, "the time-space compression of some groups can undermine the powers of others."[44]

Echoing Massey and castigating the high-tech versions of Rimspeak that became popular in the 1980s, David Palumbo-Liu asserts that "triumphalist discourse that evaporates the borderlines between east and west in the radical extension of the Pacific Rim to the entire world masks the realities of uneven access, uneven starting points of accumulation, the limits of consumerism, the shaping and warping forces of market economies, not to mention the raw physicality of labor and material. The absolute and instantaneous fluidity of capital in cyberspace, which imaginatively lifts capital off the ground into the ether, cannot long mask for the even minimally skeptical reader the rough traction of the contradictions that anchor capital in material history."[45] Protesters who gathered in the Rim city of Seattle during the 1999 World Trade Organization conference had the same issues in mind as they called attention to the structural inequities accommodating the spread of global capitalism.

Besides Cumings, Dirlik, Palumbo-Liu, and Connery, no one has done more to critique the Pacific Rim idea than Rob Wilson. Based for several years at the University of Hawaii at Manoa, where he was involved with Oahu's *Bamboo Ridge* journal and other small press publishing projects, Wilson shares with Dirlik an interest in "critical regionalism," the task of which is to "forge local spaces of difference and social tactics of resistance."[46] In the islands of the interior Pacific, this effort has involved nurturing and promoting local literary scenes filled with writers (such as novelist Epeli Hau'ofa, who eschews the European-Australian designation "Oceania" in favor of "Our Sea of Islands," and poet Joseph Balaz, who proudly asserts that Hawaii is "da mainland to me") dedicated to the reestablishment of cultural difference within a Pacific Rim discourse plagued from the start by selective mappings, universalizing rhetoric, and "global forgetting."[47] Wilson claims that his purpose in "re-imagining the American Pacific is both to dismantle stable U.S. hegemonic notions of identity, place, and region, and to create a kind of fluid and Deleuzean counterpoetics along lines of Asian/Pacific flight, place-based languages, and alternative imaginings."[48]

It is somewhat surprising, therefore, to learn that Wilson was born and raised in Connecticut, not in Hawaii. It is also interesting to note that, although he routinely deplores the hegemonic practice whereby Westerners traveling in the Pacific attempt to "become native," Wilson evidently has no problem with the act of joining Pacific citizens in a global community. In a revelatory autobiographical aside, he explains that his own "flight westward was never meant to enact a miming of the Manifest Destiny 'frontier' project, but to express (as in Jack Kerouac's 'dharma bum' quest for wilder freedoms in California and disorientation via Asian belief systems such as Buddhism and Tao) a way across and out of American common sense at the shopping mall of the soul. It traced a different, more mixed, haphazard way of 'becoming global.'"[49]

By citing the example of Jack Kerouac (another New Englander, albeit one whose westward journey stopped at the California coast), Wilson tries valiantly to put some distance between the countercultural invocation of the Asia-Pacific region, which he clearly prefers, and the more official versions of Pacific Rim discourse that have held sway in the political and economic arenas. This search for an alternative Pacific Rim discourse motivates my own study of Gary Snyder, the prototypical Dharma Bum celebrated by Kerouac in the 1958 novel inspiring Wilson's westward flight. More than any other writer in the Beat and hippie eras, Snyder made Asian cultures seem wildly attractive for Americans at odds with cold war attitudes and dictates. But some serious questions still remain. Why did the Pacific Rim loom so large for a bohemian community that, very much like Rob Wilson, sought a "haphazard way of becoming global"? Why was "the Orient," contrary to its name, regarded as a place of "disorientation"?[50] In what ways did Snyder, as the absentee leader of the San Francisco Renaissance, make the process of Oriental disorientation seem otherworldly and mystical, but at the same time, so practical and natural? How different, really, was his brand of Pacific Rim discourse from the varieties of Rimspeak already discussed?

I will attempt to answer these questions over the course of several chapters. For the moment, however, I can do little more than clarify the social context in which these questions make sense. Each of the perspectives on Asia-Pacific regionalism recounted thus far betrays the fact that the Rim is a culturally motivated invention and not a serendipitous discovery. Like all cognitive mappings, the Rim depends in large part on the movements and desires of the people who trace its contours, regardless of whether this movement takes place consciously or unconsciously, whether it exists as part of a labor diaspora or as part of a holiday tour, whether it kicks off an official presidential visit or a freewheeling countercultural quest. There are, in fact, a seemingly endless number of geographical imaginations emanating from competing positions at any given moment. For this very reason, Arif Dirlik argues, "it is necessary to define our terms by specifying *whose* Pacific—and *when*. . . . [The] apparently 'objective' forces integrating the area bear the mark of historical relationships that produced them, and they are also open to manipulation and interpretation in accordance with configurations of interest and power that have informed those relationships."[51] In putting this book together, I have realized that Dirlik's questions of who and when inform my thinking about Snyder at nearly every turn. To understand this poet's contribution to Pacific Rim consciousness, we must therefore consider his role within various regional communities, including the famous one I discuss below.

The San Francisco Renaissance
and the Countercultural Invocation of Asia

Taking a look at the development of Rimspeak in twentieth-century America, we will notice a rather large gap from 1947 to 1967. This twenty-year period marks the first half of the cold war, which stretches from the announcement of the Truman Doctrine and the demise of *Amerasia* to the first large-scale protests against the Vietnam War and the alternative strategies for American foreign policy submitted by Mansfield and Nixon. In the intervening years, Pacific Rim discourse was muted by cold war paranoia and distrust of the Asian Other. Into this breach stepped the writers and artists of the San Francisco Renaissance. Forsaking the restrictive confines of nationhood and latching on to the idea of larger geographic units or culture areas, the members of this bohemian community sought closer contact with their Pacific neighbors. In doing so, they not only revisited the spiritual rhetoric of *Amerasia*'s Philip Jaffe but also anticipated the postmodern theory of "contact zones" employed by Mary Louise Pratt in her "attempt to invoke the spatial and temporal copresence of subjects previously separated by geographic and historical disjunctures . . . whose trajectories now intersect."[52] In selected urban meeting spots (bars, coffeehouses, galleries, studios, jazz clubs, psychedelic ballrooms, public parks) where world cultures intermingled, these writers and artists discovered that cultural diversity dissolved fixed definitions of national identity and opened up the possibility of global citizenship. Indeed, it is not too much of a stretch to say that, for the pilgrims who trekked to the western edge of America in the 1950s and 1960s to participate in the counterculture revolution, it was already a Pacific Century.

In asking how the San Francisco Renaissance took place, I am proposing two different lines of inquiry, one temporal and one spatial. The first considers community formation as an event, as something traceable back to a particular moment in history. The second is more concerned with the physical "place" that a community desires to "take" or appropriate for its own uses. It is this second line of inquiry with which I am primarily concerned, since it asks the same kinds of spatial questions posed by cultural geographers who bring theories of critical regionalism to bear on Pacific Rim studies.[53] In the end, however, I find that each "take" is dependent on the other, and that together they help us grasp the implications of Snyder's unique role in twentieth-century American poetry.

The birth of the San Francisco Renaissance has been recounted much more often than has the emergence of Pacific Rim discourse. In fact, it has become the stuff of legend. On 13 October 1955, a group of five poets, along with a master of ceremonies, took their place on a hastily constructed stage at the Six Gallery. "The Six," as the gallery was commonly known, was actually an old auto repair shop at the corner of Union and Fillmore Streets that a group of six painters associated with the San Francisco Art Institute had transformed into a collaborative art space. On this particular autumn night, more than one hundred people, most of whom had received handwritten invitations from Allen Ginsberg, crammed the tiny (twenty by twenty-five feet) gallery to hear relatively unknown poets read from their work. By the end of the evening, the audience was treated to the first performance of Ginsberg's "Howl" and introduced to a cadre of young writers (Philip Whalen, Philip Lamantia, Michael McClure, and Gary Snyder) whose work would forever be linked with the Beat movement. Jack Kerouac was reportedly too shy to read on this night, but not too shy to pass around a jug of cheap California burgundy as a means of loosening up the crowd. Neither was he too timid to consecrate the event in *The Dharma Bums*: "I followed the whole gang of howling poets to the reading at the Gallery Six that night, which was, among other things, the night of the birth of the San Francisco Renaissance. Everyone was there. It was a mad night. And I was the one who got things jumping by going around collecting dimes and quarters from the rather stiff audience standing around in the gallery and coming back with three huge gallon jugs of California Burgundy and getting them all piffed so that by eleven o' clock when Alvah Goldbrook was reading his poem wailing his poem 'Wail' drunk with arms outspread everybody was yelling 'Go! Go! Go!' (like a jam session) and old Rheinhold Cacoethes the father of the Frisco poetry scene was wiping his tears in gladness."[54]

Kerouac's fictional recollection has been quoted countless times, not only because its spontaneous prose style colorfully reenacts the gyrations of Ginsberg (Goldbrook) during his reading of "Howl" ("Wail"), but also because it captures the performative and communal spirit that characterized the New American Poetry in general and the San Francisco Renaissance in particular. Kerouac's relentless narrative requires us, if we hope to make any sense of this "mad night," to keep pace with the contagious exuberance of the narrator and to picture ourselves at the creation of something big. To read Kerouac in this way is to feel the sawdust under our shoes and taste the jug wine that flowed liberally at this event, which, unlike other poetry readings in midcentury America, resembled a party. As Snyder would recall some years later, the Six Gallery reading "reminded everybody that the excitement of poetry is a communal, social, human thing, and that poems aren't meant to be read in the quiet of your little room all by yourself with a dictionary at hand, but are something to be excitedly enjoyed in a group, and be turned on by."[55] Perhaps this is why one member of the audience called the event "an orgiastic occasion."[56]

Of course, legends are notorious for their invention of origins, and Kerouac's is no exception. The San Francisco Renaissance may have reached full swing at the Six Gallery reading, but its beginning can actually be traced back to the 1940s, when Robert Duncan, William Everson, Josephine Miles, Jack Spicer, and Kenneth Rexroth were writing poetry in open forms and preaching anarcho-pacifist resistance to military adventurism overseas. In *The Dharma Bums*, old Rheinhold Cacoethes, the laureled but somewhat weepy paterfamilias, is meant to portray Rexroth, the man who, more than any of the other poets just mentioned, laid the groundwork for the West Coast counterculture. Rexroth was reading poetry to jazz accompaniment, translating Chinese and Japanese poetry, and advocating left-wing political causes (especially in San Francisco's Libertarian Circle) long before the Beats became famous for doing the same things. As a cofounder of and weekly contributor to KPFA "Pacifica" Radio, the nation's first public radio outlet, he introduced poetry to a wider cross section of Bay Area citizens, and in general he served as the central switchboard in San Francisco literary matters for the first half of the 1950s. After all, it was he who introduced Ginsberg and Snyder to each other, and it was he who encouraged Ginsberg and McClure to put together the panel of young poets at the Six Gallery.[57] A decade earlier, Rexroth had reached out to contact William Everson (Brother Antoninus), who at the time was writing poetry and running a small press at a conscientious objectors' camp in Waldport, Oregon. Heartened by Rexroth's kind words, Everson visited him in San Francisco when he was on furlough from camp and became impressed by this father figure's "presence," eventually naming him as the primary reason he decided to settle in San Francisco after the war.[58] Without Rexroth, it seems safe to say, San Francisco's literary Renaissance would never have taken off the way it did.

Rexroth had already written a good deal of poetry before he took the stage at the Six Gallery. His early work explored European surrealist modes but failed to catch on with many critics or readers. He found greater success once he started delving into various mystic philosophies from around the world, especially those from Asia. Published in 1941, Rexroth's *In What Hour* stands as an early example of the Pacific Rim vision that Gary Snyder refined during the Beat and hippie eras. Nearly a half century after its issue, another California poet, Robert Hass, highlighted the importance of this volume when he said that it "seems—with its open line, its almost Chinese plainness of syntax, its eye to the wilderness, anarchist politics, its cosmopolitanism, experimentalism, interest in Buddhism as a way of life . . . [and] its urban and back country meditations—to have invented the culture of the west coast."[59] Rexroth made even more headway with *One Hundred Poems from the Japanese* and *One Hundred Poems from the Chinese*, translations that became best-sellers in San Francisco in the 1950s. "San Francisco is the gateway to the Orient and Rexroth extolled Pacific Basin culture," Everson recalled in an appreciative 1980 essay. Along with his interest in eroticism, pacifism, and anarchism, Everson explained, Rexroth's promotion of Pacific Rim culture "prefigured the anti-war and anti-establishment sixties, and helped bring them into being."[60]

The Asian literature that made the greatest impact on the 1950s counterculture was associated with Zen Buddhism. Although most historians agree that Buddhism made its official American debut in 1893, when Soyen Shaku gave a public presentation at the World Parliament of Religions in Chicago (he came to San Francisco six years later to give an encore presentation), the religion did not truly take hold among non-Asians in this country until about fifty years later.[61] By the 1940s, however, D. T. Suzuki, a disciple of Soyen Shaku, began teaching Asian religion at Columbia and Harvard, eventually publishing a series of popular primers on Zen. In the opinion of Philip Whalen, Professor Suzuki "practically invented [Zen] for the West."[62] Meanwhile, back in "Saffroncisco," as Whalen had taken to calling it, the East-West House (1957) and the Hyphen House (1958) were set up to accommodate the increasing number of West Coast Beats wanting to learn more about Zen and other traditions from Asia.[63] San Francisco Zen Center was established in 1962, in part to handle the overflow of Zen adherents at Soko-ji, up until that time the only Soto temple in the Bay Area.

This sudden diffusion of Zen into the San Francisco counterculture was eyed warily by the older members of the Japanese-American community, who took offense at disheveled newcomers claiming to understand a centuries-old religion after sitting *zazen* a few times. Shunryu Suzuki, the founder and abbot of San Francisco Zen Center during its first decade (and no relation to D. T. Suzuki), discovered that most Westerners aspired to a freewheeling variety of Buddhism and were therefore unwilling to subject themselves to formal training, which only added to the difficulties of teaching an unfamiliar tradition from overseas. "Establishing Buddhism in a new country is like holding a plant to a stone and waiting for it to take root," he once explained.[64] Meanwhile, San Franciscan bohemians continued to explore the world of Zen, which they believed offered an attractive alternative to European traditions. Perhaps, as Theodore Roszak once claimed, this was because Zen's "commitment to a wise silence . . . [could] easily ally with the moody inarticulateness of youth."[65] To my way of thinking, though, Snyder and other serious adherents gravitated toward Zen because its emphasis on peace and interconnectedness fit nicely with the basic tenets of Pacific Rim communitarianism.

The following anecdote about Allen Ginsberg will perhaps shed some light on the pleasures and pitfalls associated with San Francisco's counter-cultural invocation of Asia. In 1953, while he was still living in New York, Ginsberg wrote a letter to Neal Cassady, who was living in the Bay Area. In the letter, Ginsberg explains his latest intellectual fascination. "I am on a new kick 2 weeks old," he tells Cassady, "a very beautiful kick which I invite you to share, as you are in a city where you have access to the kick." The letter goes on to say that Ginsberg's new kick was spurred by his reading of D. T. Suzuki's *Introduction to Zen Buddhism*, and by his discovery of "Chink" and "Jap" paintings at the New York Public Library and the Metropolitan Museum, which, as he put it, "opened my eyes to the sublimity and sophistication . . . of the East."[66] At the same time, Ginsberg imagines that a better access to the Orientalist kick exists in San Francisco, not because of that city's museums and libraries, presumably, but because of its social demographics and its geographic location on the Pacific Rim. Within a year, Ginsberg would travel to the West Coast (carrying a letter of introduction to Kenneth Rexroth written by William Carlos Williams) in order to experience the kick firsthand.

The language Ginsberg uses elsewhere in the letter to describe his discovery of Asian traditions suggests that he and other Beat writers imagined the East as a realm of uncanny pleasure. "Tho China is a bleak great blank in our intimate knowledge, there is actually at hand a veritable feast, a free treasury, a plethora, a cornucopia of pix—pictures, like children like to see—in good libraries and museum," Ginsberg opines. "If you begin to get a clear idea of the various religions, the various dynasties and epochs of art and messianism and spiritual waves of hipness, so to speak, you begin to see the vastitude and intelligence of the yellow men, and you understand a lot of new mind and eyeball kicks."[67] What better bond between friends, Ginsberg implies, than a shared secret about Asia's cultural "feast"? Asians, for their part, are summoned forth primarily as embodiments of the new hip spirit, here labeled "vastitude." Though it has not garnered much attention in critical circles, Ginsberg's letter stands as an early example of just how strong the link between Oriental knowledge and intimate personal relationships was to become for members of the San Francisco Renaissance. Sharing the mysteries of the East and telling one another about the kicks that D. T. Suzuki and other Asian writers held in store, bohemian writers in search of Pacific Rim community were able to satisfy several desires at once.

Besides D. T. Suzuki and Shunryu Suzuki, Alan Watts was the most notable proselytizer of Zen Buddhism in midcentury America. Watts was born in England in 1915, and as a young man he met D. T. Suzuki and studied with Zen Master Sokei-an in New York City. In the 1950s he relocated to Marin County, just across the Golden Gate from San Francisco, where he became actively involved in the West Coast counterculture. By the time the Beat revolution reached its apex, he was attracting a good deal of notice for his KPFA radio show, a "Sunday sermon," which was broadcast back-to-back with Rexroth's show under the banner "Pacifica Views."[68] Watts found his greatest measure of fame with *The Way of Zen*, a best-seller he published in 1957. Interestingly, he did not hesitate in labeling his books and radio broadcasts as popularizations of the more scholarly work on Zen produced by D. T. Suzuki, R. H. Blyth, and Ernest Fenollosa. Speaking and writing in a relaxed, nonpedantic tone, Watts took Buddhism out of academia and put its "delights" into the hands of novices.

A disclaimer Watts included in the preface to *The Way of Zen* illustrates his unpretentious approach. "I cannot represent myself as a Zenist, or even as a Buddhist, for this seems like trying to wrap up and label the sky," he admits. "I cannot represent myself as a scientifically objective academician, for—with respect to Zen—this seems to me like studying bird-song in a collection of stuffed nightingales. I claim no rights to speak of Zen. I can only claim the pleasure of having studied its literature and observed its art forms since I was hardly more than a boy, and of having had the delight of informal association with a number of Japanese and Chinese travelers of the same trackless way."[69] While his approach is admittedly more apologetic, the argument Watts articulates here resembles Ginsberg's giddy effusions about the Zen "kick." After reading these breathless advertisements for Zen, many members of the San Francisco Renaissance—a community founded on pleasure, not on legal right, and enhanced by flights of fancy, not by objective academic study—were inspired to follow their Pacific Rim desires to the limit. As Ginsberg would say in a biographical sketch he contributed to *The New American Poetry*, they hoped to "fade awhile in [the] Orient."[70]

Over time, Rexroth and Watts, as elder statesmen of the movement, came to detest the dilettantish attitudes about Asian religions pervading the bohemian community. In particular, they lamented the fact that Zen's emphasis on "the void" was being transformed by the counterculture into a program of irresponsibility and destructiveness. In a 1957 essay entitled "Disengagement: The Art of the Beat Generation," Rexroth warned that "the utter nihilism of the emptied-out hipster" threatened the artistic potential of the anarcho-pacifist community he had worked so hard to create. Without a redirection of attitude, he predicted, the San Francisco Renaissance would go the way of the Surrealist group or the Paris Commune, which devolved into the "desperation of the shipwreck—the despair, the orgies, ultimately the cannibalism of a lost lifeboat."[71]

Jack Kerouac, toward whom this warning was no doubt directed, was subject to a cascade of criticism from Rexroth during the late 1950s. The paterfamilias of the San Francisco scene never really forgave the young upstart for his portrait of weepy Rheinhold Cacoethes in *The Dharma Bums*, and the ill feelings were only exacerbated when Kerouac, accompanied by Ginsberg and Snyder, showed up drunk and belligerent for dinner at the Rexroth household one evening. The last straw came when Rexroth suspected that Kerouac had acted as panderer for Robert Creeley, who upon coming to the West Coast reportedly spirited away Rexroth's beloved wife, Marthe, for an adulterous interlude in New Mexico. Quite tellingly, Rexroth's personal ire was transferred to literary matters, especially to what he perceived to be the young generation's superficial knowledge of Asian traditions. He was especially fond of recounting how Kerouac received his comeuppance from San Francisco's established Orientalists, who knew a fraud when they saw one. "I have always said the greatest shock Kerouac ever got in his life was when he walked into my house, sat down in a kind of stiff-legged imitation of a lotus posture, and announced he was a Zen Buddhist . . . and then discovered everyone in the room knew at least one Oriental language," Rexroth gloated in a 1969 interview.[72]

Although he was more circumspect in naming specific individuals, Watts concurred with Rexroth's assessment. In the summer of 1958, Watts published an essay entitled "Beat Zen, Square Zen, and Zen" in the special Zen issue of the *Chicago Review* (which followed on the heels of its New San Francisco Poets issue). Watts begins his essay by reasserting the pleasure inherent in Zen practice. It is no mistake, he says, that Zen's "itchy fascination" with "humorously human" sages struck a chord with the free spirits of San Francisco's emerging counterculture. And yet Watts regrets the fact that the Beats turned to Zen primarily to escape the "American Way of Life," forsaking any real engagement with the religion in the process. Apart from Snyder and Ginsberg, he asserts, the young Beats were straying from the true path, a real possibility even on the "trackless way" of Zen. At their worst, Watts argues, the Beats were "justifying sheer caprice in art." On the whole, he believed that the members of this community were "a shade too self-conscious, too subjective, and too strident to have the flavor of Zen." A damning sentence near the end of the essay sums up his judgment of them: "The true character of Zen remains almost incomprehensible to those who have not surpassed the immaturity of needing to be justified."[73]

On certain occasions, self-conscious Beats realized the folly of their ways. Often, this would happen when their need for justification ran up against an unexpected obstacle. Kerouac could be obstinate when faced with criticism, claiming in a pair of letters sent to Snyder that Rexroth was "[making] his career off us 'unmannerly geniuses'" and that Watts had failed at "trying to establish himself as the Buddhist authority in America."[74] But even Kerouac expressed some doubts about the desperate nature of the Beats' spiritual quest. At one point in *The Dharma Bums*, Ray Smith (Kerouac) and the rest of the poets who read at the Six Gallery drive over to Chinatown to eat at a Chinese restaurant recommended by Japhy Ryder (Snyder). During this late-night feast, Ray recalls, "Japhy showed me how to order and how to eat with chopsticks and told anecdotes about the Zen Lunatics of the Orient and had me going so glad (and we had a bottle of wine on the table) that finally I went over to an old cook in the doorway of the kitchen and asked him 'Why did Bodhidharma come from the West?' (Bodhidharma was the

Indian who brought Buddhism eastward to China). 'I don't care,' said the old cook, with lidded eyes, and I told Japhy and he said, 'perfect answer, absolutely perfect. Now you know what I mean by Zen.'"[75]

In a 1969 interview, William Everson contributes a similar anecdote about counterculture Orientalists. "I'll always remember a story about Allen Ginsberg seeking across India for the absolute guru," Everson says. "Finally, he found this ragged holy man, half gone with visionary rapture, sitting by a path in the lotus position. Allen rushed up to him and in broken Hindi stammered: 'O Master! I have come all the way across the ocean to find you! Tell me, have you experienced the *Paranirvana*, the nirvana beyond nothingness?' The old adept opened his eyes and focused them blankly on Allen for a long moment. Then he replied in perfect English: 'None of your fucking business!'"[76]

Despite the sour evaluations the Beats received from Asian sages around the world, their special brand of "Zen lunacy" spread through San Francisco with all deliberate speed. Before long, their interest in Zen attracted the notice of the East Coast literary establishment, which treated countercultural spirituality with a mixture of fascination and disgust. Writing in the *Partisan Review*, Norman Podheretz railed against "Know-Nothing Bohemianism." In a *Life* article entitled "The Only Rebellion Around," Paul O'Neil called the Beats "the hairiest, scrawniest and most discontented specimens of all time."[77] Richard Eberhart offered a more balanced assessment in the *New York Times Book Review*, praising the "vital group consciousness" of San Francisco poets who, "however unpublished they may be," have "through their many readings [acquired] a larger audience than more cautiously presented poets in the East."[78] Far more typical, though, were the disparaging remarks Herbert Gold included in the February 1958 issue of *Playboy*, which took aim at the Buddhist intonations emanating from the West Coast branch of the Beat literary movement. "In recent years," Gold explains, "some have taken to calling themselves Zen Hipsters, and Zen Buddhism has spread like the Asian flu, so that now you can open your fortune cookie in one of the real cool Chinese restaurants of San Francisco and find a slip of paper with the straight poop: 'Dig that crazy Zen sukiyaki. Only a square eats Chinese food.' Promiscuity in religion stands, like heroin, for despair, a feverish embracing of despair, a passive sinking into irrationality. Zen and other religions surely have their beauties, but the hipster dives through them like a sideshow acrobat through a paper hoop—into the same old icy water of self-distrust below. The religious activities of the hipsters cure their unease in the world the way dancing cheek to cheek cures halitosis."[79]

Even by the standards of satirical discourse, Gold's mixed metaphors are dizzying. As we sort through them, though, we are given a chilling reminder of the way Orientalism has traditionally operated: the East is delicious in its exotic mysteries and heartily consumed by those in the know, even as gluttony threatens to push these connoisseurs over some unspecified brink. Over the centuries, Orientalism's search for epistemological origins has walked a fine line between lethal and salvational knowledge, and Gold works that boundary for all it is worth, especially when he claims that the promiscuous pleasure of the East has spread like the Asian flu. The tendency in the West to locate the origin of ravaging disease in the East dates back to medieval explanations for the Black Death. In his contemporary variation on this theme, Gold would have us see that San Francisco's gluttonous consumption of Buddhist culture, of the kind found in Kerouac's ramblings or Ginsberg's breathless letter to Cassady, also contains some rather harmful side effects. To consume and share this exotic religion from the other side of the Pacific, Gold suggests, is ultimately to communicate a deadly strain of nihilism and existential despair.

Despite Gold's bitter assessment, Zen and other Eastern religions continued to win converts in San Francisco's bohemian enclaves, the most famous of which was located in the Haight-Ashbury district. Throughout the 1960s, Asian cultures were marketed, consumed, and generally co-opted in the city's head shops and bookstores, at rock festivals and "excitements." Like the Beats, the hippies viewed foreign cultures as something to share among themselves. "I want to turn you on" was this era's operative phrase, and the transcendent realms the hippies turned to, and passed on to one another, usually reflected what they took to be Asian ideals: tribalism, sexual freedom, mysteriousness, exoticism. At public events like the "Human Be-in," a hippie "powwow" held at Golden Gate Park in January 1967 (where Snyder, Ginsberg, and McClure chanted mantras from the stage), or the Monterey International Pop Festival, a groundbreaking concert held later that year (where throngs of young people, bedecked with Hawaiian orchids flown in specially by express plane, sat transfixed by the music of Indian sitar player Ravi Shankar), Pacific Rim culture provided San Franciscans with a completely different way of envisioning American citizenship. No wonder the Gray Line Bus Company advertised the "Hippie Hop," its route through the Haight-Ashbury carnival, as "the only foreign tour within the continental limits of the United States."[80]

By the early 1970s, the changes put into motion by the participants of the San Francisco Renaissance began to filter into mainstream culture. Books such as *Zen and the Art of Motorcycle Maintenance* and *The Tao of Physics* became surprise best-sellers, and before long Asian religions were being invoked alongside Native American traditions and environmental causes in an eclectic mixture known as New Age spirituality. At the same time, San Francisco Zen Center's mountain monastery at Tassajara Springs was attracting high-profile guests, including transplanted New York poet Diane di Prima and California governor Jerry Brown. Eventually, Brown's frequent occupancy of Zen Center's Guest House and his appointment of counterculture luminaries (including Snyder and Peter Coyote) to the California Arts Council resulted in front-page exposés in the *Los Angeles Times* and the *San Francisco Chronicle* of a "Zen Center connection," but the California electorate appeared to take the news in stride.[81] During these years, Governor Brown liked to refer to his state as the seventh largest economy in the world—as though it were an independent nation—giving critics and supporters alike the notion that he was identifying more with an unofficial commonwealth of Pacific Rim nations than he was with the rest of the continental United States. California's westward tilt toward the Asia-Pacific region was doubtless confirmed when its young governor, clad in a suede jacket, walked silently up to the stage during one of Snyder's poetry readings and proceeded to sit in the lotus position.[82]

TAKE TWO

To this point, I have described the San Francisco Renaissance primarily in terms of its participants, its events, and its use of Asian culture as a bonding mechanism. Another crucial consideration involves the means by which this literary community appropriated certain physical locations as points of imaginative departure. To better understand the ways in which Pacific Rim consciousness took hold in the West Coast counterculture, it is necessary to survey the specific places where people gathered to share ideas, solidify alliances, and dream of new and better ways of being-in-the-world. Previous scholarship has analyzed this dialectical relationship between community and place, to be sure. Michael Davidson, for instance, speaks about the "possibilities for a new social and theological order" that the San Francisco scene provided, arguing that "these possibilities, however indebted to the 'spirit of place,' could not be realized without the sustaining fact of community—the circles, salons, and bars in which artists could invent out of the earthly city a heavenly city of fulfilled potential." According to Davidson, the city's spirit of place is attributable first and foremost to readings and performances—occasions when "the poem enacts its own realm of forces (whether psychological or physiological) that structure the natural world"—and only secondarily to the physical locations in which these events take place. In other words, poems and poets tend to shape the natural world, instead of the other way around.[83]

Davidson's communitarian emphasis is supported by Geoff Ward, who in his own version of this chicken-and-egg game asserts that the "excitements" that took place in San Francisco between 1955 and 1965 "can only offer a reminder of a general truth, that only culture makes locality real, and that the City is an 'omen of what is,' a folded field of words and ideas grown tall in concrete and glass, but not reducible to them."[84] I am indebted to this scholarship, for I too believe that language and social dynamics help to provide a city like San Francisco with its sense of place. Even so, I want to approach the topic of place and community from a different direction, reversing Ward's dialectical formula to account for an alternative (if no less general) truth, namely that "locality makes culture real." In particular, I am curious to know whether the routes traveled by influential writers can cause milieus to emerge in certain localities and not in others, or instead whether it is the physical topography of those localities that prompts groups of like-minded writers to say "this is the place." In an indirect and somewhat quirky way, I suppose I am trying to provide the San Francisco Renaissance and its legendary events with the kind of legend one normally finds on maps, with the slight difference that my project of cultural geography charts the distribution of *mobile* figures and the spacing of *far-flung* physical coordinates. In the final analysis, I believe that the local history of the San Francisco Renaissance will mean much more if it is viewed as part of a larger spatial narrative, one that includes a diverse array of global citizens.

Considering its colossal geographical aspirations, the San Francisco Renaissance's first gathering space seems surprisingly intimate. Arguably, the city's literary rebirth did not originate within the tiny confines of the Six Gallery, as Kerouac famously claimed, but instead in the even smaller (and far less raucous) space of Kenneth Rexroth's living room. In the late 1940s and early 1950s, Rexroth hosted a Friday night salon at his apartments on Eighth Avenue and Scott Street. These at-home gatherings provided a private space where a new public art could be envisioned and forged, and for a time they served as a forum for serious philosophical debate, storytelling, poetry readings, and a good deal of literary gossip. Networking was another important activity. It was at Rexroth's salon that Snyder, Ginsberg, and McClure first learned about each other and about other young writers dissatisfied with cold war culture. Once the Six Gallery reading and the *Howl* censorship trial ushered in an era of spectacle, however, the younger members of the literary community left Rexroth's intimate circle to gather in more public places. One such place was the San Francisco State Poetry Center, run by Ruth Witt-Diamint, a regular participant at the Rexroth salon. From its official inception in 1954, the Poetry Center invited poets from around the world to give readings. Over the years, these readings drew increasingly larger crowds, and the less-than-humble Rexroth liked to say that the Poetry Center was a natural outgrowth of the forum his "at homes" could no longer contain.[85]

Around the same time, the city's North Beach neighborhood witnessed a proliferation of places where the New American Poetry could be read or listened to, and its visions shared, by members of a newly imagined community. At North Beach venues like The Cellar, The Place on Upper Grant, and the Co-Existence Bagel Shop, the Beats extended the Six Gallery's coming out party. Poetry readings took place everywhere: from the traditionally orphic setting of the Poetry Center's Gallery Lounge to the jazz club atmosphere of The Cellar (where Rexroth read his poetry to musical accompaniment); from the gritty unionist enclave at the Longshoreman's Hall in the Tenderloin District to the impromptu spectacle of a soapbox recitation on Grant Avenue. On each occasion, the spirit of the poetry had much to do with the place one found it.[86]

In *Birth of the Beat Generation*, his popular account of this era, Steven Watson provides a map of "San Francisco 1950s Bohemia." The map shows a cross section of neighborhoods on the city's northeast quadrant (the Embarcadero, Chinatown, Russian Hill, South-of-Market, North Beach) and lists thirty-two sites where the Beats once assembled. Among the hangouts listed are City Lights Bookstore, Caffè Trieste, Fugazi Hall, and the Hotel Wentley, as well as the apartments of writers who made the neighborhood their home (Gino and Carlo's, a bar in which Jack Spicer and Jack Kerouac were known to hold court, is an unexpected omission).[87] With Watson's map in hand, fans of Beat literature can trace the footsteps their heroes made fifty years ago. "Here is where Blabbermouth Night occurred," a pedestrian on Grant Avenue might say as she approaches the old site of the Co-Existence Bagel Shop. "Bob Kaufman fought the cops here when they denied him free speech." "There is where the Bread and Wine Mission once stood," another might remark. "Remember? It was in movie version of *The Subterraneans*." I offer such hypothetical statements merely to show that San Francisco, as it has been mapped by scholars and visited by literary devotees, does indeed possess a spirit of place. As tourists flock to bars like Vesuvio's, situated opposite City Lights Bookstore on an alley renamed Jack Kerouac Way, they seek to recapture the aura of a bygone era and pay homage to a countercultural crescendo whose subversive spirit still lingers in American cultural memory.

For all its detail, though, Watson's map fails to account for the outside influences that gave these in spots their exotic flavor. At some point, we must recognize that these places are not merely physical givens but rather semiotic significations constructed and transformed by habitations, traversals, sightings, and meetings. Since every geographic landmark is at some level a cultural or literary construction—literally an inscription (*graph*) on the earth (*geo*)—we must try to address the way urban space gets written as a language. In "Semiology and Urbanism," Roland Barthes investigates the connection between city life and the semiotic possibility inherent in language. According to Barthes, urban spaces that give free rein to combinatory identity and cultural mobility eventually get marked as central places, such that they become "the privileged site where the other is and where we ourselves are the other."[88] In cold war America, this meant that people judged to be outside mainstream culture in their hometowns could travel to a cosmopolitan city like San Francisco or New York and belong to an identity otherwise denied them. "In the spiritual and political loneliness of America of the fifties you'd hitch a thousand miles to meet a friend," Gary Snyder recalled in an essay from the 1970s. "Whatever lives needs a habitat, a proper culture of warmth and moisture to grow. West coast of those days, San Francisco was the only city; and of San Francisco, North Beach" (OW 45). During the counterculture revolution, Snyder wants us to remember, people who were labeled "outsiders" or "others" were willing to travel vast distances in order to be a part of something larger than themselves. The fact that these folks hailed from New York (Ferlinghetti), Kansas (McClure), or Oregon (Whalen) was not important, for they had faith that the magical spot of San Francisco would give them a new lease on life.

But why is it, exactly, that certain places are able to set us free, when other places are not able to do so? An incontrovertible answer to this question is not immediately forthcoming, at least not to me. Even so, I cannot help but notice that the New American Poetry, like so many artistic movements at midcentury, tended to flourish in large coastal cities, especially in San Francisco and New York, where creative people had a hand in establishing an internationally flavored milieu. After all, if a city is a semiotic text, as Barthes says it is, its semiology probably has something to do with the diverse groups of people who gather there. In *Postmodern Geographies*, Edward Soja reminds us that "semiotics" derives from the Greek word *semeion*, "which means sign, mark, spot or *point in space*. You arrange to meet someone at a *semeion*, a particular place. The significance of this connection between semiotics and spatiality is too often forgotten."[89] In such cosmopolitan meeting spots, the pejorative character of otherness vanishes and is replaced by a different variety of foreignness that is more aleatory and thus more liberatory. For Soja, as for Barthes and the poets who gathered in North Beach, a *semeion* represents a place where one can "play" at being the "other" and meet other outsiders who are similarly interested in exploring their fundamental otherness.

To a significant degree, the semiotic city described by Soja and Barthes resembles the "other space" that Michel Foucault calls a "heterotopia": a new kind of utopia built on difference and alienation. Like the imago in Jacques Lacan's "mirror stage," to which Foucault refers, the identity of the heterotopian space is fundamentally split. It is "at once absolutely real, connected with all the space that surrounds it, and absolutely unreal, since in order to be perceived it has to pass through this virtual point which is over there."[90] To put it another way, heterotopian spaces, and the identities forged within them, are real sites that are at the same time radically contingent upon fantastical spaces outside their circumscribed domain. To visit a heterotopian site, therefore, is to subject one's prescribed role in society to a semiotic crucible within which individual identity and local place undergo a process of estrangement, dissolution, and rearticulation. To my mind, something similar took place in San Francisco at midcentury. Perched as it is on the rim of the Pacific, a vast realm that dwarfs the North American continent, this city was cherished by Beats and hippies as an uncanny place where cultural diversity and geographical liminality dissolved fixed definitions of American citizenship. As an "other space" in cold war America, this urban heterotopia (or *semeion*) became a pilgrimage site for intellectuals seeking a carefree variety of global identity. To cite Julia Kristeva, whose psychoanalytic work on pilgrimage traces a trajectory similar to the one described here, we might say that San Francisco in the 1950s and 1960s became a semiotic location where "meeting balances wandering. A crossroad of two othernesses, it welcomes the foreigner without tying him down."[91]

During the counterculture era, San Francisco writers championed the heterotopian character of their city in a series of manifestos, which tended to be defensive and celebratory by turns. The one thing they had in common was a geographic emphasis. Michael Davidson has located a "western gate" motif that held sway with many of these writers, including Robert Duncan, for whom San Francisco signified "the westward edge of dreams, / the golden promise of our days." Like others writing in this vein, Davidson explains, Duncan invoked the city "both as geological fact and metaphysical principle."[92] As I see it, another example of the western gate motif exists in a review of Pacific Coast artist Morris Graves written by a defiantly proud Kenneth Rexroth in 1955. "People in the United States and in Europe have difficulty in adjusting to the fact that the Pacific Coast of America faces the Far East, culturally as well as geographically," Rexroth states. "There is nothing cultish about this, as there might be elsewhere. The residents of California, Oregon, and Washington are as likely to travel over the Pacific as across the continent and the Atlantic."[93] A dozen years later, at the height of the hippie movement, Lawrence Ferlinghetti used similar language to explain San Francisco's unique allure for Pacific Rim cosmopolitans, offering "the premise that none of us are really a part of any nation, that I myself am not a part of America nor of any nation, that San Francisco itself is, at least in some sense, and in a sense not even possible for any other city in the United States today, not really a part of America. Its physical characteristics, its look, its location, perched high on the northern tip of its low peninsula, all contribute to San Francisco not feeling like the rest of America. . . . [T]he west coast is not only the last frontier but also the place where the Orient begins, where the Far East begins again."[94]

The mappings offered by Rexroth and Ferlinghetti stand as bookends of San Francisco Renaissance Rimspeak. Ultimately, they represent something more than regionalism writ large, for they situate San Francisco as a point of departure, a place where one never belongs exclusively to city or nation, or even to one's prior conception of self. Both writers intimate that an individual's feelings of plurality and otherness in San Francisco are channeled through an external frame of reference—in this case the oceanic realm that lies further to the west—such that the city being mapped becomes an embarcadero, a launching pad from which one can travel to far-flung (but interlinked) locations across the Pacific. In their minds, San Francisco Beats did not conceive of their community as a six-block radius in North Beach. Neither did the hippies restrict themselves to the Haight-Ashbury district and Golden Gate Park. Instead, each group pictured the city as a nodal point in an interconnected hemisphere. In addition to cafes and head shops, an accurate map of the San Francisco Renaissance must account for the oceanic routes its members were imagining as they let their thoughts and desires drift westward toward the Asia of their dreams.

Gary Snyder: Pacific Rim Voyager

Kenneth Rexroth, Lawrence Ferlinghetti, and other writers based on the West Coast (Everson, McClure, Ginsberg, Kerouac) clearly had a hand in articulating the American counterculture's Pacific Rim desires, but it would take someone else to fully realize the dimensions of their dream, someone who was willing to travel west of America's western terminus in order to chart the mysterious oceanic region that held their gaze. This was the task taken up by Gary Snyder, a writer whose geographically contoured poems, anthropologically informed prose writings, and constant movements along the Rim made him the leader of a heterotopian community coming to terms with its strong desire for cultural difference. With a solid knowledge of the West Coast's indigenous populations and a growing interest in Asian cultures, Snyder settled in the San Francisco area in 1952, after a brief period of graduate study at Indiana University. At the time of his arrival, the Beat revolution had not yet taken root in San Francisco, though something subversive was certainly in the air at Kenneth Rexroth's apartment. Snyder met Rexroth soon after his return to the West Coast and spent nearly every weekend with him over the next three years.[95] Under Rexroth's tutelage and with an increased store of knowledge he was receiving at the University of California–Berkeley's oriental languages program, Snyder emerged as a talented newcomer on the scene. Notable for his mysterious allure and indefatigable energy ("My Buddhism is activity," Japhy Ryder tells Ray Smith in *The Dharma Bums*), he became a mainstay in the city's literary gatherings as well as a living example of the counterculture's Zen ideal, its homegrown source of Asian wisdom.

In a letter written a month or so before the Six Gallery reading, Allen Ginsberg tells a friend about his first encounter with Snyder, a charming character possessing just the right mix of intellectual gravitas and Zen lunacy. In the letter, Ginsberg describes "a bearded interesting Berkeley cat name of Snyder, I met him yesterday (via Rexroth suggestion) who is studying oriental and leaving in a few months on some privately put up funds to go be a Zen monk (a real one). He's a head, peyotlist, laconist, but warmhearted, nice looking with a little beard, thin, blond, rides a bicicle [*sic*] in Berkeley in red corderoy & levis & hungup on Indians (ex anthropology student from some indian hometown) and writes well, his sideline besides zen which is apparently calm scholarly & serious with him. Interesting person."[96] We glimpse here the beginning of a lifelong friendship. A year after meeting Ginsberg, however, Snyder left San Francisco to begin a twelve-year pilgrimage in Japan, where he studied at the Zen Institute of America and at various Buddhist temples.

During this time, the far-flung Snyder served as San Francisco's offshore representative, its Oriental knowledge in situ, returning periodically to disseminate the new knowledge he had received overseas. What made his Pacific Rim mappings more effective than those put forward by his Beat and hippie cohorts was the fact that he actually had firsthand contact with people on the other side of the ocean. He was the first poet of the San Francisco Renaissance to travel extensively in Asia, the first to master Asian languages, and the first to embark on serious study of Asian religions. He urged others to do the same, but with mixed results. In the statement on poetics he contributed to Donald Allen's *New American Poetry*, Snyder lamented that "travel is the sense of journey that modern people have lost."[97] For this very reason, his own travels along the Rim assumed fundamental importance in the literary community he left behind but never really abandoned. Even though friends like Ginsberg and Phil Whalen would later follow his example and travel in Asia, most San Francisco bohemians seemed content to enjoy vicariously the adventurous route he was mapping out.

Although Snyder would not use the term "Pacific Rim" until the 1970s, we might choose to regard his early writings as another variety of Rimspeak.

Unlike the official versions promulgated by politicians and investment advisers, however, his is distinguished and strengthened by a sophisticated sense of the Pacific Rim as it initially came into being, both topographically (according to the volcanic eruptions and tectonic alignment that gave the extended shoreline its shape) and culturally (according to the process of geographic diffusion that brought diverse traditions into intimate contact with one another). Indeed, by traveling from the West Coast of America to Japan and by pushing further westward into Southeast Asia and India, Snyder effectively reversed the direction by which human populations and their cultures made their way to the American continent so long ago. In so doing, he came away with a deep appreciation for the trajectory of cultural flows across time and space. To survey Snyder's Pacific Rim writings, therefore, it is appropriate to take a long view, both spatially and chronologically, and I have tried to arrange the chapters of this book accordingly. Each is titled after a type of movement or practice that was relevant to the poet's development as a writer and geographic thinker during the 1950s and 1960s.

Chapter 1, "Migrating," tracks the long foreground of Snyder's fascination with the Pacific region, from his boyhood rambles along Puget Sound, to his work as a fire lookout and logger in the mountains of Washington and Oregon, to his anthropological study of Northwest Indian tribes at Reed College, to his first volume of verse, *Myths & Texts* (1960). Of particular importance in each instance is the way that the dissemination of mythological traditions across space aligns closely with the laws of nature. Nowhere is this more evident than in *Myths & Texts*, a complex lyric sequence in which Snyder tracks the small "creaturely" movements made by a variety of sentient beings on both sides of the Rim and highlights their importance in foundational mythological narratives. Influenced by Snyder's readings in anthropology and by his own observations of natural phenomena along the shore and in the mountains, *Myths & Texts* shows the Pacific Rim to be a region of traveling creatures, of which humans are but one species.

Chapter 2, "Translating," focuses on Snyder's second volume of poetry, *Riprap* (which was actually published in 1959, a year before *Myths & Texts*), and on his translations of T'ang dynasty poet Han-shan, also known as "Cold Mountain." The first part of this chapter features a detailed linguistic analysis of Snyder's "riprap poetry," the rhythms of which were indebted to his physical labor on a Yosemite trail crew during the summer of 1955, and to his study of Chinese poetics at UC–Berkeley's oriental languages program during that academic year. After showing how *Riprap*'s portrayal of the American West was influenced by Asian rhythms, I turn my attention to "Cold Mountain Poems" (1958). On this occasion, Snyder translates the poetry of a Chinese mountain sage by drawing upon his own experiences in the mountains of California. To read Snyder and Han-shan this way, I suggest, is to hear two great poets engaged in dialogue across vast stretches of time and (interconnected) space. Language barriers magically dissolve in the minds of poets dedicated to a common Pacific Rim vision.

My third chapter, "Embodying," follows Snyder offshore as he begins his long pilgrimage in Asia. As the title of this chapter indicates, I am interested here in the way that bodies of "others" get marked or "mapped" as people try to realize their personal desires. In the early part of the chapter, I focus discussion on the separation anxiety suffered by certain members of the San Francisco counterculture as Snyder prepared to set sail for Japan in 1956. Curiously, and rather disturbingly, this anxiety resulted in a series of "yellowface" portraits of Snyder. In published writings and offhand comments offered by fellow Beats such as Lew Welch and Jack Kerouac, Snyder "becomes oriental," his body representing everything the counterculture desired and feared about the Asian cultures he was about to encounter. The remainder of the chapter analyzes *The Back Country* (1968), Snyder's spherical travelogue in verse of his extended tour of the Pacific Rim, from California to Japan to India and back again. As Snyder maps foreign locations in Asia and plots the coordinates of his eventual return to America, he depicts the women of the Pacific region (Beat women in San Francisco, prostitutes and bar girls in Japan, Hindu deities in India) as metaphysical figures. My sense is that Snyder may have deflected some of the unwanted attention he received from his friends in San Francisco onto the bodies of Pacific Rim women, and that this libidinal fixation in turn allowed him to claim a literary "return" (or dividend) on his community's initial psychological investment. To the extent that these women were geographically situated, they helped Snyder come to terms with each stage of his Pacific Rim odyssey. At the same time, their appearance in his published writings must have piqued the interest of male Beats back in San Francisco, whose appetite for erotic tales in exotic locations seemingly knew no bounds.

I carry some of these gender issues over into my next chapter, "Communing," a substantial portion of which is devoted to a discussion of *Regarding Wave*, a 1970 volume of verse that Snyder dedicated to Masa Uehara, a

Japanese woman he married in 1967. In the "songs" of *Regarding Wave*, Masa's Asian body is depicted as the watery vessel through which a tangible form of Pacific Rim community (including Snyder's sons, Kai and Gen) becomes possible. Through her offering of "grace," Masa sanctifies the poet's journey to cultural discovery, though in the end we are left to ponder just how far her own agency extends. I also devote a significant part of this chapter to a discussion of *Earth House Hold* (1969), Snyder's first volume of essays, many of which take up the topic of tribalism, an alternative approach to modern living that he and Masa encountered as members of Japan's *Buzoku* counterculture in the late 1960s. These essays, which were extremely popular in San Francisco's hippie community, tell of Snyder's continued effort to reconcile ancient familial practices with a new model of geographic belonging. Because their publication roughly coincides with his permanent return to America with Masa and his interracial family, *Earth House Hold* and *Regarding Wave* show Snyder closing the circle on his long sojourn abroad.

My epilogue, "Digging In," addresses Snyder's life in the early 1970s, a time when his poetry and prose became increasingly ecological and local in their focus. This epilogue takes its title from the poet's description of his homesteading practice at Kitkitdizze, the rustic farmhouse he constructed in the Sierra Nevada foothills north of Sacramento. It was here, in the Yuba watershed, a bioregion that is itself part of the larger Pacific Rim drainage, that Snyder returned to Native American themes. Throughout the 1970s and 1980s, he stressed the importance of "becoming native" and "knowing one's place," which in part meant knowing where one's water comes from and being able to identify native species of flora and fauna.

Snyder's preoccupation with indigeneity was spelled out most clearly in *Turtle Island* (1974), which won the Pulitzer Prize but inspired a backlash from some American Indian writers, who accused the poet of appropriating native cultures to advance his program of "white shamanism." At the same time, other leading voices of Native American literature (Vine Deloria Jr., Simon Ortiz, Scott Momaday) rushed to his defense, praising his work for making indigenous ways known to a larger reading audience. Through it all, Snyder continued to implement the lessons he had learned overseas, building bridges among various native communities along the Rim. In addition to the time spent caring for his new family, he organized a Buddhist community at Ring of Bone Zendo (loosely based on the Banyan Ashram community on Suwa-no-se Island, where he and Masa wed in 1967), established contact with the environmental activists in the Earth First! and Planet Drum groups, and became a leading voice in a globally conscious political constituency that made substantial inroads under the gubernatorial administration of Jerry Brown.

In a career that has spanned more than half a century, Snyder has worn many hats. He has been (and continues to be) a mountaineer, a homesteader, a traveler, a scholar, a Buddhist, and an environmental activist, in addition to being an award-winning poet. He has a profound understanding of a geographic realm where the diffuse movements of animals, people, folk tales, and other literatures have given rise to a distinct set of interconnected cultures. In the 1950s and 1960s, Snyder looked back to the archaic foundation of the Pacific Rim regional structure in order to promote spiritual harmony and resist the hegemonic appropriations resulting from cold war geopolitics. Occasionally, it is true, we discover within Snyder's early writings the kind of occlusions and hierarchies plaguing official versions of Rimspeak. Particularly in the last half of this book, I reveal how Snyder's countercultural vision has at times been compromised by his complicity with dominant discourses, especially those involving gender relations.

As many readers may know, Snyder's sexual politics during the Beat and hippie eras relied on certain chauvinistic conceptualizations (the equation of uncharted terrain with available female bodies, for instance). And yet, as perceptive critics like Patrick Murphy and Julia Martin have pointed out, Snyder's stance on gender issues is more complex than commonly thought.[98] The primary reason for this complexity is that Snyder has always taken advantage of lyric poetry's potential for critical self-reflection. Because Snyder is a Buddhist, many critics (Murphy and Martin among them) have chosen to focus upon his proclivity for sacrificing the "I" to a larger field of force, a process that helps him fade effortlessly into interconnected landscapes, which he often codes as feminine. Equally vital, though, are those self-conscious moments where we glimpse Snyder reexamining his role as a white male traveler in such spaces. As a Zen adherent dedicated to the eradication of hierarchical distinctions, Snyder comes to some painful realizations about his privileged status as a globetrotting Western male and about his extolment of a utopian regional structure, especially as he moves among native Pacific peoples whose sexual and geographic identities have afforded them few such opportunities for celebration.

Rather than simply taking Snyder to task for the sexist language imbuing some of his early writings, I have decided instead to examine the libidinal character of these works in light of the poet's self-consciousness and to read them alongside other dimensions of his life, including his central role in a homosocial West Coast literary community. On the macrolevel of cultural geography, such an approach allows me to account for the poet's erotically charged investment in a multiracial/transnational Pacific Rim regional idea and to gauge the reception of that idea within the West Coast's most liberal literary community. On the microlevel of literary analysis, it allows me to critique Snyder's perilous negotiation of the border separating a male lyric self from an exotic female "other," a negotiation that could seem rambunctious and reflective by turns, depending upon the ability of that "other" to speak back and challenge stereotypical gender assignments.

All mappings cut certain borders, delineate certain zones, and disenfranchise certain populations. Snyder's cultural geography is no different. And yet no other American writer did more during the early years of the cold war to advocate inclusiveness and peace in a region marked out by those in power as a military frontier or an economic fantasy space. In an age fraught with conflict and distrust, Snyder attracted notice by making foreign locations seem familiar and cultural hybridity seem pleasurable, sometimes by eroticizing such phenomena and sometimes by linking them to the core values of his popular primitivist agenda: practicality, partnership, and respect for all sentient beings. William Everson put it best when he said that Snyder "typifies that aspect of the Westward thrust which leaps to the Pacific to retouch the origins of civilization in the Orient. Jeffers had looked westward to the vast expanse of water, and Kerouac and Ginsberg both responded to the sweep beyond, but more than any other American poet Snyder followed that gaze to its conclusion."[99] What follows is the story of an intrepid cultural voyager whose vital role in the development of Pacific Rim consciousness remapped the world at the dawn of the postmodern era.

MIGRATING

Exploring the Creaturely Byways of the Pacific Northwest

In *Routes: Travel and Translation in the Late Twentieth Century*, anthropologist James Clifford discusses a variety of postmodern predicaments resulting from increased contact among global or "traveling" cultures. Travel, as Clifford attempts to define it throughout his book's collage of essays and personal notes, encompasses "an increasingly complex range of experiences: practices of crossing and interaction that [have] troubled the localism of many common assumptions about culture." Although Clifford occasionally apologizes for his imperfect explanation of travel and its effects, he reminds all members of "heterogeneous modernity" how difficult it is to see the interactive processes that condition or "translate" our being. Part of the problem is our own myopia. As Clifford and other contemporary scholars of diaspora would have us recognize, we tend to focus on "roots" of culture while ignoring the "routes" that make cultural contacts possible. We focus too much of our attention on the location of culture and too little on the displacement of culture resulting from an endless series of global/local encounters.[1]

Clifford's thesis finds it apotheosis in "Fort Ross Meditation," the luminous personal essay that closes *Routes*. "I'm looking for history at Fort Ross," Clifford writes, journal-style. "I want to understand my location among others in time and space." Clifford's location, geographically speaking, is on the northern California coast, at the site of a Russian-American Company fort abandoned in 1842, yet the routes he espies extend far beyond that site. As his perspective shifts from local place to global space, Clifford comes to understand that extended movements along the rim of the Pacific—arrivals and retreats of human populations, migrations of animals, introductions of plant species—affect his sense of place and "may provide enough 'depth' to help make sense of a future, some possible futures."[2] By "making room for other stories, other discoveries and origins, for a United States with roots and routes in the Asian Pacific," Clifford's meditation draws a new cognitive map, a space of contingency where "contact relations, borders and powers, line up differently" before "definitive" histories of westward expansion and geopolitical fantasies about Pacific Rim community.[3]

Clifford's work is exciting, inasmuch as it challenges Americans to rethink the spatial and historical contours of their nation by locating a space of interactive identity, or "contact zone." Still, I cannot help but think that a certain poet had formulated a similar geographical paradigm years earlier. From an early age, Gary Snyder has regarded the Pacific Rim as a migratory space, the configuration of which can be determined simply by observing the interactive movements of its many forms of wildlife (humans included). For centuries, the Rim has conditioned basic subsistence practices, spurred migrations, and fostered exchanges, thereby accommodating an extended community of living beings and preserving an ancient cultural continuum. Glimpsed from this perspective, the ways (methods, practices, rites, literatures) of West Coast culture are inseparable from the various byways (trajectories, routes, paths) through which they physically make landfall and through which they psychically come to consciousness.

As Snyder's personal aura was to evolve during the Beat and hippie eras, other writers in the San Francisco community would sometimes liken him to an animal, primarily because of the way he moved effortlessly through the landscapes and seascapes of the Pacific region. If Snyder did in fact move like an animal, it was probably because he had already studied the migratory pathways taken by the creatures he calls "critters" (after frontier lingo) or "animal-people" (after Native American oral legends). In a long career devoted to recovering the "old ways" of Pacific Rim culture, he has repeatedly summoned the example of migratory animals, and the mythologies they have inspired, in order to challenge official national histories, resist capitalism's destruction of natural resources, and engage the multitude of biological and cultural currents that have been forgotten, repressed, or otherwise obscured. This chapter tracks the emergence of Snyder's migratory sensibility, following the poet from his boyhood on Puget Sound, to his college years in Portland, to the composition of his first volume of verse. Even at this early juncture, we shall notice, Pacific Rim consciousness was shaping his thinking.

Early Movements

The experience of moving came early for Snyder. Born in San Francisco in 1930, he moved at age two to Lake City, Washington, just north of Seattle, where his father tried his hand at dairy farming (with less than stellar results). During his boyhood forays into nearby wilderness areas, some of which lasted for days on end, he honed his survival skills and learned about the natural powers that dwarf human pretension. Because he sensed that the natural world was profoundly interconnected, he lost patience with philosophies or religions that privileged one group of living beings over another. The son of confirmed atheists, he held a particular aversion to Christian doctrines maintaining that animals do not have souls, a precept he knew instinctively to be false.[4] Through his contact with the wilderness areas of the Pacific Northwest, he came to respect native cultures that live close to the land. Snyder was particularly struck by the fact that an old Salish Indian who occasionally visited the family's dairy farm had a more intimate knowledge of that place than his parents ever did. As Snyder would say years later, the Salishan man "knew better than anyone else I had ever met *where I was*." The descendents of white settlers, by contrast, had only a rudimentary sense of the place they had bought into. "Looking back at all the different trees and plants that made up my second-growth Douglas-fir forest plus cow pasture childhood universe, I realized that my parents were short on a certain kind of knowledge. They could say, 'That's a Doug fir, that's a cedar, that's a bracken fern,' but I perceived a subtlety and complexity in those woods that went far beyond a few names" (PS 183–84).

Canoeing, fishing, clamming, gathering bark, and picking blackberries were the other first steps Snyder remembers taking in order to gain a more nuanced understanding of his place in the Pacific Northwest. His second step involved traveling to a Seattle Public Library branch in the university district, where he read as much as he could, including mountain writings by John Muir, poems by D. H. Lawrence, and accounts of American Indians by Ernest Thompson Seton.[5] He also began hanging out at the University of Washington Anthropology Museum, studying its excellent collection of Indian artifacts and reinforcing his "idea that the local folks knew something that the white folks didn't know."[6] Confronted with such documentary evidence, Snyder realized that humans had the choice of whether they wanted to destroy large ecosystems or preserve them. As was often the case, though, Snyder found that the wilderness was an even better teacher than a library or museum. In an interview with Bill Moyers, he recalled that his family's property bordered a "clear cut where some of the largest conifer forests in the world had been." In the midst of this deforested area, he dedicated himself to reversing the cycle of ecological abuse. "Right back of our cow pasture there were stumps twelve feet high and twelve feet across, the giant Douglas fir and Western hemlock and Western red cedar of Puget Sound, and I played among them as a kid. I became so tuned in and, in a certain sense, radicalized so early that I like to think the ghosts of those giant trees were whispering to me as a kid, 'Do something about this.'"[7]

By his teens, when he moved with his mother to Portland, Oregon, Snyder was increasing his store of ecological knowledge with a series of mountaineering adventures. Before he left high school, he had already scaled many of Washington's and Oregon's major peaks, including Mount Hood and Mount Adams, as well as Mount Saint Helens, an active volcano he climbed on 13 August 1945, just one week after the Hiroshima bombing provided an earthshaking eruption of an entirely different sort.[8] On treks up these mountains, which he came to know by their Indian names (Wy'east, Klickitat, and Loowit), Snyder remembers being afforded a panoramic view of the Pacific Northwest and "an initiation by all the great gods of the land."[9] In the 1970s, when he had children of his own, he would take them to the tops of mountains so that they could "see our place." For Snyder, climbing a peak to gain a new perspective "is the way the world should be learned. It's an intense geography that is never far removed from your body."[10]

From his mountain perches, Snyder came to understand that the Puget Sound and Portland areas are not fixed places, but rather nodal points constructed by movements, exchanges, and traversals. Weather patterns, animal migrations, and tectonic rumblings, when taken together or combined with other kinetic variables, create a spatial vortex lending each place on earth its unique character. A place that appears to be local actually has far-flung origins, which in turn have far-reaching consequences for other places around the world. As Snyder would explain decades later, as he attempted to pinpoint the location of Kitkitdizze, the farmhouse/compound he built in the Sierra Nevada foothills in 1970, a place is "but one tiny node in an evolving net of bioregional homesteads and camps" (PS 262). In the Pacific Northwest, it just so happens, the majority of nodal relationships are routed along the ecological and cultural zone we call the Pacific Rim. "The geographical significance of East Asia to the west coast was palpable, as I was growing up," Snyder once told me. "Seattle had a Chinatown, the Seattle Art Museum had a big East Asian collection, one of my playmates was a Japanese boy whose father was a farmer, we all knew that the Indians were racially related to the East Asians and that they had got there via Alaska, & there were freighters from China and Japan in Puget Sound, a constant sense of exchange."[11]

While still a boy, Snyder attended two exhibits that further enhanced his Pacific Rim consciousness. The first was the Golden Gate International Exposition in San Francisco, where he saw a performance of Chinese acrobats along with other attractions devoted to Pacific culture. The second was an exhibit of Chinese *sumi* landscape paintings, done in ink brush, on display at the Seattle Art Museum. To the boy's great surprise, the depiction of Chinese mountains in the *sumi* paintings looked hauntingly familiar. "When I was eleven or twelve," Snyder recalled in a 1977 interview, "I went into the Chinese room at the Seattle art museum and saw Chinese landscape paintings; they blew my mind. My shock of recognition was very simple: 'It looks just like the Cascades.' The waterfalls, the pines, the clouds, the mist looked a lot like the northwest United States. The Chinese had an eye for the world that I saw as real. . . . It was no great lesson except for an instantaneous, deep respect for something in Chinese culture that always stuck in my mind and that I would come back to again years later" (TRW 93–94). Snyder reiterates the germinal importance of the *sumi* paintings in his unfinished "Hokkaido Book" manuscript, where he refers to the museum experience as a "seed in my store-house-consciousness to be watered later when I first read Arthur Waley's translations of Chinese poetry and then Ezra Pound's. I thought, here is a high civilization that has managed to keep in tune with nature. The philosophical and religious writings I later read from the Chinese seemed to back this up. I even thought for a time that simply because China had not been Christian, and had been spared an ideology which separated humankind from all other living beings (with the two categories of redeemable and unredeemable) that it naturally had an organic, process-oriented view of the world."[12]

For Snyder, and for anyone else who subscribes to a "process-oriented view of the world," the various landscapes of the Pacific are all of one piece, since they not only share an ocean but also a historical and cultural development based on similar topographical wonders. What we need, Snyder realized early on, is an art that is able to translate these natural connections to civilized people who have long forgotten them. Importantly, his early observations suggested that Asian and Native American arts and literatures were more adept than those in Western civilization at registering these kinds of connections. Little wonder, then, that Snyder's magnum opus, *Mountains and Rivers without End*, took its inspiration from Chinese scroll paintings, which Snyder appreciated for their "energies of mist, white water, rock formation, air swirls—a chaotic universe where everything is in place" (MR 153). Operating on the Buddhist premise that humanity itself is less important than a landscape full of interconnected and mutually respectful sentient beings, the painters of the Chi'ing and Sung dynasties pictured a realm in which arbitrary boundaries of civilization were subject to natural dissolution and reconfiguration. Behind Snyder's "shock of recognition" there existed an ancient impulse to shrink distances and reestablish communal ties.

I Want to Create Wilderness out of Empire

When it came time to go to college, Snyder chose not to migrate very far. As a double major in literature and anthropology at Reed College, located in his new hometown of Portland, Snyder received the scholarly training that helped him delve more deeply into the Pacific Rim cultures and ecological concerns that had fascinated him since childhood. By his own account, the education he received at Reed was rigorous. "They wouldn't tolerate bullshit. . . . It was an intensive, useful experience" (TRW 64). But classroom rigors constituted only one part of Snyder's education. One of the most fruitful outcomes of his college experience was the close friendship he forged with fellow students Philip Whalen and Lew Welch. As they discovered common literary interests, these fledgling poets established the Adelaide Crapsey–Oswald Spengler Memorial Society, an outsider intellectual clique inspired by a poet renowned for her five-line hokku experiments and a historian famous for his prophetic and weighty tome, *The Decline of the West*. The decline theorized by Spengler, and eventually picked up by the Beats on both coasts (including Jack Kerouac and William Burroughs), did not signify imminent cultural oblivion so much as it heralded new discoveries of what lay beyond traditional Western comprehension.[13] As Snyder, Whalen, and Welch came to understand it, the decline of the West meant the rise of Pacific Rim consciousness, for it encouraged Americans to look beyond the western horizon in search of alternative cultural roots/routes.

This is not to say that the members of the society turned their backs on all things Western. In fact, all three men were drawn to the work of modernist experimentalists in the Anglo-American tradition, including Ezra Pound and William Carlos Williams, although it must be remembered that these two poets were among the first in the West to incorporate Asian rhythms into their own verse. When Williams visited Reed during a 1950 lecture tour, he found time to meet with three young admirers named Snyder, Whalen, and Welch, and they in turn initiated him into their society.[14] Over the next decade, Williams was to become an outspoken champion of the New American Poets, writing the introduction to Allen Ginsberg's *Howl and Other Poems* and helping other young writers make their way in the literary world. Still, except perhaps for Welch, whose senior thesis was a study of Gertrude Stein, the members of the society were moving toward a more natural and primitive aesthetic, one they felt the Anglo-American modernists had either ignored or misrepresented. While Snyder and his friends continued to respect Pound and Williams for their literary daring, and especially for their Asian-inflected poetics, they found themselves edging closer to a rugged West Coast style grounded in local landscapes and the oral literatures of indigenous cultures.

It was in this regard that Snyder emerged as the group's standard-bearer. Through his living example, he anticipated the confluence of artistic and organic forms that would characterize the New American Poetry. Welch, who while serving as editor for the Reed College publication *Janus* was among the first to publish a Snyder poem, began to trumpet his friend's post-Poundian aesthetics, calling him "the mountaineer" and "the only urbane hill-man in the Kulture."[15] If Anglo-American modernism could be rewritten to honor the particularities of the West Coast, Welch surmised, his college buddy was certainly up to the task. As he explained to Snyder in one letter, "Pound didn't get the point of those great big mountains, and you do. So make a language that talks about them better than his did."[16] Snyder, for his part, lived up to Welch's challenge; in fact, he seemed to thrive on it. As he told Whalen in a 1954 letter, "that Pound has left something undone is a great virtue."[17]

As it happened, Snyder employed his rustic knowledge not just to fashion an aesthetic paradigm but also to counteract the grasping tendencies of modern nation-states. By opposing the policies of governments seeking to seize, control, and regulate territories, Snyder developed a more radical (after *radix*, or "root") and intimate relationship with the earth. No doubt he would have agreed with the estimation of his hero Thoreau, who near the end of *Walden* claimed, "the government of the world I live in was not framed, like that of Britain, in after-dinner conversations over the wine."[18] For Snyder, as for Thoreau, proper governance of the land derives not from a handful of isolated aristocrats or bureaucrats, but instead from interactions among various communities of living creatures with the most basic investment in their particular geographic region. If cold war nationalism was basically a high-tech updating of Manifest Destiny on a global frontier, Snyder's early call for wise primitivism and ecological sensitivity was a challenge to the legitimacy of his country's latest forward thrust. Essentially, he wanted to turn back the hands on America's futuristic cultural clock. "I want to create wilderness out of empire!" his classmates at Reed remember him shouting gleefully.[19]

Before he graduated, this curious student from the backwoods of the Pacific Northwest attracted a throng of admirers. Not for the last time, Snyder's magnetic personality threatened to supersede his intellectual reputation. In a pointed critique offered decades later, David Perkins maintains that the reputations of several well-known Beat and hippie writers stemmed as much from their lifestyles as from the quality of their writing. As the American counterculture came of age, Perkins asserts, it required sages to express and even enact its moral resistance to the nation's imperial impulses. According to his argument, poets like Snyder and Ginsberg offered transvaluations of culture as they acted out, through their rebellious lifestyle choices, the visions articulated in their poems. These "gurus," as Perkins calls them, "sometimes write very well, but their general influence has derived from the image of their lives in conjunction with their poems."[20] Whatever Snyder may think of such evaluations, the Reed years mark the beginning of this trend, for it was at this juncture that he was hailed by others as an exemplar of alternative living and Pacific Rim exoticism.

At Reed, Snyder resided with Whalen, and eventually with Welch, in a seven-room Victorian house at 1414 Southeast Lambert Street in Portland. Here the three friends found a communal atmosphere conducive to their shared interests as well as to a burgeoning intellectual network. The house became an off-campus hot spot, and Snyder was regarded as the keeper of the castle. One college friend provides us with an interesting look at how Snyder's sexual allure, minimalist lifestyle, and Asian mysteriousness contributed to his special reputation: "Gary acted as sometimes-manager [of the Lambert Street house] in return for the privilege of living in the basement between the furnace and the laundry tub: an area about eight by ten feet. A casement window provided a view of the heavens and a steady stream of water whenever it rained. Typically, Gary defined the leak as a waterfall and running brook, which he channeled across the basement floor to serve a miniature Japanese garden. This 'Zen retreat,' with Gary as its centerpiece, attracted a constant stream of beautiful young ladies, especially children of the rich and famous. With a simple bed—a mattress on the floor—a Japanese print or two, and a draped cloth here and there, Gary somehow evoked the aura of a sheik of Araby."[21] We can see in this exotic portrait the kind of attention bestowed upon Snyder in later years, when his habitats (in Berkeley, Mill Valley, Kyoto, and San Juan Ridge) attracted a stream of admirers enamored of the geographical alternatives the poet defined and cultivated. To catch a glimpse of Snyder in these spaces was to understand the simple yet glorious path one could travel on the way to a non-Western mindset. His social aura, fully in place during his time at Reed, would accompany (and sometimes burden) him throughout the heyday of the San Francisco Renaissance and beyond.

In the midst of campus fame, Snyder still found time for serious scholarship, inside and outside the classroom. During a visit to a Portland art museum, Snyder had an experience rather similar to the shock of recognition he experienced a decade before in the Seattle museum. The new revelation came courtesy of an exhibit by Morris Graves, who together with Mark Tobey and Guy Anderson composed the "Northwest School of Painters." Like Snyder, each of these artists was steeped in Asian aesthetics and religion (Tobey was a Bahai, Graves a Vedantist and Buddhist) and believed that the landscapes of the Pacific Northwest and East Asia had much in common. Fascinated with the *sumi* style of Chinese scroll painters, they experimented with tempera, ink, and rice paper, working with quick, light brush strokes and representing lines of landscape as though they were an interconnected series of effortless movements.

Reviewing his intellectual development, Snyder lists Graves as an important influence.[22] It is easy to see why. Like the young poet, Graves had an intimate knowledge of rugged Pacific Coast landscapes, keeping a studio on Fidalgo, one of the San Juan Islands in Puget Sound. Graves was also a devotee of Zen, entering a Buddhist temple at age twenty-six, as Snyder himself would in 1956.[23] Even more attractive to Snyder, perhaps, was the fact that Graves registered deep-seated emotions by recourse to animal movement and behavior. In his paintings of shorebirds, especially, we can catch a glimpse of the creaturely sensibility that would later infuse Snyder's Pacific Rim poetry. For example, in a 1939 composition simply entitled *Shorebirds*, Graves depicts a group of eleven sandpipers warily measuring the steps to the edge of the Pacific Ocean, as the foam of a spent breaker curves gently on either side of their little assemblage.

By placing themselves in this particular location, these diminutive birds, which migrate by night high above these same waters, actively confront the elements of the vast ecosystem in which they move. With their close-up view of ocean waves, the birds are able to measure the fluid boundaries of their being. Graves once admitted that this painting "is more concerned with the flow across the page, the movements of the birds, than it is with the characters of the birds."[24] Still, I cannot help thinking that the movement and the character of the sandpipers are inseparable aspects of their creaturely identity. The same might be said of *Consciousness Assuming the Form of a Crane*, a series of paintings Graves completed in 1945. According to Kenneth Rexroth, who wrote a laudatory review of the painter's work in 1955, *Consciousness Assuming the Form of a Crane* illustrates how order and unity can emerge from formlessness, in an "ephemeral simplicity . . . as quiet as some half-caught telepathic message."[25] The title of Graves's series certainly suggests the extent to which migratory animals influence human thinking as they reveal a formal pattern, a fluid boundary of consciousness made visible.

The potential of animals to aid humans in their search for meaning had a profound effect on the way Graves represented trauma, an important consideration at any time, but especially at midcentury, when much of the Pacific region was marked out as a military frontier. In one of his most stunning pieces, *Bird Wearied by the Length of the Winter of 1944*, Graves uses another shorebird to register a complaint against the hostilities he saw raging across this oceanic realm. According to the painter, "the disheveled plumage and the general feeling of the line of shattered fragility—almost no bones underneath it—was a comment on how neurotic the continuation of the war was making us—how unsettled and shattered and wearied by the length of the winter of 1944 we were. One of these drawings I rolled up and packaged and addressed to Prime Minister Winston Churchill as a communication."[26] Clearly, this painting showcases the artist's pacifist tendencies.

Around the time of its composition, Graves visited a conscientious objectors' camp at Waldport, Oregon, where poet William Everson (Brother Antoninus) was interned.[27] While there, he inspired Everson to register his own variety of creaturely pacifism. Within a few years, Everson was following Graves, as well as Saint Francis, using a poem entitled "A Canticle to the Waterbirds" to advocate "the strict conformity that creaturehood entails." Neither was the painter's message lost on Lawrence Ferlinghetti, who in "A Coney Island of the Mind" explains that "the wounded wilderness of Morris Graves / is not the same wild west / the white man found / It is a land that Buddha came upon / from a different direction."[28] In *Bird Wearied by the Length of Winter* and other shorebird paintings, Graves not only pays witness to the world war's devastating effect on Pacific Rim ecosystems but also suggests that the westward thrust of American Manifest Destiny is to blame. If Graves's birds can so cogently express the feelings of a war-weary population, Snyder and other West Coast poets must have mused, how could anyone venture to say that animals do not have souls?

We must remember that the "creaturely" sensibility evoked by Graves and championed by San Francisco Beats does not belong to any particular person, or indeed to any one era or tradition. It belongs to the West as well as to the East, and to the present time as well as to the archaic past. A brief look at how other writers have invoked creaturely consciousness provides clarification. In the "General Prologue" to *The Canterbury Tales*, for instance, Geoffrey Chaucer suggests that the call to pilgrimage is inspired by the awakening of the land and its creatures, including the "smale fowles" who feel the springtime energies passionately and deeply, to their very heart ("So pricketh hem Nature in his corages"). In the tales that follow, Chaucer's animals often lend wry commentary on human nature. In "The Reeve's Tale," a freed horse's "wehee" represents the whinny of sexual delight signaling the climax of the fabliau plot. Animals also figure prominently in "The Squire's

Tale," where a male tercelet's desire for the "newfangleness" of a female kite exposes both "love's ypocryte" and the primal need to escape bounded spaces. Canacee, one of the tale's human subjects, will understand this harsh lesson of love only after listening to the testimony of the tercelet's abandoned wife, a lovesick peregrine falcon.[29]

We can locate a creaturely sensibility in modern literature as well, although by this juncture there is a greater likelihood that it will be referred to as something long gone or dangerously repressed. Walter Benjamin, who made the recovery of lost aura his life's mission, once praised Franz Kafka's tales for allowing animals to function as a "receptacle of the forgotten."[30] He lauded Spanish theater along these same lines, for he thought that its complex interplay of tragedy and comedy "permitted . . . the creaturely exposure of the person."[31] In the post-Freudian theory of Gilles Deleuze and Felix Guattari, too, we find several occasions in which a vast network of animal movements and spacings gives rise to delightfully quirky theses promoting natural interconnectedness. Wolves that run in packs, birds that sing forth in order to mark a territory, even the small molecular life that circulates so forcefully as to frustrate larger forms of organization: all of these actions convey the natural genius that Deleuze and Guattari, in their inimitable terminology, call "Becoming-Intense, Becoming-Animal, Becoming-Imperceptible."[32]

After reviewing the premodern invocation of pastoral nationhood found in Chaucer, the modern sense of nostalgia found in Benjamin, and the postmodern fluidity found in Deleuze and Guattari, we will notice that animal behavior speaks to different concerns at different times. What these writers share, however, is a belief that animals possess the most astute knowledge of the earth's fundamental structures and the keenest sense of its symbiotic relationships. Through their simple motions, animals are always at work constructing (and deconstructing) a world that civilized humans find exceedingly difficult to comprehend. Graves's wearied shorebird stands as a case in point. In 1944, as governments founded on principles of reason engaged in a war of unreasonable destruction, a migratory animal accustomed to traveling the periphery of the Pacific Rim without hindrance or peril, but suddenly prohibited from doing so, silently reminded viewers of the damage committed in the name of humanity. Clearly, the pathos of *Bird Wearied by the Length of the Winter of 1944* is strong enough to make observers choose wilderness over empire. Having already made this choice, Snyder used his college thesis to develop his creaturely sensibility.

Diffusion and Transformation:
He Who Hunted Birds in His Father's Village

Back in the classroom, Snyder began charting new paths of intellectual discovery. His early interests in Native American culture and West Coast wilderness areas, when combined with his predilection for communal living arrangements and creaturely consciousness, led to the interesting lines of inquiry shaping his senior thesis, *He Who Hunted Birds in His Father's Village: The Dimensions of a Haida Myth.* According to Snyder's thesis adviser, David H. French, *He Who Hunted Birds* is the "most copied Reed thesis of all time."[33] In it we discover Snyder's characteristic attention to natural detail along with his growing interest in a wider range of Pacific cultures and their oral literatures. "It's curious how in my thesis I mapped out practically all my major interests," Snyder told San Francisco Renaissance bibliographer David Kherdian in 1965.[34]

The Haida people make their home on the Queen Charlotte Islands, near Vancouver, British Columbia. The archipelago is situated along the extensive coastline of bays and inlets where Snyder grew up, although it turns out that he first learned about the Haida's "He Who Hunted Birds" myth by reading Bureau of American Ethnology *Bulletins* while at Reed. Snyder remembers that the "Memoirs and Reports" and "myths and texts" series included in these *Bulletins* often translated Haida songs, Tlingit and Kwaikutl mythology, and other native literatures of the Pacific Northwest (TRW 58). The particular Haida myth that Snyder chose to study is a story of creaturely transformation, and behind its simple telling lies a rich and complex history of crosscultural transmission and meaning. Snyder organizes his thesis accordingly. The first chapter provides a transcription of "He Who Hunted Birds" as it was "told to Walter McGregor of the Sealion-town people" and recorded by John Swanton for a 1905 *Bulletin* (HWHB 1, 115n).[35] Each ensuing chapter explores some aspect of that myth's dimensionality: its culture, its different versions, its sources, its literary role, and its function.

The original myth tells the tale of a chief's son who, while hunting, hears the cry of geese. Following the sound, he comes across two goose-women bathing naked in a forest lake. Their skins lie upon the shore. The hunter is immediately struck by the beauty of the younger goose-woman and asks her to marry him. The older goose-woman, who reveals herself as the sister of the young beauty, claims that she is the smarter one, but the hunter insists on his choice of the younger. Upon her marriage and entry into the bridegroom's household, the young goose-woman experiences a severe case of culture shock and refuses to eat. At night, however, she puts on her goose-skin and forages for food that suits her diet: sea grass, clover, and the *tclal* roots found at the mouths of creeks. After a long period of suffering, she decides to leave this unfamiliar situation and fly back to her family's home, where, as Haida matrilineal descent dictates, she and her husband should have gone in the first place.

In his retelling of the myth, McGregor describes the husband's search for the goose-wife who had (quite literally) taken flight. In order to reclaim her, though, he must wander some unfamiliar paths. Luckily, this chief's son is assisted in his mission by a number of creaturely guides, including a Lice Man, a Mouse Woman, and a woman who carries the mountains of Haida Island on her back. However bizarre these guides initially appear to the husband, they at least have a familiarity with the supernatural realm in which he now finds himself. They eventually lead him to a pole extending into the sky. Cloaked in a mouse skin given to him by the Mouse Woman, the husband climbs the pole and reaches the celestial realm, where the goose-woman and her family make their home. Here he is given further assistance by several more animal guides—Eagle, Heron, Kingfisher, Black Bear—and is finally reunited with his wife and accepted by her people. It is not long, however, before he experiences the same kind of acculturation difficulties his wife had suffered back in the earthly realm. Suddenly, it is he who wishes to take flight. Having no wings of his own, however, he must be transported by someone else. Raven, the predominant trickster figure in the Indian mythologies of the Pacific Northwest, accedes to his request and begins to fly the chief's son back to his father's household. During the course of their downward flight, Raven deposits the husband on a seaside reef, far short of his destination. The myth ends rather abruptly, as the chief's son is left alone on the reef, there to be transformed into a seagull.

Snyder's structural analysis of "He Who Hunted Birds" is affected by the psychoanalytic models of Sigmund Freud and Carl Jung and by the comparative folklore of Stith Thompson. Taking additional cues from mythologist Joseph Campbell, Snyder argues that this Haida parable should be classified as a quest romance or "monomyth." In this type of story, Campbell explains, a protagonist (in this case, the chief's son who weds the goose-woman) undergoes a threefold process of "separation-initiation-return" during which "a hero ventures forth from the world of common day into a region of supernatural wonder: fabulous forces are there encountered and a decisive victory is won: the hero comes back from this mysterious adventure with the power to bestow boons on his fellow man. . . . The passage of the mythological hero may be overground, incidentally: fundamentally it is inward—into depths where obscure resistances are overcome, and long lost, forgotten powers are revivified, to be made available for the transfiguration of the world" (Campbell, quoted in HWHB 70, 71). With Campbell's model in mind, Snyder says that the goose-woman in "He Who Hunted Birds" symbolizes the "totality of what can be known." So potent is her wisdom, in fact, that the tale does away with the final stage of the monomyth, whereby the chief's son would have returned to his village. Once the husband is reunited with the wife in the celestial realm, Snyder postulates, he has already "reached the ultimate boon of knowledge." There is therefore no need for the husband to return to his people, Snyder claims, since "he has—in a psychological sense—been reborn and taken new form. As seagull, he has symbolically transcended his old ordinary human self" (HWHB 71).

Structural matters aside, I cannot help but notice that "He Who Hunted Birds" takes on a geographical cast, and that its obsession with foreign spaces is spoken about in gendered terms. Apparently, the goose-woman's celestial realm needs to be explored and mapped if the husband and the members of his earthly community hope to transform their worldview or enhance their self-understanding. The chief's son regards his goose-bride not as an individual so much as a site of foreign knowledge, hunting her down and appropriating what she represents until at last it accords with his own transformed identity. By the end of the myth, the hunter has become what he has hunted all along, and thus fulfilled his quest, while the goose-woman is relegated to the status of a throwaway prop.[36] The male hero's propensity here to cathect the "foreign" woman as the temporary site of unconscious truth would resurface from time to time in Snyder's later poetry, especially in *The Back Country*. In the Haida myth, the goose-woman exists primarily to lure the male voyager to foreign climes, where (and only where) he is able to find out more about himself. She would thus seem to share the fate of *Pacifica*, the mammoth female statue Ralph Stackpole unveiled at the 1939 Golden Gate International Exposition, for she too has become the focal point of an imagined community of males whose cartographic tastes run to sublime female forms. Similarly, in *The Back Country*, Snyder turns repeatedly to supernatural women inhabiting unfamiliar spaces beyond the golden periphery of the Pacific Rim in order to understand the dark secrets shaping his utopian conception of hemispheric community (see Chapter 3, "Embodying").

Somewhat more pertinent to Snyder's early poetry, especially *Myths & Texts*, is his emphasis on the diffusion of culture in the Pacific region. In his study of Haida mythology, Snyder describes history as the remembrance of ancient cultural transmissions across vast stretches of geographical space. "'Historical study,'" according to this budding scholar, "does not mean explication of chronological development, or search for ultimate origins, but rather correlations of geographical distribution with the different versions of demonstrably historically related myths and tales. For the majority of tales, it will never be possible to know the place of origin, owing to the immense time-depth and complexity of oral literature. Knowledge of origins, at present, is not even considered as valuable as the understanding of processes in diffusion and adaptation" (HWHB 35). For Snyder, a tale or myth is historical only insofar as its dissemination within or across geographic spaces exposes it to a new audience of listeners. Here, as in his best poetry, Snyder concentrates not so much on how Pacific Rim traditions are born, but rather on how they are *borne* across geographically linked localities. As his thesis unfolds, he suggests that those who travel from one locale to another, along with those who live along cultural boundaries and those whose mixed marriages introduce them to foreign cultures, have the most unique opportunities to disseminate, translate, and thus preserve the archaic histories of which he speaks (HWHB 36). In the 1950s and 1960s, Snyder himself would fulfill this role in the San Francisco Renaissance.

In *The Masks of God: Primitive Mythology*, a volume first published in 1959, nearly a decade after Snyder completed his undergraduate thesis, Joseph Campbell explains that archaeologists and anthropologists in the modern era were already developing a working thesis for the geographical diffusion shaping Pacific cultures. One of the first intellectuals to advance such a theory was Leo Frobenius, whose 1898 article outlining a new approach called *Kulturkreislehre* (or "culture area theory") challenged the prevailing anthropological theory of "parallel development," which contended that the astonishing similarities among cultures on different continents arose from the universal impulse of humans to civilize themselves gradually and independently, free from any external models or overseas influences. According to Campbell, Frobenius countered this trend once he "identified a primitive cultural continuum, extending from equatorial West Africa eastward, through India and Indonesia, Melanesia and Polynesia, across the Pacific to equatorial America and the northwest coast." His discovery of similar types of primitive planting villages stretching from the Sudan to Easter Island was unique insofar as it "brought the broad and bold theory of a primitive trans-oceanic 'diffusion' to bear upon the question of the distribution of so-called 'universal' themes." "In our study of Oceania," Frobenius wrote in a separate study, "it can be shown that a bridge existed, and not a chasm, between America and Asia."[37]

Campbell also notes that in 1950, or about a half century after the Frobenius thesis, Carl Sauer weighed in with his own contribution, listing the various cultivated plants (bottle gourds, Asiatic cotton, cocopalms, amaranth, plantains, maize, and sweet potatoes) that grew on both sides of the Pacific. For Sauer, this seemed to indicate that agricultural innovations traveled across the ocean both eastward and westward. Robert Heine-Geldern followed a year later with his idea of a "prehistoric circum-Pacific culture zone, represented by an art style probably native to eastern Asia and perhaps dating from as early as the third millennium B.C." Heine-Geldern emphasized the fact that similar kinds of birds, fish, humans, and other creatures could be found in various locations of the Pacific Rim, particularly as figures in the region's art designs, including those carved onto totem poles, traced in tattoo motifs, woven into bark-cloth, and sculpted in bas-relief. Taken together, he argued, these artworks told of an "Old Pacific Style" that stretched from the northwest coast of America to parts of Melanesia, Borneo, Sumatra, and the Philippines. In 1952, linguists A. Meillet and Marcel Cohen made the notion of a "single culture realm" seem even more incontrovertible when they highlighted the spread of a single linguistic complex stretching from Madagascar to Easter Island. By 1960, when shards of Japanese pottery dating from 3000 B.C.E. were dug up on the coast of Ecuador, Campbell found the "possibility of an early trans-Pacific diffusion of culture traits to the New World" extremely difficult to deny.[38]

In his college thesis, Snyder does not refer to the work of Leo Frobenius, and he could not have cited the work of the other researchers even if he wanted to, since they had not yet published their findings. Even so, Snyder clearly addresses the topic of geographic diffusion, especially when he refers to "culture areas," spaces where a certain type of myth is likely to be found. Indeed, much of his commentary in *He Who Hunted Birds* is devoted to the emergence of a "North Pacific Coast Area," which runs from northern California to Prince William Sound, on the eastern side of the Rim. In the anthropological and ethnographic reports he was reading, Snyder learned that much of the mythology that flourished in this region had come from Asia after having been routed eastward and southward along the northern arc of the Pacific Rim. Here we can see Snyder moving in a somewhat different direction from the researchers Campbell cites in his study of primitive mythology. Whereas Frobenius and researchers like Paul Rivet argued that the diffusion of culture followed an equatorial sea route and was most likely transported by seaworthy catamarans built in the South Seas or balsas built in Peru, Snyder suggests that Asian people and their culture traveled to America along coastal routes. A first indication comes when he cites a 1933 report by Franz Boas, who argues that if the slat-armor used in indigenous cultures of West Coast America "should have developed from Chinese and Japanese patterns it would be proof of long-continued cultural influence that extended northward and south-eastward" along an extensive Pacific Rim shoreline (quoted in HWHB 42). A more obvious indication arrives as Snyder moves away from a discussion of material culture to talk about the transmission of the archetypal swan-maiden motif, which forms the basis of the "He Who Hunted Birds" myth. At this point, Snyder calls attention to the work of folklorist Gudmund Hatt, who asserts that the swan-maiden motif, which is "very common in Indonesia, Melanesia, and Australia . . . has reached America by the northern way, over North East Asia. A transmission via Polynesia is unlikely." Like the human populations that arrived in America by way of the Bering land bridge, that is, the Haida myth Snyder studies has traveled across the Pacific by hugging the coast.

In any geographic region, physical surroundings and natural phenomena shape migratory patterns. Thus, near the beginning of his commentary on the Haida myth, Snyder decides to concentrate on the contour of the southern Canadian coastline, with its "maze of islands, its deeply indented fjords, natural waterways and inlets"; the Japanese weather currents that arc southeastward, bringing rain and moderate temperatures to America's western shores; the rain forests that thrive in this misty climate; and the animals that thrive in such an ecosystem (HWHB 11–12). It is also important to mention, as Snyder does not in his thesis, that human migration in the Pacific Rim region was precipitated by the movement of animals in search of food. Bison, mammoth, caribou, and reindeer were the first creatures to cross the

Bering land bridge into America; humans who traveled this route were only following their prey.[39] When they were hunting these animals, aboriginal peoples would track their pathways and in some cases even mimic their movements. They would often do the same when they were formulating creaturely mythologies. Although his college thesis does not point explicitly to this historical evidence, Snyder seems to believe that the myths common to Northeast Asia and Northwest America are as naturally routed as the weather patterns and animal migrations that accompanied, and in some sense governed, their transmission and articulation.

Of course, the diffusion of mythology across geographic space also depends upon the way tales get told. It is in this context that Snyder discusses the role of the shaman. In primitive societies, the shaman plays an overtly public role. Even though the shamans suffer intense personal pain, they are able to project this pain outward to narrate the unconscious fears and concerns of the entire community. As Joseph Campbell explains in *The Hero with a Thousand Faces*, the trancelike spectacle of the shaman's dance, which at first looks to be nothing more than the contortions of a tortured being, is "simply making visible and public the systems of symbolic fantasy that are present in the psyche of every member of adult society" (quoted in HWHB 94). By likening the shaman to I. A. Richards's figure of the poet, Snyder conveys his belief that the shaman should be "pre-eminently accessible to external influences and discriminating with regard to them." His talents may appear crude on the surface, Snyder admits, but like the poet celebrated by Richards, the shaman emerges as a key figure in a society hoping to recover its cultural connections, simply because he can "recast them in symbolic form" (HWHB 94).

Significantly, the shaman's quest for lost connections is almost always aided by the presence of animals, for they possess an uncanny knowledge of "the old ways." For Snyder, part of the allure of Northwest Indian culture was its belief that animals do indeed have souls. The wily animal guides that populate "He Who Hunted Birds," such as the trickster Raven or the supernatural Thunderbird, make it known that humans are hardly the most soulful beings roaming the land or even the most powerful. According to P. E. Goddard's study of Northwest Indians, the "sea-otter people, salmon people, grizzly people, [and] geese people" in Haida mythology "are considered practically equals of man in intelligence, and [are seen to] surpass him in the particulars for which each animal is noted" (quoted in HWHB 25–26). The shaman is the one responsible for tapping into this reservoir of creaturely knowledge, for as Snyder explains, it is he who knows better than anyone else in the community that the magic of ritual and myth "never controls [human affairs] according to principles that run counter to physical fact in nature" (HWHB 107). Little wonder, then, that Snyder, at various junctures of his writing career, appeared to take on the role of the shaman, awakening in the minds of contemporary Americans a latent knowledge of their Pacific Rim heritage while making the recovery of creaturely consciousness seem both practical and palatable.

When *He Who Hunted Birds* was published as a book in 1979, Snyder wrote a foreword in which he looks back to his days as a "green would-be scholar." After going through a list of his intellectual shortcomings, he emphasizes the foundational importance of his thesis on Haida myth. "I went on to other modes of study and writing, but never forgot what I learned from this work" (HWHB x). Among Snyder's most crucial findings is his discovery that "all peoples in all places share in a rich pre-historic international lore—no group is 'culturally deprived' until oppressed by an invader or exploiter. The *indigenas* are bearers of the deepest insights into human nature, and have the best actual way to live, as well. May this be realized before they are destroyed" (HWHB xi). Whether we regard these *indigenas* as the animals of the Pacific region or as the tribal cultures that live in harmony with these animals, it is clear that various creaturely communities spurred the poet to begin the first phase of a long-term reclamation project. In *He Who Hunted Birds*, Snyder is less concerned with a search for origins than he is with finding locations where historical time and geographic space are continuously (e)merging. More than anything, Snyder learns from his early study of Pacific Rim mythology that "geographical continuity" is relevant to the cultural narratives we live by (HWHB 39).

A Postgraduate De-education

His thesis completed, Snyder graduated from Reed in the spring of 1951. He set forth the following autumn for Indiana University, where he enrolled in the graduate program in anthropological linguistics. Snyder's scholarly path over the next few years would take several twists and turns, and his tenure at Indiana would be short-lived. While hitchhiking alone on Route

40 in eastern Nevada en route to Indiana, he began to read the work of D. T. Suzuki, at that time the most renowned scholar of Zen Buddhism in America. The book's effect on Snyder was immediate and powerful. "It catapulted me into an even larger space," he recalled three decades later, "and though I didn't know it at the moment, that was the end of my career as an anthropologist."[40] Another influential book was the one Snyder pulled from the library stacks at Indiana University. It was a collection of verse by Kenneth Rexroth, the San Francisco poet who would soon become one of his mentors.[41] Like Suzuki's Zen philosophy, Rexroth's Asian-inflected nature poetry evoked a mind space that the four walls of a classroom could not accommodate. It was only a matter of time before Snyder was obliged to make a "complete and total choice, consciously turning my back on the professional scholar's career in anthropology . . . and setting myself loose in the world to sink or swim as a poet."[42] He left Indiana after one semester and returned to the West Coast.

Over the next few years, Snyder began to "de-educate" himself in an effort to get closer to the lands and waters of the Pacific Northwest. In Snyder's opinion, the years immediately after one's graduation from college should be devoted to a rigorous reevaluation of the teaching one has received up to that point. The theories, concepts, and methods imparted in the classroom should have to withstand a practical litmus test; they must be applicable in the real world. Pressed by an interviewer to explain what he means by "de-educate," Snyder answers, "I mean get back in touch with people, with ordinary things: with your body, with the dirt, with the dust, with anything you like, you know—the streets. The streets or the farm, whatever it is. Get away from books and from the elite sense of being bearers of Western culture, and all that crap. But also, ultimately, into your mind, into original mind before any books were put into it, or before any language was invented. . . . It's what you call higher education" (TRW 64–65).

In the early 1950s, Snyder's de-education took him deep into the backcountry. During the summers of 1950 and 1951, just before and just after his senior year at Reed, Snyder worked for the National Park Service, excavating the archaeological site at old Fort Vancouver, and scaled timber at the Warm Springs Indian Reservation in Oregon. When he returned to the West Coast from Indiana in the spring of 1952, he took a series of odd jobs in San Francisco before heading north to Washington, where he served as a fire lookout on Crater Mountain, in Baker National Forest. He returned to Baker in the summer of 1953, this time to work on Sourdough Mountain. In 1954, however, the job he had lined up at Gifford Pinchot Forest was taken away, since the federal government, under whose auspices the forest was managed, cited him as a "security risk" and summarily fired him, over the protests of his supervisors. As Patrick Murphy explains, Snyder eventually discovered that he had been "branded a subversive" by two separate governmental agencies, the Federal Bureau of Investigation and the Coast Guard, which targeted him for using a communist-affiliated maritime union to procure his seaman's card back in 1948. Fortunately, Snyder found employment back at Warm Springs, where he spent the remainder of 1954 working as a choker-setter in the local tribe's lumber company.[43] During the summer of 1955, he found work in Yosemite National Park as a member of a trail crew that was not regulated by the federal government. As his early poetry attests, each of these experiences helped Snyder gain a fuller appreciation of his natural habitat.

Ironically, in the midst of his de-education process, Snyder decided to return to graduate school, this time at UC–Berkeley's oriental languages program. As he traveled from Berkeley up to Washington and Oregon and back down the coast again, Snyder likened himself to "a migratory bird going north in the summer and returning south in the winter" (TRW 95). Why this sudden return to the classroom? The primary reason was that he wanted to go to Japan to study Zen Buddhism. He knew that learning Japanese and Chinese would allow him to read Buddhist texts in the original and help him find work in Asia as a translator. As it happened, though, Snyder's studies at Berkeley aided him even before he set sail for Japan, for he discovered that Buddhist texts describing wilderness areas of Asia shed light on his own observations in the lookout cabins and along the logging trails of the American West Coast. His understanding of Pacific Rim culture was thus thrown into relief. This complex interplay between education at Berkeley and de-education in the mountains is on full display in Snyder's first volume of verse, *Myths & Texts*.

Hatching a New Myth:
Myths & Texts

The title that Snyder chose for his first volume of poetry pays homage to writings he referenced in his college thesis: the myths and texts series that appeared in the Bureau of American Ethnology *Bulletins*. In *Myths & Texts*,

Snyder tapped into his ever-growing knowledge of Pacific Rim anthropology and ecology to craft a complex lyric economy. A three-tier sequence of forty-eight short poems weaving together the legends and cultural practices found in Native American, Indian, Chinese, and Japanese literatures, *Myths & Texts* stands alongside the magisterial *Mountains and Rivers without End* (1996) as Snyder's most difficult work. Yet its multitude of Pacific Rim voices speaks cogently to the various influences affecting this poet's life: environmental ethics, bioregionalism, geographic community, animal rights, manual labor, and Buddhist practice.

Influence is the word that Snyder scholars puzzle over as they try to decipher this text (or is it a myth?). Snyder was not yet twenty-six when he completed the volume, yet its numerous mythic allusions, fragments of dialogue, logged journal entries, oral histories, and practical instructions—all of them cross-hatched by a series of indigenous animal tracks—indicate a precocious mind's ability to receive, collate, and synthesize a wide array of cultural and physical data. As he took his undergraduate thesis on Haida mythology, combined it with the Asian traditions he was learning about at UC–Berkeley, and integrated this knowledge with the working rhythms and animal patterns he saw transforming the West Coast landscape he loved, Snyder went from studying the mythic patterns of Pacific Rim culture to "hatching a new myth" of his own (MT 19).

That having been said, Snyder was never so bold as to claim sole authorship of *Myths & Texts*. Indeed, despite its tripartite structure, I do not believe that the volume portrays the classic individual quest romance of separation-initiation-return, as Lee Bartlett and other scholars have argued.[44] As the lyrics themselves make clear, the "new myth" hatched by Snyder is not a singular journey, or "monomyth," so much as it is an archaic collaboration: a plural inscription indebted to the various creaturely agents whose movements through the centuries have traced the geographic boundaries of a Pacific Rim culture area and to the diverse array of oral literatures that have kept their stories alive. More than any American poem I can think of, *Myths & Texts* honors the geographic diffusions that make culture, community, history, and region recognizable if somewhat unstable (because interdependent) paradigms. With its dedication to the heterogeneous and diasporic character of geographic structure and its respect for ecologically centered communities able to withstand the destructive forces of advancing civilization, *Myths & Texts* reads like no other myth of our time. Because its Pacific

Rim themes and images are so densely concentrated and intertwined, I think it best to analyze this volume closely, phase by phase.

Phase I—Logging Ecological Communities

Much of the material in "Logging," the first phase of *Myths & Texts*, derives from the summers of 1951 and 1954, when Snyder was working as a timber scaler and log setter in Washington and Oregon. During those summers, Snyder saw firsthand the havoc that greedy lumber companies, and Western civilization in general, had inflicted on his beloved West Coast wilderness areas. In an epigraph to *Myths & Texts*, Snyder cites Acts 19:27, as if to reproduce the destructive mindset he confronts: "Goddess Diana should be despised, and her magnificence should be destroyed, whom all Asia and the world worshippeth" (MT vi). By citing this scripture, and by setting his ensuing ruminations on creaturely community in direct opposition to its clarion call for forbearance and destruction, Snyder implies that the Judeo-Christian tradition of the West is too narrow for his purposes. Throughout the "Logging" phase, Snyder will continue to supply an ecological foundation for his countercultural aesthetic.

"Logging 1" begins peaceably enough. "The morning star is not a star" might indicate that Venus is a planet, not a star, although it is also notable for approximating Thoreau's meditation in *Walden* ("The sun is but a morning star"). The similarity here is not all that surprising. In the late 1960s, Richard Howard famously labeled Snyder the "true heir to Thoreau," and we know from Snyder's journal entries that he carried a paperback edition of *Walden* to the Sourdough Mountain lookout station.[45] Like Thoreau, one of America's first literary Orientalists, Snyder finds in the wilderness a space where he can meditate on hemispheric interchange, a space where the Judeo-Christian proscriptions referred to in Acts 19:27 can be newly contextualized and possibly overcome. This is not to suggest that Snyder and Thoreau—by wandering, working, and meditating in the wilderness—categorically reject Western thought. On the contrary, both men seek balance and union between Eastern and Western traditions. Since the morning star of the eastern sky is the same entity as the evening star in the western sky, these writers have happened upon a fit symbol for their respective projects. Enlightenment is universal and therefore belongs to both East and West, as

Gautama Buddha, who found enlightenment under the Bodhi tree once he gazed upon the morning star, realized centuries ago.[46]

Still, Snyder is clearly fed up with what he knows about most modern European traditions, and in the remainder of "Logging 1" we see him moving away from deleterious brands of consciousness. Whatever European images remain are distinctly premodern and sometimes even prehuman. As Io, the moon heifer, arrives "Girdled in wistaria"; as the May Queen comes to announce "the survival of / A prehuman / Rutting season"; and as "Green comes out of the ground / Birds squabble / Young girls run mad with the pine bough," the reader is presented with scenes of earthy virility and creaturely commentary. Snyder's pagan joy is short-lived, however, since such fruitfulness is exposed as a dream from which the contemporary sleeper must awake. To mark a harsher reality, the poet provides another biblical passage, this one from Exodus 34:13, as the epigraph to "Logging 2": "But ye shall destroy their altars, break their images, and cut down their groves." For Snyder, the Hebrew God's injunction to destroy the altars and images of the pagan gods is bad enough, but the actual destruction of the groves, the very places in which Thoreau and the Buddha meditated upon East-West unity, represents the ultimate transgression.

However much Snyder tries to remove himself from Western civilization, he knows that monomythic conceptions of distinction and separation are never as cut and dry as they seem, since forces of good and evil circulate everywhere. As "Logging 2" proceeds, the story of ecological destruction on the West Coast of America is laid bare, but not before we get a glimpse of similar abuses committed on the other side of the Pacific:

The ancient forests of China logged
     and the hills slipped into the Yellow Sea.
Squared beams, log dogs,
     on a tamped-earth sill.

San Francisco 2 x 4s
     were the woods around Seattle:
Someone killed and someone built, a house,
     a forest, wrecked or raised
All America hung on a hook
     & burned by men, in their own praise. (MT 3–4)

Exploring the Creaturely Byways of the Pacific Northwest | **69**

To his credit, Snyder has never romanticized Asia to such an extent that he fails to acknowledge the ecological atrocities its nations have sometimes condoned. In this instance, China's faulty environmental policies are juxtaposed with similar policies on the other side of the Pacific Ocean. Just as the felled forests of China were once transformed into "squared beams," so too are the "woods around Seattle" transformed into the "2 × 4s" that aid the construction of San Francisco homes. More than just a reminder of where houses come from, the juxtaposition of logging practices in "Logging 2" presents the poet with a rather sober version of trans-Pacific mimesis. In the Seattle Art Museum, Snyder saw Chinese landscapes that reminded him of the Cascades. A decade or so later, at work on a logging crew, he notices that the same clear-cutting practices that permanently damaged China's natural resources threaten to do the same to the Pacific Northwest. It is a much uglier picture, to be sure.

As "Logging 2" continues, the logger-poet claims to "wake from bitter dreams," but it might be more apt to say that he *awakens to* the greedy dreams of capitalist development. "250,000 board-feet a day / If both Cats keep working / & nobody gets hurt": this is not only the end of "Logging 2," but the Machiavellian ends that justify the means, at least as far as Weyerhaeuser is concerned. "Nobody gets hurt," the clichéd closing argument for many a shady business scheme, is the phrase upon which Snyder's distinction turns. Of course, if a forest is "killed," as "Logging 1" had hinted, no one can say that "nobody gets hurt." Indeed, it makes more sense to hear the phrase homophonically as "nobody gets heard," since the "Cats" in this poem are not felines but rather the roaring Caterpillar tractors that drown out the voices of displaced wildlife. It therefore seems likely that Snyder, a poet who believes that all sentient beings have souls and that a single life in the forest is vital to many other forms of life, has an ecological agenda in mind, albeit a subtly registered one. What makes Snyder's early poetry so difficult, but in the end so rewarding, is that it avoids the heavy-handed moralizing that plagues other environmentalist discourses. Presumably, the poet ends "Logging 2" with an ironic repetition of a business-speak cliché instead of a flat-out indictment because he wants readers to travel the same forest paths and determine for themselves whether the same beings who do not "get heard" may in fact "get hurt" during logging operations.

The "Logging 3" through "Logging 11" sections include the multitude of living beings who populate the forest wasteland. Some are clearly in danger of getting hurt, while others have proved their ability to endure. Consider the hardy species of trees and insects, like the lodgepole pine and the cicada, which have adapted to this environment and accompany anyone who moves within it. Or consider the migratory animals that make their way along these forest paths. Bear, salmon, and birds are not fully conscious of civilization; they just follow their instincts and move to a better place. In "Logging 4," the bear who "grunts, stalking the pole-star," represents a freer migratory sensibility that primitive religions, like the Circumpolar Bear Cult of the Bella-Coola, understand and respect. Unlike the colonizing Anglo-Americans, who appropriated the image of the bear and polestar for the California state flag, members of this primitive cult have no designs on terri-torializing the migratory bear's extensive domain.

Other creatures continue to appear, including a number of creaturely men with whom Snyder has worked. Ray Wells, "a big Nisqually" Indian, and Ed McCullough, "a logger for thirty-five years," are just two of the labor-ers the poet mentions by name. Their bemused attitude toward work in the woods is emblematic of a sentiment that appears throughout Snyder's oeu-vre (see *Riprap*'s "Hay for the Horses" and *Turtle Island*'s "Why Log Truck Drivers Get Up Earlier Than Students of Zen"). Although these men work for the logging industry, their close connection with the land and its variety of life-forms suggests that they want to resist the violent tendencies of an encroaching civilization. Then again, the logging practices of American Indians differed quite a bit from those of greedy conglomerates. As Patrick Murphy cogently argues, "It is important to remember that Snyder worked these summers on the Warm Springs Reservation involved in selective cut-ting rather than clear-cutting. As Snyder states in *The Practice of the Wild*, 'I had no great problem with that job' because 'I don't doubt that the many seed-trees and smaller trees left standing have flourished, and that the forest came back in good shape.' Thus one can argue that, while Snyder is aware of destructive logging and will condemn it in this section of *Myths & Texts*, he also has experienced a native-influenced alternative way of working that makes the power of Spring/fertility myths not merely psychic supports in dream time but also cultural supports for economic decisions in real time."[47]

Quite often in *Myths & Texts*, we hear a chorus of disembodied voices echoing through the forests of the Pacific Northwest. A first fragmentary quotation arrives in "Logging 6," when the poet includes a testimonial about blackberry picking. Not until Howard McCord's *Notes* do we learn that the passage derives from an audiotape of Harold Snyder, recorded by his son on the sly when the two were drinking together. Equally mysterious dialogue emanates from ghostly forms parading through the wilderness or lurking in its shadows. They include five members of the Wobblies who were shot down in the Everett Massacre of 1916 ("Logging 7") as well as a flea-infested "ghost logger" ("Logging 10") who functions as an unconscious reminder of the havoc wreaked by "Xtians out to save souls and grab land." As this belea-guered ghost says of white Christians who settled on the West Coast: "They'd steal Christ off the cross / if he wasn't nailed on." Literary ghosts linger, too. Significantly, they tend to hail from Asian communities along the western side of the Rim. Hsu Fang, a Chinese mystic, appears briefly ("Logging 3"), as do Noh play masters Kwanami and Seami Motokiyo ("Logging 4" and "11"), the latter of whom wrote a play entitled "Takasago" about pine trees. But they all soon disappear through the pines, as the D8 Cat tractors continue to fell trees and tear through the "piss fir" seedlings. Sadly, the roar of heavy machinery permeates the background of every meditation, and the ghosts are forced to run for cover.

"Logging 12" is a pivotal section. Its diverse mixture of creaturely and cultural references evokes an environmental and ethical atmosphere that is genuinely Snyderian. As "Logging 12" opens, the Cats continue to do their work as hundreds of displaced butterflies "flit through the pines." By this juncture, such tales of destruction are well known. But soon another quotation arrives to add resonance and usher in a prophecy: "You shall live in square / gray houses in a barren land / and beside those square gray / houses you shall starve." The image of a barren house returns the reader to the "squared beams" of "San Francisco 2 × 4s" in "Logging 2," while the image of a "barren land" connects more generally with the wasteland motif that Lee Bartlett and Tim Dean emphasize in separate analyses. We should take a closer look, however, at the source of the quote, which Snyder cites in the next line:

—Drinkswater. Who saw a vision
At the high and lonely center of the earth:
Where Crazy Horse
    went to watch the Morning Star,
& the four-legged people, the creeping people,
The standing people and the flying people
Know how to talk. (MT 13)

This convergence of vision upon a central spot, "Where Crazy Horse / went to watch the Morning Star," recalls Buddha's enlightenment, previously described in "Logging 1." In his dissertation on Snyder's Native American sources, William Jungels informs us that the citation of Drinkswater, a Sioux prophet, comes from *Black Elk Speaks*.[48]

A century ago, Drinkswater gazed upon the freedom of mobile animal-people on the prairies, even as he forecast the cramped conformity awaiting his own tribe. Whether they would come to live on reservations or in cities, Drinkswater knew that the displaced and starving Sioux would soon occupy the square gray houses mentioned in his prophecy. "Everything an Indian does is in a circle," Black Elk was fond of saying. From the roundness of the earth to the starry spheres, to the circular cycles of the seasons, to the conical tepees that housed their people, the circle was the Sioux's primary organizational principle. "For the Sioux," Jungels explains, "the circle was a means of integration of his life with natural cycles of motion and time, a way of seeing his life as part of the whole. His circular home was a sacred space, a microcosm that communicated to him the power that drove all things. The breaking of the hoop which shattered this home was on another level the intrusion of the white man's sense of history and destiny on the Indian's time which had moved for centuries in ritualized and mythic cycles. It meant the beginning of his loss of the Holy, the beginning of secularization of life."[49]

By invoking Native America's plight in the context of circular design, Snyder implies that Western civilization's fortune, by which I mean both its wealth and its fate, is a squared-off version of the holistic relationship whose ruination and loss Drinkswater sadly prophesies. "Are we all destined to live in square gray houses?" Snyder seems to be asking in the margins of "Logging 12." "Must we all be squares?" "Square," we should remember, was the epithet San Francisco Beats applied to anyone they regarded as conformist, uptight, or otherwise out of touch with deeper consciousness. In "Logging 12," "square" represents another kind of boxed-in conformity Snyder wants to escape.

As is the case with so many sections in *Myths & Texts*, the sheer power of natural cycles is able to transform Snyder's consciousness, and before long he is granted a vision of the alternative pathways he wants to travel. All the poet need do is look and listen closely, and he will encounter the creaturely vibrancy that perseveres in the woods and along the shorelines of the Pacific Northwest:

Sea-foam washing the limpets and barnacles
Rattling the gravel beach
Salmon up creek, bear on the bank,
Wild ducks over the mountains weaving
In a long south flight, the land of
Sea and fir tree with the pine-dry
Sage-flat country to the east.
Han Shan could have lived here,
    & no scissorbill stooge of the
    Emperor would have come trying to steal
    His last poor shred of sense
On the wooded coast, eating oysters
Looking off toward China and Japan
"If you're gonna work these woods
Don't want nothing
That can't be left out in the rain—" (MT 13–14)

Snyder could have continued to listen to Cats tearing down trees, but the Drinkswater prophecy spurs him to adopt an alternative sensory mode. Even at the shoreline he could have chosen, like Matthew Arnold above Dover Beach, to hear in the roar of waves and gravel the "turbid ebb and flow / Of human misery."[50] Instead, he turns back to the creaturely world for a lesson in survival. The "salmon up creek" suggest a connection between mating and moving that the poet would explore more explicitly in a later section of *Myths & Texts* ("Hunting 9") and again in the love poems he dedicated to Masa Uehara in *Regarding Wave*. The bear on the bank is perhaps the same one that stalks the polestar in "Logging 4," worthy of an archaic community's worship. The wild ducks, for their part, establish a directionality and a territory with their flight patterns. All of these coastal creatures know when and where to move in order to escape undue hardship and locate pleasure.

With the introduction of Han-shan ("Han Shan"), we get an early indication of Snyder's eventual departure from America in 1956 to travel along the northern arc of the Rim en route to Asia. Han-shan was a poet who lived in China during the T'ang Dynasty. In the autumn of 1955, in the midst of gathering and organizing the lyrics of *Myths & Texts*, Snyder began to translate the poems of Han-shan as part of an assignment at UC–Berkeley. According to legend, Han-shan left his position as a government official (some say he was a military officer) for a wilderness retreat in the T'ien-t'ai Mountains, where he composed his enigmatic poetry on the bark of trees and the faces of rocks. "Han-shan" is usually translated as "Cold Mountain," and thus it is understood that the identity of this man was inseparable from his position in nature. In *Myths & Texts*, Snyder's invocation of Han-shan suggests that the Chinese poet's special brand of nonconformity is as practicable in postmodern America as it was years ago in the remote regions of East Asia.

If he could just avoid complicity with greedy loggers and escape the "scissorbill stooges" of his own government—including the McCarthyites who branded him a "security risk"—Snyder feels as though he might edge closer to Han-shan's holistic vision. Later in this passage, we notice Snyder glancing across the Pacific: "On the wooded coast, eating oysters / Looking off toward China and Japan." This new line of vision might have been prompted by the example of Han-shan or perhaps by the migratory paths of animals. More likely is some combination of these two influences. While eating oysters, Snyder seems suspended, as in a dream, as he gazes across the ocean toward the lands whose philosophy and literature have long inspired him. Not until a bit of pragmatic advice is offered by a crusty old logger does the young poet seem to stir from his meditation on Pacific Rim cultures.

"Logging 15," which ends the first phase, has been variously interpreted. As Patrick Murphy notes, "critics tend to emphasize either an apocalyptic or a regenerative interpretation."[51] Another answer, as I see it, would seem to lie (or "lodge," if we wanted to follow the pun suggested by the poet's beloved lodgepole pine tree) somewhere between these two "poles." Snyder's Pacific Rim vision is regenerative, to be sure, but it is a regeneration born of (and borne by) destruction. "Logging 15" announces the end of a *kalpa* cycle. Howard McCord defines a *kalpa* as a night and day cycle in the universe of Buddha, which computes to approximately 8,640,000 years. Positioning Shiva "at the end of the kalpa," as Snyder does here, suggests that a new incarnation, or a new devotional mode, is looming on the horizon, since the fall of one *kalpa* means the birth of another. Further analyzing Snyder's references, we discover that Shiva, a Hindu god known as the "Lord of Destruction," is succeeded by the beneficent and nongrasping Ganesh, also known as the "Remover of Obstacles." This is a first hint that the destructive tendencies espied in the "Logging" phase are about to give way to something better during the next phase of *Myths & Texts*.

In characteristic fashion, Snyder beseeches good karma by way of natural example, examining a lodgepole pine whose "cone / seed waits for fire." Snyder had already introduced this tree back in "Logging 4" and "Logging 8." Upon first mention, a rather free-floating quotation was offered:

"Lodgepole Pine: the wonderful reproductive
power of this species on areas over which its
stand has been killed by fire is dependent upon
the ability of the closed cones to endure a fire
which kills the tree without injuring its seed.
After fire, the cones open and shed their seeds
on the bared ground and a new growth springs up." (MT 4)

In "Logging 15," the lodgepole pine's resiliency is juxtaposed with the cyclical rebirth promised in the *kalpa* cycle. By this point, the tree has become a companionable form for the poet, for he believes he too can survive the trauma civilization metes out. The pine's branches are brittle, as Snyder notes in "Logging 8," yet its regenerative capabilities cannot be denied. Thus, while the poet continues to rail against "Men who hire men to cut groves / Kill snakes, build cities, [and] pave fields," his larger aim is to identify with the forms of forest life that survive secretly in such an atmosphere:

Pine sleeps, cedar splits straight
Flowers crack the pavement.
    Pa-ta Shan-jen
(A painter who watched Ming fall)
    lived in a tree:
"The brush
May paint the mountains and streams
Though the territory is lost." (MT 16)

The pine sleeps through destruction, knowing that, although its brittle branches snap easily whenever the D8 Cat approaches, its seeds can endure any type of firestorm. Forest flowers also refuse to die, sprouting in such a way as to ruin the "paved fields" of encroaching urbanization. Pa-ta Shan-jen, a Pacific Rim artist, is another symbol of resiliency, since his habitat—a tree rather than any type of squared or artificial abode—allows him to outlast the governors of fleeting dynasties like the Ming. As Snyder explains in the notes to *Mountains and Rivers without End*, Chinese landscape paintings "are at their most vigorous . . . exactly when much of China was becoming deforested" (MR 159). Hence the relevance of the proclamation quoted at the end of "Logging 15": "The brush / May paint the mountains and streams / Though the territory is lost." The artist's ability to give lands and waters their due, this passage implies, will save Pacific Rim locales from the losses they suffer at the hands of civilized men. Thus, an ancient Asian *sumi* painter like Pa-ta Shan-jen, whose fluid brush strokes are attuned to the dynamic energies conditioning his landscape, becomes a role model for an ecologically sensitive poet writing in cold war America.

In the first third of *Myths & Texts*, the reader is presented with a treasure trove of circulating life-forms, testimonial histories, and literary fragments, all of which decry the tendency of human beings in the West to separate themselves from the creaturely populations in their midst. By contrast, the poet feels as though he is never alone. Whether the lessons are offered by those damaged by assaults on nature (Drinkswater and the ghost logger) or by those who managed to escape those ravages (Hsu Fang, Pa-ta Shan-jen, and the various "animal-people"), it is clear that Snyder is informed by others on every step of his mythic journey. The crafty creatures pulsing through the wasteland show him that all is not lost, since alternative trails to salvation still exist within the forests, along the flyways, and on the shores of the Pacific Rim. Looking at "Logging" in this way, we might say that the title refers not merely to the chopping down of trees, but also to the poet's recording of various escape routes. By "logging" these routes for posterity's sake as well as for his own sanity, Snyder strives to sustain the ecological integrity of the Pacific Northwest despite formidable opposition.

Phase II—Hunting Animal Wisdom

Myths & Texts' second phase, "Hunting," solidifies the poet's instinctive connection with wildlife. As defined and practiced by Snyder, hunting promises the restoration rather than the killing of creaturely community. For the indigenous cultures of the Northwest, from which the poet takes instruction, hunting an animal is never to be equated with the kind of wholesale slaughter that is the unfortunate legacy of Anglo-American frontiersmen. Instead, the hunter and the hunted conclude a sacred compact, a union of souls in which mutual respect is the predominant feature. On such occasions, creaturely hybridity and cultural harmony supplant the rugged individualism and frontier aggression associated with more destructive forms of hunting.

The first clue of this interrelationship is offered in "Hunting 1," the subtitle of which reads: "*first shaman song.*" As previously discussed, the shaman articulates the communal unconscious by reference to archetypal animal behaviors. To attain this status, Snyder must first disavow the hierarchical attitude of civilized cultures, forsaking precepts that place humans above other animals. In a passage that foreshadows his study of *zazen*, the Zen practice of emptying the mind through disciplined sitting posture, the suddenly cut-loose poet sets his future course: "I sit without thoughts by the log-road / Hatching a new myth." We should notice that it is creaturely reproduction, a "hatching," that provides Snyder his foundational knowledge. Accordingly, as the "Hunting" section continues, the poet repeatedly imitates animal behavior in such a way as to nurture and provide for his new myth, but makes no claims for original creation. As he grows into his role of creaturely caretaker, Snyder realizes that the new myth he has "hatched" is actually the combination of several older myths, and that the animals that appear in them were most likely the first makers of myth, since they seem to hatch, move, and communicate rather instinctively.

In his role as shaman, Snyder hunts animals for their knowledge, not for their hides. This is not to say that he does not occasionally partake in more violent forms of hunting. Even in these hunts, though, the emphasis is on communication and understanding rather than thoughtless slaughter. In "The Wilderness," an essay he included in *Turtle Island*, Snyder explains that humility and respect for the animal are basic tenets of the Native American hunt. Pueblo "still hunters," for example, will remain motionless, singing a song that asks the hunted deer to be willing to present itself and die for the sake of their community (TI 109). In the 1973 "Craft Interview" with *New York Quarterly*, Snyder explains that this style of hunting not only helps him understand the predilections of certain wild animals but also helps him access the creaturely thoughts in his own mind: "You sit down and shut up and don't move, and then things in your mind begin to come out of their holes and start doing their running around and so forth, and if you just let it happen, you make contact with it" (TRW 34).

Besides humility and detached observation, good hunting practices require that every part of the deceased animal be used. In "Hunting 2," a horn-tipped shaft constructed from the remains of a mountain goat enables the hunter to shoot another goat, whose own horns will probably be used to construct the next arrowhead. In "Hunting 5," the whole head of a mountain goat lies waiting in a corner, possibly because it is the last part of the animal to be used. As this section proceeds, we come upon the Kwakiutl instruction for "the making of the horn spoon." Snyder, who had learned about this ritual from Franz Boas, ends the section with a Kwakiutl chant: "Wa, laEm gwala ts!ololaqeka . ts!Enaqe laxeq," which McCord translates as "Now the black horn spoon is finished after this." For members of this tribe, the chant gives religious significance and a sense of closure to the hunt.

Notwithstanding the extensive use made of deceased animals like the goat, the predominant motif in the "Hunting" phase involves the lessons that living animals provide. In the sections dedicated to birds, bear, and deer, Snyder thanks these animals for the paths they have blazed and the communitarian examples they have offered. In "Hunting 3," which contains the subtitle *this poem is for birds,*" the poet recognizes a geographical pattern that most Americans have chosen to ignore:

Birds in a whirl, drift to the rooftops
Kite dip, swing to the seabank fogroll
Form: dots in air changing line from line,
         the future defined.
Brush back smoke from the eyes,
         dust from the mind,
    With the wing-feather fan of the eagle. (MT 20–21)

The whirling motion of these birds, which follow closely upon (or "swing to") the misty "seabank" weather currents of the Pacific Rim, establishes a pattern whereby the future might be defined. In the last few lines of this passage, the observer finds that the birds allow him to see with new clarity, since smoke is brushed back from the eyes, and dust is brushed back from the mind. Their wisdom is emphasized even more clearly in the final lines of the section:

The whole sky whips in the wind
Vaux Swifts

Flying before the storm
Arcing close hear sharp wing-whistle
Sickle-bird
    pale gray
    sheets of rain slowly shifting
    down from the clouds,
Black Swifts.
    —the swifts cry
As they shoot by, See or go blind! (MT 21)

The migrating birds, the rolling fogbank, the whipping wind, and the sheets of rain from a Pacific storm arrive together in one fell swoop. All move in a way that is patterned, and the arcing, banking, sickle-shaped maneuvers of the swifts indicate that they follow a circular path. Indeed, like the majority of weather currents that hit the coasts of Washington, Oregon, and northern California, many species of birds hug the curved shoreline of the Pacific Rim as they travel from the northwestern reaches of Asia, across the Aleutian archipelago, and southward along America's West Coast.[52] Their travels would be depicted more explicitly in "Migration of Birds," a 1956 poem Snyder included in *Riprap*, and again in "Night Herons," a poem in *Turtle Island*. Yet even at this early juncture, the poet senses that flying creatures possess knowledge of Pacific Rim interrelatedness that "dusty" human minds have somehow repressed. The "arcing" Vaux's swifts that herald the storm and the dipping kites that ride the fogbank summon an alternative mind-space, an ancient geographic community Snyder wants to rediscover and join.[53]

In "Hunting 6," a section whose subtitle reads *"this poem is for bear,"* Snyder reinforces his creaturely message in the wilderness with some help from the sacred traditions of native peoples. In McCord's *Some Notes*, Snyder states that the epigraph to "Hunting 6" "is referring to Marius Berbeau's Bella-Coola collections plus an article on the Circumpolar Bear Cult by A. I. Hallowell, about 1914, & my own encounters with bears."[54] As Joseph Campbell reveals in his study of primitive mythology, the Circumpolar Bear Cult extends across the northern stretches of the Pacific Rim, for it is evident among the Ainu of the northern islands of Japan as well as among the Nootka, Tlingit, and Kwakiutl tribes of the Pacific Northwest.[55] The migratory paths of bears, regarded by cult members as divine visitors, thus define a cultural space. Snyder wants to preserve this way of thinking. Unfortunately, as often happens in the "Logging" phase, he finds himself in the company of humans who exhibit far more destructive forms of behavior. Things come to a head in "Hunting 8" as Snyder recounts an experience amid a frustrated and drunken hunting party. For the hunters on this outing, a missed opportunity to shoot a buck is quickly avenged by shooting the head off a defenseless cottontail hare. So much for hunting as sport. In twentieth-century America, animals are no longer visitors from a divine realm; they are merely interchangeable targets for our misplaced aggression.

Like "Hunting 4" and "Hunting 6," "Hunting 8" is prefaced by a subtitle, *"this poem is for deer."* The deer faces a more perilous predicament than do the birds or the bear, however, and thus the subtitle will read like an epitaph by the time the episode is concluded. After the hare is shot, the poet pauses to address the majestic creature that has only temporarily escaped the wrath of the drunken hunters:

Picasso's fawn, Issa's fawn,
Deer on the autumn mountain
Howling like a wise man
Stiff springy jumps down the snowfields
Head held back, forefeet out,
Balls tight in a tough hair sack
Keeping the human soul from care . . . (MT 27)

The first line of the passage reveals that baby deer have inspired European painters and Asian poets alike. Snyder, too, wants to honor the howling deer, insofar as its wild character aids him in "Keeping the human soul from care." But how secure is this animal, really, from the shotguns being wielded? The proud posture of the deer, with its "Head held back, forefeet out, / Balls in a tough hair sack," proves that it has evaded the fate of the tethered and gelded ponies in "Logging 11." It might also, for the moment of artistic representation, symbolize the unbridled energy that civilized humans can never approach but only hope to imitate.[56] Nevertheless, underpinning these ruminations is the reminder that people hell-bent on destruction wander the same woods. As the section continues, Snyder is forced to ponder a tough mystery: what does the freedom of the deer signify when a drunken group of men, with a number of technological weapons at their disposal (cars as well as guns), pays that freedom no heed?

Home by night
                drunken eye
Still picks out Taurus
Low, and growing high:
                Four-point buck
Dancing in the headlights
                on the lonely road
A mile past the mill-pond,
With the car stopped, shot
That wild silly blinded creature down.

Pull out the hot guts
                with hard bare hands
While night-frost chills the tongue
                and eye
The cold horn-bones.
The hunter's belt
                just below the sky
Warm blood in the car trunk.
Deer-smell,
                the limp tongue. (MT 27)

One presumes that the "horn-bones" of this "silly blinded" animal will not end up in an arrowhead or a sacred spoon, as they had within the Kwakiutl rituals described in "Hunting 2" and "Hunting 5." If they are to be used at all, they will most likely be as part of a taxidermist's trophy, a false badge of honor for an undeserving vanquisher aided by his vehicle. By intimating that the slaughtered deer was frozen in the headlights, Snyder is reworking our era's clichéd euphemism for confusion or bewilderment. Temporary befuddlement is certainly deadly for the deer run down by the car, and yet I think Snyder wants to argue that the real confusion lies not with the deer so much as with the civilization that does it harm. If this trend holds, the poet fears that the creaturely freedom that defines his culture region will fall prey to the diseased consciousness represented by the blinding headlights, with disastrous results for all involved.

It is up to Snyder to "hunt" for alternative answers, and those he locates lead him back to the instinctive movements of other animals. In contrast to the vulnerable deer, the "offshore" creatures of the Pacific region enjoy unrestricted mobility and free love. By this juncture of *Myths & Texts*, Snyder has already depicted the movements of fish, ducks, shorebirds, and other sea creatures. In "Hunting 9," he chooses to represent this movement in explicitly libidinal terms:

Sealion, salmon, offshore—
Salt-fuck desire driving flap fins
North, south, five thousand miles
Coast, and up creek, big seeds
Groping for inland womb

Geese, ducks, swallows,
        paths in the air
I am a frozen addled egg on the tundra. (MT 28)

The sexual appetite of these animals (elementally represented as "salt-fuck desire") occasions a drive or movement, which in turn makes visible certain long-distance routes ("five thousand miles / Coast"), certain bodily contortions (fins flapping), and certain geometric patterns ("paths in the air"). Such movement may even help to fertilize the embryo of one's far-flung identity ("I am a frozen addled egg on the tundra"). The key to understanding this culture region, as Snyder is laying out its terms and mapping its dynamics, is inextricably tied to the various creatures populating, holding a desire for, moving toward, and seeking release within its permeable boundaries.

In the opening to the "Hunting" phase, we learned that Snyder, as shaman-poet, occasionally takes on the guise of animals in order to reach a deeper understanding of Pacific Rim culture. He augments his store of creaturely knowledge in "Hunting 11" when he returns to John Swanton's *Haida Texts and Myths*, the book that contained "He Who Hunted Birds," to summon the example of Big-Tail. In the "He Who Hunted Birds" narrative, we will recall, a chief's son drapes a mouse skin around himself for protection as he climbs the pole leading to the celestial realm of the swan-maiden. A similar motif is in evidence as Snyder transcribes the speech of Big Tail, a Haida spokesman who wore a raven skin so that he might discover new knowledge in foreign realms. As Bert Almon explains, in Haida legend "Big-Tail descends into the ocean in order to meet a supernatural being called 'He-at-whose-voice-the-Ravens-sit-on-the-sea' and to gain power in the form of a magic hat to save people from famine."[57] Interestingly, back in "Logging 12," Snyder added He-at-whose-voice-the-Ravens-sit-on-the-sea to the catalogue of animal-people who "know how to talk." In "Hunting 11," Big-Tail returns from his meeting with this supernatural being and challenges modern readers to face up to their current environmental crisis, repeating the same question posed to him by the "fern women" (vegetable-people?) after his foray into the supernatural animal realm: "What will you do with human beings? / Are you going to save the human beings?"

Of course, readers need not take on the role of shaman to ponder the fate of humanity. A simpler way to wisdom, one similar to the method of "still hunting," will also do quite nicely. By the time of "Hunting 12," the wandering poet has not eaten for several days. Whether his abstinence is due to ritual deprivation or to his disgust with the slaughter waged by drunken hunters is never explicitly stated. What seems most likely is that the poet, just down from the mountains, has been granted a moment of natural communion:

> Out of the Greywolf valley
> in late afternoon
> after eight days in the high meadows
> hungry, and out of food,
> the trail broke into a choked
> clearing, apples grew gone wild
> hung on one low bough by a hornet's nest.
> caught the drone in tall clover
> lowland smell in the shadows
> then picked a hard green one:
> watched them swarm.
> smell of the mountains still on me.
> none stung. (MT 30–31)

In this version of Eden, the poet is granted knowledge before he takes the apple. In his coming-to-consciousness in the wilderness, he has found a way to combat destructive behavior and is therefore allowed to pick the fruit without retribution. Importantly, his common sense derives as much from the scent of the mountains still on his body as it does from any intellectual process. In the beautifully delivered final line, after having picked the wild apple amid wild hornets—creatures that civilization has mistakenly yet routinely associated with unmitigated anger (i.e., "mad as a hornet")— Snyder recalls rather stoically that "none stung." The harmoniousness of this episode is reinforced by the internal rhyme the poet couches in these monosyllabic words, as the brief extension of the same low sound evokes the resonant hum of the swarm. By acceding to a natural sensibility, learned in the mountains and brought back to the lowlands, the poet himself has become part of the swarm or movement of living things. He is more ready than ever to provide a working model for how the diverse beings of this culture region can get along.

The final sections of the "Hunting" phase are significant primarily for their introduction of Eastern religions that, when combined with Native American traditions, form a complex devotional mode. In "Hunting 11," the Hindu god Prajapati, "Lord of Creatures," mingles freely with Haida shaman Big-Tail. In "Hunting 16," Zen Master Chao-chou, who wrote a treatise on the Buddha-nature, is mentioned alongside Coyote, the Native American trickster figure, who as it happens is the only beast not to have the Buddha-nature. As these figures circulate and congregate, Snyder prepares us for another look at Pacific Rim community in "Burning," the last phase of *Myths & Texts*.

Phase III—Burning Matter

Once *Myths & Texts* moves on to consider the Dhyana (South Asian), Ch'an (Chinese), and Zen (Japanese) traditions of Buddhism, Jungels has noted, "the use of or allusion to Native-American myths thins out."[58] Even so, the backwoods lessons of "Logging" and "Hunting" do not disappear. Rather, they are set alongside the literatures Snyder was exposed to in UC–Berkeley's oriental languages program and the Jodo-shin (or "Pure Land") devotions he was practicing at the Berkeley Buddhist Church. Inspired in part by Buddha's Fire Sermon, "Burning" provides new contexts for the cyclical destruction and creaturely adaptation Snyder saw taking place along the eastern Rim.

"Burning 1" opens with a *"second shaman song,"* signaling Snyder's intention to summon the spirit of an archetypal animal or life force. On this occasion, Snyder depicts himself as a figure squatting in a swamp. "Seawater fills each eye" of this figure, and exactly where the muddy water ends and where the body of the shaman-poet begins is hard to determine. Indeed, the identity of the poet seems to dissolve in the primordial soup of this swamp, which because it contains seawater is probably a Pacific estuary:

> Streaked rock congestion of karma
> The long body of the swamp.
> A mud-streaked thigh.
>
> Dying carp biting air
>   in the damp grass,
> River recedes. No matter.
>
> Limp fish sleep in the weeds
> The sun dries me as I dance (MT 37)

"A frog was made to live in a swamp, but a man was not made to live in a swamp," Emerson once wrote in a chastening journal entry addressed to Thoreau.[59] Clearly, Snyder would be more apt to side with the creaturely Thoreau than with the civilized Emerson, for in this section he reminds humans, by virtue of a Darwinian mud dance, that we all did live in a swamp at one time. In the estuaries and inlets of the Pacific coast, creatures continue to mate and be born, while the shaman-poet who goes there to dance harks back to the "inland womb" toward which the offshore creatures driven by "salt-fuck desire" gropingly made their way in "Hunting 9." The "streaked rock" suggests a sedimentary "congestion of karma," or a visible failure to free oneself from the endless cycle of suffering. This is a trap the poet wants to avoid. The phrase "No matter" indicates that the shaman-poet tries not to attach himself to any previous life cycle, and that he similarly attempts to steer clear of the material cares of modern civilization.[60] According to Lawrence Buell, this section "conveys as rigorous a relinquishment of homo-centrism as one could expect a human lyric to achieve."[61]

In "Burning 2," we find an even better synopsis of the creaturely mind-set Snyder has tapped into:

> One moves continually with the consciousness
> Of that other, totally alien, non-human:

Humming inside like a taut drum,
Carefully avoiding any direct thought of it,
Attentive to the real-world flesh and stone.

Intricate layers of emptiness
This only world, juggling forms
    a hand, a breast, two clasped
Human tenderness scuttles
Down dry endless cycles
Forms within forms falling
           clinging
Loosely, what's gone away?
—love (MT 38)

The difficulty of this passage is immediately apparent, but after unpacking its swirl of images and statements we get a sense of the poet's creaturely consciousness. In the first two lines, nonhuman energies are viewed as accompaniments to any movement a human makes. To call these energies "totally alien" is to provide an ironic misnomer, for they actually form the most intimate core of our being. The enjambment between the first two lines highlights the indeterminate relationship described in the first two prepositional phrases. In a first reading, we might understand "consciousness of that other" to refer to the persona's conscious acknowledgement of an "alien" creature lurking in his midst, and perhaps even within his own breast ("Humming inside like a taut drum"). But a second reading leads us to believe that this "non-human" character possesses a "consciousness" all its own, so long as we agree that the second preposition ("of") directs us toward whatever is possessed by the object of the second prepositional phrase ("that other"). Read either way, the passage suggests that consciousness belongs to all creatures, and that the human being who gains the clearest understanding of the world is one who acknowledges the importance of the creaturely realm to human thoughts and actions. Without the influence of these natural soul mates, Snyder seems to say, human life would remain static (it could not physically move) and uninspired (it could not be emotionally moved in any way).

As it happens, the human agent in "Burning 2" carefully avoids "any direct thought" of creaturely consciousness, and this evasion eventually results in a fixation on other forms, including the "real-world flesh and stone." As I will discuss in detail in a later chapter, Snyder would often employ the real-world phenomena of flesh (of female bodies) and stone (of craggy Pacific Rim landscapes) as sites of transference whereby his desires, and those of the countercultural community, could be satisfied. Here, though, Snyder seems more interested in the basic tenets of Buddha-mind, which forbid grasping and attachment. As the poet mentions in "Burning 2," and indeed throughout the entire "Burning" phase, the forms in this world are fleeting and eventually give way (or are burned away) to "intricate layers of emptiness" or to "forms within forms falling." The question that remains is how to act in the face of such formlessness. In the passage cited above, it is not clear as to whether "clinging loosely" is a verbal or a participial phrase, nor is it clear as to which subject the phrase is modifying. What does seem likely, however, is that a lack of love has resulted in the tendency of this human agent to cling, however "loosely," to physical matter. A Buddhist like Snyder would know this to be a fundamental mistake.

The imagery at the end of "Burning 2" is also hard to interpret, although we will notice the repetition of a few key terms, which allow us to get a better idea of the love the poet is talking about:

> Bones & flesh knit in the rock
> "have no regret—
> chip chip
> (sparrows)
> & not a word about the void
> To which one hand diddling
> Cling (MT 38)

Stone and flesh, the real-world materials of the section's first verse paragraph, reappear here as an intricately knitted skeletal structure (bones, flesh, and rock). "Have no regret," another of *Myths & Texts'* disembodied quotations, is a phrase I have trouble deciphering, although I believe "chip chip" to be a continuation of this speech, since the preceding line does not have any closing quotation marks. "Chip chip" is surely the song of the sparrows and, as Sherman Paul points out, may even provide sonorous counterpoint to the "jug jug" sung by the debased nightingale in "The Fire Sermon" section of *The Waste Land.*[62] "Have no regret" could therefore refer to the sexual aggression "so rudely forc'd" upon Philomela in Eliot's poem, especially since she, like the chief's son in "He Who Hunted Birds," was transformed into a bird once she received the (in)appropriate (carnal) knowledge. More crucial, though, is the next line, which implies that the sparrows find no need to utter a word about "the void": a kind of formlessness-made-visible that they accept without reservation. A fundamental precept of Zen Buddhism, surrendering to the void requires that one not cling to any entity, whether it exists in the form of a person, an identity, a landscape, or even a thought. For a brief moment in "Burning 2," this nongrasping variety of love is invoked. But the moment does not last. The last image of the section shows a body suspended over the void, clinging precariously to something, when the way to enlightenment would be to let go entirely. At this juncture, though, only the sparrows seem to understand the propriety of abandonment.

As "Burning" proceeds, the Ch'an/Zen freedoms represented by Chaochou ("Hunting 16") and other unself-conscious beings of the Pacific Rim are complemented by references to Mahayana Buddhism, which tends to emphasize sexual and sometimes violent, albeit ultimately compassionate and available, methods of abandonment. Maitreya, whom Mahayana eschatology worships as the "future Buddha" chosen specifically by Gautama, appears in "Burning 4."[63] Another Mahayana deity is represented by the "statue of Prajna / from Java," who emerges as the key figure in "Burning 7." Prajna, "whose body is the Universe / Whose breasts are Sun and Moon," is known in the Mahayana pantheon as the mother of all bodhisattvas. She gives birth and succor to those who would bring enlightenment to all the world's creatures and express compassion for living beings going to their slaughter. By this point, the reader should understand that Snyder wants to replace the masculine world of phallic aggression and frontier violence, represented by Shiva's *kalpa* cycle ("Logging 15") and the drunken deer hunters ("Hunting 8"), with the feminine world of creativity, fecundity, and kindness promised by Prajna.[64]

With the Prajna image indelibly imprinted in his mind, Snyder is now ready to engage more rigorously the issue of "clinging." "Burning 8" opens with an episode in the life of John Muir that originally appeared in *The Mountains of California*.[65] During a precarious climb on Mount Ritter, Muir faces the realization that any move he makes will cause him to tumble off the mountain to his death. And yet he is able to save himself by adopting a new way of thinking. In the following passage, Snyder assumes Muir's voice to revisit the actual moment of crisis:

     About half-way
To the top, I was suddenly brought to
A dead stop, with arms outspread
Clinging close to the face of the rock
Unable to move hand or foot
Either up or down. My doom
Appeared fixed. I MUST fall.
There would be a moment of
Bewilderment, and then,
A lifeless rumble down the cliff
To the glacier below.
My mind seemed to fill with a
Stifling smoke. . . . (MT 43–44)

As Snyder first intimated in "Burning 2," the way out of this predicament is not to cling to the face of the rock but rather to surrender to the void of space beyond the cliff. As Patrick Murphy explains, Snyder is summoning forth the Taoist doctrine of *wu wei*, or "the action of nonaction," in the hopes of locating a *kensho*, or Zen epiphany.[66] Only after Muir acknowledged the wisdom of *wu wei*, Snyder asserts in his recounting of the parable, was the celebrated mountain man able to clear his mind and move with necessary abandon:

     . . . This terrible eclipse
Lasted only a moment, when life blazed
Forth again with preternatural clearness.
I seemed suddenly to become possessed
Of a new sense. My trembling muscles
Became firm again, every rift and flaw in
The rock was seen as through a microscope,
My limbs moved with a positiveness and precision
With which I seemed to have
Nothing at all to do. (MT 44)

Murphy is quite right to mention the doctrine of *wu wei*, for Muir seems to have accepted the nongrasping attitude laid out in chapter 43 of *Tao Te Ching*, the imagery of which is strikingly similar to the description of the epiphany on Mount Ritter. "The most submissive thing in the world can ride roughshod over the hardest thing in the world—that which is without sub-stance entering that which has no crevices," Lao Tzu says. "That is why I know the benefit of resorting to no action. The teaching that uses no words, the benefit of resorting to no action, these are beyond the understanding of all but a very few in the world."[67] Then again, readers might want to recall Snyder's own fearless activities in the mountains. Consider the following episode, recounted by Jack Kerouac in *The Dharma Bums*, in which the greenhorn climber Ray Smith takes instruction from Japhy Ryder, whom he sees bounding down the slopes of the Matterhorn without any fear of falling off. "Suddenly everything was just like jazz," Ray marvels; "it happened in one insane second or so: I looked up and saw Japhy *running down the mountain* in huge twenty-foot leaps, running, leaping, landing with a great drive of his booted heels, bouncing five feet or so, running, then taking another long crazy yelling yodelaying sail down the sides of the world and in that flash I realized *it's impossible to fall off mountains you fool.*"[68]

What Huston Smith once said about *wu wei* holds true in each of these examples: "creative quietude combines within a single individual two seem-ingly incompatible conditions—supreme activity and supreme relaxation."[69] In Muir's case, the newfound ability to see "as through a microscope" brings forth a "preternaturally clear" connection with a landscape that had seemed so foreign and off-putting just moments beforehand. I find it particularly sig-nificant that Snyder includes the image of smoke being brushed back from Muir's eyes and mind, for this signals an epiphany first represented in "Hunt-ing 3," when the "birds in a whirl" spatially defined the future. In "Burning 8," Muir is similarly defining the future, not just for himself, but for Snyder and other West Coast Beats, who would locate an uncanny affinity between Eastern mind and Western landscape in the years to come.

If we believe that poetry helps us gain a foothold in a vast and mysteri-ous universe, "Burning 13" is the section that should stand out, for it is here that Snyder utters his famous precept: "Poetry a riprap on the slick rock of metaphysics." Snyder offers a more commonplace definition of riprap on the title page of the 1959 volume bearing its name, calling it "a cobble of stone laid on steep slick rock to make a trail for horses in the mountains." By equating poetry with a riprap trail in "Burning 13," Snyder presumably wants to emphasize the lyric mode's diminutive yet essential functionality, its ability to make travel on the slick roads of philosophy an easier if no less daunting exercise. Metaphysical connections between East and West may be difficult to ascertain, owing to physical and psychical distances and to countless other factors, but the phenomenological quality of riprap poetry helps us to travel the path to Pacific Rim enlightenment if we wish to do so.

As "Burning 13" proceeds, we notice Snyder putting his textured verse to rather different uses. "As long as you hesitate, no place to go" is a phrase that may be taken as a cliché or perhaps as a Zen koan. More likely, it refers to the lesson that John Muir had learned on Mount Ritter, a lesson that takes on a peculiarly gendered aspect later in the section:

> Bluejay, out at the world's end
> > perched, looked, & dashed
> Through the crashing: his head is squashed.
> > symplegades, the *mumonkwan*,
> It's all vagina dentata
> > (Jump!)
> "Leap through an Eagle's snapping beak"
>
> Actaeon saw Dhyana in the Spring.
>
> > it was nothing special,
> > misty rain on Mt. Baker,
> > Neah Bay at low tide. (MT 49)

The jay at world's end recalls the seagull perching on a reef at the end of "He Who Hunted Birds." On both occasions, crashing ocean breakers threaten to squash the heads of those who go beyond world's end, into the roiling nothingness. "The *mumonkwan*," as Snyder told McCord, refers to a global folklore motif he had found in the "Gateless Gate" series of Asian texts edited by R. H. Blyth. But the next image suggests an altogether different kind of gate. The "vagina dentata" is one of many images Snyder would employ in the early stages of his career in an attempt to connect the void with the female body as a means of finding Buddhist enlightenment. In this instance, the vaginal void is guarded or "gated" by a set of teeth, thus invoking an image first seen in "Burning 6": "Where the sword is kept sharp / the VOID / gnashes its teeth." In the later section, the moist cavity protected by those teeth seems to be the perfect space available for the male poet who wants to pass from one realm to another.

The parenthetical injunction to "jump" reiterates the lesson learned by Muir on Mount Ritter: abandon yourself to the void, no matter how dangerous the consequences may appear. "Don't hesitate," the poet advises us, even as his detailed recollection of the void's genital imagery betrays the fact that he looks before he leaps. Patrick Murphy tells us that the witty substitution of "Dhyana" for Diana (mentioned in the epigraph from Acts 19:27 at the beginning of the volume) refers to the Sanskrit word for "absorption; the form of meditation," but it is the gendered basis for this Pacific Rim meditation that seems most troubling here.[70] Indeed, by equating the body of a woman with the site of the void, "Burning 13" perpetuates stereotypes of hysterical and empty women, whose primary function is to test the mettle of men who want their phallic mythos "kept sharp."[71]

Fortunately, the gender equations end there. In "Burning 14," Snyder describes a peaceful hike on Mount Tamalpais, in Marin County, most likely with Alison Gass, his first wife. In "Burning 15," he views a logging site after a burn. As the poet gazes down from a lookout station (probably on Crater Mountain), the burnt landscape of the Pacific Northwest transforms itself into a wider cultural panorama full of curious characters, including Native Americans ("Siwash strawberry pickers"), hobos hitching flatcars from Sacramento to Fresno, and librarians from New York and Europe, who together constitute "the whole spinning show / (among others) / Watched by the Mt. Sumeru L.O." McCord explains that Mount Sumeru is the peak or pole at the center of the earth, representing the Heaven of Indra in the Hindu-Buddhist world. By placing Sumeru in the Cascades, Snyder offers a syncretic model shaped by Pacific Rim consciousness.[72] In this instance, Indra, whose "jeweled net" would become a key image for Snyder in the 1960s and 1970s, is on hand to reflect a wide-angle view of interconnected landscapes.

Like the seascape James Clifford meditates upon at Fort Ross, the landscape Snyder sees from atop Mount Sumeru is fleeting and formless, but not at all uninhabitable. "It's all falling or burning," he explains, and yet "what is imperfect is best." As "Burning 15" comes to a close, smoke from a forest fire blots out the sun and stings the poet's eyes, but life goes on: "The hot seeds steam underground / still alive." This image, reminiscent of the regenerative species of lodgepole pine introduced in "Logging 3," offers a natural example of a Buddhist ideal emphasized throughout this phase: the ability to abandon oneself to traumatic experience in order to be born anew.

"Burning 17" closes the final phase and returns us to the "burning" issue of the entire volume: the ways in which the interrelationship between texts and myths, or the close connection between everyday occurrences and the legends they inspire, helps us locate our collective identity and placement along the Pacific Rim. To highlight the terms of this discussion, Snyder splits this final section into two verse paragraphs, "the text" and "the myth." Both describe a fire and subsequent rainstorm on Sourdough Mountain, where Snyder was working as a lookout in 1953. The text of "Burning 17" tells the story of the forest fire with the kind of clipped and direct phrasing we could imagine firefighters using on their walkie-talkies: "Sourdough mountain called a fire in: / Up Thunder Creek, high on a ridge. / Hiked eighteen hours, finally found / A snag and a hundred feet around on fire." What follows is a description of digging a fire line and the welcome arrival of an overnight rain, a sequence representing man and nature working in partnership to put a halt to destruction. Tired firefighters recall what has just transpired: "We slept in mud and ashes / Woke at dawn, the fire was out, / The sky was clear, we saw / The last glimmer of the morning star." Although the Sourdough Lookout station has spotted a fire, the best efforts of man and nature have put it out, and a placid morning rewards their work. To invoke a line from "Burning 13," we might say that this experience "was nothing special"; it happens all the time. Such is the text of life in the woods according to this latter-day Thoreau.

In contrast to the stoic tone of the text, the myth makes this forest fire and rainstorm the center of an apocalyptic vortex. This time, the rain represents a spiritual calm characteristic of the Dharma, the set of Buddhist teachings that act as a salve for the vicious traumas we suffer in the material world:

Fire up Thunder Creek and the mountain—
        troy's burning!
The cloud mutters
The mountains are your mind.
The woods bristle there,
Dogs barking and children shrieking
Rise from below.
Rain falls for centuries

Soaking the loose rocks in space
Sweet rain, the fire's out
The black snag glistens in the rain
& the last wisp of smoke floats up
Into the absolute cold
Into the spiral whorls of fire
The storms of the Milky Way
"Buddha incense in an empty world"
Black pit cold and light-year
Flame tongue of the dragon
Licks the sun (MT 53–54)

A fire in the Cascades is equated with the burning of Troy, but the poet's reminder that "the mountains are your mind" indicates that the fall of civilization is less important than our attainment of ecological consciousness (as Aldo Leopold once claimed, it is important that we know how to "think like a mountain").[73] Similarly, while the image of "dogs barking and children shrieking" recalls the fearful flight of sinners on the Day of Judgment, the array of scurrying forest critters on Sourdough Mountain suggests the more creaturely invocation of this religious theme found in Chaucer's "Nun's Priest's Tale."[74] The rain that douses the fire represents the natural world's own sweet caretaking, while the last wisp of smoke signifies a "Buddha incense" vision that urges us to abandon ourselves to the elemental workings of an "empty world." Buddha made it clear in his Fire Sermon that one must go through the fire if one hopes to find the way to compassion. But Buddha's gentle explanation of "Dharma Rain" in the Lotus Sutra is even more relevant on this occasion, for by the end of *Myths & Texts* it appears as though compassion truly does rain down everywhere, saving a countless number of sentient beings and granting all the gift of cosmic release.[75] Snyder implies that Buddha's beneficent spirit is ours to cherish, and he does not hesitate to shift the scene of this compassionate rainstorm to the Pacific Northwest, a region accustomed to such downpours.

Ultimately, the sparking and dousing of the forest fire provide us with a natural commentary on the human condition. We all need to be able to weather firestorms, as the lodgepole pine is able to do, in order to renew ourselves in a cyclical universe. As if to make the cyclical nature of life unmistakable, Snyder closes *Myths & Texts* by returning to the image with which he began the entire sequence. Back in "Logging 1," the poet revealed the fact that "the morning star is not a star." "Burning 17" closes this way:

The sun is but a morning star.

    Crater Mt. L.O. 1952—Marin-an 1956

    end of myths & texts (MT 54)

The first line is a direct quotation from Thoreau, who used it to conclude his own wilderness meditation in *Walden* a century beforehand. In one sense, Thoreau's words deflate the mythic ambitions Snyder has just offered, and yet in no way do they suggest a hasty return to scientific empiricism. Thoreau believed in precise calculations, to be sure, but he also acknowledged in his journal that in a purely scientific world the "sun no longer dazzles us and fills the universe with light."[76] By the same token, he thought that moving away from solar centrality would open our eyes to other wonders of the universe. By saying that "the sun is but a morning star," the author of *Walden* did not mean to imply that the sun is no longer worthy of our adoration or wonder, but merely to suggest that it is one of countless phenomena that deserve our attention. After all, if the sun, a star that just happens to become visible in the morning, can have a mythology built up around it, why cannot the same hold true for any other natural "text"? This seems to be Snyder's realization as well, for in his first volume of verse he introduces a wide variety of myths and texts to pay tribute to the Pacific Rim's abundant wonders.

The penultimate line of *Myths & Texts* provides the time and place of the volume's composition. Crater Mountain Lookout, which functions as the American stand-in for Mount Sumeru in "Burning 15," is the place where Snyder first wrote these lines of verse in 1952. In a journal entry written that summer, Snyder renamed the location for the first time, calling it "Crater Shan," after the Chinese word for mountain (EHH 4). "Marin-an" suggests a similar type of syncretism. As Katsunori Yamazato points out, the suffix "an" is Japanese for "hermitage."[77] The juxtaposition of Crater Mountain (or Crater Shan) with Marin County (or Marin-an) thus represents the combinatory energy driving Snyder's thinking about Pacific Rim community. Whether he was in a lookout tower in the Cascades, gazing out upon a mountainous landscape resembling the kind he saw in *sumi* paintings, or in a rustic cabin in Mill Valley, telling Jack Kerouac about his plans for establishing a series of "bhikku hostels" for Buddhist wanderers in America, Snyder was constantly promoting East-West exchange.[78]

Near the end of 1955, Marin-an was the place where the fragments of *Myths & Texts* came together for the first time. In his small cabin, Snyder tried to re-create the vantage point of a lookout station in order to make sense of what he had written over the preceding four years. According to Snyder, "that was done in part by taking pre-existing material, all of which I perceived to be related, and redefining my understanding of what the relationships were. What I did was I laid out everything that I had done so far on the floor. Then I got on a stepladder so that I could look down and see it all in a panoramic way. I would then get down and rearrange the poems; studying it, I saw what order they belonged in. Then I saw the gaps, and proceeded to write the poems which filled in the gaps within a two week period. That's what you call field composition."[79] Throughout his career, Snyder's statements about his composition process have shed light on his use of geographic models. In this case, he is invoking a more literal variant of Charles Olson's "composition by field," the main thrust of the elder poet's "projective verse" movement.[80] At the top of a mountain or at the top of a stepladder, the novice poet clearly had a predilection for panoramic vistas. In *Myths & Texts*, he captured this sweeping vision on the page.

The "end of myths and texts" signals that this volume is now finished, but I prefer to read the end as a goal toward which Snyder frequently pointed during the counterculture era. By negotiating metaphysical mysteries, marking out territories, and paying homage to creaturely communities that establish themselves there, Snyder invokes his culture region as both text and myth. As a text, the Pacific Rim is a natural outcropping of shoreline, a migratory route for animals, and a bioregion conducive to a variety of plant life. As a myth, the Rim is a visionary space, an ancient realm where philosophical sages hold court, and a far-flung community of diverse but likeminded souls who celebrate diffusion and oppose ecological destruction. By the close of *Myths & Texts*, Snyder looks out over the Pacific and completes the "impossible translation exercise" that James Clifford would describe years later in "Fort Ross Meditation," for like Clifford he locates "a specific sense of the real becoming visible at the fraying limits of a triumphant West."[81] Tracking the biotic and creaturely movements within our natural texts, recovering the lost myths that first made sense of these movements, and "hatching a new myth" that replaces contemporary versions of Manifest Destiny with an ancient and far more equitable model of Pacific Rim community: these are the true ends of Snyder's justly celebrated and rather difficult first volume.

2. TRANSLATING
The Poetics of Linking East and West

In the spring of 1956, after reaching the end of *Myths & Texts*, Snyder handed the completed manuscript to Robert Creeley, whom he entrusted with the task of seeking a publisher. He could not have predicted that *Myths & Texts* would remain in the trunk of Creeley's car for months on end, despite the best efforts of Phil Whalen to get Creeley to finish and distribute the typescript. "ANY NEWS OF CREELEY?" Snyder asked Whalen in a December 1956 letter. "I'll bet he sold my MSS to Metro-Goldwyn-Mayer for a million clams and beat it to New Zealand." Fortunately, these fears were unfounded. Creeley eventually made contact with LeRoi Jones, whose Totem Press published the influential volume of verse, rather belatedly, in September 1960.[1] Snyder would have done the literary legwork himself, but just weeks after completing the manuscript he embarked for Japan, beginning a residence in Asia that lasted the better part of twelve years.

In the months leading up to his departure, Snyder was trying his hand at a different poetic mode, one more clearly indebted to the Asian verse forms and Buddhist philosophies capturing his attention. Although *Myth & Texts* (especially its last phase, "Burning") was notable for its allusions to Asian traditions, Snyder's new poems seemed to absorb those traditions as never before. The result was a complex interplay between Eastern mind and Western landscape. Snyder selected twenty-one of these new poems for a volume he entitled *Riprap*. When Cid Corman's Origin Press published *Riprap* in 1959, it became the first of Snyder's volumes to see print. Snyder and Corman printed the volume in Japan and sold it out of City Lights Bookstore in San Francisco, which had trouble keeping it in stock.[2]

Like *Myths & Texts*, *Riprap* is shaped by Snyder's work experiences. It should be noted, however, that during the summer of 1955 the poet was doing rather different work in an unfamiliar locale. Instead of migrating northward to work in the lookout cabins of the Cascades or the logging camps of eastern Oregon, Snyder decided to stay in California, where he found work in Yosemite National Park as a member of a trail crew. As he labored to learn the intricacies of cobblestone mountain trails, he not only practiced the art of "riprapping," but also adopted a new technique for writing verse. Snyder has frequently cited this summer as the time he became a real poet. Back in 1955, though, the experience of staying put in California struck him as somewhat strange. "I just can't adapt to not packing up & traveling this time of year & my rucksack & boots hang accusingly on the wall," he confessed to Phil Whalen in a letter from June of that year.[3]

Augmenting Snyder's new work experience was his growing understanding of Asian religious traditions. While living in the Bay Area, he immersed himself in the study of Buddhism and came to hold a special affinity for the Jodo-shin or "Pure Land" variety practiced by Japanese immigrants at the Berkeley Buddhist Church. To his great delight, Snyder discovered that this place of worship was "warm, relaxed, and familial," with an atmosphere of "infinite generosity" (MR 154). Buddhism was "cosmopolitan and open to everyone," he would later explain, since unlike most American Indian traditions it did not require that one be "born into" the culture in order to participate in its rites (TRW 94, 95). Encouraged by Reverend Kanmo Imamura and other friends at the Berkeley Buddhist Church, Snyder set forth to learn a wide range of devotional practices. "I soaked up Mahayana sutras and traditional commentaries, Chinese and Japanese Ch'an texts, and Vajrayana writing through those years," he remembers, "taking delight in their scale of imagination and their fearless mytho-psychological explorations" (MR 154).

During this same period, Snyder continued his studies at UC–Berkeley's oriental languages program. In the autumn semester of 1955, having completed his summer work in Yosemite, he enrolled in a class taught by Professor Ch'en Shih-hsiang. It was in Ch'en's class that Snyder chose to translate the poetry of Han-shan, a mountain mystic who lived in T'ang Dynasty

China. Han-shan was the perfect poet for Snyder to study. From an academic standpoint, translating Han-shan's "Cold Mountain Poems" provided Snyder with a lesson in classical Chinese prosody and form. Even more important, Han-shan's poems depicted a topographical mind space not unlike the one Snyder himself had encountered as a hiker, a lookout, and a trail crew worker on the West Coast of America. As members of the San Francisco Renaissance would soon realize, the kinship between the poets was uncanny. To read Snyder's translations of Han-shan is to hear two mountain sages, from vastly different times and places, speaking clearly and serenely in dialogue across the Pacific Rim.

Snyder's translation of the "Cold Mountain Poems," first published in a 1958 issue of the *Evergreen Review*, has appeared alongside *Riprap* since 1965, when Donald Allen's Four Seasons Foundation put out a dual edition. The pairing of these projects makes sense, since both are exercises in translation. In *Riprap* Snyder employs the rhythms of Chinese poetics to make sense of American landscapes, whereas in "Cold Mountain Poems" he draws upon his knowledge of American landscapes to make sense of Chinese poetry. Walter Benjamin has stated that the task of the translator is "to release in his own language that pure language which is under the spell of another, to liberate the language imprisoned in a work in his recreation of that work. For the sake of pure language, he breaks through decayed barriers of his own language."[4] To my mind, something similar happened in 1955 when Snyder wrote his Yosemite trail poetry and embarked on his study of Han-shan, for on both occasions he came to understand that the category of the "foreign" is often more familiar than it first appears. Then again, echoing Benjamin, we might say that Snyder's twin projects "broke through decayed barriers" of a familiar language to place various words and images from cold war America "under the spell" of Pacific Rim consciousness. By taking this approach, Snyder was able to locate an interstitial contact zone where things are gained, not lost, in translation.

Riprap:
Laying the Groundwork for a New Poetics

I no doubt take some liberty (call it poetic license, if you like) in labeling *Riprap* a project of translation. At one level, I am arguing that these poems, though "original," adhere to a process by which a familiar language is substituted for something foreign (usually another language, but in some cases an unusual set of concepts, perhaps even an unfamiliar landscape) in order to make that entity more understandable. At the same time, I am inspired by Benjamin's way of thinking, which maintains that the most successful translations are those that destabilize familiar language, freeing it from restrictive rules or normative expectations and bringing to light thoughts that might otherwise have remained hidden. Snyder would have certainly appreciated translation's revelatory power as he worked on the Yosemite trail crew. As a laborer, he needed to find a foothold in the unfamiliar terrain of the Sierra Nevada mountains. As a poet, however, he wanted those mountains to retain their mysteriousness and sublimity. His challenge was to find a language that could accurately describe the new terrain and still allow that landscape to shape his poetic language according to its rugged specifications. As Snyder explained in a 1994 interview, "Languages seem to have their own ways of moving from place to place. Languages travel with human beings. But they obviously pick up vocabularies and strategy and become transformed in some way by the locale."[5] Some forty years prior to making this statement, Snyder showed in *Riprap* the potential of language and landscape to transform each other and point to trans-Pacific connections others tend to miss.

Crucial to Snyder's development as a Buddhist poet was his adoption of physical labor as a means of spiritual meditation and literary composition. Manual labor has been a fixture of Buddhist practice ever since Po-chang established the first working monastery in T'ang Dynasty China.[6] Realizing that labor and meditation were but two sides of the same activity, Snyder tried incorporating the rhythms of trail work into his Zen-inflected poems. Accordingly, in a statement on poetics he submitted to Donald Allen for inclusion in *The New American Poetry*, Snyder says: "I've just recently come to realize that the rhythms of my poems follow the rhythm of the physical work I'm doing and life I'm leading at any given time—which makes the music in my head which creates the line. . . . 'Riprap' is really a class of poems I wrote under the influence of the geology of the Sierra Nevada and the daily trail-crew work of picking up and placing granite stones in tight cobble patterns on hard slab."[7]

For Snyder, the result of such labor was a poetry that, compared to *Myths & Texts*, looked different on the page and sounded different to the ear. Whereas his lookout work in the Cascades gave him a wide-angle view of Pacific cultures, "riprapping" in the Sierras prompted him to take a closer look at geological structure, which resulted in a more focused purview. The effect of trail crew work on Snyder's prosody was also quite unmistakable. In *Myths & Texts*, lines of verse tended to flow into one another as Snyder traced the trajectory of Pacific Rim animals on the move. In *Riprap*, by contrast, the poet uses shorter lines, chiseled and somewhat teasing phrasing, and the kind of sharp, clear imagery found in Chinese and Japanese versification. Where *Myths & Texts* is fantastical, geographical, and global, *Riprap* is practical, topographical, and local (though no less visionary) in its outlook. In subtle yet powerful ways, *Riprap* takes an American landscape notable for its grandeur, alters our perception of it with techniques gleaned from Asian poetic traditions, and thereby conceives of a new spatial register, one in which Eastern and Western cultures are allowed to meet and flourish.

Although they are indebted to fundamental Buddhist tenets, the poems in *Riprap* contain few references to Asian deities or philosophers. Instead, they describe the way of Zen as a hard-working California mountain man might practice it. Throughout the volume, Snyder edges closer to an egoless ideal known as "Buddha-mind." In this state of consciousness, Joseph Campbell tells us, "there is no hero-monad to be saved, released, or found. All life is sorrowful, and yet, there is no self, no being, no entity, in sorrow. There is no reason, consequently, to feel loathing, shock, or nausea, before the spectacle of the world; but, on the contrary, the only feeling appropriate is compassion (*karuna*)."[8] Campbell's summary certainly seems to describe the sensibilities Snyder was developing as he began to write *Riprap*. Only rarely, for instance, will he use the word "I" in these poems. Like Taoist and Buddhist poets from China and Japan who renounced first-person pronouns, Snyder is less concerned with individual experience than with the circulation of physical and psychical energies that exist in the natural realm. A similar case might be made when talking about the "migratory" poems in *Myths & Texts*. In *Riprap*, however, Snyder is more interested in local landscapes that complicate notions of individuality than he is with the diffusion of culture. As we shall see, this new way of looking had a profound effect on his poetic translations.

A Last View from Sourdough

In the first poem of *Riprap*, Snyder revisits an old haunt in the Pacific Northwest but registers this experience in the new poetic style he was perfecting in the mountains of California. "Mid-August at Sourdough Mountain Lookout" has become one of Snyder's most frequently anthologized pieces, and for good reason. Although it seems simple on its surface, the poem shows a complex mind at work. The opening stanza provides three directional words that seem to fix the time and place of Snyder's meditation:

> Down valley a smoke haze
> Three days heat, after five days rain
> Pitch glows on the fir-cones
> Across rocks and meadows
> Swarms of new flies. (RRCM 3)

"Down" and "Across" help the reader navigate the wild terrain, and "after" provides a clue about the time frame in which natural processes occur. On second consideration, though, these directions are anything but clear. "Down valley" implies that the persona is on a mountaintop, looking down onto a hot, hazy valley.[9] But after this juncture, the syntax of the poem allows for a variety of interpretations, which is most often the case when enjambment blurs causal relationships.

In the *shih* (Chinese) and hokku (Japanese) traditions Snyder was studying at UC–Berkeley, a line is written with a set number of characters or syllables (usually five or seven) and is understood to be end-stopped regardless of whether punctuation is employed at the end of its phrasing. Enjambment never occurs in these Asian poems, Robert Kern tells us, since "our movement through a poem, and even through a line, is continually arrested by the unitary nature of the line and the frequent heavy stressing of its rhythm." Kern refers to this style of versification as "colloquial mental shorthand, whose meaning, like that of most metonymic styles, depends almost entirely on external context," and as a "paratactic series of elliptical phrases that are autonomous rhythmic units."[10] Kern would have us read *Riprap* in the same way, and yet I find that Snyder substantially modifies the rules of *shih* and hokku throughout this volume, constructing his lines in such a way as to blur imagistic thought processes.

Laszlo Géfin therefore comes closer to the point when he says of the poet that "even strict oriental forms such as the haiku become in his hands singularly Snyderian." For Snyder, Géfin goes on to argue, a basic ideographic form like a haiku "conforms in structure to the 'riprap' of things in nature, and is [therefore] essentially an open, projective poem."[11] Snyder himself spoke to the issue of natural form and prosody in a 1992 interview published in the *Paris Review*: "There is one sort of poem I write that is highly compressed and has a lot of ear in it. As a poem comes to me, in the process of saying and writing it, the lines themselves establish a basic measure, even a sort of musical or rhythmic phrase for the whole poem. . . . I don't count syllables or stresses, but I discover after the fact what form the poem has given itself, and then I further that" (GSR 333). Offering a similar explanation, Snyder once told me, "*Riprap* is entirely North American, with just a trace of Chinese flavor, and is actually not a play of Chinese poetics, which is formal, rhymed, strict, parallelistic and elegant."[12]

While I believe that *Riprap*'s Chinese flavor is a bit more piquant than its author lets on, I think he makes clear in both statements his willingness to deviate from *shih* and hokku traditions whenever circumstances seem to demand it. This is most often the case when the indeterminate nature of a vast American landscape transforms lucid phrasings into something more mysterious and unfixed. Fittingly, enjambment plays a key role in many of these instances. In the first stanza of "Mid-August," for example, the prepositional phrase "after five days rain" could be read as the natural complement to "Three days heat," a simple connection surely strengthened by the caesura that arrives after the third syllable. But because "after five days rain" flows uninterruptedly into the beginning of the next line, it might also refer to the time when "Pitch glows on the fir-cones." The ambiguous position of this phrase suggests that a rainstorm is anything but an isolated incident; rather, it is an event that establishes weather patterns (three hot days) and sustains various forms of life (it bathes the fir-cones and incites swarms of flies to carry themselves aloft, much as Keats's gnats do in "To Autumn").

"Across," the directional word that begins the fourth line of the poem, is also subject to an enjambed construction. In the kind of end-stopped reading common in Asian prosody, "Across rocks and meadows" would indicate the place inhabited by the flies in the fifth line. Alternatively, in an enjambed reading, the phrase would cause us to read backward against the grain of Snyder's syntax, making us realize that "across rocks and meadows" signals the location where the "Pitch glows on the fir-cones" "after five days [of] rain." In yet another enjambment, this one between the fourth and fifth lines, "meadows" and "Swarms" are juxtaposed, which suggests that wide-open spaces are conducive to the kind of creaturely communion Snyder says he once enjoyed amid a swarm of hornets after picking an apple in a lowland meadow (MT 30–31). As is perhaps the case with the word "glows" (which could conceivably function as a noun describing a type of pitch formation on pinecones), "Swarms" and "flies" are descriptive nouns that take their names from the kind of movement or action that makes them recognizable entities in the wilderness. Snyder has clearly learned from their example, for his words elude strict rules of syntax and fly across arbitrary boundaries of form, thereby multiplying the ways the landscape and its creatures get translated into thought.

Notwithstanding his predilection for syntactical experimentation, Snyder hesitates to believe that his writing is the final arbiter. Unlike Jacques Derrida or Paul de Man, postmodern theorists who hold that the truth or meaning of any text is a façade that can be deconstructed through rigorous or playful readings of its language, Snyder believes that the construction and deconstruction of knowledge are always and at base natural actions. Accordingly, in his poetry, words are often subject to the vicissitudes of the natural objects they reference rather than the other way around. With this dynamic in mind, the second stanza of "Mid-August" takes on new resonance:

I cannot remember things I once read
A few friends, but they are in cities.
Drinking cold snow-water from a tin cup
Looking down for miles
Through high still air. (RRCM 3)

Upon first glance, these lines seem to reinforce the commonly held assumption that isolation is a prerequisite for the composition and enjoyment of introspective nature poetry. Actually, this passage echoes poems composed by other Pacific Rim nature lovers through the ages, including Basho in Japan ("Just as a stag's antlers / Are spilt into tines, / So I must go willy-nilly / Separated from my friend") and, as Beongcheon Yu has noted, Tao Yuanming in China ("Plucking chrysanthemums by the eastern hedge, I gaze afar at the southern hill").[13] Taking a slightly different look at the issues of isolation and Pacific Rim influence, we should note the countercultural significance of Snyder's mountaintop location for members of the West Coast literary community in the 1950s.

In 1965, Snyder told bibliographer David Kherdian that his summertime work in the Cascades marked a "solitary period" with "almost no social contact." And yet he was quick to point out that the time he spent in the mountains was also a "period of great excitement and growth."[14] In retrospect, I wonder whether some of Snyder's excitement was attributable to his serving as a role model for Beat writers like Phil Whalen and Jack Kerouac, who followed his lead and did some of their most interesting writing in lookout cabins, or to his influence on other writers like William Stafford, whose first volume of verse (*West of Your City*) depicted the satisfying life one could lead in the remote regions of the American West.[15] Snyder might also have had in mind occasional visits from city friends like Dick Brewer (the subject of another Sourdough Mountain poem he included in *The Back Country*), who literally hitched hundreds of miles from San Francisco to see Snyder in the wilderness of Washington before heading onward to New York. Then, too, Snyder's excitement and growth may have stemmed from his ability to communicate with the various nonhuman beings filling the isolated landscapes of the American West. Whatever the cause, the poet's retreat to mountain hideaways did not mean that he was frightfully alone.

It is rather pertinent, given this context, that the word "I" does not appear until the second stanza of "Mid-August." As Patrick Murphy notes, Snyder's decision to delay the introduction of the personal pronoun may have been based on Asian linguistic patterns, for "in both conversational and written Japanese 'I' is almost never used."[16] Though Murphy's observation rightly urges us to consider the effects of Snyder's scholarly training, I regard the Cascade Mountains as the poet's primary influence here. After all, he has spent the first stanza trying to refine himself out of existence, or rather *into* the plural existence of his place. His confession in the second stanza that he can no longer remember things he once read indicates to me that the de-education process he began after graduating from Reed has come to fruition, and that he no longer has to contend with outdated, irrelevant, or overly abstract theories.

Meanwhile, the final three lines of the poem, which reenact the opening's meditative gaze down the valley, acknowledge the rhythmic activities that make locodescriptive verse possible. Just as the first stanza depicts a landscape conditioned by gentle processes (rising mists, the slow growth of pitch, flies borne aloft), so too does the poet hoping to commune with his natural surroundings partake in a series of simple actions. He clears his mind of old memories and distant commitments, drinks snowmelt from a tin cup, and gazes once more down a valley that is suddenly indistinguishable from his own being. Taken together, these uncomplicated activities situate the poet in the here and now. He is rewarded with a moment of satori, or Buddhist enlightenment, which as D. T. Suzuki explains in *An Introduction to Zen Buddhism* "consists of acquiring a new viewpoint for looking into the essence of things."[17]

By avoiding fixation (the most basic of Zen tenets) and by granting the land and its creatures their own agency, Snyder distances himself from the anthropomorphic and appropriative tendencies plaguing most Romantic landscape poetry. In "Mid-August," and in several of the other new poems he was writing, the push and pull of a landscape's diverse elements, among which the persona is no more (and no less) than one integral part, affect the psychology of whoever chooses to travel the same pathway. Wild landscape is not a companionable form for Snyder so much as it is a companionable force pushing him forward to consider new possibilities and take on new identities. As he moves within, and is emotionally moved by, the landscapes and seascapes of the American West, the poet writes verse that is elastic enough to accommodate his rapidly developing religious sensibilities, yet precise enough to record the natural phenomena shaping his consciousness. But as we shall see, the Sierra Nevada mountains presented Snyder with a significant challenge on both personal and aesthetic levels.

Trail-Building in the Sierras

In 1955, Snyder's feelings about remaining in California for the summer were ambivalent, at best. The painful circumstances of the previous summer's blacklisting affair were apparent in a June letter he sent to Whalen, who was planning to work on Sourdough Mountain that summer. "If you go," Snyder tells his friend, "I will make a brave effort to come up north and visit you en Lookout. I am physically sick for wanting to be in the mountains so bad." When Snyder ended up taking the trail crew job in California a few weeks later, his mood failed to improve. "The fucking Sierras are disappointing," he tells Whalen in a letter written that July. "I climbed a 10,000 foot mountain Sunday—which did not have the alpine quality of even Sourdough, and a much less entertaining purview. Awful hard old granite rock, though. But none of the 'presence' of the Cascades. These hills are dead."[18]

As it happened, the Sierras afforded Snyder a unique opportunity to grow as a writer. "It was in Yosemite Park that I found myself as a poet," he admitted to David Robertson, three decades down the line. "I had given up ideas of being a writer, and had quit writing poems for three to four years, after having written quite a bit." Snyder's admission that he had ceased writing for "three to four years" is questionable, given the number of lookout and logging poems that found their way into *Myths & Texts*. Still, it seems clear from his conversation with Robertson that the grandeur of the Sierras was forcing him to think of new ways to translate landscape into words. "It was like going to bed with a totally new woman," Snyder recalls. "It was exciting and scary. I was used to a very different kind of terrain—much more moisture, much more snow, not the quality of rock, not the quality of light. I think the first thing that struck me about the Yosemite Sierra is the very high quality hard, white granite. The glacial slick, the exfoliating domes were fascinating to me. I thought the light too bright, very *yen* [sic]. It was a little unsettling: everything is very intense, very sharply contrasted, definite, even harsh. I was disturbed sometimes by the intensity of light and the steadiness of it. You have to adjust to it, and these adjustments have psychic analogues."[19] In a way, Snyder's reminiscence of his first summer in the Sierras does not sound all that different from John Muir's famous account of this "Range of Light" in *My First Summer in the Sierras*: "Probably more free sunshine falls on this majestic range than any other in the world I've ever seen or heard of. It has the brightest weather, brightest glacier-polished rocks, the greatest abundance of irised spray from its glorious waterfalls, the brightest forests of silver firs and silver pines, more starshine, moonshine, and perhaps more crystalshine than any other mountain chain, and its countless mirror lakes, having more light poured into them, glow and spangle most."[20]

Muir tends toward a breathless Romantic style. Snyder, by contrast, is more measured and, as Tim Dean might say, more "grounded" in his description of locality.[21] But just because Snyder seeks grounding in the earth does not mean that he is beyond resorting to "psychic analogues" on occasion. The most striking example arrives as he equates the intimidating power of the Sierras with the excitement of "going to bed with a totally new woman." Snyder once told me that a gendered relationship to the land became crucial for him as he came to "explore [the] unfamiliarity, new forms, new smells, new climates, [and] new sounds" of the California mountains. "For one who loves landscapes," he said, "a new landscape offers the kind of awe, beauty, unfamiliarity, etc., that a new lover offers. It needn't be heterosexual, this has mainly to do with newness. As I once joked in a talk I gave, 'I'm a monogamist in marriage, but promiscuous about landscapes and ecosystems.' I do hope the Yuba watershed is tolerant with me in this regard."[22]

Snyder's linkage of gender, sexuality, and landscape has huge implications for human geography, a subject I take up in earnest in the following chapters, where I analyze the love poems of *The Back Country* and *Regarding Wave*. At this point, I will simply say that the question of whether the women who populate that Pacific Rim and the Yuba watershed in northern California are in fact tolerant of such a linkage remains highly debatable. It is both ironic and unfortunate that a poet who has dedicated himself to the eradication of frontier mentality should adopt a mode of thought that Annette Kolodny and Louise Westling, among others, have exposed as sexist and imperialist by turns. In her pioneering study on this subject, *The Lay of the Land* (1975), Kolodny maintains that masculine exploitation of American landscapes, which she likens to rape, will not truly disappear until men abandon sexual metaphors, such as "virgin land," that they have traditionally used to negotiate unfamiliar terrain.[23] Although I would classify Snyder as a lover and not a rapist, a *blason* poet and not a rampaging imperialist, his complicity in the aggressive discourse Kolodny deplores haunts his work from time to time, especially when he represents the male poet as an active agent and the feminized landscape as a passive reservoir awaiting his arrival.

In *Riprap* it was manual labor, much more than sex, which helped Snyder negotiate an unfamiliar and dangerous mountain environment, though we will notice that his metaphors about work were similarly situated within a masculine symbolic economy. In later poems and prose statements, Snyder often refers to something he calls "the real work," the main purpose of which is to "make the world as real as it is, and to find ourselves as real as we are within it" (TRW 82). Importantly, Snyder believes the work of writing poetry is no different from other kinds of work he does: "Poetry does no more than woodchopping, or automobile repair, or anything else because they're all equally real" (TRW 82). In *Riprap*, more than in any other volume, Snyder takes pains to avoid academic pretension, presenting himself as just another laborer. Hence his decision to dedicate the book to twelve coworkers, all of them men.

That the young poet's inspiration came from an odd collection of Whitmanian "roughs" squared perfectly with his ongoing process of de-education. "The indigent seasonal-working male is a wonderful species," Snyder tells Whalen in a letter written during the summer of 1955. "In this camp, as elsewhere, they are fairly rational, organized creatures until con-fronted with liquor."[24] Snyder reiterated this point a decade later, telling bib-liographer David Kherdian, "As much as the books I've read the jobs I've had have been significant in shaping me. My sense of body and language and the knowledge that intelligence and insight, sensitivity, awareness and bril-liance [bring] are not limited to educated people, or anything like it. That's why I dedicated *Riprap* to that list of fellow-workers. . . . I felt I owed them as individuals, as persons, as much as I owed my books. They were real teachers, they were all men of no education, but men of great natural brilliance and life. Some real fuck-ups too, of course."[25]

Reading *Riprap*, we can gauge the degree to which real work affected Sny-der's syntax and phrasing. We notice, for instance, that the new poems differ significantly from the logged notebook entries in *Myths & Texts*, insofar as they edge closer to what David Robertson, in his article on *Riprap*, calls a "trail-talking" or "trail-building" style.[26] "Walking, climbing, placing with hands. I tried writing poems of tough, simple, short words, with the com-plexity far beneath the surface texture," Snyder explained in the statement on poetics included in *The New American Poetry*. "In part the line [of riprap poetry] was influenced by the five- and seven-character line Chinese poems I'd been reading, which work like sharp blows to the mind."[27]

Paying further tribute to his "trail-building" poetics, Snyder placed the following definition on *Riprap*'s title page: "Riprap: a cobble of stone laid on steep slick rock to make a trail for horses in the mountains." We might remember that in "Burning 13," a late section of *Myths & Texts*, Snyder had provided the following aphorism: "Poetry a riprap on the slick rock of metaphysics" (MT 48). In both cases, a riprap trail becomes a tactical means of negotiating tricky terrain. The slippery slopes of the West Coast may exist on the physical register (the windswept shale beaches of Nootka Sound and the mountain pastures of southern China that appear in "Burn-ing 13"; or the "exfoliating domes," "glacier-polished rocks," and "glorious waterfalls" in the descriptions of the Sierras offered elsewhere by Snyder and Muir), in the metaphysical realm (the sublime musings that Pacific landscapes and seascapes have long inspired in American writers such as Herman Melville and Robinson Jeffers), or in a gendered relationship that contains elements of both. In any event, these slopes can be daunting for the first-time climber and would seem to require the trail-building expert-ise of an experienced hand.

The extent to which *Riprap*'s trail-building poetry actually kept the poet "on the trail" is open to some debate. As a seasonal laborer and practicing poet, Snyder was certainly influenced by the fixity of the trails he was building and the Asian verse forms he was learning about in Berkeley classrooms. On the other hand, during his spare time, he was just as likely to wander "off the trail" in search of wisdom and enlightenment. As Snyder recalls in his discussion with Robertson, the mountains of California sparked in him a desire to explore new pathways. "In the Sierra I . . . got a sense of mobility that I had never experienced before," he explains. "You are not working in and out of steep brushy gorges, like you are in the Cascades and the Olympics. There you don't leave the trail lightly. You are in for some real brushwacking. Or if you are up on a ridge, you have to negotiate steep snow fields, cornices, and overhangs any time of year. Whereas in the Sierra Nevada, especially in Yosemite, you could put a blindfold on and practically take off—although there are places where you might want to see where your feet are going [chuckle]. I just reveled in the freedom of movement."[28]

Snyder's love of unrestricted mobility, on or off the trail, aligns with the basic tenets of Taoism. "The Way that can be *followed* is not the true or correct Way," Snyder tells Julia Martin in a 1990 interview, explaining that he prefers this translation of the opening lines to the *Tao Te Ching*—which substitutes the verb "followed" (literally "wayed") for "spoken of"—because it places Lao Tzu's aphorism (*Dao ke dao fei chang dao*) in the field of physical action instead of the realm of thought and speech.[29] Then again, in "On the Path, Off the Trail," an essay he included in *The Practice of the Wild*, Snyder presents a strong case for locating the tao in all sorts of creative activities, telling readers that "from the earliest days of Chinese civilization, natural and practical processes have been described in the language of the path or way. Such connections are explicit in the cryptic Chinese text that seems to have gathered all the earlier lore and restated it for later history—the *Dao De Jing*, 'The Classic of the Way and the Power.' The word *dao* itself means way, road, trail, or to lead/follow. Philosophically it means the nature and way of truth. . . . Another extension of the meaning of *dao* is the practice of an art or craft. In Japanese, *dao* is pronounced *do*—as in *kado*, 'the way of flowers,' *bushido*, 'way of the warrior,' or *sado*, 'tea ceremony'" (PW 155).

Even when the philosophy of the tao charts a route to enlightenment, it encourages adherents to diverge from that route and go into uncharted territory. According to Snyder's understanding, "there are paths that can be followed, and there is a path that cannot—it is not a path, it is the wilderness. There is a 'going' but no goer, no destination, only the whole field" (PW 162). A little discipline never hurts, of course, especially at the beginning of one's studies or endeavors. Just as many accomplished free verse poets and abstract artists benefited from formal training early in their careers, some freewheeling members of San Francisco's counterculture might have done better to study Asian religion and culture with experts before going off to "do their own thing." As Snyder tells Martin in their interview, "you have to learn how to go on a way before you quit following it."[30]

Apparently, Snyder took this lesson to heart in the mid-1950s, when he was educating and de-educating himself by turns. In a linguistic context, this exercise meant that he had to learn Chinese literary traditions at UC–Berkeley before discovering that he really wanted to make them applicable to his experience in the Sierras. In a religious context, it signified that he had to train as a Zen monk in Japan before realizing that he really wanted to become a lay disciple and bring his practice back to America. In a natural context, it connoted that he had to build mountain trails before figuring out when and where to leave them behind and take his own path into the wilderness, where the facts of life are not so neatly organized and notions of singular identity are not so clear. As Snyder would say in "On the Path, Off the Trail," an essay clearly indebted to the teachings of the *Tao Te Ching*: "The actuality of things cannot be confined within so linear an image as a road. The intention of training can only be accomplished when the 'follower' has been forgotten" (PW 161).

Learning to appreciate the ambiguous nature of roads and trails makes reading *Riprap* a richer experience. Snyder's best Yosemite poems—"Piute Creek," "Milton by Firelight," and "Riprap"—chronicle the summer of 1955 in the short, clipped phrasing commonly associated with Asian poetics and therefore stand as good examples of the trail-building style he was perfecting at that time. Avoiding the drawing-room preciosity that imbued earlier Orientalist verse experiments by Imagist poets such as Ezra Pound and Amy Lowell, Snyder opted instead for a rugged and pragmatic style forged in the mountains. And yet—as grounded in good, honest work and literary craftsmanship as they seem—the poems in *Riprap* point to something far more mysterious and unfixed, since they are constantly on the lookout for the dark tangles and shadowy presences that lurk somewhere off the trail, beyond our pragmatic understanding, out there amid "the relentless complexity of the world" (PW 155). The writer of these poems does not abandon himself entirely to the slippery slopes of sublimity, but neither is he so tied to the trail as to avoid the more uncertain aspects of an unfamiliar mountain landscape.

"Piute Creek" and "Milton by Firelight" should be read as a pair, not only because they appear side by side in *Riprap*, but because they were written around the same time and in the same location. Piute Creek was visible to Snyder throughout most of his summer in the Sierras, since the riprap trail he was building, which ran from Pate Valley to Kerrick Canyon in the northern reaches of Yosemite National Park, skirted its banks. Decades later, Snyder has an amazingly precise memory of the space that gave rise to "Piute Creek" and "Milton by Firelight," telling me in correspondence that "both poems were composed in the best camp and pasturage area along that part of Piute Creek, called Pleasant Valley. That was trail camp headquarters for some weeks. You can find it named on the . . . quad called Hetch Hetchy, up near Irwin Bright Lake."[31]

Notwithstanding this detailed recollection, Snyder begins "Piute Creek" by summoning a more hypothetical locale, a relatively sparse and uncomplicated landscape that, if it only existed, would more accurately match the concise and simple phrasings of his Asian-inflected verse:

> One granite ridge
> A tree, would be enough
> Or even a rock, a small creek
> A bark shred in a pool.

With its indefinite articles and conditional verb, this passage hardly adheres to the conventions of locodescriptive verse. Instead, these short lines mark a first step in the poet's shuttling back and forth between newly learned poetic techniques and a topographical register that prevents him from measuring up to their strictures. Indeed, as the poem continues, Snyder intimates that the sublimity of the Sierra Nevada mountains has overwhelmed the spare riprap style he has been attempting to perfect:

> Hill beyond hill, folded and twisted
> Tough trees crammed
> In thin stone fractures
> A huge moon on it all, is too much.
> The mind wanders . . .

At the same time, I suspect that the poem might be lamenting the tendency of well-known writers and artists (Muir, Jeffers, Joaquin Miller, Albert Bierstadt, Ansel Adams) to focus on the vast and powerful aspects of the American West while ignoring this landscape's tiny energies. By offering such a reading, I am contesting an argument put forth by Tim Dean, who links Snyder with Bierstadt, Adams, Georgia O'Keeffe, and other ambitious artists whose main purpose, he claims, was to determine "how any subject can find a space for itself in such landscapes."[32] To my mind, Dean's frequent recourse to theories of the Romantic Sublime—an appropriative and self-aggrandizing scenario in which a subject initially falls prey to a powerful object or force, only to end up introjecting that entity and claiming the power for his own—fails to account for what is going on in "Piute Creek," for in this poem the persona blends into the landscape and then *stays there.* Snyder's emphasis here is on plurality. As a result, the temporary loss and convoluted recuperation of the poet's singular subjectivity, a complex process tracked rather rigorously by Dean and theorists of the Romantic Sublime, becomes a moot point.[33]

As "Piute Creek" comes to a close, Snyder lists the uncertainties circulating in his mind and finds that they summon a state of consciousness that is altogether real, though nearly impossible to explain. Surrounded by "endless mountains," the poet experiences a moment of satori not unlike the one in "Mid-August":

All the junk that goes with being human
Drops away, hard rock wavers
Even the heavy present seems to fail
This bubble of a heart.
Words and books
Like a small creek off a high ledge
Gone in the dry air.

A clear, attentive mind
Has no meaning but that
Which sees is truly seen.
No one loves rock, yet we are here.
Night chills. A flick
In the moonlight

Slips into Juniper shadow:
Back there unseen
Cold proud eyes
Of Cougar or Coyote
Watch me rise and go. (RRCM 8)

Here we will notice that a number of the writer's everyday tools and assumptions (words, books, the present time, and "all the [other] junk that goes with being human") are subject to processes of diminution, precipitous tumbling, and outright failure. The brute reality of Yosemite will not allow for any excess, on the part of the poet or anyone else, and all who hope to survive there must first learn to alter their daily lives according to its austere topography. The poem's short lines are well suited to the task, since words are constantly dropping from the end of one line to the beginning of another in cascading fashion. Snyder's clever positioning of words such as "Drops" and "Gone" at the enjambed beginnings of lines serves to reinforce metrically and formally the process he is portraying imagistically. As words cut across, run up against, and cascade down the lines of this poem, their status becomes just as tenuous—and every bit as powerful—as drops of water going over a rocky cliff.

The last verse paragraph of "Piute Creek" opens with a statement that is mysterious enough to be a Zen koan. Curiously, no comma is supplied before the word "but" in the second line. A reader is therefore conditioned by the uninterrupted syntax to understand "but that" to mean "except for that." According to the logic of this reading, "that / Which sees" (presumably some visionary creature, and quite possibly the cougar or coyote mentioned in the penultimate line) would signal the last vestige of meaning in a "clear, attentive mind." Strange to say, the syntactical flow of the poem would actually get bogged down were we to read the second line of the paragraph without a pause, since the purely objective status of "that / Which sees," a status guaranteed by the quantitative comparison this combination of phrases sets up, would strip this visionary creature of its subjective agency, implied by the verb "is" in the next line. After all, once an object is earmarked as the exception to the rule in a main clause, it cannot function as a subject unless a non-restrictive clause happens to provide this object with a measure of agency somewhere down the line, in a subordinate part of the sentence. Our reading of "Piute Creek" is thus thrown into confusion. Accustomed as we are to the rhythms of everyday speech, we want to read the second line as though there were a comma before the word "but," and yet Snyder's refusal to supply such punctuation keeps his meaning ambiguous. This is the case in nearly every one of *Riprap*'s Yosemite poems, which piece together but ultimately refuse to cement the constitutive elements of syntax and image, thereby forcing us to weigh the merits of various readings.

Because riprap poetry ends up fragmenting its own meaning, the poet who writes it must learn to align himself with the disparate elements affecting his understanding of particular localities. It is in this respect that the final lines of "Piute Creek" loom large, for they suggest that Snyder, alone at night on a hillside above the Piute drainage, writing the notes for his first Yosemite poem, has stumbled upon a pluralistic way of thinking about nature and humanity. "No one loves rock, yet we are here" is a characteristically economical sentence about an isolated place and might even imply a conscious decision to steal away to that place. But in the mind or on the part of whom? As was the case in "Mid-August at Sourdough Mountain Lookout," the first pronoun in "Piute Creek" does not arrive until late in the poem, well after this location has been charted. Furthermore, the pronoun is plural and may therefore refer to both Snyder and the unloved rock. The "we" may even be construed to include the titular creek and the poet's own words, both of which cascade down the ledge of rocks/lines they have helped to carve and shape. The sheer power of the Sierras cuts many ways and is distributed among sites and presences that may at first appear to be unpoetic. In *The Waste Land*, a despondent T. S. Eliot complains, "Amongst the rock one cannot stop or think." In *Riprap*, Snyder not only stops and thinks, but also reclaims a rocky environment as an imaginative site, one with abundant footholds for the philosophical adventurer.[34]

In the closing lines of "Piute Creek," Snyder reintroduces the concept of the gaze, a prolonged and powerful way of looking he had already invoked in the final lines of "Mid-August on Sourdough Mountain Lookout," when he described his peaceful and panoptic view from on high: "Looking down for miles / Through high still air." Many postmodern theorists have argued that gazing is an appropriative activity undertaken by a human subject who cathects or otherwise utilizes (identifies with, projects something upon, transfers something to) a viewed object (in the case of "Mid-August," the mountainous landscape) as a means of satisfying a desire or resolving a psychological predicament. In "Piute Creek," however, this power dynamic is effectively reversed, since it is the land and its creatures that eye the poet, not the other way around. All the poet notices is that a "flick / In the moonlight / Slips into Juniper shadow."

The fleeting nature of Snyder's observation brings to mind Jacques Lacan's description of an elusive human Unconscious, which he once likened to a fading neon light on a Baltimore morning. For Lacan, the Unconscious should be regarded as a line of movement or a trajectory, not as a fixed object or a bounded space. One cannot locate the Unconscious simply because it is always just beyond our grasp, disappearing around the bend or fading into the light of day.[35] The same dynamic holds sway in "Piute Creek." As happens in those fleeting moments when unconscious energies threaten to break through the surface of our everyday routine, Snyder is not exactly sure of what he sees moving in the shadows, or whether he sees anything at all. His experience in this particular location leaves him neither here nor there. All his imagination can get him is lost.

Once this "flick / In the moonlight" unsettles the poet's sense of self and place, he must learn to let go in the same way that young Ike McCaslin, in Faulkner's environmentalist fable, "The Bear," had to take off his watch and hang his compass around a tree in order to catch a glimpse of the proud and elusive beast, Old Ben. Or in the way that John Muir, in the Mount Ritter episode Snyder recounted in *Myths & Texts*, had to let himself fall off the cliff in order to survive. But where, and to what, should the poet of "Piute Creek" abandon himself? Any answer would have to come from the "flick" guiding Snyder to a place "Back there": a wild and uncharted location he would later refer to as the "back country of the imagination."[36] Once again, Snyder's ambiguous syntax indicates just how difficult it is to locate the site of unconscious knowledge. Since it is preceded by a colon, the phrase "Back there unseen" would seem at first to refer to the spot where Snyder loses the flick in the moonlight in the "Juniper shadow." At the same time, the following line positions "unseen" as an adjective modifying the "Cold proud eyes" of a lurking animal. In either case, the word "unseen" indicates that Snyder cannot see the eyes of the animal (Cougar or Coyote) he believes (but cannot prove) is looking at him. Ultimately, the poet's identity derives not so much from his own subjective gaze as it does from multiple and intersecting lines of vision, the vast majority of which remain invisible to him at any particular time, in any particular place.

Accustomed as he is to looking for traces of the Romantic Sublime in Snyder's poetry, Tim Dean argues that these "weaker" final lines, in which "the subject becomes aware of itself as object of another's watchful gaze," contradict the highly subjective character of the rest of the poem, insofar as they are "acknowledging not the consciousness of another person but of an animal, a consciousness which can count in the realm of nature." The human subject of this poem "is not excessive of the natural," Dean admits, yet the effect Snyder strives for "is only achieved by attributing to nature a consciousness which has been revealed as excruciatingly lacking by the poem's opening lines. The problem is not whether or not nature can have a consciousness that can count in relation to human consciousness, but rather whether consciousness can possibly be conceived in other than human terms."[37]

As I have argued in my preceding chapter, however, I believe that Snyder *has* indeed been able to articulate a nonhuman or creaturely consciousness. He rarely if ever succumbs to the anthropocentric tendencies Dean hints at, simply because he refuses to accept the dualistic thinking that arbitrarily separates humankind from the rest of nature and makes psychoanalytic theories of sublimity applicable. His strategy in "Piute Creek," rather, is to make the poetic subject invisible to himself, for only after shucking off the constraints of visibility and self-consciousness can he enter the unseen realm of interconnected gazes, where one finds his true bearings. A visionary poet must give up the role of seer and become instead "that / Which is truly seen" if he wants to see things as they really exist. Years later, Snyder would define the practice of meditation as "the problematic art of deliberately staying open as myriad things experience themselves" (PS 113). In "Piute Creek," an underlying simplicity and respect for wild nature lend credence to Alan Watts's assertion that the "'peripheral' aspect of the mind works best when we do not try to interfere with it, when we trust it to work by itself—*tzu-jan*, spontaneously, 'self-so.'"[38]

In "Milton by Firelight," Snyder's treatment of unseen energies takes on a somewhat different tenor, for he implies that the kind of blind surmising he practiced at the end of "Piute Creek" is largely irrelevant, and perhaps even dangerous, if it is not tethered to a strong sense of place. A great many prophecies from the civilized world simply do not apply in the mountains of California, since the land itself refuses to accommodate their existence. Snyder sorts through a set of competing influences as he picks up a copy of *Paradise Lost* by the campfire one summer night:

> "O hell, what do mine eyes
>   with grief behold?"
> Working with an old
> Singlejack miner, who can sense
> The vein and cleavage
> In the very guts of rock, can
> Blast granite, build
> Switchbacks that last for years
> Under the beat of snow, thaw, mule-hooves.
> What use, Milton, a silly story
> Of our lost general parents,
>   eaters of fruit? (RRCM 9)

The opening question is Satan's, uttered in Book Four of *Paradise Lost* as he looks down from Mount Niphates to behold Adam and Eve in the realm of Paradise. The closing question is Snyder's and is indirectly addressed to Milton, asking the English poet to defend the usefulness of his "silly story." In between these framing questions, Snyder describes the process of building a trail. Here we learn that an "old / Singlejack miner" (quite possibly Roy Marchbanks, the leader of the trail crew in 1955) knows more about the "unseen" energies of the wilderness than do either Snyder or Milton, for he possesses a tactile expertise. Indeed, the fact that he "can sense / The *vein* and *cleavage* / In the very *guts* of rock" (my emphasis) suggests that he has the dexterity of a surgeon. In this context, the "switchbacks"—the zigzagging trails that Marchbanks and Snyder build—are surgical stitches that "last for years" through constant use in a harsh climate. The practical nature of the miner's "real work," which is designed to prevent people from falling off the mountain, causes Snyder to question the relevance of the metaphysical fall described in Milton's seventeenth-century epic.

In the next verse paragraph, an "Indian, a chainsaw boy, / And a string of six mules" come down from the mountain, hungry for the "green apples" a mountain meadow offers, providing another reminder of Snyder's creaturely activity among the hornets in *Myths & Texts*. Unlike Adam, these characters are not afraid to pluck the fruit from the tree. Their California is a new kind of Eden, immune to the harsh dictates of English Puritanism. Their earthly utopia is subject to the ravages of time, but is no less comforting for all that:

> In ten thousand years the Sierras
> Will be dry and dead, home of the scorpion.
> Ice-scratched slabs and bent trees.
> No paradise, no fall,
> Only the weathering land
> The wheeling sky,
> Man, with his Satan
> Scouring the chaos of the mind.
> Oh Hell! (RRCM 9–10)

A "weathering land," a "wheeling sky," an approaching scorpion: these natural entities, neither human nor divine, urge the poet to move alongside them, to mimic them, to abandon outdated modes of knowledge, in order to locate a realm worlds apart from the kind *Paradise Lost* has offered generations of readers. "Oh Hell!" marks Snyder's final frustration with Milton. A vituperative outburst, it approximates the language uttered by Satan at the beginning of the poem while also paying heed to the kind of expletives trail workers use. "Oh Hell!" is something we might imagine Roy Marchbanks muttering if he tried to reconcile the moral lessons of *Paradise Lost* with the lessons he had gleaned from years of hard work in the Sierras.

We half expect Snyder to throw the book in the campfire at this point, but there is not enough rhetorical hot air to sustain any fire, let alone the fires of Puritanism. Instead, by the end of "Milton by Firelight," we see the poet taking on a rather bemused sense of Buddhist calm:

> Fire down
> Too dark to read, miles from a road
> The bell-mare clangs in the meadow
> That packed dirt for a fill-in
> Scrambling through loose rocks
> On an old trail
> All of a summer's day. (RRCM 10)

Snyder borrows the final line from Book One of *Paradise Lost*, where Milton describes the fall of Mulcibur (Vulcan): "From morn / To noon he fell, from noon to dewy eve, / A summer's day" (ll. 742–44). In Snyder's universe, by contrast, a summer's day is just a simple occasion. It is sufficient to know the details of the land one traverses, as Roy Marchbanks does; it is permissible to take and enjoy the fruits of that land, as the Indian, the chainsaw boy, and the mules do; and it is proper to realize when it is too dark to read a literature that no longer applies, as Snyder does here, in one of his most marvelous poems.

In "Riprap," the final poem in the volume bearing its name, Snyder reinforces the messages of his previous poems, which include the need to respect natural processes, the need to learn from one's work experiences, and the need to look upon oneself as a vital link in an interconnected universe. In this treatise of trail-building poetics, Snyder maintains that a trail, however much it acts to guide us or keep us on course, prompts us to consider more inclusive possibilities inherent in nature:

> Lay down these words
> Before your mind like rocks.
>   placed solid, by hands
> In choice of place, set
> Before the body of the mind
>   in space and time:
> Solidity of bark, leaf, or wall
>   riprap of things:
> Cobble of milky way,
>   straying planets,
> These poems, people,
>   lost ponies with
> Dragging saddles
>   and rocky sure-foot trails.
> The worlds like an endless
>   four-dimensional
> Game of Go.

A number of items, ranging from the earthy bark to the cosmic Milky Way, are linked by the colons in lines six and eight, until they form a riprap trail writ large. Although Snyder is not necessarily leaving the trail in "Riprap," he is looking up to the sky to show just how far the trail extends. "On those clear nights in the High Sierra I saw the stars as further rocks and trails leading onward and out," Snyder recalled years afterward.[39] The game of Go is important in this context. Snyder tells David Robertson that this Asian game, which is played with black and white stones on a board of intersecting lines, functions as a "structural image" as well as a "metaphor of interconnectedness." Summoning an image strikingly similar to that of Indra's Net, Snyder mentions Go in order to show that the "universe is like a huge network with crystal beads at each juncture. Each of the beads contains within itself the entire universe by reflecting all the others."[40] In the board game, as on the trail, a few well-placed stones can lead a player off the straight-and-narrow path to consider the grander mysteries of the universe. As the game of Go is played, as the stars shine down, and as the lines of riprap poetry wend their way (with the indented typography forming a zigzag or switchback pattern on the page), Snyder spots a design of infinite belonging.

John Muir once remarked that any writer who hoped to represent California accurately needed to know when to put down the pen and read the land itself as an unfinished manuscript, a work-in-progress.[41] In the final lines of "Riprap," Snyder realizes that the poems he is writing, like the trails he is building, are dependent not so much upon the fruits of his own labors as they are upon ancient (and ongoing) geological processes:

> . . . ants and pebbles
> In the thin loam, each rock a word
>   a creek-washed stone
> Granite: ingrained
>   with torment of fire and weight
> Crystal and sediment linked hot
>   all change, in thoughts,
> As well as things. (RRCM 32)

The Sierras are born of change, and it is up to the poet to register this truth. He succeeds brilliantly with the phrase "Granite: ingrained," since the colon inextricably fastens the noun to its adjective. The poem's inverted syntax, in which the adjective follows the noun, suggests that whatever looks to be solid (in this case granite) is actually the result of a long formative process (of "ingrained" sedimentation). That the words "granite" and "ingrained" are nearly anagrammatic only reinforces this causal relationship. Snyder is being quite clever with his word play here, and yet he is also acknowledging a primal creativity that issues forth from the earth, not simply from his own pen. By describing the "torment of fire and weight" that has helped to shape the rocky landscape he stands upon, he honors an ongoing process affecting the different kinds of work he does.

Trip-Stop Mind-Points

When Snyder came down from the Sierra Nevada mountains after his summer on the trail crew, he could hardly have predicted the literary explosion that was about to take place. But the October reading at the Six Gallery kick-started the San Francisco Renaissance, and a countercultural mythology was born. It was in this heady atmosphere that the poet who had spent so much of his time working in the mountains and studying in the classroom became newly socialized. For the remainder of 1955, Snyder lived in Berkeley, not far from Allen Ginsberg, whom he met just prior to the Six Gallery event. Early in 1956, he moved to Mill Valley, in Marin County, where he shared a small cabin with Jack Kerouac. In May of that year, Snyder left for Japan, but not before commemorating the important friendships he had recently forged and reflecting upon his decision to leave the San Francisco scene. Two poems from *Riprap* are illustrative of this period.

Snyder has told me that "Nooksack Valley" was composed on a hitchhiking trip that he made with Ginsberg in January and February of 1956, when the two poets left Berkeley for the Pacific Northwest, in part to escape the fishbowl atmosphere that had emerged in the Bay Area (Ginsberg had just debuted Part Two of "Howl" at a big Berkeley reading).[42] After stops in Portland, Seattle, and Bellingham, Snyder settled in at a remote cabin owned by one of his friends. While there, he reflected upon where he had been and where he was going in his life:

> At the far end of a trip north
> In a berry-pickers cabin
> At the edge of a wide muddy field
> Stretching to the woods and cloudy mountains,

Feeding the stove all afternoon with cedar,
Watching the dark sky darken, a heron flap by,
A huge setter pup nap on the dusty cot.
High rotten stumps in the second-growth woods
Flat scattered farms in the bends of the Nooksack
River. Steelhead run now
    a week and I go back
Down 99, through towns, to San Francisco
              and Japan.

Like "Mid-August at Sourdough Mountain Lookout," this poem opens with directional prepositions that guide us to a place of meditation. High rotten stumps and scattered farms make the Nooksack Valley read like a manuscript, and the tale being told attests to a cycle of settlement and destruction Snyder had pondered since childhood. The "edge" of the muddy field signals a boundary beyond which true wilderness begins, a boundary that is receding every year. The shrinking forest supplies the settlers of Washington with cedar, which in turn feeds their stoves, which in turn emit the smoke that darkens an already darkened sky. "Heron flap by" and "steelhead run," but we are left to guess whether these creatures are instinctively migrating or consciously choosing to flee civilization's deleterious effects. In a show of sympathy, Snyder suggests that he too will be migrating soon. Of course, he will be taking a north–south highway rather than a stream or flyway. In the end, he hopes that Route 99 will take him off its asphalt trail and lead him beyond this continent, across the Pacific to Japan. Geographic coordinates continue to appear as the poet plots his next move:

All America south and east,
Twenty-five years in it brought to a trip-stop
Mind-point, where I turn
Caught more on this land—rock tree and man,
Awake, than ever before, yet ready to leave.
    damned memories,
Whole wasted theories, failures and worse success,
School, girls, deals, try to get in
To make this poem a froth, a pity,
A dead fiddle for lost good jobs.

the cedar walls
Smell of our farm-house, half built in '35.
Clouds sink down the hills
Coffee is hot again. The dog
Turns and turns about, stops and sleeps. (RRCM 17)

When reading this passage, I am reminded of Thoreau, who, while standing on the beach at Provincetown, Massachusetts, famously claimed that he was able to "put all America behind him."[43] One hundred years later, Snyder stands on the western edge of the same continent, with "All America south and east," trying to distance himself from daily concerns in cold war America. Education, girls, deals—all the things that the mainstream society of the 1950s defines as masculine markers of "success"—are poor substitutes for the "good jobs" he had before the blacklisting affair of 1954. The cedar cabin, meanwhile, reminds him of his father's failure as a farmer back in 1935, a failure the son certainly does not want to repeat. Presumably, neither Ginsberg (who goes unmentioned) nor any of the other poets associated with the San Francisco Renaissance are able to quell the restlessness Snyder feels during this "trip-stop / Mind-point." He feels "caught" on the land and in the past, and is anxious to begin the next stage of his Pacific Rim odyssey.

"Migration of Birds" is a creaturely variation on the same theme, for it too talks about following a visionary trail off the American continent. Composed two months after "Nooksack Valley," this poem describes a lazy afternoon that Snyder and Kerouac spent together in Mill Valley. It opens with a vague pronoun, and thus it is difficult to determine Snyder's reason for writing the poem as well as the cause of his sudden insight on this particular April day:

It started just now with a hummingbird
Hovering over the porch two yards away
                           then gone.
It stopped me studying.

In keeping with his theme of de-education, Snyder finds something that incites his intellectual curiosity, even as "it" stops him from studying. Whatever "it" is, the hummingbird appears to be the one who can bring "it" to light. The bird hovers close enough for the poet to catch a glimpse, but soon

this winged creature is gone, its elusive flight pattern indicated by the radically indented typography of the third line.

As the poem progresses, Snyder describes the foliage around his Mill Valley cabin, then mentions two other winged species: the "white-crowned sparrows" that sing in the trees and a rooster that crows "down the valley." To this
point, Snyder has concerned himself with birds that stay close to home. Tiny
hummingbirds are notable for their ability to suspend themselves in midair,
not for their ability to cover large distances. Sparrows are more migratory, but
they do not travel very far compared to some other birds. And roosters cannot
fly for more than a few feet at a time and are thus restricted to the barnyard.
By the end of the poem, though, Snyder is turning his attention to shorebirds
whose movements foreshadow his own leave-taking:

Jack Kerouac outside, behind my back
Reads the *Diamond Sutra* in the sun.
Yesterday I read *Migration of Birds*;
The Golden Plover and the Arctic Tern.
Today that big abstraction's at our door
Broody scrabblers pick up bits of string
And in this hazy day
Of April summer heat
Across the hill the seabirds
Chase Spring north along the coast:
Nesting in Alaska
In six weeks. (RRCM 19)

While Kerouac reads his favorite Buddhist text, Snyder reflects upon the
knowledge he has gleaned from *Migration of Birds*, a book written by Frederick
C. Lincoln, a biologist employed by the Fish and Wildlife Service of the U.S.
Department of the Interior. Ostensibly a field guide to birds of North America, Lincoln's book nevertheless examines the instincts and environmental
conditions that prompt some species of birds to travel far beyond this continent. As the restless poet looks up from his book to gaze at the spring migrations along the Pacific flyway, he no doubt envies long-distance flyers like
the golden plover and the Arctic tern. The Pacific golden plover, Lincoln
explains, heads north in April to nest and breed in Alaska, a fact Snyder
acknowledges in the final two lines of his poem. What "Migration of Birds"

fails to remark upon, even though it is representative of Snyder's impending journey, is the Rim-like contour of the golden plover's migratory route. According to Lincoln, this bird "breeds chiefly in the Arctic coast region of Siberia and merely overflows onto the Alaskan coast, some of the birds probably migrating south along the coast of Asia to winter quarters in Japan, China, India, Australia, New Zealand, and the Low Archipelago."[44]

The Arctic tern, the other bird Snyder mentions (called the "champion globe-trotter" by Lincoln), covers an equally vast distance on the other side of the Pacific Ocean, hugging the western coast of the Americas as it travels between the Arctic Circle and Antarctica. Interestingly enough, when the path of the tern is combined with that of the plover, one can see the full outline of the Pacific Rim. Fittingly, these winged creatures, which have inspired other Asia-Pacific artists (Basho, Morris Graves, Albert Saijo, Hawaiian hula dancers) over the years, appear at the door of a postmodern American poet who, having learned about their "coastwise" routes in Lincoln's book, no longer regards the Rim as just another "big abstraction."[45] It remained for Snyder to follow their lead, to "Chase spring north along the coast" and head to Japan. He did so a month later, in May 1956.

Japan First Time Around

Birds do not need passports, but humans traveling between Pacific Rim nations certainly do, and in the mid-1950s the blacklisting affair was proving to be quite an obstacle for Snyder. For months on end, the State Department denied his requests for a passport, finally relenting when he wrote a long letter—"a loyalty statement of sorts," according to Patrick Murphy— disavowing any connection to communism. As Murphy duly notes, Snyder was anything but repentant in this letter. Although he agreed to refrain from criticizing the American government while stationed abroad, he used the rest of the letter as an opportunity to denounce the nationalist fervor that made cold war America such an unwelcoming place for political dissent. Accordingly, he stood by a statement attributed to him that he "would rather go to a concentration camp than be drafted" for the Korean War. The letter also includes an early instance of the bioregional politics Snyder would champion in the 1970s. "In opposition to large, centralized modern nation states," Murphy explains, after reviewing this letter, "Snyder supports decentralized land-based social organizations. These would be communities based on more ancient models of traditional societies, with territories defined by the lines of the natural boundaries and regions of a particular place."[46] The State Department could hardly have agreed less with Snyder's bioregional viewpoint, but after one more round of rejection, it finally agreed to grant him a passport.

Fortunately, Ruth Fuller Sasaki not only offered Snyder a job as her personal secretary at the First Zen Institute of America in Kyoto (the board of the institute rejected his scholarship application because of the political trouble it might bring them) but also agreed to save this job while he and the ACLU fought the bureaucracy back in the States. She knew all too well about the duplicity of the American government, having agreed to marry New York–based Zen Master Sasaki Sokei-an in the 1940s primarily to prevent his forced removal to a Japanese-American internment camp. Snyder would express quite a bit of frustration with Ruth Sasaki over the years, and he gladly left her employment in the early 1960s, but he must have been grateful that she at least allowed him the chance to realize his dream and travel to Japan.

The Zen Institute of America was housed at Ryosen-an, a small temple located at the grand Daitoku-ji complex on the northern outskirts of Kyoto. Here, Snyder worked alongside a handful of other American expatriates, translating Japanese texts. At the time of his arrival, Ruth Sasaki was particularly intent on finishing a project her late husband had started: an English-language translation of *Lin-chi lu*, the foundational document of the Lin-chi or Rinzai school of Zen Buddhism. Snyder worked diligently on this project and published two related translations in mimeographed editions: *Ryosen-an Zendo Practices* (1960) and *The Wooden Fish: Basic Sutras & Gathas of Rinzai Zen* (1961), the second of which was modeled on the traditional sleeve manuals carried by Zen monks. Although these guides were intended solely for use at the Zen Institute, some copies of *The Wooden Fish* made their way to San Francisco, where they were sold at City Lights Bookstore. Snyder also sent a copy to Philip Whalen.[47]

Despite all the work that went into these translating activities, Snyder has claimed that his "main reason for being in Kyoto was to do Zen Buddhist practice" (MR 156). As he has explained in an interview, poetry does not often come to him while he is meditating.[48] He therefore gave little attention to his own writing during his first stay in Japan. The poems Snyder did write in late 1956 and early 1957 are few in number, modest in scope, and uneven in quality. As had been the case in the Sierras, Snyder had to learn how to modulate his writing to make it conform to the realities of a new place. "Kyoto: March" is one of the few poems to succeed in this regard. This poem may do little more than provide a simple and sentimental portrait of humanity, but its gentle spirit signals a welcome development in a country only a few years removed from the catastrophe of war and the humiliation of the American occupation. As the poem comes to a close, Mount Hiei, a sacred mountain dusted with snow, looms in the distance, protecting Japanese citizens who in turn nurture a new generation destined for more peaceful times:

> Beneath the roofs
> Of frosty houses
> Lovers part, from tangle warm
> Of gentle bodies under quilt
> And crack the icy water to the face
> And wake and feed the children
> And grandchildren that they love. (RRCM 22)

In "Toji," Snyder shifts to talking about the religious culture he encounters overseas. At one juncture, the poem provides details of a Buddhist statue, which Snyder, employing the lingo of the San Francisco Beats, equates with Asia's inscrutable mysteries:

> Peering though chickenwire grates
> At dusty gold-leaf statues
> A cynical curving round-belly
> Cool Bodhisattva—maybe Avalokita—
> Bisexual and tried it all, weight on
> One leg, haloed in snake-hood gold
> Shines through the shadow
> An ancient hip smile
> Tingling of India and Tibet. (RRCM 20)

Beat Orientalism never had it so good, simply because it never had such a close look at the Asian culture it desired. In this poem, San Francisco's native son, suddenly freed from the restrictive policies and conservative atmosphere of cold war America ("Nobody bothers you in Toji," he explains at poem's end), is able to let his guard down and set his sights on a realm of pleasure that is new and yet ancient, cynical and yet beatifically haloed, and best of all, totally hip. To the extent that Snyder shared such discoveries with his Beat friends back home, he solidified his reputation as an Orientalist hipster in situ (for more on this score, see the following chapter, "Embodying").

"A Stone Garden," the final poem in *Riprap*'s Japan sequence, was actually written aboard the *Sappa Creek*, an oil tanker upon which Snyder worked from August 1957 to April 1958. Curiously, this poem is written in iambic pentameter, hardly the meter (or métier) of a New American Poet interested in Asian poetics. Its decasyllabic lines are relatively loose and Latinate in syntax, and its phrasings parallel and rhetorical. Even though the images in "A Stone Garden" are recognizably Japanese, the language that seeks to capture these images is more reminiscent of Anglo poetry written by Wordsworth, Coleridge, and Eliot. Sanehide Kodama points out that the poem's narrative is adapted in part from the Japanese poetry of Ariwarano Narihara and Otomo no Yakamochi and in part from the "Economy" section of Thoreau's *Walden*.[49] More pertinent for my own study is this poem's account of how American imperialists constructed a new Asia in their own image in the wake of World War II. To a certain extent, Snyder felt that he had traveled thousands of miles only to discover another version of the Western civilization he had been trying to escape. He would develop this premise more rigorously in "This Tokyo," a superior poem he published in *The New American Poetry* and eventually included in the "Far East" section of *The Back Country*.

Snyder did not write his finest poetry aboard the *Sappa Creek*. Even so, employment on its decks (actually in its engine room) allowed him to see a greater portion of the world. His travels between the Persian Gulf and various Pacific oil ports took him to locations "on the Rim" (Yokohama, Singapore), "inside the Rim" (Samoa, Midway), and "off the Rim" (the Bay of Bengal, Sri Lanka, Suez). Snyder's thoughts of this time are recorded in "Tanker Notes," a journal he published in *Earth House Hold*, and in a handful of poems from *Riprap*, including "The Sappa Creek," "T-2 Tanker Blues," and "At Five A.M. Off the North Coast of Sumatra." Although these poems are a bit better than "A Stone Garden," they show Snyder struggling to find an appropriate register for his Pacific Rim journeys. Meanwhile, back in the States, another of his poetry projects was being readied for publication.

A Meeting of Sensations: The "Cold Mountain Poems"

As mentioned in the previous chapter, Snyder's fascination with Pacific Rim culture dates from early childhood. Surprisingly, though, his interest in Asian literature was not really sparked until his final years at Reed College, when Charles Leong, an older Chinese-American student attending school on the G.I. Bill, and Professor Lloyd Reynolds taught him Asian calligraphy and encouraged him to branch out from his readings in Native American mythology.[50] Reading Asian texts in translation gave Snyder his first sustained engagement with Zen thought, which in turn made him want to read Buddhist texts in their original language. In a 1999 interview with David Meltzer, Snyder recalls, "When I came onto Zen, I said, ah, this is where it all comes together. I got interested in trying to study Zen first hand. Sort of broke off my anthropology career [at Indiana University] mid-stream . . . and said, 'I'm going out to Berkeley to study Chinese.'"[51] In 1952, Snyder entered UC–Berkeley's oriental languages program, where he received instruction in Chinese from Professor Ch'en Shih-hsiang. In 1955, during his final semester, Snyder was given an open-ended translation assignment by Professor Ch'en. In light of his burgeoning interest in Zen, Snyder expressed his desire to translate some Buddhist poems. He asked Ch'en whether he could recommend some, especially if he knew of any written in the vernacular. "Of course, Han-shan is the poet you should work with," Snyder remembers his professor saying.[52] Neither Ch'en nor Snyder could have known at the time that this recommendation would pave the way for one of the most intriguing documents in the New American Poetry.

At first, Professor Ch'en criticized his young charge for his unruly translations of Chinese texts. "I am engaged in a bitter fight with my teacher of Chinese poetry at the moment," Snyder admitted to Whalen in a letter dated 2 November 1953. "He called for polished translations of four poems from everybody in the class, & says he won't accept mine because they're too experimental and 'wild.'. . . He's a nice man but he just doesn't understand English poetry."[53] Ch'en quickly reversed course once he acknowledged Snyder's gift for American plain speech. In a letter he wrote just ten days after the one containing his initial complaint about Professor Ch'en, Snyder tells Whalen, "Poetry has improved slightly here; I handed a translation to Mr. Ch'en in forbidden form, & he liked it so much he reversed his stand on the matter. I now have complete freedom in the matter of translation, a special dispensation. Chinese poetry is indeed more complex, obscure, allusive, than I had ever dreamed. It is, as the translations indicate, tranquil, peaceful, sublime, and full of charming & accurate observation of nature. But also it has (especially Tu Fu) all the logical complexity and allusiveness of Donne, Eliot, etc. Simply fantastic."[54]

One wonders whether Professor Ch'en sensed his student's ability to make Han-shan's poetry jibe with his rucksack lifestyle in the American West. Actually, Snyder already knew about this T'ang Dynasty poet. He recalls his first encounter with Han-shan in the prefatory note appended to the twenty-four "Cold Mountain Poems" he published in a 1958 issue of the *Evergreen Review*:

> In the Japanese art exhibit that came to America in 1953 was a small *sumi* sketch of a robe-tattered wind-swept long-haired laughing man holding a scroll, standing on a cliff in the mountains. This was Kanzan, or Han-shan, "Cold Mountain"—his name taken from where he lived. He is a mountain madman in an old Chinese line of hermits. When he talks about Cold Mountain he means himself, his home, his state of mind. He lived in the T'ang dynasty—traditionally 627–650, although Hu Shih dates him 700–800. This makes him roughly contemporary with Tu Fu, Li Po, Wang Wei, and Po chu-i. His poems, of which three hundred survive, are written in T'ang colloquial: rough and fresh. The ideas are Taoist, Buddhist, Zen. He and his sidekick Shih-te (Jittoku in Japanese) became great favorites with Zen painters of later days—the scroll, the broom, the wild hair and laughter. They became Immortals and you sometimes run onto them today in the skidrows, orchards, hobo jungles, and logging camps of America.[55]

Snyder's half-serious assertion that he has "run onto" Han-shan and his "sidekick," Shih-te, in the skid rows and workplaces of America suggests that the Chinese poet was part of a larger Pacific Rim community he already knew, even though he had not yet traveled to Asia (he would not visit mainland China until 1983) and was just learning how to read Chinese characters. The various Han-shans Snyder claims to have seen, be they laconic loggers in Oregon or "wild-haired" Beats in San Francisco, are simply latter-day manifestations of the "Immortal" Chinese recluse. The tone of Snyder's note implies that, in a mythological region where time and distance are subject to compression, anyone who cultivates a Taoist or Zen sensibility may come to share the greatness of Han-shan, for to appreciate this poet is merely to recognize another dimension of one's immortal Pacific Rim identity. Such a belief may seem impractical, and yet there was something in Pacific Rim religious traditions that made fantastic feats seem possible. "Throughout the literature of the Occident defeat is typical of such superhuman adventures," Joseph Campbell explains, referring to the tragic consequences befalling those who try to overcome their separation from the gods (just think of the lesson in *Paradise Lost*), "whereas it is not so in the Orient, where, as in the legend of Buddha, the one who sets forth to gain immortality almost invariably wins."[56]

Arriving as it did immediately after his summer work in the Sierras and his experimentation with trail-building poetics, Snyder's decision to translate Han-shan's poetry established a continuum of sorts, for like the poems in *Riprap*, these translations indicated that his real-life experiences and his literary endeavors could find fruitful combination. In a 1977 roundtable discussion on Chinese poetry sponsored by the Academy of American Poets, Snyder spoke about the propitious combination of influences he encountered in 1955:

> I had just been on a four month's season in the high country of the Sierra Nevada, totally out of touch, supplied every two weeks by a packstring that dropped by with groceries, and then left alone to work with rocks, picks, dynamite, and a couple of old men who really knew how to do rockwork and an Indian who was a cook. So when I came back [to Berkeley], I was still full of that; and when I went into the Han Shan poems . . . when he talked about a cobbly stream, or when he talked about the pine-wind, I wasn't just thinking about the pine-wind in English and then the pine-wind in Chinese, but I was hearing it, hearing the wind. And when a phrase like "cloudy mist" or "misty mountain" or "cloudy mountain" or "mountain in the cloud" comes up . . . the strategy ultimately is this: you know the words in Chinese, you know the words in the original text, so drop them and now remember what it looks like to look at cloudy mountains and see what they look like, in your mind—go deep into your mind and see what's happening; an interior visualization of the poem, which means that you have to draw on your senses, your recollection of your senses. And it certainly helps if you've had some sensory experiences in your life, to have a deep storehouse to pull it out of and re-experience it from, or if you can't re-experience it, go out and look at it again.[57]

The experiences Snyder spells out in this reminiscence—manual labor ("rockwork"), de-education (being "totally out of touch"), and visualization ("see what [words] look like, in your mind")—contributed greatly to the poetry he was writing in the mid-1950s. Visualization was especially critical for Snyder as he translated the "Cold Mountain Poems," which he regarded primarily as an exercise of the mind's eye. He even went so far as to tell the other poets assembled at the roundtable that "the reason I have not translated more is that I discovered how to translate a poem by visualizing."[58] As Snyder told Dell Hymes in 1965, "I get the verbal meaning into mind as clearly as I can, but then make an enormous effort of visualization, to 'see' what the poem says, nonlinguistically, like a movie in my mind, and to feel it. If I can do this (and much of the time the poem eludes the effort) then I write the scene down in English. It is not a translation of the words, it is the same poem in a different language, allowing for the particular distortions of my own vision—but keeping it straight as possible."[59] As Snyder told Lee Bartlett on a more recent occasion, "I was able to do fresh, accurate translations of Han-shan because I was able to envision Han-shan's world, because I had much experience in the mountains and there are many images in Han-shan which are directly images of mountain scenery and mountain terrain and mountain weather that if a person had not felt those himself physically he would not be able to get the same feel into the translation—it would be more abstract. I think that was the success of the translations—a meeting of sensations."[60]

As Snyder reflected upon the hardscrabble education he had received in the Sierras and the Cascades, he realized that walking upon a mountain was itself a poetic activity. And as he worked closely with the poetry of Han-shan at UC–Berkeley, he saw that writing poetry was in turn a natural activity. In the field of translation, few American poets had ever been in as good a position to explore the full dimensionality of Pacific Rim literatures. "Pound didn't get the point of those great big mountains, and you do," Lew Welch had told Snyder during their college days. "So make a language that talks about them better than his did." If the poems in *Myths & Texts* and *Riprap* provided the first indication that Snyder was meeting Welch's challenge, the "Cold Mountain Poems" proved that, unlike other translators, he was able to honor an ancient Asian tradition while maintaining the bohemian flavor of 1950s San Francisco.

In contrast to Pound's translations of Chinese verse, which Snyder regarded as "quite a ways off from the original" and Whalen thought "lumpy," Snyder's translations were unique and sharp.[61] In contrast to both Pound and Kenneth Rexroth, whose *One Hundred Poems from the Japanese* (1955) and *One Hundred Poems from the Chinese* (1956) were huge hits in the San Francisco literary community, Snyder dispensed with previous translations and worked directly from the Asian languages.[62] The twenty-four "Cold Mountain Poems" that appeared in the *Evergreen Review* were not just hip, they were authentic. Whalen called Snyder's translations "the best thing going in the industry since Pound's *Propertius*," probably because they suggested that the traditions we refer to as foreign are simply the underdeveloped aspects of our collective identity.[63]

Who Was Han-shan?

Although Snyder's visual recognition in the mountains of the American West provides a clue as to why he would have liked Han-shan, the true identity of this eccentric and charismatic Chinese poet is less than clear. Exact dates are impossible to pinpoint, but it appears as though Han-shan lived sometime during the T'ang Dynasty (618–907) and was influenced by Taoism and Ch'an Buddhism, the forerunner of Zen. Buddhism was not widely practiced in China until the early days of the sixth century, when a Mahayana monk from India named Bodhidharma traveled there, bringing a "special transmission outside the scriptures" to a civilization known for its devotion to Confucian and Taoist teachings. The Dharma (or body of Buddhist teachings) that the visiting monk brought with him was similar to the Taoist "way" in many respects, with the significant difference that Mahayana Buddhism went beyond individual escapism to preach universal compassion and collective responsibility. "The Taoists got tipsy and wrote poetry by the light of the moon, or they practiced breathing exercises aimed at making them immortal," Richard Bernstein explains in his book on Hsuan Tsang, the seventh-century Chinese monk who retraced Bodhidharma's path back to India to find the Ultimate Truth. The Buddhists, on the other hand, "prayed to the various Bodhisattvas, who, rather than achieve nirvana and disappear beyond life and death, stayed around to help the rest of humankind achieve enlightenment."[64]

Ch'an Buddhism, which took its name from the Chinese word for intense personal concentration or meditation, effectively split the difference between Mahayana and Taoist traditions. Ch'an was compassionate, to be sure, but also creative enough to attract and influence poets such as Wang Wei (c. 699–761) and Meng Hao-jan (c. 689–740). Han-shan was a contemporary of these poets, and yet he has received relatively little attention from scholars in the West, many of whom deem him too colloquial in his speech, too bizarre in his behavior, and too removed from mainstream society to be representative of his age.[65] As a result, his poems are underrepresented in English language anthologies of Chinese poetry. In China, it is a different story. Commentaries on Han-shan's work have circulated regularly since the ninth century, when Tu Kuang-t'ing and Pen Chi put out editions, and his poetry has been popular in various Buddhist monasteries for nearly the same length of time.[66]

Han-shan is believed to have been a government official, perhaps even a military general, who left his family and privileged position to retreat to the T'ien-t'ai Mountains, a coastal range situated south of Shanghai near the East China Sea. The given name of this poet remains unknown. "Han-shan"—which translates as "Cold Mountain," and sometimes as "Cold Cliff" or "Cold Creek"—most likely refers to his place of retirement. By the early years of the T'ang Dynasty, the T'ien-t'ai range was well known for its Buddhist and Taoist monasteries as well as for the collection of mountain men and mystical spirits thought to reside in its backcountry. Those who gathered in this region tended to be positively countercultural in their outlook. In his introduction to the most recent Han-shan translations to appear in English, John Blofeld explains that "some were Buddhist monks who had turned their backs on the 'world of dust,' bent on treading the rugged path towards Enlightenment that led to Nirvana's bliss. Some were Taoist recluses cultivating joyous tranquility by studying nature's cyclic changes and learning to flow effortlessly with life's current, instead of battling upstream against formidable odds like the status-minded, power-and-wealth hungry city-dwellers. Yet others were people of no religious faith who, like our own hippies, had decided to sever the restraints of conventional and social ties and create a new life in accordance with an image built of their own dreams."[67]

Han-shan was so eccentric, however, that he made most of these monks and mountain men look like buttoned-down businessmen. According to prevailing legend, known almost exclusively through a preface written by a T'ang prefect named Lu Ch'iu-Yin and attached to a manuscript of 311 poems, Han-shan would frequently leave his cave at the base of Hanyen, or "Cold Cliff," to visit one of the nearby monasteries, Kuo-ch'ing Temple, where his friend Shih-te ("The Foundling" or "Pickup"), an orphan who worked in the dining hall, would give him leftover food. The monks who caught sight of Han-shan described him as old, raggedy, and "beat": an utterly mysterious apparition. Unfazed, Han-shan responded to their derisive inquiries by clapping, laughing, and shouting "Ha Ha!" "Yet in every word he breathed," Lu Ch'iu-Yin tells us, "was a meaning in line with the subtle principles of things, if only you thought about it deeply. Everything he said had the feeling of the Tao in it, profound and arcane secrets" (RRCM 35–36). With their birch bark hats, wooden shoes, and keen wit, Han-shan and Shih-te played the role of the original Dharma Bums. For years, these two mountain mystics poked fun at the civilized monks at Kuo-ch'ing, offering them an endless string of koan riddles, and laughing at their misguided attempts to solve them.

"No one knows just what sort of man Han-shan was," Lu Ch'iu-Yin admits in his preface, but it was not for lack of trying. Lu himself, in his authoritative role as governor of T'ai Prefecture, ordered the monks of Kuo-ch'ing to track down Han-shan and Shih-te, having heard from a third mountain mystic, Feng-kan ("Big Stick"), that these unconventional men were true bodhisattvas. But when the prefect's messenger traveled to Cold Mountain to deliver gifts to Han-shan, the raggedy sage yelled "Thief!" and retreated into his cave, which closed behind him. He was not seen again. Shih-te also disappeared (an Indian monk later claimed that he found his remains on a mountain near the Kuo-ch'ing Temple).[68] The only firsthand testimony we have from the two mountain men, Lu Ch'iu-Yin explains, is contained in the writing they left behind: "poems written on bamboo, wood, stones, and cliffs . . . and also . . . on the walls of people's houses" (RRCM 38). In both name and deed, Han-shan dedicated himself to organic composition. More than just a signature inscribed on the cliff of a cold mountain in China, Han-shan refers to the poet, his poems, and his place, as they exist in an earthy and nearly secret relation to one another.

A few attempts were made in the twentieth century to discover Han-shan's identity. In an important article published in 1957, Chinese scholar Wu Chi-Yu chronicles the reception of Han-shan in his native land, perusing records of personal contacts, changes in the naming of places, histories of Buddhism, and patterns of readership in order to get a better understanding of how this poet lived. After reading this lengthy article, one is led to believe that "Han-shan" was the pseudonym of Hua Chih-Yen, a brave general known more for his kindness to animals and his respect for opponents than for his exploits on the battlefield. A gentle soul, Hua beat a hasty retreat from military life, choosing instead to live in the mountains, where he made friends with wolves, tigers, and other creatures that civilized humans tended to fear. By reliable historical accounts, Hua was visited in his place of retirement by one Lu Ch'iu-Yin, a former army buddy who was at the time (either 623 or 624) the governor of T'ai Prefecture (Taichou). Working by inference, Wu claims that Hua Chih-Yen must be Han-shan, the hermit poet mentioned in Lu Ch'iu-Yin's preface.[69]

In recent decades, scholars have found a few problems with Wu's proposal. Robert Henricks claims the only Lu Ch'iu-Yin who lived during the T'ang Dynasty was a prefect in Lichou, a region some two hundred kilometers to the west of Taichou.[70] Red Pine (Bill Porter), another translator of the "Cold Mountain Poems," has dug a bit deeper, unearthing old Chinese records that do in fact list a Lu Ch'iu-Yin who served as prefect of Taichou from 642 to 646. This certainly fits the time frame for composition of the "Cold Mountain Poems." Even so, the official insignia of the office that Lu Ch'iu-Yin lists before his name was not in use before 650. What is more, the name he assigns to the district where Han-shan lived, Tanghsing, was not in use until 761, a full century later, leading Red Pine to surmise that "either someone altered the preface to conform with later usage or Lu Ch'iu-Yin's name was appropriated to give another person's preface and Cold Mountain's poems the imprimatur of official sanction as well as the stature associated with greater age."[71] Regardless of the inconsistencies in dating, this Lu Ch'iu-Yin was probably the prefect Wu had in mind, and there is ample evidence to suggest that he visited an old army friend at his mountain retreat. What fails to line up, of course, is the fact that the Lu Ch'iu-Yin who writes the preface claims not to know the man he searches for, whereas Wu's story would have us believe that he and Han-shan were longtime friends. With this breakdown in logic, the identity of Han-shan is once again thrown into question.

In the wake of the controversy surrounding Wu's findings, some scholars have suggested that "Han-shan" was actually a pseudonym employed by several Buddhist monks, who composed the Cold Mountain poems over the course of three centuries, from the late Sui period (589–618) to the late T'ang period (880–907). Professor Iriya Yoshitaka, whom Snyder would end up meeting at the Zen Institute in Kyoto, was among the first to advance the idea of collective authorship in 1958, a year after Wu's article.[72] This contention was bolstered in the 1970s by E. G. Pulleybank, who took the Han-shan poems he believed were composed during the early days of the T'ang Dynasty and contrasted them with those purportedly written during the late T'ang era. The early poems (called "Han-shan I" by Pulleybank) are generally considered superior to the later poems ("Han-shan II"), which are overly didactic and self-conscious, like much of the poetry composed in the monasteries at that time. In any event, the inconsistencies in rhyme schemes, Buddhist references, and place-names suggested to Pulleybank that Cold Mountain poems were written by many people over several centuries.[73]

In the end, all attempts to determine the identity of the "Cold Mountain" remain shrouded in mystery, and that is probably the way that the reclusive Han-shan, whoever he was, would have wanted it. All we have for primary sources are the 311 poems and Lu Ch'iu-Yin's awestruck preface. Snyder probably knew little about the controversy surrounding Han-shan's identity, having completed his translations before Wu published his article and before he met Iriya Yoshitaka in Kyoto. When Snyder started his Cold Mountain assignment in 1955, Arthur Waley's "27 Poems by Han-shan," published in a 1954 issue of *Encounter*, was the only English translation that existed.[74] Snyder claims not to have read Waley's version until after completing his own translations, even though a typescript of Waley's translations accompanies the manuscript of Snyder's "Cold Mountain Poems" housed at Kent State University Library. Regardless of whether Snyder read Waley beforehand, his translations are so unique, so tied to his countercultural vision of the Pacific Rim, that many scholars consider his version to be the best. In fact, Snyder remembers that, soon after "Cold Mountain Poems" appeared in the *Evergreen Review*, "Waley graciously wrote me and said he thought he preferred mine."[75]

Han-shan's Habitat

What Snyder says he admires most in Chinese poetry is its recognition of habitat. Tellingly, it is habitat's relationship to natural domesticity, or what Snyder calls the "capacity to live," that suffuses his version of the "Cold

Mountain Poems." As he makes clear in the 1977 roundtable on Chinese poetry, Han-shan and Shih-te (and other Ch'an or Taoist poets who considered themselves to be outside the mainstream of T'ang society) nurtured their understanding of habitat as they sought peace and sanity in nature. With Han-shan there is no wasted energy and no empty rhetoric, only the example of a life well lived. Snyder believes that Americans should take courage from his unconventional, but wholly natural, practice. "If we are grounded in a clear sense of habitat," Snyder explains to those gathered at the roundtable discussion, "we don't get caught either in the artificiality of a preservationist wilderness mentality, or in the artificiality of creating a kind of genius-craziness adversary idea as being the only way to run counter to your times. For me, one of the most useful discoveries in Chinese poetry was that you don't have to be crazy to be a poet."[76] In contradistinction to conservationists like John Muir, who regarded the natural and the human as separate categories, or Beat writers like Jack Kerouac, who regarded Han-shan as the epitome of Zen lunacy, Snyder wants to celebrate the simple actions of a man for whom nature, humanity, and habitat were different words for a peaceful state of mind.

If, as Sherman Paul asserts in his study of poetic primitivism, "Snyder's art is a matter not solely of re-visualizing the poems but of selecting those that propose the journey he has begun," then his careful selection of "Cold Mountain Poems" warrants some attention.[77] The 311 poems that Han-shan left behind examine various persons and themes: court ladies, the fleetingness of human life, family matters, and so on. As we might expect, many of them refer to the Chinese poet's isolated habitat. These "Han-shan poems," as Robert Henricks classifies them, are those in which the poet "describes the place where he lived and speaks of the difficulties of reaching the top of that mountain. Many of these are no more than description, and as such, they are beautiful landscape poems; yet many of these poems are more than that, for they symbolize the spiritual quest for enlightenment and the difficulties and obstacles one encounters along the way."[78] Significantly, each of the twenty-four translations Snyder published in the *Evergreen Review* belongs to this grouping. Today, thanks in large part to Snyder, Han-shan's poems about habitat are those for which the Chinese poet is best remembered.

Snyder's first Cold Mountain translation introduces the mind space that he and Han-shan hold in common. In this instance, Snyder tries to maintain the prosody and form employed by the T'ang Dynasty recluse:

The path to Han-shan's place is laughable,
A path, but no sign of cart or horse.
Converging gorges—hard to trace their twists
Jumbled cliffs—unbelievably rugged.
A thousand grasses bend with dew,
A hill of pines hums in the wind.
And now I've lost the shortcut home,
Body asking shadow, how do you keep up? (no. 1, RRCM 39)

A typical Han-shan poem consists of eight lines, each of which contains five Chinese characters. The task of the English language translator is to supply just enough syntax to connect the characters, or word pictures, so that they make a coherent statement. Since each translation is radically dependent upon the mindset of the translator who molds these ideograms into syntactical, phrasal, and narrative sequences, versions can vary quite a bit. Consider, for instance, the different beginnings of the poem cited above:

Wonderful, this road to Cold Mountain—
Yet there's no sign of horse or carriage. (Burton Watson, translated 1962)

Delightful! The road to Han-shan
Yet one finds no trace of horses or carts. (Robert Henricks, translated 1990)

It's fun to be on Cold Mountain Road,
Yet it has no tracks of horses and carts. (Stephen Owen, translated 1996)

The Cold Mountain Road is strange
no tracks of cart or horse. (Red Pine, translated 2000)[79]

The second line is translated similarly in all four examples. The translators differ somewhat in their translation of the first line, but not nearly so much as they collectively differ from Snyder, who employs the word "laughable" to describe Han-shan's habitat. In Snyder's opinion, the Cold Mountain "path"—a more metaphysical variant of "road" (and therefore closer to the Taoist "way" to enlightenment)—is not merely "wonderful," "delightful," or "fun." It is far more mysterious than that. At the same time, Han-shan's route to higher knowledge is not to be taken too seriously, for it is as ridiculous as it is sublime.

As he continues with his sequence of twenty-four translations, Snyder repeatedly pays tribute to the carefree nature of Han-shan and Shih-te. In the twentieth selection, for example, Han-shan offers this rejoinder to a critic who says his poems "lack the Basic Truth of Tao": "I have to laugh at him / He misses the point entirely, / Men like that / Ought to stick to making money" (no. 20, RRCM 58). If a man is truly in tune with his habitat, Han-shan argues, he need not concern himself with politics, wealth, or status: "If I hide out at Cold Mountain / Living off mountain plants and berries — / All my lifetime, why worry?" the insouciant hermit asks. "One follows his karma through / . . . I'm happy to sit among these cliffs" (no. 17, RRCM 55). Because he is convinced that his unconventional choice marks a path of right action, Han-shan leaves traces of his contentment for others to find:

> Once at Cold Mountain, troubles cease —
> No more tangled, hung-up mind.
> I idly scribble poems on the rock cliff,
> Taking whatever comes, like a drifting boat. (no. 19, RRCM 57)

In the centuries following Han-shan's death, the poet's carefree spirit was represented pictorially, especially in Japanese woodblock prints, one of which Snyder provides on the page opposite Lu Ch'iu-Yin's preface in the 1969 edition of *Riprap and Cold Mountain Poems*. In the woodcut, Han-shan points to the ground, as if to show his friend Shih-te that "Cold Mountain" is just where he belongs. The two men are shown smiling and laughing, probably at one of their many jokes.[80] Not all scholars of T'ang poetry are amused by such pictures, however. In a background note he supplied for an influential anthology of Chinese poetry, Edward H. Schafer complains that such representations of Han-shan fail to match the content of his poetry, insofar as they depict him as "a freak in tattered garments, grinning imbecilely, a happy social reject."[81] On the other hand, we can see how Snyder, a translator with his roots in the rambunctious and irreverent San Francisco literary community, would have cherished an illustrated example of two friends using exhibitions of frivolity to disrupt the forces of civilization. He would have also admired the happy companionship depicted in this woodcut illustration.

Intimate friendship was a prevalent theme not just in Beat circles, but among T'ang era writers as well, especially Taoist poets, who often wrote about getting drunk together and staring at the moon, or about engaging in inebriated writing contests. In a letter he mailed to Phil Whalen from Kyoto, Snyder himself speaks about getting drunk "in some poetical oriental manner." In another letter, he tells his college buddy, "I like to get drunk but in the Chinese manner—with a few close friends & long easy drinking while discussing the Classics or the Muse or Friendship," going on to explain that "just getting drunk and balling won't make the gods appear."[82] Regardless of whether they got drunk together (and if they were Buddhist monks, they may not have), Han-shan and Shih-te proved that sharing good times and engaging in serious discussion are not mutually exclusive endeavors. Other Chinese poets of their day came to similar conclusions. Little wonder, then, that Snyder once listed "the spirit of friendship" and "karmic empathy" as reasons why he enjoys Chinese poetry even more than he enjoys Native American and Japanese literatures (GSR 324, 328).

And yet, for all its initial lightheartedness, the first Cold Mountain poem Snyder decided to translate contains a hint of sadness in its penultimate line: "now I've lost the shortcut home." The path to Han-shan's mountain retreat may be "laughable," but following that path to its conclusion is not always so delightful. Quite often, Han-shan describes the loneliness that arrives after one abandons his family and his societal obligations and "follows his karma through." After awhile, all ties to the past seem to be irrevocably severed. "For ten years I haven't gone back home," Han-shan explains in poem 5. "I've even forgotten the way by which I came" (RRCM 43). He also begins to wonder whether anyone truly cares about him anymore. "Who knows that I'm out of the dusty world / Climbing the southern slope of Cold Mountain?" he laments in poem 13 (RRCM 51).

As Sherman Paul has speculated, Snyder also may have been wrestling with feelings of loneliness and regret as he translated these poems. In the 1950s, he withstood a failed marriage to college classmate Alison Gass, a breakup with another woman from Reed named Robin Collins, and temporary estrangement from his mother. It is possible that some of these events were precipitated by his stubborn insistence to seek enlightenment on his own terms. Although Snyder would wait until *The Back Country* to express his regrets about the failed relationship with Collins, the melancholy tone of his "Cold Mountain" selections suggests that Paul is right in his assertion that this breakup weighed heavily on him during the translation process. Snyder's tenth selection is particularly bleak:

> I have lived at Cold Mountain
> These thirty long years.
> Yesterday I called on friends and family:
> More than half had gone to the Yellow Springs.
> Slowly consumed, like fire down a candle;
> Forever flowing, like a passing river.
> Now, morning, I face my lone shadow:
> Suddenly my eyes are bleared with tears. (no. 10, RRCM 48)

Here we glimpse a prodigal son's unique brand of survivor guilt. While he has traveled away to live in spiritual solitude, more than half of his friends and relatives have gone to their mortal destination, "the Yellow Springs." Arthur Waley translates "the Yellow Springs" as "The Springs of Death," and Wu Chi-Yu translates it as "the other world." Japhy Ryder, Snyder's fictionalized self in *The Dharma Bums*, simply points to the phrase and tells Ray Smith (Jack Kerouac), "That means death."[83] Each of these translations speaks powerfully to the undeniable reality staring Han-shan in the face: the fact that, once he comes down from his mountain and rediscovers the "shortcut home," he must leave his "laughable" path to enlightenment and reconcile himself to the mortal cares of this world.

Like every other translator I have listed, Snyder uses the word "shadow" in the penultimate line, thereby establishing a connection with images found in the first and fourth selections: "Body asking shadow, how do you keep up?" (no. 1, RRCM 39); "I waggle my shadow, all alone" (no. 4, RRCM 42). But the primary reason Snyder's tenth selection packs such a wallop is that he is one of only two English language translators (Henricks is the other) to use the word "morning" in the penultimate line. Read as an appositive for "Now," the word "morning" marks the precise moment when Han-shan wakes up to find himself alone. Heard as a homonym, however, "mo(u)rning" becomes a participle describing the process Han-shan is undergoing after losing family members and friends. Also telling is Snyder's use of the word "bleared" in the final line. Some of the other translators describe Han-shan's tears as falling down in two streams, and such an image certainly works well to position the poet's grief in the appropriate topographical register. But

Snyder's version is just as nuanced, since his use of "bleared" reveals just how foggy Han-shan's thinking is at this difficult moment. The mountain recluse has a hard time reacquainting himself with his "slowly consumed" family for the simple reason that his shadow and tears (his constant companions in later life) end up blurring his view, darkening his landscape, and throwing a veil of mourning over his eyes.

Though it may not be true in the case of poem 10, Snyder's translations are usually the most adept at showing the topographical features of Han-shan's retreat. In poem 1, for instance, Snyder includes three mountain images ("converging gorges," "jumbled cliffs—unbelievably rugged," and "hill of pines") reminiscent of those found in *Myths & Texts* and *Riprap*. "Unbelievably rugged" is the key modifier here. None of the other translators, with the possible exception of Red Pine (who speaks of a "piled-up ridge"), speaks so forcefully about the harsh nature of Han-shan's habitat, probably because none of them could lay claim to any extended residence in a Pacific Rim mountain range. Of course, as Snyder once admitted to Ling Chung, his "Cold Mountain" translations are based on his knowledge of the Cascades and the Sierra Nevadas, not the T'ien-t'ai Mountains.[84] The result is a hybrid combination of Eastern mind and Western place, a combination portrayed vividly in poem 8:

> Clambering up the Cold Mountain path,
> The Cold Mountain trail goes on and on:
> The long gorge choked with scree and boulders,
> The wide creek, the mist-blurred grass.
> The moss is slippery, though there's been no rain
> The pine sings, but there's no wind.
> Who can leap the world's ties
> And sit with me among the white clouds? (no. 8, RRCM 46)

As in his first selection, Snyder chooses the word "gorge" rather than "valley" (chosen by Watson, Henricks, and Waley) or "river" (chosen by Red Pine). Compared to a valley or river, both of which can be quite broad, a gorge is an exceedingly narrow passage, with steep and often dangerous slopes. Snyder would have encountered many gorges during his summer in the Sierras, including those littered with the "scree and boulders" left by ancient glaciers in cols and moraines. It is important to note, however, that such traces of glacial activity are not found in the T'ien-t'ai range where Han-shan resided. For this reason, I am inclined to regard Snyder's inclusion of "scree," a word derived from Scandinavian languages and common in the writings of John Muir, as evidence of his need to combine elements from several landscapes and thereby achieve Pacific Rim harmony.

The process by which Snyder translated Chinese characters shows more clearly how he tried to make Han-shan's "Cold Mountain Poems" align with his own vision of the Sierra Nevada mountains. According to Ling Chung, the Chinese manuscript of "Cold Mountain Poems" Snyder is most likely to have read includes the following set of characters for the third line in poem 8 (the Wade-Giles and English language equivalents are Ling Chung's additions):

谿	長	石	磊	磊
ch'i	ch'ang	shih	lui	lui
(deep gorge)	(long)	(stones)	(the abundance of boulders)	

As Ling Chung notes, "the ideograph *lui* is composed of three piled-up boulders (磊). The reader of the Chinese original can receive the visual effect of abundant heaping boulders."[85] On the other hand, a translator has a very difficult task in trying to capture the same effect in English. For this reason, Snyder's translation process required several painstaking steps, each of which had him reflecting upon familiar mind pictures.

Jacob Leed, a scholar who has worked closely with the manuscript of "Cold Mountain Poems," reveals that Snyder initially wrote out the five Chinese characters in each line in his own hand, using calligraphy. He then limited himself to five English words in order to get the truest, most austere sense of Han-shan's language. In this most literal stage of translation, Snyder's third line reads: "Gorge long stones stony stony." In his next draft, Snyder added and rearranged words, then supplied punctuation in order to flesh out a recognizable lyric: "The long gorge—stones: stony, stony." Dissatisfied with this version, he scribbled a variant in the margin of his manuscript: "rocks in great piles—heaps." In ensuing drafts, Snyder translated *lui* as "boulders and talus" before finally settling on "scree and boulders," the image he thought most accurately represented the Sierra Nevada landscape he held in his mind's eye. Throughout the succession of drafts, Leed deduces, Han-shan's original Chinese characters are "expanded to images that the literal version does not specifically designate."[86] In other words, as Snyder refines his meaning, he distances himself more and more from Han-shan's original habitat, having fallen back upon his own California habitat as the final measure for imagistic portrayal and word choice. Translations that purport to express the spirit of the T'ien-t'ai Mountains therefore end up containing images we would just as likely expect to find in the poems of *Riprap*. Defying all sense of cartographic logic, Snyder's translations nonetheless work well to capture the mystical realm that Han-shan claimed as his own, centuries ago and thousands of miles away.

Try and Make It to Cold Mountain

Even more than the poems in *Riprap*, the "Cold Mountain Poems" are allegories about paths and trails. As Snyder and Han-shan stand on their respective trails, they challenge readers to imagine themselves seeking the true path to enlightenment (satori, in the Zen tradition). The paradox of Zen teaching is that it urges adherents to discover that the road to satori is really a trackless route to which they already have access. Until one accedes to the right mindset, though, all paths to enlightenment will remain obscured. Snyder's decision to concentrate on Han-shan's habitat is significant in this regard. Consider the following aphorisms about finding the "way" to Cold Mountain:

> The path to Han-shan's place is laughable,
> A path, but no sign of cart or horse. (no. 1, RRCM 39)

> In a tangle of cliffs I chose a place—
> Bird-paths, but no trails for men. (no. 2, RRCM 40)

> For ten years, I haven't gone back home
> I've even forgotten the way by which I came. (no. 5, RRCM 43)

> Men ask the way to Cold Mountain
> Cold Mountain: there's no through trail. (no. 6, RRCM 44)

> Clambering up the Cold Mountain path,
> The Cold Mountain trail goes on and on . . . (no. 8, RRCM 46)

Rough and dark—the Cold Mountain trail,
Sharp cobbles—the icy creek bank. (no. 9, RRCM 47)

To make it to Cold Mountain, these excerpts suggest, travelers must overcome physical obstacles, come face-to-face with infinitude, and be willing to forget their prior existence. The trail to enlightenment is elusive, and might not even exist, according to conventional understanding: "There's no through trail." And yet this is hardly a dead end Han-shan is pointing to. Travelers can reach Cold Mountain once they know the right "way."

Like Thoreau, Han-shan recommends leaving the pretensions of civilized life behind and returning to an elemental relationship with the land. In Snyder's seventh and sixteenth selections especially, the poet known as "Cold Mountain" argues that gratuitous luxuries cannot compare to the domestic arrangements one makes in a natural setting:

Men don't get this far into the mountains,
White clouds gather and billow.
Thin grass does for a mattress,
The blue sky makes a good quilt.
Happy with a stone underhead
Let heaven and earth go about their changes. (no. 7, RRCM 45)

I've got no use for the kulak
With his big barn and pasture—
He just sets up a prison for himself.
Once in he can't get out.
Think it over—
You know it might happen to you. (no. 16, RRCM 54)

The architecture of civilization, whether it exists in the form of a bed or a barn, becomes superfluous once one has found the path to satori. Snyder makes this lesson relevant to modern times by updating the Chinese poet's language and extending his frame of reference. By choosing the word "kulak" instead of "farmer" in poem 16, for instance, he calls to mind the prosperous Russian landowners targeted by Soviet revolutionaries in the early years of the twentieth century. In another selection, Snyder updates one of Han-shan's rhetorical questions so that it strikes a chord with conspicuous consumers in cold war America: "Go tell families with silverware and cars / 'What's the use of all that noise and money?'" (no. 2, RRCM 40).

In another move indicative of this trend, Snyder makes a concerted effort to articulate Han-shan's teachings in the vernacular of the American hipster. In Snyder's sixth selection, Han-shan issues one of his most direct challenges, asking his readers to revitalize their meaningless lives. Of course, the question of whether readers in San Francisco would respond positively to such a challenge depends on their ability to understand and appreciate the language in which it is couched. For the sake of comparison, consider the following translations of poem 6:

> How, you may ask, did I manage to get here?
> My heart is not like your heart.
> If only your heart were like mine
> You too would be living where I live now. (Waley, translated 1954)

> How can you hope to get there by aping me?
> Your heart and mine are not alike.
> If your heart were the same as mine
> Then you could journey to the very center! (Watson, translated 1962)

> imitating me how can you get here
> my heart and yours aren't the same
> if your heart was like mine
> you'd return to the very center (Arthur Tobias, translated 1982)[87]

> How has someone like me arrived?
> My mind and yours are not the same
> If your mind, sir, were like mine,
> You too could come right to the center. (Henricks, translated 1990)

> How did someone like me get there?
> my heart is not like yours.
> If your heart were just like mine
> then you could get there the right way. (Owen, translated 1996)

how did someone like me arrive
our minds are not the same
if they were the same
you would be here (Red Pine, translated 2000)

The translations by Waley and Henricks provide the most formal challenges, whereas those by Owen and Red Pine seem closest to the American vernacular. But even they cannot match the informality of Snyder's version, which (like Tobias's) substitutes "was" for the grammatically correct conditional verb ("were") and proceeds from there:

How did I make it?
My heart's not the same as yours.
If your heart was like mine
You'd get it and be right here. (no. 6, RRCM 44)

In Owen's translation, the word "get" refers to an ability to move from one location to another. In other words, Han-shan is saying that if you have the right heart, you will know the right path to take to Cold Mountain and thus "get there" in due course. Although this ability to travel is undoubtedly important, Snyder's different sense of the word "get" raises the ante. In asking, "How did I make it?" Snyder's Han-shan refers not only to a journey but also to an achievement, his sense of having made something out of his life. With his closing boast—"If your heart was like mine / You'd get it and be right here"—the mountain sage implies that mental understanding, the ability to "get it," is just as important as physical movement when one is seeking the right place. In Snyder's translation of this colloquial Chinese poet, "making it" and "getting it" emerge as street-savvy expressions for discovering a fulfilling spiritual life in postmodern America.

Snyder saves Han-shan's ultimate challenge for his last selection. In poem 24, the mountain mystic encourages humans to look beyond the misunderstandings perpetuated by civilized society in order to locate the place where all trails disappear:

When men see Han-shan
They all say he's crazy

And not much to look at
Dressed in rags and hides.
They don't get what I say
& I don't talk their language.
All I can say to those I meet:
"Try and make it to Cold Mountain." (no. 24, RRCM 62)

By this point, readers should realize that Han-shan's craziness is actually a form of sanity, and that most misunderstandings about his character derive from civilized men who "don't get" what he says. Once again, Snyder's translation succeeds brilliantly, capturing Han-shan's wisdom in the idiomatic language used by contemporary American speakers. Waley, Watson, Wu, Henricks, Tobias, and even Red Pine never achieve the same level of proficiency. Here are the last four lines of poem 24 as they exist in their translations:

"What we say, he cannot understand;
What he says, we do not say."
You who spend all your time in coming and going,
Why not try for once coming to Han-shan? (Waley, translated 1954)

My words they do not understand,
And when they speak, I remain silent.
But I say to the passers-by:
"You may come here!" (Wu Chi-Yu, translated 1957)

"The things we say he doesn't understand;
The things he says we wouldn't utter."
A word to those of you passing by—
"Try coming to Cold Mountain sometime!" (Watson, translated 1962)

they don't understand what I say
I don't speak their kind of jabber
I want to tell all of you passing by
You can come up and face Cold Mountain (Tobias, translated 1982)

But my words they don't understand,
And *their* words are things I wouldn't say!

My response to these visitors is,   .
"You too can come look at Han-shan." (Henricks, translated 1990)

they don't understand my words
their words I won't speak
this is for those to come
visit Cold Mountain sometime (Red Pine, translated 2000)

Each of these translations highlights the distinction between Han-shan's speech and that of civilized men (Waley and Watson even go so far as to quote these men). But with the possible exception of Watson, Snyder is the only translator to infuse the final line with a sufficient display of pride, such that we hear Han-shan laying down a warning to a group of ignorant contestants: "try to make it here, *if you can*." It is quite possible that Snyder is making a grammatical error here, saying "try and make it" when he should be saying "try *to* make it." Then again, Snyder's choice of syntax could mean that he wants the last line to remain ambiguous. When Han-shan says "Try and make it to Cold Mountain," he could very well be presenting a challenge, but he might also be extending a heartfelt invitation and a motivational pitch, in effect telling seekers, "*if you try, you can and will make it* to Cold Mountain." Whichever way the final line is read, this poem, like the others in Snyder's sequence, is built upon the assumption that readers would in fact want to follow the Cold Mountain trail. And who would not want to do so, if only for a short while, after having heard of Han-shan's unorthodox account of enlightenment, humor, and peace?

Following New Trails

In an essay from the 1990s entitled "What Poetry Did in China," Snyder claims that studying Chinese poetry in the 1950s forced him to "break open ways out of the accustomed habits of perception [and] slip into different possibilities—some wise, some perhaps bizarre, but all of them equally real, and some holding a promise of further angles of insight" (PS 93). Translating the "Cold Mountain Poems" certainly seems to have given Snyder a new angle on the trail-building poetics he had practiced in *Riprap*. Working high in the mountains in California, he was able to assert, in a poem entitled "Above

Pate Valley," "I found my own trail here" (RRCM 11). Once down from the Sierras, he made contact with a Chinese poet who had made the same boast several centuries beforehand. In his own time, Han-shan challenged others to locate new paths to understanding. Playful and elusive, he called to his audience from a point that was always a bit further up the trail, shrouded in the mist of the T'ien-t'ai Mountains. For Snyder, who was at a crucial "trip-stop mind-point" in his burgeoning Pacific Rim consciousness, there was no better trail guide.

During 1955 and 1956, Snyder kept constant company with Han-shan. While organizing and adding sections to *Myths & Texts*, he looked back upon his logging experiences in Oregon and uttered, "Han Shan could have lived here" (MT 13). While walking the streets of Berkeley, he imagined that he saw Han-shan walking alongside Walt Whitman and Hitomoro, and recorded this sighting in a poem entitled "The Rainy Season" (LOITR 50). While noting his first impressions of Kyoto in his journal, he wrote about an "old dark smoky kitchen where Han Shan might have worked" (EHH 36). Cold Mountain thus became for Snyder a kind of alter ego, a figure from the past he could not shake.

For Snyder, composing the "Cold Mountain Poems" was not an end in itself, but part of an ongoing project of translating East and West. Geoff Ward once said that Snyder's "Cold Mountain Poems" contain "no serious attempt at a *change* of language to match the change of mind described," adding that, "perhaps like all occidental orientalia," the sequence is "confined by its charm."[88] I could not disagree more with Ward's statement. Whether he was employing the prosody of Chinese poetics to perfect his "trail-building" style of riprap poetry or visualizing his experience in the Sierras as a way to translate poems written during the T'ang Dynasty, Snyder was constantly altering language so that it would fit into a Pacific Rim paradigm. *Riprap* and "Cold Mountain Poems" thus stand as complementary translation exercises in a geographic project Snyder had already begun. While living and traveling in Asia, he would serve as a translator on a much grander scale.

3. | EMBODYING
| *Human Geography and the Way to the Back Country*

Some readers might find it surprising that Snyder picked up and left for Japan just as he was becoming a fixture on the San Francisco scene. But his journey to Asia had been planned for some time, and for him it was the natural course of action after taking graduate courses at UC–Berkeley and making contact with various Pacific Rim mythologies and literatures. All the same, Snyder could not have known exactly what awaited him on the other side of the ocean. After boarding the *Arita Maru* and setting sail for Japan in May 1956, the cultural geography filling the young man's imagination began to take on a whole new meaning. Except for short stints back in America in 1958 (when he met Joanne Kyger, soon to become his second wife), 1964 to 1965 (when he taught at UC–Berkeley), and 1967 (when he participated in the Human Be-in and other countercultural happenings), Snyder pitched his stakes on the other side of the Pacific Rim and stayed there for the next twelve years.

Despite his long-term residence in a distant land, Snyder continued to play a key role in the San Francisco counterculture. As his community's offshore representative, he became the channel through which the mystical visions and cosmic vibrations emanating from the Far East found their way back to America. The successive publication of "Cold Mountain Poems,"

Riprap, and *Myths & Texts* in 1958, 1959, and 1960 kept his name before the reading public during his early residence in Asia, as did a selection of poems appearing in Donald Allen's *The New American Poetry*. In addition, Snyder published two revelatory prose accounts of his first months in Japan. "Letter from Kyoto" appeared in a 1957 issue of the *Evergreen Review,* and "Spring Sesshin at Shokoku-ji" in a 1958 issue of the *Chicago Review*. Many more people came to know him through Jack Kerouac's hagiographic portrait of Japhy Ryder in *The Dharma Bums.* A Kerouac hero in the tradition of Dean Moriarty (the Neal Cassady figure in *On the Road*), Japhy Ryder is more than just a typical Beat wanderer; he is a Pacific Rim folk hero who combines the rugged individualism of the American West with the ascetic selflessness of a Buddhist adept. Throughout *The Dharma Bums* narrative—an interesting mixture of rambunctious mountain climbs, quiet Zen lessons, and raucous parties—Japhy teaches Ray Smith (Kerouac) the ways of the wilderness and the rewards of Buddhist mindfulness. As millions read the novel, they felt as though they too were gaining a new appreciation for the mysteries of an ancient culture and having a good time doing it.

Snyder also remained closely linked with the San Francisco community on a more intimate level. He kept up a voluminous correspondence with his friends back home, especially Phil Whalen. In these letters, one learns about Snyder's initial disappointment and occasional frustration with Buddhist practice in Asia, as well as his gradual acculturation process and growing respect for the Japanese way of life. Once he settled in to his new habitat, Snyder found that he was glad to host Americans willing to meet him overseas. These visitors kept him apprised of what was happening in America. In turn, they were able to report back on what San Francisco's offshore representative was up to, thousands of miles away from the city he called home.

The Back Country (1968) records events and travels in Snyder's life from the mid-1950s up to 1965, the year he wrapped up an extended visit to California. Arguably the centerpiece of Snyder's poetic oeuvre, *The Back Country* shows the poet coming to terms with social and physical environments that had, up to this time, existed largely in his imagination. A lyrical tour of Snyder's spherical journey along the Pacific Rim, from America to Asia and "back" again, this book is at one level a quest romance played out on a geographic register. On another level, though, its author moves beyond the individual concerns of monomyth to conceive of a spatially defined human community. Like *Myths & Texts* and *Riprap, The Back Country* utilizes the insights of a gifted lyric observer to consecrate the lands and waters of the Pacific region, and yet it goes much further than those earlier books in its portrayal of the human populations who live in that region and share (or compete for) its resources. In *The Back Country*, the Pacific Rim emerges as a space of "human geography," the contours of which are subject not merely to the history of mythological diffusion (as in *He Who Hunted Birds in His Father's Village* and *Myths & Texts*) or to the vagaries of linguistic experimentation (as in *Riprap* and "Cold Mountain Poems"), but primarily to pressing social concerns involving race, gender, class, and sexuality.

In the first part of this chapter, I examine two key events from the 1950s in order to illustrate the coping process that the San Francisco community was forced to undergo as its avatar of Pacific Rim consciousness prepared to travel overseas. The first is the bittersweet send-off Snyder received just prior to his departure for Japan in May 1956. The Beats were excited about Snyder's impending adventure, to be sure, but they were also clearly anxious about his departure from their ranks, and a few of them used insensitive racial remarks to express their feelings of uneasiness. As Kerouac and Lew Welch wrung their hands at Snyder's leave-taking, for instance, they implicitly suggested, through explicit depictions of the poet's body, that their friend was becoming a little too Asian for their liking. In a series of "yellowface" portraits written by Kerouac and Welch, Snyder's "Asian" body became a palimpsest upon which the counterculture's Pacific Rim desires were duly (if somewhat indirectly) recorded. The result of such portraits was an insidious variety of Orientalist discourse that spiraled beyond Snyder's control. I follow this discussion with an analysis of the letters and essays Snyder wrote in Japan during the late 1950s. Many of these letters show that the young American poet who had retreated to Kyoto's Buddhist temples was acting as a countercultural ambassador for the West. As he spread word about the virtues of the American Beats, Snyder not only made himself popular among a new generation of Japanese writers but also established himself as a central player in Kyoto's burgeoning expatriate community.

The second part of this chapter examines the cultural duality and self-consciousness affecting Snyder during his extended residence in Asia. I am particularly interested here in tracing the socially inflected mapping processes that gave rise to the four distinct sections of *The Back Country*. My main thesis is that the Beat community's fixation on a "yellowface" poet was replaced in turn by this poet's fixation on Pacific Rim women who, besides offering sexual pleasure, helped him come to terms with his own incommensurable cultural desires, especially as he plotted the coordinates of his Pacific Rim journey. Eventually, however, the women who Snyder depicted in this volume—sex industry workers in Japan, Asian goddesses in India, and girlfriends left behind in America—came to complicate his fantasy, either by visually revealing their geographical fixity or displacement, or by speaking back in such a way as to challenge his privileged status as a globe-trotting white male. After analyzing Snyder's travels in the Asia-Pacific and his poetic portrayals of the human populations in that region, it becomes apparent to us, as it did to the poet himself in the late 1950s and early 1960s, that the path to the "back country" wends its way through spaces where notions of identity and place, always mutually constitutive, are transformed by culturally specific desires, many of them pertinent to ongoing academic debates about race and gender.

Countercultural Desire and the Color Line

During the mid-1950s, when he was studying Japanese and Chinese languages at UC–Berkeley, Snyder received a rigorous introduction to Asian literatures and cultures. And yet, because he also belonged to a bohemian community of "Zen lunatics," he found himself mired in a series of playful (but still harmful) appropriations based on racial stereotypes. Indeed, despite his proclivity for hermetic isolation in the mountains, Snyder became a central figure in the San Francisco Beat community's Orientalist fantasies, a good number of which fixated upon his body. As I hope to show throughout this section, race-based depictions of Snyder in the 1950s lend credence to arguments made by David Palumbo-Liu, who in *Asian/American* asserts that "the body is a multiply inflected sign and a somatic entity demanding sustenance and satisfaction for its particular needs. The fulfillment of those needs and desires is in turn implicated within the discursive formations that award recognition to that body across and within a racialized social logic."[1] During the Beat Generation heyday, Snyder himself may have had little say in how the white San Francisco counterculture was sizing him up. Nonetheless, he was clearly tapped to signify and facilitate that community's "racialized social logic." By the time he left for Japan in 1956, the poet who Allen Ginsberg once described as having a "little red beard and a bristling Buddha mind" had become subject to a barrage of fawning portraits by white male Beats who worshiped him as the West Coast's homegrown source of Asian wisdom.[2]

Such characterizations actually had a long history. We will recall that Reed students thought Snyder resembled a "sheik of Araby" presiding over the Zen garden he improvised in the basement of the Lambert Street commune. Snyder's closest friends made similar judgments in the years that followed. In a 1953 letter, Phil Whalen urges his charismatic friend to start his own "Puritan, Neo-Orthodox Purified Anabaptist Nonepiscopal Zenshu of Inward Grace," illustrating his point with a pen and ink sketch of himself picking tomatoes in a temple garden while a serene Snyder sits *zazen* on the temple's veranda.[3] Lew Welch was another who welcomed Snyder's immersion in all things Asian, even if he was much more anxious than Whalen about his friend's acculturation process, which he feared was going too far. Often, writers of the San Francisco Renaissance discovered that the study of Asian traditions formed the basis of their friendships. "I will treat you as the Chinaman treats someone who has saved his life," a grateful Welch wrote Whalen, who agreed to help Welch with his move from Chicago back to the West Coast in the mid-1950s.[4] At other times, though, the Orientalist brotherhood of white bohemians drew an arbitrary line separating a sublime variety of Asian culture from a more stultifying variety of racial terror, which only increased as the date of Snyder's departure grew near.

An early example of racial anxiety in the San Francisco Renaissance can be found in the rather tasteless joke that Welch included in a 1952 letter to Snyder. In the joke, Welch brags about his own Zen prowess to his friend, who at the time was about to leave graduate school in Indiana to enroll in the oriental languages program at UC–Berkeley:

> STUDENT: Sir, I hate to waste your time, but I've got a question that's eating
> me inside out, eating me out . . . Sir, do I exist?
> DR. COHEN (COLUMBIA): Who wants to know?
> So not only your slant-eyed son of a bitches play this game.
> Lew[5]

Welch's commentary on the joke implies that one need not be Asian (or "slant-eyed") to appreciate the existential mysteries of Zen. It also hints at the prevailing tendency within the San Francisco counterculture to co-opt Asian cultures while ignoring the immigrant communities situated on the other side of Grant Avenue. Equally as important, it shows that the Beat community believed an interest in Asian cultures could run dangerously deep.

Welch, for one, needed some reassurance that white writers could "play" the Zen "game" expertly and on their own terms, without interference from Chinese or Japanese practitioners. In all likelihood, it was Snyder, with his vast store of Pacific Rim knowledge, who provided Welch and other white bohemians with this reassurance. Over time, however, Welch began to trace the emergence of Asian features on Snyder's body, a sure sign that his friend was immersing himself a bit too deeply in Oriental subject matter. For instance, in June 1955, after Snyder had been studying Asian languages at Berkeley for several years, Welch mailed him a letter with the following salutation: "Trust the local carriers will ferret you out and put this in good order before your worthy, and no doubt by now slanted, eyes."[6] By this point, apparently, Snyder himself had become one of the "slant-eyed son of a bitches" that Welch admired but also feared. Taken together, Welch's communiqués suggest that it was only a matter of time before the Beat community's search for a Pacific Rim ambassador got transformed into an anxiety over losing that person to total racial otherness.

In October 1955, Snyder was announced to a larger audience during the Six Gallery reading, where he closed the evening's events, immediately after Ginsberg's passionate performance of "Howl," by reading "A Berry Feast," an American Indian fable featuring the trickster Coyote. Even though Snyder's source for this poem was an indigenous tale he had heard while working at the Warm Springs Reservation in Oregon, and even though the Six Gallery event has generally been considered as a watershed moment in the New American Poetry, a letter Welch sent to Whalen two years after this reading suggests that their Reed buddy was already looking across the Pacific for his inspiration. "Snyder's 'Berry Feast' was very good," Welch writes. "By long odds the best of his I've seen. Still, you get the impression he's looking a little to the left—which is not to bring him down either, I know that's precisely why he went to Japan."[7]

While Welch's description of Snyder's offshore gaze ("looking a little to the left") might refer in part to his friend's political leanings, it also recalls Charles Olson's description of Herman Melville, whom he praised for being "long-eyed enough to understand the Pacific as part of our geography."[8] Because it was written in 1957, Welch's assessment would have certainly been colored by the realization that Snyder had already embarked on his Asian pilgrimage. Welch probably wanted his college friend to follow his dream and become more intimately acquainted with Asian cultures, although not to such an extent that he would actually pick up and leave America. But that is exactly what happened. In the early 1950s, Welch anxiously anticipated Snyder's line of flight through Orientalized depictions of his body. Once Snyder left for Japan, Welch retroactively marked his friend's (slanted) eyes with the directionality of his movement westward along the Rim.

The Dharma Bums, published in 1958, is the most obvious place to look for Orientalized portraits of Snyder, since Kerouac's novel is mostly a paean to the poet's "lumberjack Zen" lifestyle. Perhaps even more than Dean Moriarty, the freewheeling protagonist in *On the Road*, Japhy Ryder embodied the Beat Generation's "new vision," which by 1958 was looking west from California shores for its inspiration. In the spirit of "Zen lunacy," the main characters in the novel dream of having half-breed babies, organizing naked bonfire orgies, and climbing mountains. In the background of their frolicsome activities, though, is an unsettling anxiety about Japhy's impending departure for Japan. Once again, this anxiety is played out on the poet's body.

From the very beginning of *The Dharma Bums*, narrator Ray Smith depicts Japhy as "strangely Oriental looking," with "eyes [that] twinkled like the eyes of old giggling sages of China."[9] As Snyder's classmates at Reed had done, Ray also pays close attention to his exotic friend's living quarters. Surveying the Berkeley cabin and making a list of "typical Japhy appurtenances" (which included an unused pair of wooden shoes, thrift store lumberjack sweaters, an orange crate that served as a table, and tatami mats, not to mention "the complete works of D. T. Suzuki and a fine quadruple-volume edition of Japanese haikus"), Ray cannot help but marvel at the simple beauties of his friend's ascetic life. After all, it was not every man who possessed the strength to climb a mountain and also had the artistic sense to bring back the rocks he had found and place them in a "Japanese tea garden" next to a pine tree in his front yard.[10]

At other junctures in the narrative, Japhy is celebrated for looking like an Indian, scaling mountains like a goat, making "mysterious Chinese dishes," having a "Chinee girlfriend" in Seattle, and being a "grunge-jumper with the women."[11] The last two characterizations bring to mind ribald descriptions of Neal Cassady, whom Ginsberg famously celebrated in "Howl" as "cocksman and Adonis of Denver," a man whose appetites for space and sex were seemingly inseparable.[12] But if "what got Kerouac and Ginsberg about Cassady was the energy of the archetypal West, the energy of the frontier," as Snyder told Ann Charters some years later, what "got" Kerouac about Snyder was his ability to push Cassady's libidinal frontier spirit ever westward, beyond the edge of the continent, until it was linked with a usually feminized Orient.[13]

It is important to remember that most Beats stopped their ramblings once they hit the Pacific coastline. "No more land," Dean Moriarty shouts to Sal Paradise upon reaching their western terminus in *On the Road*. "We can't go any further 'cause there ain't no more land."[14] In another famous piece of spontaneous prose, Kerouac spoke of San Francisco in terms of its "end of land sadness."[15] It thus remained for Snyder, San Francisco's Pacific Rim voyager, to point the way offshore. His intellectual curiosity and indefatigable wanderlust made him superbly suited for this task. "I need some of your gaiety and natural bhikku openness in the way you move and get around," Kerouac gushed in a letter he sent to Snyder on Valentine's Day, 1956.[16]

As was the case with Welch, it was only a matter of time before Kerouac shifted from celebrating Snyder's invocation of Asian cultures to expressing fear that his friend might accede to racial otherness. Again, the primary locus for this anxiety was Snyder's body. In *The Dharma Bums*, Ray Smith refers to Japhy Ryder as a contemporary incarnation of Han-shan, the T'ang Dynasty poet Snyder was translating when Kerouac first met him. Actually, Kerouac's fixation on the Han-shan figure in his midst was registered on two separate occasions. The more public mention arrives late in *The Dharma Bums* narrative, as Smith and Ryder hike Mount Tamalpais just days before Japhy's departure for Japan. Ray, who is clearly upset about the prospect of losing his friend, has a dream in which he sees "a little seamed brown unimaginable Chinese hobo . . . with an expressionless humor. . . . This one was a Chinese twice-as-poor, twice-as-tough and infinitely mysterious tramp and it was Japhy for sure. . . . I woke up at dawn, thinking 'Wow, is that what'll happen to Japhy? Maybe he'll leave that monastery and just disappear and we'll never see him again, and he'll be the Han Shan ghost of the Orient mountains and even the Chinese'll be afraid of him he'll be so raggedy and beat.'"[17] We see here the importance of Snyder in the San Francisco community. Ray feels that Japhy will become more Oriental than the Oriental once he lands in Asia, and that he will eventually track further westward, from the Buddhist monastery in Kyoto to the mountains of China, where he will never be seen by Westerners again. Japhy will become so Oriental, Ray anxiously surmises, "even the Chinese'll be afraid of him."

Curiously, Kerouac presents a rather different version of the dream when he describes it to Snyder in a letter dated May 1956. "O what a vision I had of Han Shan!" Kerouac declares. "He was standing in the market place in China on a Saturday morning, with a little peaked hat very much like yours with the rope, and a seamed and weatherbrowned little face, and very short, and hopelessly tangled legs hanging from him all over, and a small bundle bindlestiff bundle, he looked very much like you but smaller and he was old. Cant you find someone like that in Japan?"[18] Notice that, although he uses the same imagery, Kerouac does not signal to Snyder, as Ray Smith would to Japhy Ryder in the soon to be written novel, that the latter is destined to become a hermit like Han-shan. Instead, he merely tells Snyder that Han-shan looks "very much like" him and asks whether he might find a figure like that during his travels. Apparently, Kerouac does not want to admit to Snyder what *The Dharma Bums* admits to the reading public at large: the Beat community's frustration over the impending loss of its countercultural icon. By 1956, Snyder had become a reliable resource for matters relating to the Pacific Rim, but his quest for more knowledge threatens to render him inaccessible to those in San Francisco who so clearly depend on him. If Snyder could just "find someone like" Han-shan, Kerouac postulates, he would not have to disappear in Asia. Even more important, he could remain a white bohemian. Like Welch, Kerouac apparently wants Snyder to embody the mystery of the East without becoming fully Asian in the process. Snyder can satisfy San Francisco's Orientalist fantasies, according to this logic, only if he straddles the color line his Beat friends have drawn for him.

Lacking any assurance that Snyder will in fact abide by his role as an Orientalist (but not Oriental) sign, Kerouac is forced to rely on faith and imagination. With Japhy in Japan, Ray Smith's last resort is to envision his friend's body as it was during his final days stateside. As Ray treks up the aptly named Desolation Peak to spend the summer of 1956 as a fire lookout (a job that Snyder helped Kerouac procure), he imagines that his absent cohort is on hand to provide guidance, "as though Japhy's finger were pointing me the way."[19] Imitating an ancient monastic practice from China, Ray hitchhikes on the wrong side of the road and then looks off toward the "Pacific-ward skies that led . . . to the Hokkaido Siberian desolations of the world." At this point, Ray finally steadies himself, but not without a little help from a mysterious figure, an "unimaginable little Chinese bum standing there, in the fog, with that expressionless humor on his face. It wasn't the real-life Japhy of rucksacks and Buddhism studies and big mad parties at Corte Madera, it was the realer-than-life Japhy of my dreams, and he stood there saying nothing. 'Go away, thieves of the mind!' he cried down the hollows of the unbelievable Cascades. It was Japhy who had advised me to come here and now though he was seven thousand miles away in Japan answering the meditation bell . . . he seemed to be standing on Desolation Peak by the gnarled old rocky trees certifying and justifying all that was here."[20] Interestingly, the words Japhy shouts down the mountain closely resemble those used by Han-shan as he eluded Lu Ch'iu-Yin's messengers and disappeared into his Cold Mountain cave. Like Han-shan, Japhy is now absent in body, and yet he lingers in Ray Smith's mind as a "certifying and justifying presence," sanctioning his Dharma buddy's countercultural Buddhist visions and pointing the way toward Pacific Rim community, even though in real life Kerouac and Snyder would never meet again.

Understandably, Snyder was a bit chagrined when *The Dharma Bums* hit the street and created such a fuss. Kerouac had sent him the dust jacket in advance, telling him, "You're a Whitman in this book," before asking him to sign a libel release form for Viking Press.[21] By that point, Snyder knew that nothing would be the same. "*Dharma Bums* is out & we are discovered! Flee for your life!" he warned Phil Whalen (Warren Coughlin in the novel). In response, Whalen sounded a similar alarm: "[*Dharma Bums*] is beautiful, but god only knows how the young of the Bay Area (or elsewhere) will understand it & how they'll react (not to mention the Luce organization). Be brave." Snyder wrote back with his own assessment of Kerouac's work: "Drammy Bums is quite a chronicle. I hope we all won't be arrested. I do wish Jack had taken more time to smooth out dialogues etc., transitions are rather abrupt sometimes. I have stayed fearfully home since I got back but for one brief foray into The Coffee Gallery. Everybody's reading it."[22] According to one report, Snyder sent a chastening letter to Kerouac, suggesting that his tongue be cut out in hell. Regardless of whether this story is true, additional letters exchanged over the next few years caused Kerouac to feel that his old Zen buddy was growing distant from him. Even today, Snyder is quick to dismiss Japhy Ryder as a fiction, chalking up all the tall tales and the Han-shan comparisons to "Jack's romanticism."[23]

It is somewhat surprising, in light of the uneasiness he expressed in his letters, that Snyder chose to refer to Orientalized portraits of himself in his own writings. But on several occasions, we can find additional evidence of his "becoming Oriental." In the lewd banter spewed by coworkers on oil tankers and in forest service camps and chronicled in Snyder's published poems and journals, we find that the poet continues to get teased about taking on the features of the Asian peoples he studies. "Why don't you be more like the Japanese you talk about?" he was asked aboard a freighter on the way to Japan in May 1956. "They don't bother about being loved. They keep themselves taut in their own selves—there, at the bottom of the spine, the devil's own power they've got there" (EHH 32). Snyder also recalls that once, aboard a freighter in the Indian Ocean, after he had "spread [a] mat on the boat-deck, slipped off [his] zori, sat down crosslegged, faced the sunset, [and] poured *ocha*," a shipmate turned to him and said, "'Snyder, you've gone totally Asian'" (GSR 386). In "To the Chinese Comrades," a poem included in *The Back Country*, Snyder attests to hearing similar outbursts in the wilderness areas of the Pacific Northwest:

Old loggers vanish in the rocks.
They wouldn't tote me rice and soy-sauce
            cross the dam
"Snyder you gettin just like
        a damned Chinaman." (BC 113)

When Andy Wilcox, the crusty muleskinner who guided forest lookout workers to their stations in the Cascades, assigned the "Chinaman" epithet to Snyder during the summer of 1952, he probably thought it was part of some good-natured ribbing. As John Suiter points out in *Poets on the Peaks*, "Gary wore it like a badge for the next two years."[24] Still, there is a hidden anxiety that underlies comments like these. As Alexander Saxton, Ronald Takaki, Maxine Hong Kingston, and Lisa Lowe have noted, there is a long tradition of xenophobia among white laborers on the West Coast who fear that they will lose their jobs to Asian immigrants.[25] In the comments cited above, Snyder may be doing nothing more than acknowledging the ugly racism to which he, a white worker who happened to study Zen, was also subjected. At the same time, these citations read more like off-color jokes, and the fact that Snyder quoted and disseminated these comments, and prefaced one of them with a pidgin English pronoun, suggests that he took them as such. In either case, Snyder's publication of such material indicates that he has played a small role in embellishing his iconographic value as an Oriental sign, probably as a way of meeting the expectations of others.

Snyder's correspondence with friends in the Beat community sheds more light on the matter. In a letter he mailed to Lew Welch in May 1957, Snyder proudly declares, "I wear me Buddhist robes & look just like a blooming oriental."[26] Japhy Ryder tells Ray Smith much the same thing in *The Dharma Bums*. "What are you going to wear in the monastery, anyway?" Ray asks on the eve of Japhy's departure for Asia. "Oh man, the works," Japhy answers, "old T'ang Dynasty style things, long black floppy with huge droopy sleeves and funny pleats, make you feel real Oriental."[27] From Kyoto, Snyder sent pictures of himself outfitted in monastic attire. He also purchased a kimono, a *koromo* robe, and ceremonial accoutrements (including a tea set and a bell-and-clapper set) and shipped them to Phil Whalen, who clearly appreciated the gift. "I'm sitting here in me chopsuey costume," a gracious Whalen wrote back, "drinking wine & feeling splendid."[28] A few years later, Snyder told Welch, who had grown frustrated over the years because he was never able to raise enough money to visit Asia, how he could make his own Tibetan robe back in California simply by snipping and dyeing an everyday bathrobe. Thousands of miles removed from the scene, Snyder remained the cohesive force by which members of the San Francisco Renaissance recognized and satisfied their Pacific Rim desires.[29]

To a certain degree, the poet who edged closer to East Asian lifestyle in looks and practice during these years emerged as a character in "yellowface," a West Coast version of the blackface minstrel tradition once popular in the American South. While John Tchen has shown that yellowface pageantry in America dates back to the early part of the nineteenth century, Frank Wu and David Palumbo-Liu remind us that this dual expression of cultural desire and anxiety continued to manifest itself well into the 1990s, when white British actor Jonathan Pryce appeared as the Engineer, an Asian character, in the Broadway staging of *Miss Saigon*, and when the Clintons and Al Gore were depicted with Asian features on the cover of the *National Review* during the Asiagate fund-raising scandal.[30] In Beat-era San Francisco, bohemian writers probably thought that casting Snyder as a yellowface character would give them a safe and effective way of imagining their Oriental fantasies. Here was a man who seemed exotic, perhaps even Asian, but at the same time familiar and ruggedly American.

To be singled out as the counterculture's yellowface character was not Snyder's aim, of course, nor was it really his fault. But it is clear that his status as a "white Asian" prompted a series of reactions, from the desirous longings of Kerouac, to the anxious jokes of Welch, to the xenophobia of white laborers, to his own slightly amused evaluations of his looks. That these various responses to Snyder's person betray feelings of fear and pleasure is not anomalous. As Eric Lott has argued, the white American's anxiety over racial difference often begins as an internal fantasy of enjoyment, which he subsequently chooses to locate externally, at the site of a racial "other." Before long, though, his externalized racial fantasy (whether it is of black masculinity or Asian exoticism) gets introjected back into his own being. He therefore experiences the joy of *becoming* the other without necessarily *being* the other. The end result is a loop of enjoyment that uses people of color as throwaway props or colored masks. Paraphrasing Slavoj Zizek, Lott explains the complex trajectory of racial desire: "Whites organize their enjoyment through the other . . . and access pleasure precisely by fantasizing about the other's 'special' pleasure. Hatred of the other arises from the necessary hatred of one's own excess; ascribing this excess to the 'degraded' other and indulging it—by imagining, incorporating, or impersonating the other— one conveniently and surreptitiously takes and disavows pleasure at one and the same time."[31]

Viewed as a character in yellowface, Snyder became the accessible Asian other to whom white San Francisco writers routinely paid homage. At the same time, he got chided for taking his act to an anxiety-provoking extreme. The jokes at his expense only thinly mask his community's worry that they too might get caught up in Asian excess. Snyder was tapped by writers like Kerouac and Welch to lead the Beats to the edge of the Pacific Rim, a spherical space of unified otherness resembling Zizek's loop of enjoyment. But once there, he was only supposed to signify Zen pleasure and bohemian subversion; he was not supposed to accede to total racial otherness. In the minds of his peers, it was fine for Snyder to disavow cold war paranoia about, say, China, and he was allowed to look and act as if he were Chinese ("very much like" Han-shan), but he was certainly not encouraged to slide over the color line and become "more Chinese than the Chinese" (or actually become Han-shan).

It is ironic, to put it mildly, that the San Francisco Beats played out their Orientalist fantasies on the body of a white poet when Chinatown was just a block or two away from their North Beach hangouts. The Beats went to Chinatown on occasion, but most of their stories about the neighborhood involve eating (see the dinner celebration after the Six Gallery reading, as recounted in *The Dharma Bums*) or the search for other forms of pleasure ("When I go to Chinatown I get drunk and never get laid," Ginsberg lamented in his poem "America"). Rarely did their journeys into that space include conversations with Asian-Americans. Indeed, for all the talk about Asian religion and philosophy during these years, Albert Saijo (whom Kerouac disguised as the "hepcat" George Baso in *Big Sur*, and Welch once referred to as a "very swinging but repressed little Jap, really beautiful . . . with the open little moon face of the children of his race") and Shigeyoshi Murao (the manager of Lawrence Ferlinghetti's City Lights Bookstore) are the only Asian-Americans to receive much mention in the literature and popular accounts of the Beat era.[32] The language barrier was responsible for much of the cultural distance, and since Snyder knew Asian languages better than Rexroth or any other writer on the scene, and since he had established friendly contact with the Japanese immigrants at the Berkeley Buddhist Church, he was picked as the most convenient (read: white) source of Asian knowledge. The only crisis the Beats suffered came when he crossed the Pacific. At that juncture, they were forced to imagine just how Oriental he had become.

A Hipster Looks at Asia

Alas, Snyder did not disappear in Asia, anymore than he became racially Asian once he settled there. After a three-day party, which by some accounts turned into an orgy, Snyder left San Francisco on 7 May 1956.[33] Two weeks later, he arrived in "the long smoggy Osaka Bay leading finally up to Kobe" (EHH 33). Two days after that, he entered Kyoto, Japan's ancient capital and cultural center, which at the time was receiving an increasing number of visitors from the West. It was here, as an expatriated San Francisco Beat, that he began the next phase of his Pacific Rim odyssey. Meanwhile, his friends back in the States waited for letters and an eagerly anticipated manuscript of poems. "There you sit, waiting to flop into the pond so we can all screech 'Basho!' on the wildest side of the frantic Pacific," Phil Whalen wrote Snyder in January 1957, echoing the Japanese poet's famous haiku.[34]

As mentioned earlier, Snyder's main purpose in Kyoto was to serve as a translator and aide to Ruth Fuller Sasaki at the First Zen Institute of America. But he also found ample time for Buddhist practice. His activities included lengthy and intense *sesshin* meditation, which he practiced as an *unsui* (or monastic novice) under the tutelage of Isshu Miura Roshi at Shokoku temple and eventually as a *koji* (or lay disciple) with Oda Sesso Roshi at Daitoku temple. He also had the opportunity to take a break from the rigors of Rinzai practice and meet with the Yamabushi, Kyoto's local Mountain Buddhists, whose rituals involved walking the sacred landscape near Mount Hiei, especially the Omine Ridge (MR 156). Snyder, who had written a short article on the Yamabushi sect for a Zen Institute newsletter in 1954, took to the Mountain Buddhists almost instinctively. He would employ their walking practice in future mountain climbs, including formal circumambulations of California's Mount Tamalpais. Snyder would also use their concept of "walked-in landscapes" in several of the poems he included in *Mountains and Rivers without out End*. Although he would move on to study other branches of Buddhism in the 1960s, Snyder took from these first contacts with Japanese Buddhists lessons that would last a lifetime.[35]

Snyder shared the more formal aspects of his Buddhist training with American readers in "Spring Sesshin at Shokoku-ji," an essay the *Chicago Review* featured in its popular Zen issue in the summer of 1958. "Spring Sesshin" describes the strict regimen that *unsui* (meaning "cloud, water") monks must withstand during their residence in a monastic training school (or *Sodo*). During seasonal *sesshin* weeks, a monastic novice engages in long periods of sitting meditation (*zazen*), short periods of walking meditation (*kinhin*), the study of riddles (koans), rounds of begging (*takuhatsu*), intensive interviews (*sanzen*) with a Zen Master or Dharma heir (*Roshi*), and a good deal of manual labor. At Shokoku temple, where *unsui* novices were kept busy from 3 A.M. to midnight and were whacked on the back whenever a *Roshi* or a *Jikijisu* (the head *unsui*, who acts as a silent drill sergeant) suspected a lack of concentration, Snyder learned that Buddhist practice involved a lot more than just walking mountains or sitting *zazen* for a brief period in the morning. Evidently, the Dharma required that one be more than just a Dharma Bum. Americans who read this essay received an introduction to Zen Buddhism starkly different from the kind regularly disseminated in Beat literature.[36]

Although his training schedule kept him isolated for weeks at a time, Snyder still had the opportunity to make friends at the Zen Institute in Ryosen-an.

Burton Watson and Phil Yampolsky, two young scholars from Columbia University, were already at the institute when Snyder arrived. Watson, who had been in Japan since 1951, was enrolled as a graduate student in the Department of Chinese at Kyoto University, which, because Beijing was closed off to Westerners in the early years of the cold war, was regarded as the best available center for Sinology. As previously noted, Watson went on to translate one hundred poems by Han-shan, and today he is regarded as one of the best English-language translators of Chinese literature. Yampolsky, in Japan on a Fulbright scholarship, eventually became a professor of Japanese at Columbia. Snyder cavorted freely with both men. When they were not working, these young intellectuals explored the ancient city that was their new home.

The Kyoto they discovered differed significantly from the postmodern portraits of Japan that surfaced a few decades later, when cyberpunk fiction and movies like *Black Rain* and *Rising Sun* were all the rage. In the mid-1950s, American occupation of Japan was a recent memory, and the nation was still suffering the aftereffects of the Pacific War. Kyoto was lucky to have escaped the bombing, but like most of Japan it was awash in poverty and plagued by the "*kyodatsu* condition" of postwar exhaustion and despair.[37] There were few cars, hardly any flush toilets, and no sources of heat other than fireplaces and coal hibachis. On the plus side, expatriated Americans discovered that food and rent were cheap. So too were the various enjoyments the city offered. Watson recalls that he and Snyder frequently patronized Kyoto's *aka-chochin*, or red lantern stands. These were "small places seating ten to fifteen customers" and serving "bottled beer, sake, and sometimes an illegally manufactured, unrefined sake called *doburoku* (that was very cheap but could give you a nasty hangover), as well as such simple foods as the stewed vegetables known as *oden* or bean curd dishes."[38]

Yampolsky remembers that the city's "pleasure quarters" were also quite active, since the Japanese government had yet to "succumb to Western pseudo-morality."[39] After a massive effort put forth by Japanese feminist groups, nationwide antiprostitution legislation was finally enacted in the mid-1950s. Nevertheless, the sex trade still flourished. Pink districts sanctioning illicit sexual activities quickly replaced the red-light districts the Japanese government had licensed for centuries, since the early Tokugawa period. Because these pink districts were immune from policing, the antiprostitution law was largely ineffective, and the exploitation of Japanese women continued virtually without halt.[40] Additionally, around military compounds, "comfort women" (*ianfu*) were made available to occupation troops. Japanese officials hoped that these women would serve as a "dike of chastity," asking them to give up their bodies "for the nation" so that libidinous Western males would not search out and sully the general female population.[41] Despite these efforts, the sex trade flourished in several big cities. In Tokyo and elsewhere, racketeers controlled the drinking establishments, brothels, hostess bars, and gambling joints, all of which employed thousands of impoverished women in desperate need of work. Instead of a Geisha atmosphere full of ceremonial tradition and grace, the *mizu shobai* (or "water trade") that made its home in low-end pink district spots such as massage parlors and "amusement centers" offered customers titillating arousal and sexual release, but little more.

Daniel Ellsberg, who visited in Kyoto in 1960 while working for the RAND Corporation, recalls meeting Snyder in a hostess bar where the waitresses wore "nothing at all but transparent shortie nightgowns." Kyoto's bar district, Ellsberg explains, was "like nothing in America at the end of the fifties. What this district of Kyoto held out to an adult male (an oxymoron, especially in that era) was as exotic to my eyes as the Ryoanji garden where my walk had started."[42] Interestingly, Ellsberg claims that he might not have visited Kyoto at all if he had not first read about the city's cultural riches in *The Dharma Bums*. His chance meeting with Snyder in the bar was therefore colored by certain expectations. Upon being introduced to Snyder, Ellsberg recollects that he "looked hard at him and said, 'You're Japhy Ryder.' He nodded. I said, 'You're the reason I'm in Kyoto.'"[43] Even overseas, the iconographic power of this Pacific Rim voyager held strong.

As other Westerners settled in Kyoto, they formed a small but tight-knit intellectual community, with the magnetic Snyder at its center. "Kyoto in the early 1960s looked as if it might become a Far Eastern alternative to Paris," Clayton Eshelman, a young poet who arrived a few years after Snyder, recalls nostalgically. "It didn't, but probably through Snyder more than anyone else, it became an accessible and amazingly reasonable cultural outpost for some half-dozen American writers during this period."[44] Residents of Kyoto's "beat set" (Snyder's term) included lithographer and painter Will Petersen, potter John Chappell, and literary editor Cid Corman, whose Origin Press and *Origin* magazine published *Riprap* and other poems by Snyder in the late 1950s and early 1960s, making the poet's work available to the American reading public during his long residence in Asia.[45]

Kyoto may not have become another Paris, but it did serve as a *semeion*, a type of heterotopian meeting ground, as well as a Barthesian "Empire of Signs," a place where displaced Western artists could investigate the nature of their far-flung identity. By immersing themselves in a flow of significations ordinarily denied them back home and by losing their geographical bearings in the process, these bohemian expatriates sought to overturn the symbolic order of cold war America. And yet, as so often happens, the exotic Asia of their imagination did not always line up so neatly with the real Asia they discovered once they got there. They therefore found themselves clinging to familiar reference points and attitudes. Will Petersen, who proudly admitted to Snyder that he kept one Japanese room and one "S.F. Bohemian" room in his apartment, went so far as to refer to Kyoto as "a suburb of the Bay."[46]

Some of this geographical and cultural confusion finds its way into "Letter From Kyoto," a bittersweet epistle Snyder published in a 1957 issue of the *Evergreen Review*. In this open letter, the San Francisco Renaissance's far-flung correspondent excoriates the citizens of Kyoto for letting global exchange pollute their ancient sensibilities. The arrivals of Commodore Perry and General MacArthur are relatively recent events in Japan's long history, and yet Snyder has discovered that the island nation has amalgamated Western influence rather quickly and liberally. At first, he finds this troublesome. Japanese students from the provinces still arrive in Kyoto by the busload to tour ancient shrines and temples, but Snyder cannot help noticing that they come into contact with "dinky bars & coffeehouses that look like Stratford-on-Avon outside & Christina Rossetti's parlor inside (western influence)." As he sees it, the false sense of history evoked by these Western-themed tourist spots affects the way the young Japanese perceive their own Shinto and Buddhist shrines. The distinction between real history and simulated history has become cloudy, and as a result, the authentic Asian experience Westerners like Snyder had craved from afar suddenly seems like a put-on. "Many people don't take Kyoto seriously anymore," Snyder explains. "A friend in Tokyo said if you go to somebody's house in Kyoto they'll tell you the toothpick you get was handmade in a hereditary factory 500 years old. Everyone except the bargirls seems to have been doing their line of work for nine generations." It is hard to know what to expect in such an atmosphere. Whatever Snyder regards as crass and Western the Japanese treat reverentially, whereas whatever he regards as exotic or authentic the Japanese treat disparagingly or cynically.[47]

As the letter continues, Snyder's cultural compass spins out of control. Kyoto emerges as a space of humorous confluence ("Downtown like any town but funnier") where American expatriates aspire to a particularly hip version of ancient Japanese wisdom, even as "hordes" of Japanese students choose to read Percy Shelley, D. H. Lawrence, and *Vogue*. To hear Snyder tell it, the young Japanese turning their backs on Kyoto's cultural riches have become strangers in their own homeland. "Some of these students dig old Japan too; most not," he writes. "If they'd go down to Nara, back in time, to Horyuji temple & look at the dozens of really ancient statues, carved wood little waked-up cats with gone looks & secret hipster smiles, they mightn't feel so left out."[48] In short order, Snyder's initial disappointment with Japan filtered down to other members of the San Francisco counterculture. In *The Dharma Bums*, Ray Smith recalls the gist of an argument put forth by Alvah Goldbrook (Allen Ginsberg), who lamented "that while guys like us are all excited about being real Orientals and wearing robes, actual Orientals over there are reading surrealism and Charles Darwin and mad about Western business suits."[49]

The Buddhist Japan described in "Letter From Kyoto" is less a cultural heritage than it is an index by which exiled Americans "hooked on the place" calibrate their hipness quotient. I find it rather telling that Snyder evaluates this Japanese city in terms of the pleasure it provides to knowledgeable foreign travelers. Thus do ancient Buddhist sculptures appear, in Snyder's Beat lingo, as "carved little waked-up cats with gone looks and secret hipster smiles" or as "splintery sages a pleasure to see." To appreciate Kyoto, Snyder implies, is to dig it in the right way, as carefree Western expatriates like Phil Yampolsky (who is able to "thaw the stoniest old types with some American-unheard-of sudden slang") or Lindley Hubbell (who is "hung on No & never misses a performance") are supposedly able to dig it. In the middle of the letter, Snyder mentions that there are "some fine Kyoto people too," but by this point such sentiment seems like an afterthought. By letter's end, we learn that, among the Japanese, only a handful of Japanese artisans and Zen monks able to "swing in both realms" (presumably East and West) have fully engaged Snyder's imagination.[50]

The air of disappointment that pervades "Letter From Kyoto" is echoed in Snyder's private musings. In "Japan First Time Around," selected journal entries from 1956 and 1957 published in *Earth House Hold*, Snyder depicts a

scenario in which the Japanese fall prey to foppish excess while doing harm to their own cultural heritage. "It turns out you got to spend $30 for a special meditation cushion," the ascetic San Francisco transplant complains. Furthermore, he finds it bitterly ironic that "fierce-eyed" and "culture-thirsty" Japanese students sit listening to a Westerner play Haydn on a piano, "all in a land of rice paddy and green hills and rains where still deep-hatted Dharma hobos try to roam" (EHH 33, 37–38). Snyder, who is clearly befuddled by Japan's appetite for Western culture, surmises that Zen consciousness is undergoing a geographical shift. As he remembers "friends in America who are humble about their interest in the Dharma and ashamed of their profligacy while living on salvaged vegetables and broken rice," he contrasts their virtuous behavior to the halfhearted commitment to Buddhism he witnesses overseas at the Zen Institute. Eventually, he takes it upon himself to utter a prophecy: "The center in this [Zen] world is quietly moving to San Francisco where it's most alive. These Japanese folks may be left behind and they won't (in the words of Feng Kuan) recognize it when they see it" (EHH 33). As was the case in "Letter From Kyoto," Snyder cannot help but think that the Buddhist culture conceptualized by San Francisco bohemians has somehow managed to be more authentic than the Buddhist culture he discovers in Japan.

Snyder's letters to Phil Whalen reiterate his initial disappointment. "It looks to me like Americans . . . are making it—not even knowing how good they are—better than most Jap Buddhists, who take too much for granted," he writes two days after his arrival in Kyoto. He therefore advises Whalen to stay behind in San Francisco. "There's no reason for anybody to come over here except to peer about." Even the Japanese landscape fails to match Snyder's expectations. "I went up to Hiezan (Mt. Hiei) today & talked with a fine young Tendai priest in a huge mossy temple under big cryptomeria," he tells Whalen. "But Tamalpais and Muir Woods are just as lovely, for the natural beauty angle."[51] Snyder also tells Whalen about the difficulties of adapting to Rinzai Zen practice. "I goddamn near croaked," he complains after a particularly tough December *sesshin* called *Rohatsu* in 1956. Once again, Snyder measures his disillusionment against forms of enlightenment he had already experienced as a San Francisco Beat. "Organized Zen is for the birds," he tells Whalen. "Kerouac's vision of the holy bums on Gondolas is solider than the self-conscious emulation of the pictorial and literary tradition of the 'old Zen masters' these arrogant & ignorant fops are up to."[52]

In 1960, Snyder offered his analysis of East-West relations directly to the Japanese public. In two articles solicited by his friend Hisao Kanaseki for *Chuo-koron*, a highly respected intellectual journal, Snyder continued to maintain that American bohemians who were hip to the way of Zen could rejuvenate an Asian culture that had grown dull. In the first article, "Notes on the Beat Generation," Snyder rehearses the storied beginnings of the Beat movement and maps the travels its members have made around the "big triangle" of New York–Mexico City–San Francisco. He also offers basic definitions of "beat," "hip," and "square" for Japanese readers unfamiliar with those terms. Snyder ends the essay by claiming that he and his Beat cohorts "live an independent life writing poems and painting pictures, making mistakes and taking chances—but finding no reason for apathy or discouragement." Unlike other intellectuals around the world, Snyder insists, the creative types of the Beat Generation "are going somewhere." Consequently, "it would do no harm if some of their attitudes came to liven up the poets of Japan" (PS 13). In "The New Wind," the second article he published in *Chuo-koron*, Snyder reviews Donald Allen's recently published collection, *The New American Poetry*. Once again, Snyder champions the tough antinomian character of the Beats and contrasts it with the relatively feckless attitude of modern Japanese poets, who he claims have taken the "guts and brains out of poetry" (PS 15). "Let us hope this fresh wind of poetry doesn't stay just in America, but blows its way about the globe," he concludes, in a rare display of Western pride (PS 16).

By and large, the disappointed tone that characterizes Snyder's first communications from Japan is an aberration, since his long residence in Asia marked a period of artistic growth and spiritual "communionism" (his term). By the early 1960s, Snyder was roaming further into Japan and taking off to explore other Asian locales, including India in 1962. He was also delving more deeply into the religious and philosophical traditions of Asia and getting to know its people on a more intimate level. His discoveries are reflected in the organizational pattern of *The Back Country*, a volume of poetry first published in England and published complete in America in 1968. A panoramic portrait of East-West interchange, this book charts Snyder's movements from "Far West" to "Far East" and "Back" again. *The Back Country* stands as a classic study in human geography, for it provides us with a detailed glimpse of the diverse populations and cultural conditions the poet encountered during his travels along the Pacific Rim.

Human geographers sometimes disagree as to whether space is socially constructed or whether the social is spatially constructed, but the reality is that these categories are mutually constitutive. Doreen Massey, a leading voice in human geography scholarship, explains that "the very fact of social relations being 'stretched out over space' (or not), and taking spatial forms, influences the nature of the social relations themselves, the divisions of labour and the functions within them. Social change and spatial change are integral to each other."[53] Whatever way they choose to look at a given region, whether it be spatially or sociologically, scholars working in this field tend to agree that "geography *matters*," which is to say that it literally materializes our cultural desires, our excesses, and our expressions of difference, usually in terms of race, class, gender, or sexuality (and sometimes in combination). A similar dynamic holds sway in *The Back Country*, for in its pages we find Snyder confronting the material conditions underpinning his literary community's geographic desires. In a series of hard-hitting poems, the writer objectified by white male Beats as an exotic specimen comes to realize that he, too, has objectified Pacific Rim people, especially women, as part of his ongoing effort to understand the region. His deep feelings of regret are thus tied to an equally deep understanding of cultural geography. Throughout this volume, Snyder speaks with refreshing candor as he liberates himself from personal demons and begins to break free from all sorts of racial and sexual stereotypes. In the process, he stands the Beat community's Orientalist fantasy on its head.

The Back Country:
The Story of a Cultural Return

The Back Country may be Snyder's most representative volume, for it comes closest to tracing the full arc of his Pacific Rim travels and influences. The book is organized into four main sections. "Far West" is concerned with Snyder's life on the West Coast of America. "Far East" is dedicated mostly to poems about Japan. "Kali," according to the book's jacket copy, includes "poems inspired by a visit to India and his reading of Indian religious texts." The final section, "Back," contains poems Snyder wrote during his nine-month stay in America in 1964 and 1965. The circular, Rimlike organization of these four sections is anything but arbitrary. Snyder once told bibliographer Katherine McNeill that the organizational structure of his volumes is usually determined by a thematic coherence he discovers once he places poems side by side. "As poems come into existence," Snyder explains, "I begin to see what kind of force field they generate, meaning what various resonances, implications, threads, subliminal meaning networks there are. What constitutes a collection is when you see that all of those possibilities are more or less completed in a given set—it constitutes a set, and then it's ready to publish. All of the collections of poetry I've brought out have a certain internal coherence—in thematic imagery, direction and implication, to some extent in stylistics."[54]

There are many ways to read *The Back Country*. In a strictly literary sense, a reader finds evidence of Snyder's poetic growth, since poems he had composed over an extended period are charted and arranged as a loop of experience, a return route of personal discovery. One can also read this book as a kind of natural history journal. Snyder once described the intellectual journey in *The Back Country* as "starting with Douglas fir and Ponderosa pine and ending with Douglas fir and Ponderosa pine" (TRW 86), reinforcing the visual message evoked by the pine tree mandala on the cover of the New Directions paperback edition. To further emphasize his love of Pacific Rim lands and waters, Snyder chose a fitting passage from Basho for the book's epigraph: "So—when was it—I, drawn like blown cloud, couldn't stop dreaming of roaming, roving the coast up and down." As Snyder told McNeill, *The Back Country* "can be seen in the tradition of Basho's *Oku no Hosomichi*, 'The Narrow Trails to the Back Country,' the journal-poem book of his long six-month walk up the Japan Sea Coast and down."[55]

Given the cloud and water imagery in the epigraph, one might also assume that Snyder shared with Basho an appreciation for the naturalistic aspects of Zen practice, especially since he had already explained in "Spring Sesshin at Shokoku-ji" that one of the primary aspirations of an *unsui* novice during his six-month *Sodo* sessions is "to drift like clouds and flow like water" (EHH 44). All the same, by extending Basho's six-month journey so that it matched his own six-year residence in Asia from 1958 to 1964, altering the Japanese poet's description of his island seacoast so that it becomes the extended shoreline of the Pacific Rim, and translating "The Narrow Road to the Deep North" as "The Narrow Trails to the Back Country," Snyder hints at his broader agenda, which is to make a centuries-old Asian literature align with the "new vision" of a California-based Beat movement.

Of course, one can also read *The Back Country* as the chronicle of a religious quest or spiritual pilgrimage, in which case it would stand as an important precursor for other highly esteemed Buddhist journey books written by Americans, such as Peter Matthiessen's *The Snow Leopard* and Richard Bernstein's *Ultimate Journey*.[56] I think it rather significant, given this context, that *The Back Country*'s organizational pattern effectively reverses the route taken by Buddhism over the centuries as it moved from India to China with Bodhidharma, then northward to Japan, before arriving on American shores in the modern era. On a geographical register, *The Back Country* tracks Snyder's movements as he gets closer to the ancient home of Buddhism. On a psychological register, the book accounts for the changes taking place in his spiritual consciousness. Snyder himself has said that his journey from cold war America into the cradle of Buddhist civilization brought him face-to-face with archetypal images that—because they existed on the level of the subconscious, in the "back country" of his imagination—altered his life in unforeseeable ways.[57]

A return motif is relevant to each of the religious, naturalistic, and literary contexts mentioned above. Mythologist Joseph Campbell, for instance, has noted that the "myth of eternal return" is basic to Asia's daily life and its archaic religions. Ecocritic Thomas Lyon makes use of Campbell's monomyth theory when he claims that "the great mythic pattern of departure, initiation, and return" has been a staple of American nature writing since the late eighteenth century.[58] My own tendency is to read *The Back Country* as a parable of a larger-scaled "cultural return." When I employ this phrase, I do not merely wish to explain a religious devotee's psychological relocation back to a zero degree of spirituality, nor do I simply mean to refer to a traveler's physical return to his geographical starting point. Instead, I am trying to account for the return (or dividend) that a literary community receives on an initial investment made by one of its leaders (a twelve-year residence in Asia, in Snyder's case). As happens in most business transactions, an investor (a Pacific Rim traveler, in our present discussion) spends something (certain desires or physical energies) with the expectation that he and his clients (San Francisco compatriots) will gain something else in return (a sense of the exotic, perhaps, or religious salvation).

It is crucial to recognize, however, that psychological investments often use marginalized people as cultural currency to be exchanged. We have already noted one such instance in the yellowface portraits of Snyder circulating throughout San Francisco's Beat community. In other locations along the Pacific Rim, this kind of symbolic exchange has often involved impoverished women, many of them from Oceania, who are exploited in the Rim's "pleasure industry." In *The Back Country*, Snyder makes repeated reference to bar girls and prostitutes working in this industry, as well as to other poor women in Asia, goddesses in Asian religions, college girlfriends, and Beat women on the San Francisco scene. On several occasions, he expresses regret for not having recognized the plight of such women during his travels and laments the fact that he and his friends have contributed to a gender hierarchy subjugating female labor to masculine pleasure. As we analyze the poems in *The Back Country*, we should therefore try to determine where, and especially upon whom, Snyder decides to draw the line between work and leisure, desire and excess, whether it be on a map, on a female body, or on both at the same time. The intersections of these issues, and their arrangement according to a clearly defined geographical paradigm, are crucial to my understanding of Snyder's Pacific sojourn.

Far West

In the first section of *The Back Country*, Snyder describes the America he left behind in 1956, but he also looks forward to the longer journey that lay ahead. As he had done in earlier poems like "Logging 12," "Nooksack Valley," and "Migration of Birds," Snyder anticipates a line of flight he had, in fact, already chosen. He registers his restless desire to travel in subtle and effective ways. The conclusions to "August on Sourdough, A Visit from Dick Brewer" and "Home from the Sierra" are typical of his geographical approach:

Next morning I went with you
            as far as the cliffs,
Loaned you my poncho—   the rain across the shale—
You down the snowfield
            flapping in the wind
Waving a last goodbye   half hidden in the clouds
To go on hitching
            clear to New York;
Me back to my mountain   and far, far, west. (BC 19)

Down to hot plains.
Mexicans on flatcars in the San Joaquin.
cool fog
smell of straw mats
cup of green tea
by the Bay (BC 15)

In both instances, Snyder determines his geographic position by comparing his movements to those of other people. At an earlier stage of "August on Sourdough," for example, Snyder reveals that his friend Dick Brewer has "hitched a thousand miles / north from San Francisco," leading us to wonder whether this visit occasioned his statement in the "North Beach" essay: "In the spiritual and political loneliness of America of the fifties you'd hitch a thousand miles to meet a friend" (OW 45). Another celebration of long-distance friendship appears in "Rolling in at Twilight," a poem in which Snyder gets off a bus in Newport, Oregon, just in time to meet his old friend Phil Whalen, who is carrying a bag of groceries through a parking lot full of logging trucks and Caterpillar tractors (BC 23). By the close of "August on Sourdough," however, all emphasis is placed on the divergent paths that friends often take. Dick Brewer descends Sourdough Mountain after his short visit and heads "clear to New York," whereas Snyder decides to stay on his isolated peak. By claiming residence in the "far, far, west," Snyder implies that he has gone farther west than others have, entering a mind space that is so far out that it might be considered a part of the East, or at least a part of the Pacific Rim community by which West and East find union.

In "Home from the Sierra," Snyder charts his geographic trajectory in relation to Mexicans riding flatcars in the San Joaquin Valley. Since seasonal laborers from Mexico travel north and south in this long fertile valley, depending on the employment opportunities available in agricultural industries, they would at some point cross paths with the poet, who is heading down from trail work in the Sierra Nevada mountains and back to the Bay Area. The fact that Snyder sits on a tatami mat, enjoying the cool Pacific fog and drinking green tea, provides one more indication of his impulse to travel further westward, across the ocean to Japan, where these things exist in plentiful supply.[59]

Snyder's inclusion of the Mexicans in "Home from the Sierra" also highlights the issue of human labor, a main concern throughout *The Back Coun-*

try. As an ecological advocate, Snyder has always questioned the effects that certain kinds of work have on our natural environment. In "Far West," he flips this relationship upside down, speculating on the effect that endangered natural resources have had on a mobile human work force. Consider "Marin-an," a poem named for the Mill Valley shack (or "bhikku hostel") that Snyder shared with Jack Kerouac in the spring of 1956.[60] In this poem, we find Snyder isolated on a California hilltop, meditating upon the hermetically sealed automobile passengers making their morning commute into San Francisco. As he listens to the distant rush of traffic invading his natural habitat, the poet realizes that cars have altered life to such an extent that they have replaced human beings as active agents: "a soft continuous roar / comes out of the far valley / of the six-lane highway—thousands / and thousands of cars / driving men to work" (BC 8). Heard but not seen, this mechanical roar is hardly the sweet piping of a Keatsian nightingale or a Shelleyan skylark. On the contrary, it is a horrible reminder of our detachment from natural beauty and our enslavement to bottom-line thinking.

The word "driving" can be read ambiguously in this context. Ostensibly, it means that cars transport men to work, but it can also mean that cars exhort men *to work*, in which case these automobiles emerge as the commodity fetish "driving" our desires and necessitating our daily labors. Whereas Snyder would rather hike the surrounding hills of Marin County, suburban commuters are intent on driving through the landscape as quickly as possible and reaching their workplace on time. According to the specious consumer logic formulated by advertisers, these commuters will be truly successful so long as they work diligently enough to make more money and purchase the freedom represented by newer and faster models of automobile. Echoing contemporary writings by Herbert Marcuse, Snyder argues that even "progressive" Californians are out of touch with their true needs and desires, having been duped by what cultural critic Thomas Frank has trenchantly labeled "hip capitalism."[61]

"Oil" (BC 20) takes another look at American consumer dependencies and places them in the context of global trade flows. In this poem, Snyder is in the engine room of an oil tanker crossing the Pacific, "bearing what all these / crazed, hooked nations need: / steel plates and / long injections of pure oil." As he had done in "Marin-an," Snyder examines the addictive behavior of those he refers to elsewhere as "fossil fuel junkies of tremendous mobility zapping back and forth, [people] who are still caught on the myth of the frontier, the myth of boundless resources and a vision of perpetual materialistic growth" (TRW 69). The Pacific Rim has always offered a wealth of natural resources, to be sure, and its peoples have tapped them for thousands of years. Even so, Snyder suggests in "Oil" that dangerous exploitation of these resources might be avoided if consumers would see their dependencies for what they really are: modern conveniences that are not really all that necessary. At the same time, we should find it highly ironic, given this poem's message, that Snyder's travels to and from Asia were made possible by his work on oil tankers.

A related topic involves the blurred boundary between work and leisure. Importantly, this is a distinction that Snyder comes to understand and articulate in terms of gender differences. While working in the mountains, Snyder learned that labor has the potential to order a landscape. In "Fire in the Hole," for example, he describes a "valley, reeling, / on the pivot of that drill" (BC 12). Among other things, this image suggests that a site of labor has become the pivot point around which the mountains are transformed, and that the energy radiating outward from this labor creates out of the wilderness a temporary sense of order (not unlike the enigmatic scenario Wallace Stevens depicts in "Anecdote of the Jar"). Investigating the matter more generally, though, we might want to ask a few rhetorical questions. How does the site or "pivot point" of work get overdetermined? Who gets to do this work, and who or what is "ordered" by it? When, where, or with whom does work stop and leisure begin? As Snyder himself seems to argue in "Marinan," we must question the forces that "drive" us to work hard and prompt us to spend hard-earned money on objects symbolizing freedom and leisure. To answer each question, we need to examine the ways in which objects of leisure and spaces of freedom get constructed as such.

Gendered contours of work and leisure spaces are evident in "After Work." In this poem, Snyder takes a break from his labors, just as he does in "The Spring" (BC 10) and "A Walk" (BC 11), two better-known poems from the "Far West" section. The difference, in this case, is that Snyder is no longer in the company of male coworkers. Neither is he totally alone. Other than the title, no reference is made to the work that Snyder has just completed. Instead, we encounter the poet in what is ostensibly a space of relaxation:

The shack and a few trees
float in the blowing fog

I pull out your blouse,
warm my cold hands
    on your breasts.
you laugh and shudder
peeling garlic by the
    hot iron stove.
bring in the axe, the rake,
the wood

we'll lean on the wall
against each other
stew simmering on the fire
as it grows dark
    drinking wine. (BC 22)

At first glance this appears to be a harmless scenario, pleasurable for all involved. In a certain sense, the situation here resembles the one Snyder mentioned in the "Logging 9" section of *Myths & Texts*, when on a weekend leave from his job as a choker-setter at Warm Springs he enjoyed a warm bath and hours of lovemaking with his "girl" (MT 11). Regarded from a feminist perspective, however, this poem betrays an overdetermined distinction between gender roles.

In the second verse paragraph, woman is confused with hearth, the surface of her body a sensual substitute for the stove's warmth. The heat she generates comes directly from her labors, which continue over the stove even as the poet's cold hands search her body. Essentially, he seeks to transform her workspace into a lair of leisure before her work is done. To the extent that her work functions as a pivot point in this rustic cabin, it is less as a point of agency than a point of capitulation allowing a male to cease his work and begin his play. As indicated by memoirists such as Carolyn Cassady and Hettie Jones and by literary critics such as Maria Damon and Michael Davidson, this distinction between female work and male leisure was routinely fixed yet conveniently obfuscated in the annals of Beat literature. In the bohemian enclaves of New York and San Francisco, Damon explains, Beat women "hung out, married, cohabited, eloped, drank, drugged and held it together. In short, they did everything the men did in addition to childbearing and domestic 'duties' which, in accord with the tribal ideology of the movement, took on a positive aura."[62] This gendered dichotomy between work and leisure, clearly evident in "After Work," would take on a rather different dimension for Snyder once he encountered the native women of Asia.

In *The Back Country*, women often take turns as mnemonic presences or philosophic guides. They provide Snyder with an additional means of knowledge, though in fulfilling this role they rarely relinquish their primary role as objects of affection. As might be expected, pitfalls and power struggles crop up repeatedly. But in the "Far West" section, at least, such difficult instances are usually regarded as nothing more than temporary roadblocks on the path to enlightenment. "For the Boy Who Was Dodger Point Lookout Fifteen Years Ago," the poem that brings the "Far West" section to a close, stands as a case in point. This poem presents beautiful images of the Pacific Northwest throughout its story of loss, regret, and the compensatory power of memory. In a headnote to this poem, Snyder recalls a backpacking trip that he took with his first wife, Alison Gass, in the Olympic Mountains, along the Elwha River, in 1950. "Hiking alone down the Elwha from Queets basin, these years later," he explains, "brings it back" (BC 31). David Wyatt notes that the poem is rather Wordsworthian in spirit, for like "Tintern Abbey" it "brings back the memory of happiness in a beloved place" and attests to the writer's "own capacity for storing the moment away."[63]

In the opening lines of "Dodger Point," Snyder looks down from a distant rise to describe a campsite, a provisional domestic space set up in the wilderness. From this "perch," he catches sight of Alison in a snowmelt pond, "half-stoopt bathing like / Swan Maiden, lovely naked, / ringed with alpine fur and / gleaming snowy peaks." To the extent that Alison takes on the features of the mythological creature Snyder studied in *He Who Hunted Birds*, she blends in with the landscape: her hair becomes ringed with alpine fur, and her breasts become snowy mountain peaks. Suddenly, Snyder turns to behold someone else occupying the perch on which he stands. At this point, the syntax shifts from a conjugal "we" to an even more intimately addressed "you," then to another "we." Alison fades into the background as the poet confronts this unnamed presence in the mountains:

> . . . We
> had come miles without trails,
> you had been long alone.

We talked for half an hour up
there above the foaming creeks
and forest valleys, in our
world of snow and flowers.

I don't know where she is now;
I never asked your name.
In this burning, muddy, lying,
blood-drenched world
that quiet meeting in the mountains
cool and gentle as the muzzles of
three elk, helps keep me sane. (BC 31)

In the final verse paragraph, the pronoun "she" probably refers to Alison, her whereabouts unknown to her ex-husband all these years later. Curiously, neither the name nor the gender of the third being is divulged, though the title of the poem implies that it is a "boy" working as a fire lookout, a profession Snyder would take up two years later. All we know for sure is that the poet's half-hour congress with this mysterious mountain presence prompts him to ignore the marital bliss he had been describing just moments beforehand. Reading the poem through, one wonders whether, after his meeting with the unnamed being in the "world of snow and flowers," the poet now equates his marriage with other fleeting entities in the "burning, muddy, lying, / blood-drenched world," the samsara world from which the Buddhist seeks escape. Although it is true that Snyder sought similar escape from a "burning world" at the end of *Myths & Texts*, in "Dodger Point" and other poems in *The Back Country* we should notice that his escapes are more likely to involve human intermediaries. Granted a recollection in tranquility, Snyder realizes that one of these guides provides a "cool and gentle" form of companionship as well as a way of thinking that keeps him sane.

The intersections of gender, work, landscape, and memory take on added importance in the "Far East" and "Kali" sections, as Snyder begins to record his travels in Asia. As he acclimates himself to foreign cultures and the rigors of Buddhist training, the poet discovers that the presence of exotic and mysterious women grants him a better understanding of his place in the world. Accordingly, he continues to make human geography the driving force of *The Back Country*'s cultural message.

Far East

When Snyder crossed the Pacific in 1956, Orientalist imagination confronted Asian reality. Suddenly, a Western poet versed in Asian traditions encountered an Eastern population that regarded *him* as the bearer of a culture they deemed exotic. Snyder's acculturation process during his first months in Kyoto was not always smooth. The few Japan poems included in *Riprap* show him to be searching for an appropriate lyric register, while the open letters he published in the *Evergreen Review* and *Chicago Review*, together with the personal letters he sent to friends, show his initial frustration with Japanese society. "When I first went to Japan, I thought it was going to be like the Pacific Northwest," Snyder admitted in an interview conducted in the 1980s. "I was amazed at how different it was. It's 180 degrees opposite in a way."[64] In the "Far East" section, Snyder records events that transpired during his second, more extended stint in Japan, from 1958 to 1964. In this section Snyder's poetic tone is far more measured, his assessments of San Francisco Beat culture more humble, and his portraits of Japanese people more sympathetic and complex. By this juncture he was urging Phil Whalen, whom he had originally advised not to bother coming to Japan, to "rob a drug peddler and come over here."[65]

In "Far East," Snyder is concerned with the reception he receives as an American in an Asian nation ravaged by war. The section begins with a beautiful and heartfelt poem, "Yase: September," which takes as its subject "old Mrs. Kawabata," the owner of the house Snyder rented in a northern suburb of Kyoto. Although Mrs. Kawabata shows herself to be adept in practical matters (during one stretch, she cuts down twice as many spike weeds as does the much younger Snyder), it is her compassionate side that attracts the poet's notice. In the final lines of the poem, Snyder recalls that "out of a mountain / of grass and thistle / she saved five dusty stalks / of ragged wild blue flower / and put them in my kitchen / in a jar" (BC 35). Here, after all the pain that America and Japan have inflicted during the Pacific War, is a makeshift garland offered to a Western poet trying to live the contemplative life in Asia.

In other poems, though, the Japanese regard Snyder with the same curiosity the Beats regarded Asians back in the States. In "The Public Bath," Snyder's awkward status as foreigner is exposed quite literally. In the midst of listing the folks he sees in the steamy bathhouse—a baby boy who without warning "inscrutably pees," the two daughters getting scrubbed by their father, a pubescent girl who is bashful about her "little points of breasts," an old woman who is "too fat and too old to care," and old men whose shriveled bodies resemble those "tumbled on beaches" in wartime newsreel footage— Snyder realizes that he, too, is on display: "getting dressed, in the mirror, / the bath girl with a pretty mole and a / red skirt is watching me / am I / different?" (BC 41). His knowledge of Japanese language and culture aside, Snyder was, in fact, markedly different. To the Japanese, he was not only a Westerner but also a symbol of America's unique brand of rugged individualism. Hisao Kanaseki, a Japanese professor of American literature, recalls that Snyder was not one of the "*gaijin* poet maudit types" to which the Kyoto community had grown wearily accustomed in the 1950s, but rather an "educated lumberjack" or "redskin" who embodied American vibrancy.[66] An exotic specimen in his own right, Snyder attracted a good deal of attention, much of it unwanted. "The Japanese newspapers have been bugging me lately to take pictures & write articles on the queer foreigner who lives in the country," Snyder complains to Whalen in a 1960 letter.[67]

As noted earlier in this chapter, Snyder also attracted the notice of Western males on the Kyoto scene. At times, bonding rituals took place amid the company of women, especially in hostess bars. In these locations, Asian women became the pivot point for male congregation and play. As Anne Allison acknowledges in *Nightwork*, her detailed study of Japan's "water trade," hostesses or "bar girls" are not prostitutes. Their task, rather, is to provide pleasure to several men at the same time, making each of them feel comfortable in front of his male peers. After offering drinks to the men assembled at a particular table, a hostess will usually steer talk toward suggestive sexual topics and will occasionally allow the men to touch her body. While it is possible that a rendezvous may be arranged outside the club, no sustained sexual contact actually takes place inside the hostess bars. In fact, sexual liaisons are far less likely to be arranged in clubs that employ the most desirable women. "What characterizes the hostess and differentiates her service from that offered by others in the *mizu shobai* [water trade]," Allison explains, "is that her medium of service is primarily talk. The job of the hostess, as both speaker and listener, is to make customers feel special, at ease, and indulged. Or, as one Japanese man told me, the role of the hostess is to make a man 'feel like a man.'"[68]

In correspondence with friends, Snyder shared bawdy anecdotes about his visits to hostess bars and other places of masculine pleasure. One letter from Snyder to Whalen mentions "a night of crawling on bar-girls." In another letter, mailed from sea, Snyder speaks of being "befuddled with shoreside amusements" at "dockside bar-girl and jukebox scenes" in Naha, Okinawa. Snyder also tells Whalen about "making all the Tokyo scenes," including the hostess bar circuit: "It's a place that would drive Ginsberg into a delirium of pleasure, so many alleys & bars & all varieties of sex."[69] In other letters and journals, though, Snyder assumes a far more sober tone, for he seems to have realized that the majority of bar girls and other "leisure workers" are simply playing a role, and nothing more, in order to provide for their destitute families. "The language & spirit of Bar girls is nothing vulgar & limited to their jobs—simply the personality (& very pleasant) of country girls," he notes in an April 1957 journal.

Sadly, Snyder suspects that these otherwise innocent girls are succumbing to the misogynist dictates of Japan's male-dominated social sphere. Kyoto's bar section "is a strange world," Snyder tells future wife Joanne Kyger in a 1959 letter. "Most all the bars have hostesses (young chicks who serve you and talk to you) because Japanese men don't take wives or girl friends out drinking, but go drinking to talk to other (prettier) girls." In a journal entry from August 1957, Snyder praises his friend Will Petersen for pointing out the bitter irony of "wives working as part-time whores to earn money to give their husbands to go to whore-houses." At the same time, Snyder knew that water trade hostesses could be ruthless when it came to business dealings. A note in Snyder's 1958 journal repeats one no-nonsense line he recalls hearing from a bar girl: "You have money, I like you too much. You no have money, *sayanora* no sweat."[70] Little wonder, then, that in an early section from *Mountains and Rivers without End* titled "Three Worlds, Three Realms, Six Roads," Snyder explains that one of the "Things to Do Around Kyoto" is to "Get buttered up by bar girls, pay too much" (MR 29).

In *The Back Country*, Snyder introduces readers to Japan's *mizu shobai* underworld in "March," part of a long poem entitled "Six Years," a chronological compression of his six-year stay in Japan that he arranged in calendar format. The thirteen sections of "Six Years" (Snyder adds an "envoy" after the twelfth month) alternate between scenes of working and scenes of leisure. Several sections show Snyder performing chores around the Buddhist monastery between meditation periods. In "March," however, he is clearly cut loose, for we find him eating "Korean food," visiting an "okinawan awamori bar," drinking "white doboroku," and pissing "against the slab posts of highways / overhead." Significantly, a "bar girl girl-friend" is added to this list of Asian delights. According to Katsunori Yamazato, "March" describes one of Snyder's last nights in Japan before he left for a nine-month stay in America. Working with Snyder's unpublished journals, Yamazato is able to determine that the poet went into Tokyo's freewheeling Shinjuku district with Nanao Sakaki and two other Japanese friends, Mamoru Kato and Tetsuo Nagasawa, on 21 March 1964 for a night of partying. Yamazato downplays the sexual overtones evident in "March," preferring to concentrate on Snyder's exploration of East Asia's "marginalized cultures," epitomized by his friendship with members of Sakaki's "tribe," his visits to Korean and Okinawan eating establishments, and his enjoyment of cheap liquor and peasant food like raw cow's womb.

Still, I cannot help but think that "March," with its emphasis on the pleasure one seeks after a period of hard labor, ends up blurring the distinction between female work and male leisure. I wonder, for instance, not just about the fun the men were having on this particular March night, but also about the plight of the one woman mentioned in this poem: the "bar girl girl-friend with a silver trinket cup / hung on a neck chain." After determining that this bar girl was Kato's girlfriend, Yamazato would have us believe that Snyder, in saying that "she, gives us, / all beer free," is simply acknowledging her "gesture of generosity and friendship," and not, as I have argued on an earlier occasion, mimicking her speech in halting pidgin English. Yamazato is probably right on this score. But what about the other male customers in the bar? For them, nothing comes for free. Of course, the bar girl is in an even worse position, since she must spend her working hours buttering up these men with false gestures of generosity and friendship in an attempt to get them to spend more money on their leisure activities. By the end of the night, I suspect that the "silver trinket cup hung on a neck chain" will become this working girl's albatross, its weight attributable to the amount to which she allows male libido to overspill its brim. Eventually, Snyder came to the same realization. Not for nothing did he refer to female "entertainers" in his journal as "objects of a mass unpersonal desire."[71]

Even if Yamazato had not provided the precise date for the episode described in "March," the mere mention of Nanao Sakaki, whom Snyder did not meet until 1962, proves that the poet continued to visit hostess bars after Joanne Kyger arrived in Japan in February 1960. The story of the Snyder-Kyger courtship points to some of the disparities plaguing gendered relationships in the San Francisco Renaissance, especially those relating to issues of movement and travel. One of the most promising New American Poets to be left out of the famous anthology edited by Donald Allen, Kyger met Snyder on the North Beach poetry reading circuit in 1958, when Snyder returned from Japan to spend nine months in San Francisco. "I was part of a group of young writers clustered around the poets Robert Duncan and Jack Spicer," Kyger tells Beat biographer Brenda Knight. "Gary came to our Sunday poetry group and read from *Myths & Texts* sitting cross-legged on a table with Jack Spicer sitting cross-legged under the table. 'Do you like this Boy Scout poetry?' Spicer challenged me. I did indeed, very much."[72] Snyder was involved with two other girlfriends at the time, but his attraction to Kyger grew strong, in part because he thought he might help her realize her full potential as a poet. In a November 1958 journal entry, Snyder postulated that, more than anything, Kyger "needs a solid lover from outside to cut the foolish shrieking of her life down so her great perceptive self will make it cool." A month later, the two poets were expressing their love for one another, with Snyder noting in his journal that their relationship evoked the mysteries one usually finds in a Zen koan.[73]

Upon his return to Japan in February 1959, Snyder exchanged letters frequently with Kyger, confessing in correspondence from April 1959 that he missed her but maintaining all the same that "it was right for me to come back here, & from here I must go like an arrow with a single hand." Kyger, for her part, told Snyder about having recently received a warning from Lew Welch: "Gary is a Serious student of Zen and it is something that he has *Got* to do." As the date grew near for their overseas reunion, Snyder himself warned Kyger about the single-minded dedication demanded of Buddhist adepts. In a letter sent to Kyger on Halloween 1959, Snyder apologizes for having a one-night stand with a Japanese "girl," but wonders whether, "much more than my sexiness . . . you aren't going to have a hard time accepting my ascetic habits of Zen study & book-reading & day-long quiet thinking and writing."[74]

Kyger wed Snyder three days after her arrival in Asia, having been forced to do so by Ruth Fuller Sasaki, who would not allow cohabitation at Ryosen-an without a marriage certificate. Less than two weeks into the marriage, Kyger wrote in her journal that she felt "trapped."[75] According to Phil Yampolsky, Kyger "had great trepidation about the proposed union and was outraged that Mrs. Sasaki insisted that they be married at once." Kyger seems to have had an even tougher time acclimating herself to a foreign culture. In their overseas correspondence from 1959, Snyder had advised Kyger to prepare herself for Japan by reading certain books, such as Edward Conze's *Buddhism*, fearing that she would otherwise "arrive as uninformed & goggle-eyed as some illiterate Texas corporal's wife."[76] By 1960, Snyder had long since worked through his own acculturation difficulties, but for Kyger the shock of Japan was very real, with gender disparities vying with unfamiliar aspects of Buddhist culture as the leading causes of her discomfort.

"Joanne was handsome, blonde, and tall, conscious of how greatly she differed from Japanese women, terrified of the thought of going to a public bath to be stared at, self-conscious of her inability to converse in Japanese," Yampolsky remembers. "Gary was not the most tolerant of persons when judging the behavior of others. He was far too demanding, too insistent on requiring conformity to Japanese customs, too much away during his Zen practice. It was not a marriage for which a prognosis of durability could be made."[77] Matters were probably not helped when Snyder took Kyger into Kyoto's hostess bars, including Minge Place, House without a Master, and Pepe le Moko, described by Kyger as a place where "tossled girls wear shorty nightgowns, a small place with the feeling of a clothes closet." The appearance of a tall Western woman in such a place was unusual, to put it mildly. "All the girls cluster around me in curiosity," Kyger wrote in her journal.[78]

In a letter sent to Phil Whalen two months after Kyger arrived in Kyoto, Snyder speaks about his wife's intermittent unhappiness and about his repeated attempts to immerse her more deeply in Japanese culture. "Misses J. Elizabeth alternately stomps her foot & wishes she was back in San Francisco," he writes. "We have had numerous trips about the local countryside to eat dinner w/ friends & observe festivities such as the *mizu-tori* rite at Nara last weekend. She does not yet have, however, much actual interest in or curiosity about the country. I trust & hope that will come later."[79] Over time, Kyger began to meet her husband's rigorous expectations, despite her growing dismay with other expatriate wives, who she believed were subservient to the bohemian patriarchy.[80] In *The Back Country*, for instance, Snyder recounts pleasurable trips the couple took through the Japanese countryside. In "A Volcano in Kyushu" (BC 43), Snyder depicts a March 1963 trip to Nagasaki, during which he and Kyger braved overcrowded sightseeing buses in order "to view bare rock, brown grass, / space, / sulphury cliffs, streakt snow." At first, Snyder describes this land formation as "rimrock," but by the end of the poem he becomes aware of the harrowing atomic crater, no doubt because the "mouth-twisted middle age man" who wears "blue jeans, check shirt, [and] silver buckle" while inspecting the crevice is a dead ringer for J. Robert Oppenheimer. The couple's salient position in the postwar Pacific Rim landscape is highlighted again in "The Manichaeans," a poem in which Snyder and Kyger turn away from the endless trauma of the samsara world, almost as Matthew Arnold wishes to do at the end of "Dover Beach," with the notable difference that these young American poets prefer Asian role models: "We shall sink in this heat / of our arms / Blankets like rock-strata fold / dreaming as / Shiva and Shakti / And keep back the cold" (BC 83).

Among the other Japanese adventures Snyder describes in "Six Years," Kyger figures prominently in the July, August, and September sections. "July" describes a hike, with the lovers "kicking through sasa / bear grass bamboo" and gazing distantly toward a beach, where a bare-breasted woman picks up seashells. "August" is similarly picturesque in its description of a harbor scene at nightfall. It is "September," however, which provides the most intimate portrait of the couple. Recalling a journey taken on an overloaded motorcycle along a precarious stretch of coastal highway, Snyder depicts himself as the fearless navigator and Kyger as the dutiful backseat rider:

> Rucksack braced on board, lashed tight on back,
> sleeping bags, map case, tied on the gas tank
> sunglasses, tennis shoes, your long tan in shorts
> north on the west side of Lake Biwa
> Fukui highway still being built,
> > crankcase bangd on rocks—
> > > pusht to the very edge by a blinded truck
> > I saw the sea below beside my knee:
> you hung on and never knew how close.

The indented typography of lines five through seven faithfully reenacts the motorcycle's drift onto the shoulder of the highway, dangerously close to the edge of the sea cliff. Snyder comes across as a gentlemanly protector, for he never tells his wife about their perilous predicament. Instead, the young Americans continue to enjoy their idyllic retreat in the Japanese countryside:

> In Fukui found a ryokan cheap
> > washt off each other's dust by the square wood tub

ate dinner   on worn mats
        clean starcht yukata
        warm whisky with warm water,
all the shoji open, second floor,
        told each other
what we'd never said before, ah,
        dallying on mats
            whispering sweat
        cools our kissing skin—

next morning rode the sunny hills, Eihei-ji,
got the luggage rack arc-welded
back through town and to the shore,
    miles-long spits and dunes of pine

and made love on the sand (BC 64)

In no other description do Snyder and Kyger seem so happy. A private bath at the *ryokan* (inn) anoints the couple and frees them of their secrets. This bathing experience, infinitely more comfortable than the public bath experiences both were forced to endure back in Kyoto, serves as a prelude for the salt-water dip they will probably take after their roll in the sand, one day later. The closing image of the couple making love by the edge of the Japan Sea represents a natural (albeit highly romanticized) form of Pacific Rim communion. Snyder would capture this elemental confluence of the senses even more explicitly in the "Regarding Wave" poems he dedicated to his third wife, Masa Uehara, and again in family poems like "The Bath" (in *Turtle Island*). For Kyger, though, charged moments like these were not enough to sustain a failing marriage. By 1964, she had left Snyder to return to America. Phil Whalen was the only person who showed up to meet her on the Oakland docks.[81]

Joanne Kyger is not the only woman Snyder mentions by name in "Far East." A beautiful and haunting sequence entitled "Four Poems for Robin" stands as a poignant reminder of how women, landscape, and memory exist together in Snyder's lyric economy. This sequence takes as its subject Robin Collins, one of Snyder's girlfriends at Reed College. Although Snyder's Lambert Street housemate J. Michael Mahar claims that his friend's relationships with women at Reed were characterized by "a lot of bravura and not much sentiment," he notes that "Robin was the exception. She was the essence of myth and legend—lean of leg, sensitive, intelligent, and delicate in matters of the heart. She came very close to Gary but then she withdrew, and it was a very long time before Gary could accept what had happened. Perhaps she sensed his underlying fear of emotional involvement with women, a feeling he never expressed in words but which was somehow implicit in the fleeting nature of his other relationships and in his celebration of sex for its own sake."[82] Contrary to Mahar's final assertion, "Four Poems for Robin" shows Snyder admitting to his fear of emotional involvement, albeit years after the couple's breakup, which occurred when both were still in college. Perhaps Snyder just needed some time before he was able to gain the proper perspective. Then again, he was clearly taken with this woman, and in letters and journals composed in Japan, he admits to still having dreams about her.

The tone of "Four Poems for Robin" is decidedly melancholic. Snyder is always alone in these poems, thinking back to earlier times and meditating on the course his life has taken. In the opening lines of the first Robin poem, "Siwashing it out once in the Siuslaw Forest," he remembers sleeping alone in the cold of the Washington wilderness and admits that he might not have shivered so much were it not for the presence of another memory, one that burned but did not warm the man whose body and mind were exposed to the elements:

> Hands deep   in my pockets
> Barely   able   to   sleep.
> I remembered   when we were in school
> Sleeping together   in a big warm bed
> We were   the youngest lovers
> When we broke up   we were still nineteen.
> Now our   friends are married
> You teach   school back east
> I dont mind   living this way
> Green hills   the long blue beach
> But sometimes   sleeping in the open
> I think back   when I had you. (BC 47)

Just as the split typography causes the poem's syntactical flow to become interrupted, as though by shivers, the disturbed consciousness permeating this passage suggests that neither Snyder's desired route of travel (he determinedly heads west, while Robin heads east) nor his natural way of living has healed the rift he feels deep in his heart.

The other Robin poems continue in the same vein. "A spring night in Shokoku-ji" and "An autumn morning in Shokoku-ji" were influenced by meditations Snyder did at that Japanese temple. Both juxtapose the Buddhist student's quest for inner calm with the one personal trauma he cannot shake. In these poems, as in the first, Snyder sleeps (or remembers sleeping) outside in chilly conditions, where he is exposed to raw emotions as well as raw weather. "All that I wanted then / Is forgotten now, but you," he confesses in the first of these poems (BC 47). In the second, his regret surfaces as a physical symptom: "Last night watching the Pleiades, / Breath smoking in the moonlight, / Bitter memory like vomit / Choked my throat" (BC 48). In the final Robin poem, "December at Yase," Snyder seems to suffer the same kind of regret Han-shan experienced on Cold Mountain once he realized the implications of taking the ascetic's lonesome path. Operating without an alter ego this time, Snyder looks back at the brief period he spent with Robin and takes stock of his present situation:

> I thought I must make it alone. I
> Have done that.
>
> Only in dream, like this dawn,
> Does the grave, awed intensity
> Of our young love
> Return to my mind, to my flesh.
>
> We had what the others
> All crave and seek for;
> We left it behind at nineteen.
>
> I feel ancient, as though I had
> Lived many lives.
>
> And may never now know
> If I am a fool
> Or have done what my
>   karma demands. (BC 49)

Like "Dodger Point," the Robin poems are representative of a genre David Wyatt calls "poetry of the second chance."[83] Quite noticeably, Snyder halts in the middle of his headlong quest for adventure and knowledge to consider the effects his actions have had on the women he has loved. The honesty with which Snyder looks back on his past relationships with women assumes even greater importance in the "Kali" section. Some of the women mentioned in "Kali" have familiar names: Robin Collins, Alison Gass, Joanne Kyger. But others are less familiar. They tend to be the native women of Asia—real and imagined, impoverished and deified—with whom Snyder had various forms of contact during his time overseas. Wyatt and Mahar are correct when they argue, each in his own fashion, that Snyder used a series of female substitutes to try to replace the one true love he had thought he had lost (Wyatt suggests that Snyder was trying to replace Alison Gass; Mahar suggests, more correctly it seems to me, that he was trying to replace Robin Collins). Curiously, though, neither critic makes specific reference to the Asian women Snyder met before his 1967 marriage to Masa Uehara, nor, for that matter, do most critics of Snyder's work. In "Kali," however, we find Snyder speaking straight-forwardly and rather powerfully about his encounters with this very popula-tion. Reading this section with a critical eye provides a strikingly different perspective on Snyder's Pacific Rim community-building.

Kali

With "Kali," Snyder's Pacific Rim odyssey takes a detour into India, in theme and temperament, though not always in reality. Some of the poems in this section were indeed based on a trip Snyder took to India in late 1961 and early 1962 with Joanne Kyger, Allen Ginsberg, and Peter Orlovsky. During this trip, Ginsberg and Snyder, who had planned a brief reading tour in addi-tion to their sightseeing activities, were recognized by some Indians and treated like stars. To their pleasant surprise, the travelers discovered that *Howl and Other Poems* and Kerouac novels were displayed prominently in a Madras bookstore. It was a true measure of how far the "new wind" of Beat culture had spread. Before long, Ginsberg was offering LSD to the Dalai Lama, Orlovsky was basking in the adoration of young Indian men, and middle-class Western tourists were coming up to Kyger to ask whether she knew a poet named Gary Snyder. In a poem entitled "October 29, Wednesday," Kyger speaks about the attention the male writers attracted. "The crowd follows Ginsberg and Snyder out on a quick / demonstration march thru the halls of a tall building out / into the gardens, their faces among the trees as little / Chinese sages grained into the wood," she writes. "As they are on their busy / way, as groups of people pour their respect and devotion to- / wards them. Pour, pour—they're busy drinking it up all day."[84] Evidently, the East was as curious about Western poets as they were curious about the East.

Back in America, members of the San Francisco counterculture also expressed a vivid interest in what was going on. Phil Whalen showed letters Snyder had sent him from India to Lew Welch, who reportedly "laughed and laughed." Whalen then wrote back to his far-flung friend and admitted his vicarious delight, telling him, "I'm enjoying your trip enormously."[85] Meanwhile, Lawrence Ferlinghetti tossed off an adulatory note to Ginsberg. "Your meeting [with Snyder] seems to be known all over the U.S., in the bookstore circuit," Ferlinghetti writes. "Everybody saying, 'Allen got to India to meet Gary yet?' Like some kind of International sorcerer swamis' conjunction."[86] Snyder further fed San Francisco's appetite for Asian exotica by publishing "A Journey to Rishikesh & Hardwar" (a travel essay, complete with photos of himself, Ginsberg, and Orlovsky) in Ferlinghetti's *City Lights Journal* in 1963 (reprinted in EHH 83–89). The mainstream press also caught wind of this Indian adventure, with *Esquire* dispatching a reporter to Benares to see whether Ginsberg and Orlovsky "might not have a message for the hipsters back home."[87]

Although the jacket copy for *The Back Country* states that Snyder's "Kali" section was "inspired by a trip to India and his reading of Indian religious texts, particularly those of Shivaism and Tibetan Buddhism," the section includes poems that he wrote before his trip to the Asian subcontinent was even planned. For this very reason, Snyder's fellow traveler Ginsberg admitted to some befuddlement when he read *The Back Country* for the first time, telling him, "I see how you're organizing psyche thematically, but it would be also interesting to see a chronological graph of these returns to the same places in the mind." Simultaneously downplaying and acknowledging the geographical and chronological impulses shaping this section, Snyder once told me that "Kali, the dark goddess, is wherever you find her. But I was brought up against her archetypal presence quite strongly in India."[88]

Who, we may ask, is Kali? She comes in many manifestations and is known as Shakti in the Tantric tradition, but most worshipers know her as the Indian goddess of rage and destruction. She is sometimes called the "Black Goddess." Renowned as the consort of Shiva (another creator/destroyer), she has inspired cultlike devotion and fear for centuries. Interestingly, there is an elaborate temple dedicated to her in Calcutta, the city where Snyder and Kyger made landfall on the subcontinent. In his *Masks of God* series, Joseph Campbell provides a vivid if somewhat bloodcurdling description of the sacrifices made in this goddess's name: "In the temples of the Black Goddess Kali, the terrible one of many names, 'difficult to approach' (*durga*), whose stomach is a void and so can never be filled and whose womb is giving birth forever to all things, a river of blood has been pouring continuously for millenniums, from beheaded offerings, through channels carved to return it, still living, to its divine source."[89] Snyder uses much the same imagery as Campbell when, in an epigraph to the "Kali" section, he portrays a black, naked woman, with four arms, holding a sword and laughing over the decapitated corpse of one of her victims.

Huston Smith gives us an even better clue as to why Snyder might have tapped into Hindu and Tantric traditions while selecting poems for this section of *The Back Country*. According to this renowned scholar of world religions, Hinduism chooses not to suppress human desires or pleasures. Instead, it allows those desires and pleasures to run their course. At a certain point, we realize that pleasure is not the only thing, or even the most important thing, that we want out of life. "Sooner or later," Smith explains, "everyone wants to be more than a kaleidoscope of private, momentary pleasures however exquisite and subtle." Hinduism is extremely patient, Smith explains. It waits until we decide for ourselves to give up the pleasures of the body and the knowledge of the conscious mind; only then does it provide us with the tools for plumbing our subconscious, where the key to our totality lies. Before this time of decision, Hindu texts and artworks, as well as those in the Tantric (Vajrayana) tradition of Tibetan Buddhism, offer hedonistic suggestions for how to revel in samsara addictions and maximize worldly enjoyments. "Wine, flesh, fish, woman, and sexual congress: / These are the fivefold boons that remove all sin," according to the *Syama Rahasya*, a Tantric scripture. In the devotional traditions of later Hinduism and early Buddhism, Smith reminds us, "the Path of Renunciation comes *after* the Path of Desire."[90]

As I have argued in my discussion of the "Far West" and "Far East" sections, it is quite likely that Snyder was rethinking his own attitudes toward the pleasures of the body in the late 1950s and 1960s. In "Kali," those reeval-uations take on a decidedly darker and scarier tone, in part because Tantric Buddhism is far more theatrical, passionate, and confrontational than the Zen traditions Snyder had been studying up to that point. But the poet's self-questioning also appears to have been influenced by his encounter with a dif-ferent Asian population. Indeed, after taking a look at the long, journal-style letter Snyder sent to his sister Anthea (which was subsequently published under the title "Now India" in Clayton Eshelman's *Caterpillar* magazine and eventually as a book, *Passage through India*), we see how his journey to South Asia enhanced his understanding of human geography.

Leaving Japan on the *Cambodge*, a French freighter, Snyder and Kyger set sail for India in December 1961 and returned to Japan in May 1962. Their route took them along the western rim of the Pacific. Skirting the southern portion of the Japanese archipelago, they sailed through the Formosa Strait to Hong Kong, coasted past Vietnam, rounded the corner of Southeast Asia at Singapore, and exited the Pacific as they continued westward through the Straits of Malacca and into the Indian Ocean. As if to signal their entry into another cultural realm, the Sri Lankan women traveling aboard the *Cam-bodge* exchanged their Western garments for traditional saris once they crossed into the Bay of Bengal. Exiting the Pacific Rim occasioned a sea change in Snyder as well. "You don't get nothing for sheer friendliness in these parts," he wrote soon after his arrival in South Asia (PTI 12). While he was in Bombay, Snyder noted that "bars, sake stalls, teahouses, young pretty girl hostess, all that sort of thing—which exists in limited quantity in India . . . is much more degraded and dirty than it is in Japan." By the end of the trip, though, he was able to claim that India, for all its rudeness and hostility, had "a kind of honesty . . . which is ultimately lacking in Japan" (PTI 96).

Just as the passage of time allowed Snyder to look back on romantic rela-tionships with greater clarity, his passage to India, a space "off the Rim," pro-vided him with the geographic distance necessary to reevaluate his literary community's Pacific Rim desires. The Beat invocation of Asia emerged in hindsight as a pale reflection of the original truths he was now able to see firsthand in the cradle of Buddhist civilization. More pertinent to my study is the fact that the archetypal presence of Kali caused Snyder to think that purgation and exorcism were necessary if the "Great Subculture" he was envisioning hoped to avoid the pitfalls plaguing mainstream societies around the globe. "It is necessary to look exhaustively into the negative and demonic potentials of the Unconscious," Snyder wrote in a 1967 essay entitled "Why Tribe." "By representing these powers—symbolically acting them out—one releases himself from these forces" (EHH 115).

In *The Back Country*, Snyder's symbolic performance of demonic energies is most clearly evident in the poems that look back to relationships with women of the Pacific Rim region. Besides the poem Snyder dedicates to Kyger ("The Manichaeans"), two more poems about Alison Gass ("Alysoun") and Robin Collins ("Robin") make their way into this section, the latter of which shows Snyder sounding a familiar refrain, as he regrets "how many times I've / hitchhiked away" (BC 75). In addition to considering the Western women from whom Snyder runs, however, I want to draw attention to the Asian women toward whom he runs, specifically those on the western side of the Rim. We already know from reading the "Far East" section that Snyder frequented Japan's hostess bars. What we discover in "Kali," though, is a more detailed consideration of what sex meant for women of the Asia-Pacific region. Evidently, something prompted Snyder to think more deeply about the suffering he had witnessed during his travels and to reevaluate his rambunctious engagement with the material world.

In "Kali," the bohemian poet's ecstatic representations of sexuality are mysteriously troubled. Sexual partners are weighed down by self-consciousness, remorse, sometimes even boredom. In poems such as "How Many More Times" (BC 103) and "Go Round" (BC 105)—with its oversexed merry-go-round analogy, in which the "puberty devi" who rides the "plunging donkey" is watched by her "knowing" yet taciturn mother—the feeling is of ennui rather than sensual delight. Shame is another predominant theme. While sex is still occasionally praised as a spiritual elixir in poems such as "Night" and "Maya," Snyder is now more apt to acknowledge the remorse that sometimes follows pleasurable encounters. "North Beach Alba" (BC 75), an early San Francisco poem Snyder places in this section, revisits the bewilderment he felt upon "waking half-drunk in a strange pad." In another poem, "Lying in Bed on a Late Morning" (BC 99), Snyder admits to waking up with "a new girl beside me, / I hardly know." He is able to "smile the smile" that helps him consummate casual sexual relationships, but he is unable to escape the feelings of guilt that arise when he considers the effects his actions have had on another person. Snyder's awkwardness is more painfully evident in "Kyoto Footnote," a poem that contains a stilted conversation with an Asian prostitute:

She said she lived in Shanghai as a child
And moved to Kobe, then Kyoto, in the war;
While putting on her one thin white brassiere.
She walked me to the stair and all the girls
Gravely and politely said take care,
  out of the whorehouse into cool night air. (BC 81)

Like all too many Asian women, this prostitute has suffered a series of traumas
meted out by men. Japanese military men invaded China in the 1930s; American military men bombed Japan's coastal cities in the 1940s; Eastern and Western men alike sexually exploited poor women in Japan, even after prostitution
was declared illegal in the 1950s. Putting on her "one thin white brassiere," the
Shanghai prostitute leads Snyder past a group of working girls. Their wish that
he "take care" seems highly ironic in the wake of all they have suffered.

Snyder's freewheeling movements along the Pacific frontier have been
prompted by his quest for religious instruction and cultural knowledge as well
as pleasure, whereas the Shanghai prostitute's diasporic travels along the
western rim of the Pacific have been conditioned by basic matters of subsistence. The long route she has taken to the Kyoto whorehouse foreshadows
more recent journeys undertaken by Thai and Filipino women, many of them
imported by the Japanese leisure industry to fill the void left by Japanese
women once they raised their standard of living and left this kind of work. In
both cases, cultural critic Neferti Tadiar has argued, the poor women of Asia
become concubines shared by American and Japanese men. The awkwardness of their valediction in the Kyoto whorehouse says implicitly what these
women do not dare to say explicitly, namely that their travels in the region
make possible someone else's Pacific Rim fantasy, not their own.[91] As Doreen
Massey, David Palumbo-Liu, and other scholars working in the fields of
human geography and diaspora studies like to point out, it is not only one's
membership in a geographic community but also the possibility of moving
freely within its boundaries that matters.

If the other poems of "Kali" are any indication, Snyder got the message
the Shanghai prostitute was trying to convey. In "To Hell with Your Fertility
Cult," for instance, we find Snyder casting a critical eye on the libidinal economy shaping today's Pacific Rim. Partially ventriloquized, this poem is even
more explicit and direct than "Kyoto Footnote" in its indictment of heartless
men who make special use of women in order to perpetuate their global

wanderings. In an impassioned diatribe, a woman whose body has been targeted as a generative void speaks back to a man responsible for such labels:

> To hell with your Fertility Cult, I
> never did want to be fertile,
> you think this world is just
> a goddamn oversize cunt, don't you? Everything
> crowding in and out of it like a railway
> terminal   and isn't that nice?
> all those people going on trips.
> well this is what it feels like, she said,
> —and knocked the hen off the nest, grabbed
> an egg and threw it at him, right in the face,
> the half-formed chick half clung, half slid
> half-alive, down over his cheekbone, around
> the corner of his mouth, part of it thick
> yellow and faintly visible bones and it drippt
> down his cheek and chin
> —he had nothing to say. (BC 73)

In his *Masks of God* series, Joseph Campbell draws upon the work of James Frazer, Heinrich Zimmer, and Sri Ramakrishna to list a number of precedents for the scene Snyder describes here. Frazer, for instance, recounts ceremonies held in honor of an Earth Mother during which women picked up clods of earth and flung them at retreating men, who were considered lucky to have escaped ritual sacrifice. Zimmer, for his part, explains why human birth, simply because it is the first trauma we suffer, is often invoked in primitive mythology as an archetype of transformation. To pay tribute to the experience of birth, Zimmer explains, several Hindu ceremonies involve the ritual reentry into the womb or the prostration of a male supplicant to a naked goddess. Importantly, though, the supplicant is not supposed to ask questions about the origin of this archetypal Mother if he wants to avoid her curse, which is powerful in the extreme. In her most dangerous manifestations, the Original Mother becomes a cannibal ogress, the most famous of which is the "Black One" named Kali. "She is the very pattern of the sow that eats her farrow," Campbell states, "life itself, the universe, which sends forth beings only to consume them." By the same token, Campbell asserts, citing

Ramakrishna, "'she is full of bliss.' All life, all moments, terminate in her insatiable maw; yet in this frightening return there is ultimately rapture for the hero who, in trust, can give himself—like the perfect king."[92]

Snyder was not the only Beat writer to express feelings of attraction and repulsion for India's fearsome fertility goddesses. Adopting a playful persona in an early poem titled "Souffle" (1957), Phil Whalen wrote, "I'm a genuine thug, I believe / in Kali the Black, the horrific aspect / the total power of Siva / absolute destruction / BUT it don't mean / What it looks like / and the description misleads."[93] Other Beats were not as equivocal. In his lesser-known novels, Jack Kerouac refers to "Mother Kali of ancient India . . . laughing as she dances on the dead she gave birth to" (in *Vanity of Duluoz*) and "Mother Maya . . . the magic henlayer without origin" (in *Tristessa*).[94] Allen Ginsberg, during his trip to India with Orlovsky, fixated on a wailing street beggar with twisted arms and legs, whom he called "Kali Ma." Furthermore, in a journal subheading entitled "Calcutta Graffiti," Ginsberg records the following lines: "Fuck Kali. Fuck all Hindu Goddesses. Because they are prostitutes."[95] Such comments clearly show the uneasy position that Kali occupied in the male Beat imagination.

What makes Snyder's depiction of the fertility goddess even more unsettling than those of his peers, however, is its graphic fixation on her vaginal cavity, the generative void that male travelers from around the world, despite the fact that they call themselves worshipers, end up using like a railway terminal. Admittedly, the void is a key component in Buddhism, since enlightenment is dependent upon the recognition of a spatial transparency or emptiness (*shunyata*) that links all sentient beings together. To reach the level of compassion demanded by Mahayana and Tantric forms of Buddhism, one must enter *shunyata*, expose samsara as a dream, and undergo a positive ascesis that allows one to rethink and improve one's relationships with other living beings. The question that arises, though, is why Snyder routinely links the void with the female body. Despite the uncanny overlap of such imagery in his work (see the "vagina dentata" myth cited in *Myths & Texts*, for example, or the erotic poems he would dedicate to Masa Uehara in *Regarding Wave*), Snyder insists that "*shunyata*, being without concepts, is without gender or geography."[96] In "Fertility Cult," however, not only is the void speaking back, it is speaking in the voice of a powerful woman. "To be a poet you have to be tuned into some of the darkest and scariest sides of your own nature," Snyder is on record as saying. "And for a male, the darkest and scariest is the destructive side of the female" (TRW 80).

Like Freud's neurotic male patients, whose fears of being buried alive in the earth were ameliorated by the fantasy of intrauterine existence, the male persona in "Fertility Cult" searches for contact with an exotic mother figure, but becomes frightened when an uncanny combination of female destruction and female creativity presses too closely, which is precisely when the feminine body is no longer bound by the Pacific Rim sex trade or by any symbolic economy coded as masculine.[97] By the time the goddess is done speaking, this man has egg on his face and is left with "nothing to say." As a Buddhist, we would expect Snyder to make better use of his confrontation with the void. But as a man expressing regret for his past relationships with real and imagined women, his encounter with the goddess probably scares the hell out of him. The whole experience renders eerily prescient Snyder's mock invitation to Whalen, offered in a 1954 letter in which he discusses the dangers of immersing oneself too deeply in Asian lore, to "come and lobotomize me before I split into two & begin a new universe with the female monster opposite."[98] By 1962, clearly, Snyder realized that certain gender tropes had gotten the better of him.

If "To Hell with Your Fertility Cult" suggests the ways in which Asian women have been symbolically manipulated in the fantasies of male travelers, "This Tokyo" examines with unrelenting acuity the spaces in First World Asia where they have been showcased as sex industry workers. Prophetic in its tone, the poem addresses the postmodern relationship between Japan and the United States, starting with the early years of the occupation but looking forward to the "marriage" that Tadiar believes characterizes their current relationship. The unfortunate result, Snyder says in "Dullness in February: Japan," a like-minded poem that he wrote about the same time, has been "the meeting / Of the worst of East and West" (LOITR 64). Behind the façade of an emerging Pacific Rim unity, apparently, there lurks a characteristically human capacity for destruction and the mistreatment of others:

Peace, war, religion,
Revolution, will not help.
This horror seeds in the agile
Thumb and greedy little brain
That learned to catch bananas
With a stick.

All human "concoction" and thought, he now realizes, have led to "this Tokyo":

This gaudy apartment of the rich.
The comfort of the U.S. for its own.
The shivering pair of girls
Who dyked each other for a show
A thousand yen before us men
—In an icy room—to buy their relatives
A meal.

The poem's final lines echo those in Wallace Stevens's "Sunday Morning," perhaps to show that the new chaos lurking on the Pacific Rim horizon far outstrips the "old chaos of the sun" described in that great modernist poem, but also to suggest that the new economic dependencies in the region are much more vicious than "the old dependency of day and night":

We live
On the meeting of sun and earth.
We live—we live—and all our lives
Have led to this, this city,
Which is soon the world, this
Hopelessness where love of man
Or hate of man could matter
None, love if you will or
Contemplate or write or teach
But know in your human marrow you
Who read, that all you tread
Is earthquake rot and matter mental
Trembling, freedom is a void,
Peace war religion revolution
Will not help. (BC 80–81)

In this relentlessly negative epiphany, first published in *The New American Poetry*, Snyder explores the material foundation of America's postmodern global fantasy. In this Asian capital, "which is soon the world," the United States has reconstructed in its image not a shining city on a hill, but rather a squalid claptrap edifice resting uneasily upon the same "earthquake rot" destroyed by U.S. bombing raids. Similar in its scope to "Vapor Trails" (BC 37)—a signature piece for the politically conscious Snyder in which he

espies "the air world torn" by the "white blossoming smoke of a bomb"—
"This Tokyo" implies that human folly threatens to match the earth's own
gap-producing prowess. Postmodern Asia is built on a "void" of dubious origin that masquerades as "freedom." At this point, Snyder realizes that both
he and his nation's military leaders must reevaluate their incommensurable
desire to return to a state of nothingness. "Tokyo is my fault too," he admitted in his journal two weeks after this poem was written.[99]

Snyder's mention of the women who "dyked each other for a show" is
significant in another context. After reviewing revelatory articles on the sex
trade written by Tadiar and Yayori Matsui, my best guess is that these women
are pawns in a burgeoning Pacific Rim pleasure economy, their residence in
the cosmopolitan city of Tokyo enabled solely by their degradation, their
movements along the Rim motivated by the cold facts of economic necessity, their ties to their previous place of residence (be it the Japanese hinterlands or another Asian nation) held firmly intact by virtue of the money
they must send back home. Such cruelty, pernicious enough in itself, is mag-
nified by the realization that their show becomes a pivot point around
which a new geographic community organizes itself. As Tadiar notes, an
increasing number of these sex industry workers were being imported from
places inside the Rim (especially the Philippines and Oceania), which tend
to be viewed rather condescendingly in official versions of Pacific Rim discourse as the watery void around which the Rim forms (in ex nihilo fashion).

Over the years, sex workers hailing from the interior Pacific have come to
signify a pleasurable gap, an oceanic reservoir, a site in which an excessive
desire for freedom and enjoyment is allowed to overspill the Rim's symbolic
economy. In "This Tokyo," the men who gather to watch the sex show probably want some reminder of the unfathomable depths out of which their brave
new Pacific world is being constructed. Of course, if the nothingness the
women represent were to press too closely, the scenario might resemble the
one in "Fertility Cult," and the men might run screaming. But we see that
the sex workers remain safely showcased. The goal in this pleasure economy is
thus the same goal Jacques Lacan ascribes to the "*jouissance* of transgression,"
which for the male patrons assembled in the icy room means treading very
close to the (female/oceanic) void without stepping over the edge.[100]

As Hortense Spillers has shown, any fantasy formation—be it "America"
in her projects or the "Pacific Rim" in my own—should be surveyed with an

eye trained toward the gendered or racial beings who "cut its border" and therefore delineate its character. Armed with her thesis, I am prompted to ask several questions. Who is included in the geographical community of the Pacific Rim, and who gets excluded? Who is thought to occupy an unintelligible position somewhere in the middle? Could it be that the Pacific Rim's borderless world is not so borderless? After all, as Christopher Connery reminds us, "for the Pacific Rim to exist, there must be differentiated regions that are off the rim, in stagnation or decline." Then, too, as Haunani-Kay Trask and other activist writers from Oceania have reminded us, official Rim discourse loves to figure such places as an Edenic backdrop, a Shangri-La made available for Western travelers on holiday, effectively stealing the culture of native peoples who call these places their home.[101]

Snyder may have come to a similar recognition as he composed and organized the sections of *The Back Country*. In "Kali," especially, he lays out the uneven playing field of human geography for all to see. Working in a revisionist mode and tapping into ancient religious practices as well as contemporary social conditions, Snyder discovers that his search for pleasure and meaning is often dependent on women who, as markers of an original nothingness, "cut the border" of Pacific Rim community. When the Shanghai prostitute walks him to the door of the whorehouse, when the fertility goddess speaks back, when the sex industry workers shiver during their show, the suddenly self-conscious poet acknowledges a situation he first noticed when the bar girl dangled her trinket cup in "Six Years: March," namely that the fantasy of the Rim makes use of a population it marginalizes in terms of race, class, gender, and geography. Ultimately, we should join Snyder in recognizing that this regional community's utopian understanding of itself is dependent upon native bodies it displaces, deploys, and enjoys as symptoms of its own unfathomable desires.

Back

"Back," the section that closes the circle on *The Back Country*'s cultural return, avoids the rigorous examinations of self and community that we find in "Kali." A few poems, such as "For the West" and "To the Chinese Comrades," are overtly political in their sentiments. These poems reflect Snyder's participation in demonstrations against the Vietnam War and in favor of free speech during his one-year stint as a lecturer at UC–Berkeley from 1964 to 1965 and edge closer to the politically charged writing he would include in *Earth House Hold* and *Turtle Island*. More often, though, "Back" is filled with free-floating poems describing women and California landscapes. Two poems in particular, "For the West" and "Beneath My Hand and Eye the Distant Hills, Your Body," indicate the direction Snyder's poetry would take in the opening sections of *Regarding Wave*. In their combinatory register of erotic bodies and landscapes, these poems move away from public space of human geography to consider the private space of family homestead and the ecological space of local bioregion.

An apt description of Snyder's "floating" return to America comes in "The Plum Blossom Poem" (BC 124), which describes a sailboat voyage on San Francisco Bay. As his boat slips west past Angel Island, the infamous Asian immigration station, and fights the strong currents near the Golden Gate, Snyder finds solace in a lover's arms: "We hold and caress each other / Where a world is yet unborn; / Long slow swells in the Pacific— / the land drifts north." The scenario here recalls the haven-making possibilities of "After Work," except that this poem is situated on the waters that separate the Pacific (Snyder's second home) from coastal California (his original home). Casting his gaze onshore for a change, Snyder notices (or remembers) that "Two plums below Buchanan street / on Vallejo / blow blossom petals / eastward down the walk." In a journal entry dated January 1959, roughly a month before he set sail for his second stint in Japan, Snyder mentions plum trees blossoming in Berkeley alongside his recent breakup with a woman named Erika (one of the two girlfriends Snyder had when he met Joanne Kyger in 1958), pausing later in this entry to meditate upon a "sense of distance, heart of journey . . . [the] gradual lowering of the north star as you travel south."[102]

In "The Plum Blossom Poem," Snyder assumes this traveler's perspective once again. Secure now in the arms of a new lover, or perhaps in a fond memory of Erika, he drifts along, recognizing that all direction in life is relative, and that his return trip to California leaves him feeling blessed. Interestingly, and not surprisingly, Joanne Kyger offers quite a different story of male homecoming in "The Odyssey Poems," a section from *The Tapestry and the Web*. In this allegorical sequence, composed between April and December 1964, the time during which Snyder returned to America, Kyger represents Odysseus as a bewildered hero in desperate need of female aid. Hence the arrival of "the morning venus," shown in Kyger's poem "lifting [Odysseus] asleep onto the land / he has returned to / and doesn't know where he is. / outside of San Francisco / the long paths and eucalyptus / are another country."[103] Whether this "venus" is meant to represent Kyger herself is difficult to say, given the lack of available archival documentation on the subject. What does seem probable, however, is Kyger's willingness to provide wry allegorical commentary on the ways in which Snyder and other "heroic" male travelers often rely upon the kindness of women to situate themselves, geographically and existentially, in "home" spaces the men do not know as well as they think they do.

In "For the West," Snyder's commentary on his temporary return to California moves beyond personal memories to address political concerns. In the following passage, he once again seems to be speaking from a location on the water while taking stock of his nation after a long absence:

> Ah, that's America:
> the flowery glistening oil blossom
>   spreading on water—
> it was so tiny, nothing, now it keeps expanding
> all those colors,
>   our world
>   opening inside outward toward us,
> each part swelling and turning
> who would have thought such turning;
> as it covers,
>   the colors fade.
> and the fantastic patterns
>   fade.
> I see down again through clear water. (BC 117)

A gasoline stain (masquerading as an "oil blossom") spreads rapidly, much as America in the global era spreads its symbolic colors across distant oceans and continents. Like Sherwin-Williams paint (whose manufacturing plant was conspicuously visible on the East Bay shoreline during those days), American colors "cover the earth," and yet, as today's antiglobalism demonstrators have persuasively argued, American cultural aggression too often fades from critical consciousness, dissolving into a transparent homogeneity that appears to be normal even as it threatens to destroy distinctive civilizations around the globe.[104] Snyder's poem claims that this homogenizing process occurs "inside out toward us," which is to say that it arises from a primordial outpouring from the cavities of the earth. Indeed, it appears likely that this communal "us" (or "U.S.") is radically dependent on open spaces (or oceanic voids) within which an affective global unity recognizes its original essence. Snyder is granted access to one of these spaces once he stares through clear ocean water, the limitless depths of which will not easily reflect diverse sets of images. Although I am postulating that Snyder is talking about American hegemony around the globe, he could just as well be referring to official Pacific Rim ideology, which often targets a mysterious, oceanic realm as the "s/pacific" space where nations from East and West discover their origin and fight for common interests.

In "Beneath My Hand and Eye the Distant Hills, Your Body," we find an erotic variation on this theme. In this poem, Snyder forsakes political commentary in order to trace the "swimming limits" of land and body:

What my hand follows on your body
Is the line. A stream of love
  of heat, of light,   what my
  eye   lascivious
      licks
  over, watching
  far snow-dappled Uintah mountains
Is that stream.
Of power.   what my
  hand curves over, following the line.
  "hip" and "groin"
Where "I"
  follow by hand and eye
  the swimming limit of your body.
As when vision idly dallies on the hills
Loving what it feeds on.

In this passage, Snyder would have us believe that his hand is remarkably well suited for following the line of a woman's body, his eye for following the line of a mountain. His disposition in such matters is nothing new. In a 1959 journal entry, for instance, Snyder looks back to his days on Crater Mountain Lookout in 1952 and remembers that he had posted a nude photo of an old girlfriend from Portland upon the glass walls of his cabin. The result, Snyder recalls, was an erotic juxtaposition of land and body, with "her nipple just poking Mt. Challenger, Mt. Sourdough by her thigh" (GSR 342). "Natural against natural, beauty," Snyder had originally scribbled in the pages of his "Lookout's Journal" back in 1952 (EHH 7).[105]

Some years later, in "Beneath My Hand and Eye," Snyder explains that this ability to fuse woman and landscape in his mind's eye ultimately allows him to constitute his identity, his "I." Reading the poem, we notice that this "I" is preceded by a directional marker ("Where"), which indicates a geographic orientation at the heart of any self-knowledge. As in "Fertility Cult," Snyder's quest for knowledge leads him to examine the "swimming limits" of a woman's body. His experience is much more pleasant this time, of course, in part because the landscape seems to buffer the impact of her unfamiliarity and sublimity. The hip of this woman traces the poet's overland route, whereas her groin marks the region of moist streams whence he came. The "snow-dappled Uintah mountains" euphemistically refer to this woman's breasts, much as "snowy globes" became a popular substitute for breasts in the *blason* tradition of early modern European poetry.[106] Taken together, these gendered images reveal both an erotic connection with an on-the-scenes lover and a pre-oedipal connection with mother earth. In each case, the visually oriented male poet is "Loving what [he] feeds on."

As the poem continues, the female presence is summoned more directly, though still in earthly terms:

As my hand feeds on you
  runs down your side and curls beneath your hip.
  oil pool; stratum; water—

What "is" within   not known
  but feel it
  sinking with a breath
  pusht ruthless, surely, down.

Beneath this long caress of hand and eye
  "we" learn the flower burning,
      outward, from "below." (BC 123)

As Snyder's hand curls under the curved contours of hill and hip, it reaches something moist (oil pool, stratum, water) and mysterious ("What 'is' within"). The scenario described here is not unlike the one that elicited Joanne Kyger's bemused journal entry in the early 1960s: "Gary says women are always associated with water, and holes are mystic entrances."[107] Because this affective region purportedly contains the primordial outpourings "we" all share, the singular "I" mentioned earlier in "Beneath My Hand and Eye" is suddenly rendered obsolete. No narcissistic reflection emanates from these pools, which retain their unfathomable depths and become the site of shared learning. All the same, the reader is left to wonder what the female subject of this poem would say about her being conflated with landscape and seascape in this way. Indeed, the poet here seems to be making the same mistake that elicited the outburst from the goddess in "Fertility Cult," since the female body has once again become the terrain male adventurers want to traverse as they plumb the mysteries of original community.

To a certain degree, "Across Lamarck Col" (BC 120), another contemporary *blason*, provides a counterweight to "Beneath My Hand and Eye." Judging by its tone, it seems to be another Robin poem, though the lover referred to here is never named. In the poem, Snyder laments the loss of this lover's natural resources: "A giving stream you give another / should have been mine." Faced with this predicament, he reverses the *blason* gaze to take a look at his own body: "[I see] myself as a stony granite face — / You giving him because an other." Evidently, Snyder has lost this lover because his stony body was not porous enough to soak up the "stream" of her giving. As a result, she has floated down the river, out of his life. He finds some recompense at the end of the poem, however, once he finds a new lover waiting in the wings: "I also now become another. / what I / Had not from you, for you, / with a new lover, / Give, and give, and give, and / take." According to David Wyatt's reading of this poem, "a pattern of behavior that Snyder has been reviewing as careless or evasive is here seen as potentially regenerative. The history of the poet's loves is a 'giving stream' in which the abiding force of what he is losing nevertheless sends up, like a wave, the possibility of future giving and taking."[108] In other words, Snyder realizes that his exposure to the "swimming limits" of Pacific Rim community does not mean that he must now refrain from enjoying America's natural riches or its women. On the contrary, his exposure to terror and regret in "Kali" probably gives him a greater appreciation of the natural communion he searches for in "Back," an appreciation he invites others to share. This trend would continue as Snyder wrote the love poems of *Regarding Wave*.

An Economy of Exposure

In the 1950s and 1960s, Snyder and the various communities to which he belonged were constantly exposing themselves to new limits as part of their ongoing effort to understand and realize their desires. In San Francisco, Snyder (as Han-shan) was thought to embody his community's Pacific Rim visions, and his impending journey to Asia promised (but also threatened) to expose this community to a new cultural frontier. In Kyoto, Snyder was not only exposed to the rigors of Zen training but also to a Japanese populace that did not seem to appreciate its cultural past as much as he did. In Tokyo, he was exposed to a postwar leisure economy that was subjecting poor Asian women to degrading work. In India, he was exposed to the foundations of Buddhist philosophy and an impoverished society that caused him to re-evaluate past relationships. Back home again in San Francisco, Snyder turned the tables, preferring to have the gendered landscape of the American West expose itself to him. Each exposure allowed Snyder the opportunity to analyze his geographic imperative and see the Pacific Rim in a different light.

We can view Snyder's round-trip in *The Back Country* as a spiritual pilgrimage that has come full circle and as a harbinger of cross-cultural exchange celebrated in today's Pacific Rim discourse. With brutal honesty, the poet exposes his readers to an economy of goods that takes advantage of certain women and deifies others while denying them any real agency. Poking holes in a Beat Orientalist fantasy he had inspired but never fully shared, Snyder wants us to see that his countercultural odyssey along the Rim relies upon spaces where distinctions between work and leisure, materiality and nothingness, body and landscape, have become blurred and at the same time insidiously fixed. As we deconstruct today's Asia-Pacific fantasies in order to make them "Asia-Specific," we should continue to pay close attention to the spaces that cut the borders of this region as well as to the raced and gendered bodies misrecognized as empty reservoirs by those pursuing freedom and unity in an oceanic hemisphere.

4. COMMUNING

Tribal Passions in the Late 1960s

Looking back on the first half of Snyder's career, it is possible to view "Back," the final section of *The Back Country*, as the initial stage of a cultural return that continued to unfold in the late 1960s. After six consecutive years in Asia, Snyder spent nine months in America from 1964 to 1965. During this time, he taught at UC–Berkeley, gave public readings and interviews, climbed mountains, and reconnected with old friends in the Beat movement, bringing his extensive knowledge of Pacific Rim traditions to bear on a counterculture that was making the transition to the hippie era. With increasing frequency, Snyder began to introduce ancient Asian customs to the Bay Area. Along with Phil Whalen, he formally circumambulated Mount Tamalpais. The two friends also protested the Vietnam War by sitting *zazen* in front of the Oakland Navy Terminal. In his poetry and prose, meanwhile, Snyder beat the drum for various primitive cultures around the Rim. Judging by the positive response he received after delivering a lecture entitled "Poetry and the Primitive" at the Berkeley Poetry Conference in July 1965, he continued to win the admiration of counterculture types seeking to replace cold war policies with a more peaceful and tribal worldview. Snyder's emphasis on tribal values was especially cogent in the heady atmosphere of the late 1960s, when throngs of youth traveled to San Francisco in search of alternative living arrangements, different models of political constituency, and ecstatic ways of being together.

Two well-timed books cemented Snyder's reputation as Pacific Rim spokesperson. In the prose writings collected in *Earth House Hold: Technical Notes & Queries to Fellow Dharma Revolutionaries* (1969), Snyder took what he knew of Asian traditions and molded them into a practical political program. Although this volume includes material composed as far back as 1952 ("Lookout's Journal"), nearly half of it consists of essays that Snyder wrote or revised in 1967, the annus mirabilis of the hippie movement. Reflecting the anarcho-pacifist idealism coloring the hippie community's visions of a utopian future, each of these 1967 essays contains serious discussion about how the counterculture can look back into history to recover the value systems of ancient mystics and primitives. As Michael Davidson reminds us, "it is difficult to think of the [San Francisco Renaissance] as 'postmodernist' when so much of it hearkens back to 'premodern' sources."[1] Snyder's 1967 essays surely support Davidson's point, for alongside peaceful prescriptions for the future they talk about older tribal models, some of them dating back to Paleolithic times.

In another important stage of his cultural return, Snyder went back to the lyric mode, publishing *Regarding Wave* (1970), a volume of poetry he dedicated to his third wife, a young Japanese woman named Masa Uehara. In this book, Snyder offers crosscultural family units as a practical means to discovery, focusing upon the multicultural significance of his wife and son (Kai Snyder, born in 1968) in order to celebrate a Pacific Rim communion made flesh. *Regarding Wave* thus takes the human geography of *The Back Country* to a whole new level. Particularly noteworthy in this context are Snyder's erotic descriptions of body and landscape, which he articulates ecstatically in a series of "songs" dedicated to Masa. Taking the tropes of the *blason* tradition a step further, these songs "orient" the traveling poet as he and his family prepare to settle permanently on the North American continent.

Like the Beats, the hippies of San Francisco's Haight-Ashbury district took a vested interest in Snyder's Pacific Rim adventures. In the travel journal he kept in India, Snyder defines culture as "a matter of style that pervades" (PTI 34). To my mind, this definition reveals quite a bit about Snyder's unique role in twentieth-century poetry. He was absent from San Francisco for much of the 1950s and early 1960s, and yet his sense of style, his way of moving through Pacific Rim space, clearly pervaded that city's countercultural circles. The same was true in the later years of the 1960s. The only difference was that the Beat Generation's Dharma Bum, its inscrutable Han-shan figure, was now a "Dharma Revolutionary" using Buddhism and other religions to promote radical political change. The response to Snyder's primitivist political program was overwhelmingly positive in San Francisco, but in the background of such celebrations there lurked dissonant voices, many of them emanating from the American Indian community, complaining about the extent to which he and other West Coast bohemians were appropriating native cultures for their own benefit while ignoring the real Native Americans in their midst.

Drawing upon rebuttals authored by Leslie Marmon Silko, Geary Hobson, and Wendy Rose as well as upon more recent cultural criticism by Marianna Torgovnick, Philip Deloria, and Rey Chow, I shall seek to place Snyder's neoprimitive writings within this larger cultural context, not merely to examine how various tribal communities responded to the spectacle of white middle-class San Franciscans wearing feathers and singing Indian chants, but ultimately to suggest that Snyder's invocation of Pacific Rim community, as freewheeling as it may have appeared, relied upon a deeper understanding of primitive traditions. In this chapter, as elsewhere, I find that the line separating communitarian idealism from cultural co-optation is difficult to trace and is subject to lively debate. Snyder's idealistic tribal writings from the late 1960s may appear to straddle that line, but they are actually far more responsible than other counterculture documents in their articulation of a shareable Pacific heritage.

California Interlude 1965

During the summer of 1965, having just completed a successful stint as a lecturer at the University of California's flagship campus, Snyder joined Allen Ginsberg, Robert Duncan, and other leading literary figures at the Berkeley Poetry Conference. At this conference, which was closely modeled on one held two years earlier in Vancouver, Snyder presided over a three-day seminar and delivered a lecture entitled "Poetry and the Primitive." Snyder would substantially revise this talk in 1967 (see the printed essay that appears in *Earth House Hold*), but even in its early version "Poetry and the Primitive" helped Bay Area literati appreciate the newfound relevance of older familial models. After being introduced by Ginsberg and recounting his experiences among the Kwakiutl Indians on Vancouver Island, Snyder begins his lecture by repeating a pronouncement made earlier in his writing career: "As a poet I hold the most archaic values on earth." He then offers a confession to those assembled: "I think I know better now what I was saying there than I did when I said it."[2]

I cannot help but wonder whether the time spent in India accounted for some of Snyder's enlightenment. We have already seen how his trip to the Asian subcontinent brought him into more intimate contact with older forms of Buddhism and Hinduism and caused him to reevaluate his relationships with Pacific Rim peoples. In the lecture, he implies that this trip also showed him a historical continuity that has been interrupted by modernity, but might still be recovered in certain places. "In India," he tells conference attendees, "we've not been subjected to that break between the heathen or the pagan, between the old people & the elder gods—& the modern gods; those gods have survived, they're still there." In the West, by contrast, religious and political leaders have succeeded in dividing people into various sects and nation-states. "What happens with the emergence of political society is that mankind becomes more separated," Snyder states. Frightfully missing from today's world is "a sense of kinship" basic to primitive societies, a kinship "not only with each other but with the rest of the world."

Displaying his long-standing affinity for creaturely communities, Snyder explains that in a primitive society "you are literally a relative of the animals. You are literally a child of the sky—this is built into your kinship system. You can, if you like, call the sky Uncle—or certain animals Cousin— right within the language." In the idealistic spirit of the hippie era, Snyder expresses optimism as he looks forward (by looking backward) to a time when postmodern peoples will discover their common origin. "What we have in common with the Neolithic is that we are once more on the edge of having a world culture." Thinking back to the analysis offered by Michael Davidson, I am led to assume that the premodern societies Snyder worships would have shared his dismay over the tendency of modern civilizations to divide living beings into separate camps, thus dampening their natural compassion for each other, all in the name of progress.

Throughout the Berkeley Poetry Conference lecture, Snyder reads from his notes in deep tones and measured cadences, conveying authority as he draws upon a rich store of anthropological and mythological knowledge. He speaks freely and extemporaneously as occasions demand (fielding a question from Robert Duncan, at one point), as though he had been standing behind a college lectern for years instead of months. His professorial persona must have surprised those who knew him best as Japhy Ryder, Jack Kerouac's archetypal Dharma Bum. Jack Nessel spoke for this portion of the populace while conducting an interview with Snyder, Phil Whalen, and Lew Welch on KPFA radio: "You guys come on like scholars. No shit, for a long time I thought you were putting us on, like maybe you were a road cast for *Evergreen Review* or something, the real Lew Welch in the woods, Snyder still in Japan, Whalen safe and hiding."[3]

Clearly, these bohemian intellectuals were no imposters. At the same time, they believed that the pursuits of pleasure and intellectual enlightenment were closely associated, regarding anyone who sought one without the other as either hopelessly square or borderline irresponsible. Searching for the right balance, Snyder implies in his "Poetry and the Primitive" lecture that contemporary Americans would do well to take their everyday pleasures seriously, perhaps even ritualistically. "As we seek love in ecstasy & the dance in our modern American society what we have is a sort of compulsive party going," Snyder maintains. "People are looking for that Deva realm—every Friday or Saturday night with various groups of their friends—& they achieve some small segment of it sometimes with dancing, drinking, & a little necking. But it could be so much more—& it has been more—& this is on one level what we really want."[4]

Seeking a little of the serious fun offered in primitive ritual, Snyder, Ginsberg, and Phil Whalen decided to perform a formal circumambulation of Mount Tamalpais in October 1965. Situated in Marin County, "Mount Tam" was attractive to Snyder because of "its proximity to the ocean, its central relationship to the whole Bay Area, its way of relating across to Mt. Diablo and up to Mt. St. Helena and to the northern Bolinas Ridge."[5] Snyder had hiked Mount Tam several times before, initially with his aunt in 1939, then with college girlfriend Robin Collins in 1948, again while helping his father build a house in Corte Madera in 1952, and most famously with Jack Kerouac in 1956 (on the final day of Snyder's boisterous farewell party). But this would be Snyder's first formal circumambulation of the mountain, according to the Buddhist fashion.[6]

We might remember that Snyder learned about circumambulation rituals during his 1956 meeting with the Yamabushi, Japan's Mountain Buddhists, on

Mount Hiei. In a conversation with David Robertson, Snyder describes the Yamabushi as Buddhists who "sleep or hang out in the mountains" with the hope of paying homage to the spirits or gods (*kami*) who also "hang out" in that landscape when they come down from heaven.[7] In "The Making of *Mountains and Rivers without End*," Snyder explains that, during his first stint in Kyoto, he and the Yamabushi "did the five-day pilgrimage on the Omine Ridge and established a tentative relationship with the archaic Buddhist mountain deity Fudo" (MR 156), the god that inspired the *Fudo Trilogy*, a chapbook of poetry Snyder published in 1973. By the early 1960s, Snyder was telling Whalen about his intention to come back to the Bay Area and "sacredize Tamalpais." When the two college buddies actually reunited in the mid-1960s, they put this plan into motion. Snyder remembers saying, "Let's all go do a formal circumambulation of Tamalpais and establish sacred spots on it and pay our respects and do some chanting."[8]

Circumambulation is an ancient Hindu-Buddhist ritual practice of walking meditation. In a note he appended to "The Circumambulation of Mt. Tamalpais," a poem from the *Mountains and Rivers without End* sequence he dedicated to Whalen and Ginsberg, Snyder explains that during this type of meditation, also known as *pradakshina*, "one stops at notable spots to sing a song, or to chant invocations and praises, such as mantras, songs, or little sutras" (MR 161). During their 1965 circumambulation, for instance, Snyder and Whalen chanted the Heart of the Perfection of Great Wisdom Sutra, a magical spell (*dharani*) for removing disasters, and the Four Vows (the compassionate Buddhist's promise to work for the benefit of all living beings). They carried Buddhist paraphernalia as well, including a ringed staff called a *shokujo*, a conch shell (for blowing), a *juzu* bead rosary, bells called *ghantas*, and other "magical devices," such as bear claws.[9] Their directional movement around the mountain was just as ritualized, since circumambulation stipulates that one move in a clockwise direction around a sacred object or shrine. As Snyder explains in an early draft of the poem, "one circumambulates (always keeping it on your right) a stupa, a tree, a person you wish to show respect to, or a mountain."[10] Fittingly, this motion mimics the clockwise route Snyder took along the northern boundary of the Pacific Rim as he brought Asian traditions back to America.

Snyder and Whalen tell Robertson that they had three main goals during the 1965 circumambulation. The first goal was to pay tribute to a place they admired. The second was to open the mountain to ritualistic Buddhist practice. The third was to express their devotion in a physical manner, by *doing* something. But there was another goal these members of the San Francisco counterculture had in mind, and that was to engage in play. As Snyder puts it in his interview with Robertson, "all of those stops on Tamalpais were like playing with the being of the mountain, nothing fancy about it." Quite in keeping with their proclivity for playful spontaneity, Snyder and his friends declined to choose the stations in advance. "We just felt the magic vibrations," Snyder recalls. "We decided them on the day that we walked it, by being finely tuned."[11] What they wanted their circumambulation to show, at least in part, was that Asian ceremony could be used for creative as well as ritualistic purposes. As Snyder says, "It is too burdensome to say that [circumambulation] must be a Buddhist ritual. I would rather think that it is open for anyone to be as creative as they like. They can stop at those points we stopped at, or they can stop at other points. The main thing is to pay your regards, to play, to engage, to stop and pay attention. It's just a way of stopping and looking—at yourself too. In a way that is what ceremony is for."[12]

Although I do not believe that Snyder himself is guilty of appropriative behavior on this occasion, his comments portend a tendency on the part of San Francisco hippies to play or engage with other cultures, not necessarily to achieve a fuller understanding of those cultures, but primarily to enhance their understanding of themselves. In the later 1960s and again in the New Age movement of the 1970s, hippie Orientalists walked a fine line between making Asian and Native cultures accessible to Americans who were sincere in their attempts to broaden their horizons and allowing those people to co-opt exotic cultural ceremonies for their personal benefit, their own sense of freedom or liberation from mainstream culture. As they practiced and played on Mount Tamalpais in 1965, Snyder and Whalen were filled with good intentions. What is more, they possessed a detailed knowledge of, and an abiding respect for, the Buddhist and Hindu rituals they were implementing. Unfortunately, the same could not always be said for other members of the American counterculture, whose enchantment with the "magic vibrations" of Pacific Rim traditions resulted in naive and disengaged invocations of imagined community. Reading Snyder's essays in *Earth House Hold*, we gain a better appreciation for the "Great Subculture" the poet wanted to restore and nurture around the globe. At the same time, we are forced to acknowledge that many who read these essays fell prey to an appropriative mindset, one that Snyder himself was trying to eradicate.

Gathering the Tribes:
The Later Essays of Earth House Hold

For years, Snyder admitted in "Four Poems for Robin," he had been obsessed with a plan that would take him to Asia. Even so, it is important to recognize that Snyder always planned to return to his native land. Throughout his twelve years in Asia, San Francisco's far-flung voyager was committed to finding and transporting back home a communal model that would make America over in an idealized and archaic form. An early indication of Snyder's cultural return can be located in "Japan First Time Around," a collection of journal entries written during his first stay in Japan. In the final entry, dated 9 May 1957, Snyder envisions a new Berkeley that might come into being, provided that certain elements of Asian cultures could be introduced to the Bay Area: "One night I dreamt I was with Miura Roshi, or maybe an unheard of Polish revolutionary poet with a bald head—looking at Berkeley. But a new Berkeley—of the future—the Bay beach clean and white, the bay blue and pure; white buildings and a lovely boulevard of tall Monterey pines that stretched back to the hills. We saw a girl from some ways off walking toward us, longlegged, her hair bound loosely in back" (EHH 43). Here Snyder forecasts an ecological transformation of the Bay Area, which, as he noted in "For the West" (BC 117), was becoming increasingly industrialized. The longhaired girl who approaches the meditating men seems a prototype of the free-spirited hippies who would roam the Berkeley streets a decade later, even though in an unpublished portion of the journal Snyder included this afterthought: "I knew it was Robin."[13] Meanwhile, the shared gaze between the poet and his bald-headed Japanese teacher suggests a syncretic way of spotting countercultural trends.

In the years that followed, Snyder sought to realize his dreams of cultural confluence by making them more communicable and practicable, especially as he edged closer to a permanent return to American shores. "At a certain point I realized that, for the time, I'd been in Japan enough," Snyder recalled in a 1977 interview in *East West Journal*. "I began to feel the need to put my shoulder to the wheel on this continent. It wasn't just returning—the next step of my practice was to be here" (TRW 99). The workmanlike metaphor Snyder uses on this occasion attests to his abiding respect for practical action, the real work that must be done if one truly hopes to bring enlightenment to others. What the San Francisco counterculture needed most, he surmised, was a *working* model of tribal community. Two decades earlier, in *The Dharma Bums*, Japhy Ryder introduced this model rather more breezily in a conversation with Ray Smith: "Ray, by God, later on in our future life we can have a fine freewheeling tribe in these California hills, get girls and have dozens of radiant enlightened brats, live like Indians in hogans and eat berries and buds. . . . We'll write poems, we'll get a printing press and print our own poems, the Dharma Press, we'll poetize the lot and make a fat book of icy bombs for the booby public."[14]

Although I cannot imagine Snyder actually using this hipster lingo, I regard Japhy's pronouncement as prophetic, since communal hippies of the next generation came to resemble the tribes he describes. We should note in particular Japhy's mention of a printing press. As Benedict Anderson and Jürgen Habermas have shown in separate scholarly studies, the establishment of print culture has been crucial to the rise of nationalism and the creation of a public sphere.[15] The same tendency held true for a counterculture whose conception of a Pacific Rim public sphere sought to replace divisive nation-state paradigms with new models of imagined community. Max Scherr's *Berkeley Barb* (established in 1965), Allen Cohen's *San Francisco Oracle* (1966), and Jann Wenner's *Rolling Stone* (1967) fulfilled this role in the Bay Area. Before they were collected in *Earth House Hold*, several of Snyder's essays appeared in the pages of these and other underground papers, which allowed him to get his neotribal messages across to a greater cross section of the counterculture, including those people less inclined to read his experimental poetry.

The first of Snyder's essays to appear in the underground press was actually a revision of a 1961 essay, "Buddhist Anarchism," which had originally been published in *Journal for the Protection of All Beings*, a periodical put out by City Lights Books. In 1967, this essay was retooled for the Haight audience and published in the *San Francisco Oracle* as "Buddhism and the Coming Revolution." In both versions, Snyder calls for the East and West to share complementary strengths. Of course, Snyder had been advocating such a notion for some time. In a telling passage from *The Dharma Bums*, Japhy Ryder assures Ray Smith that "'East'll meet West anyway. Think of what a great world revolution will take place when East meets West finally, and it'll be guys like us that can start the thing. Think of millions of guys all over the world with rucksacks on their backs tramping around the back country and hitchhiking and bringing the word down to everybody.'"[16] In Kerouac's narrative, Japhy divulges his visions of rucksack revolution to Ray, but virtually no one else. In war-torn 1967, however, the social stakes were higher, and the call for global revolution more pressing. Snyder knew that when he revised his model of East-West exchange he would have to make it speak to a politically astute audience. "Buddhism and the Coming Revolution" therefore makes an explicit call for people on both sides of the Pacific to move away from narrow epistemological or psychological concerns (common in the Beats' existential applications of Asian traditions) in order to foster better social understanding and create new patterns of cultural exchange.

"Historically, Buddhist philosophers have failed to analyze out the degree to which ignorance and suffering are caused or encouraged by social factors, considering fear-and-desire to be given facts of the human condition," Snyder writes (EHH 90). What the East needs, he concludes, is the "mercy of the West," which is to say its unique brand of "social revolution." The East is rich in individual insights but appears to require the creative political resistance that has been the hallmark of West Coast activism during the twentieth century, from the grassroots union organizing of the Wobblies, to the "monkey wrenching" of Edward Abbey and his environmentalist gang, to the carnivalesque media stunts pulled by those who gathered in Seattle to protest globalization during the 1999 World Trade Organization conference. Returning to America in 1967, Snyder argues that any political program able to combine the relative strengths of Eastern introspection and Western compassion will have "nation shaking implications" in a divisive cold war landscape haunted by "giant appetites" and "cancerous collectivities" (EHH 91).

Given the political climate of Berkeley in the late 1960s, when protests against the Vietnam War were at their peak, the changes that Snyder made to "Buddhist Anarchism" are noteworthy. Unlike many in the antiwar movement, he was not beyond blaming Communist governments around the world for current troubles. Below I have listed a set of phrases taken from the 1961 essay and placed them alongside substitutions and modifications appearing in "Buddhism and the Coming Revolution." I have italicized portions of the 1961 version to indicate the passages that Snyder later altered:

1961 version ("Buddhist Anarchism"): "*Modern America* has become economically dependent on a fantastic system of greed which cannot be fulfilled, sexual desire which cannot be satiated, and hatred which has no outlet except against oneself or the *persons one is supposed to love*. The conditions of the cold war have turned all modern societies, *Soviet included*, into *hopeless brain-stainers."*

1967 version ("Buddhism and the Coming Revolution"): "the 'free world'" . . . "the persons one is supposed to love, or the revolutionary aspirations of piti-ful, poverty-stricken marginal societies like Cuba or Vietnam" . . . "Communist included" . . . "vicious distorters of man's true potential."

1961 version: "Have this much faith—or insight—and you are led to a deep concern with the need for radical social change and personal commitment to some form of *essentially non-violent* revolutionary action."
1967 version: "hopefully non-violent"

1961 version: "From one standpoint, governments, wars, or all that we con-sider 'evil' are uncompromisingly contained in this *illuminated realm*."
1967 version: "totalistic realm."

1961 version: "The mercy of the west has been *rebellion*; the mercy of the east has been insight into the basic *self*."
1967 version: "social revolution" . . . "self/void"

1961 version: "This last aspect means, for me, supporting any cultural or eco-nomic revolution that moves clearly toward a free, international, classless society."
1967 version: "world"

1961 version: "Fighting back with *civil disobedience, pacifism, poetry, poverty—and violence, if it comes to a matter of clobbering some rampaging redneck or shoving a scab off the pier*. Defending the right to smoke pot, eat peyote, be polygamous, polyandrous, or *queer—and learning from the hip fellaheen peo-ples of Asia and Africa attitudes and techniques* banned by the *Judeo-Christian West*.
1967 version: "civil disobedience, outspoken criticism, protest, pacifism, vol-untary poverty and even gentle violence, if it comes to a matter of restraining some impetuous redneck" . . . "homosexual" . . . "worlds of behavior and custom" . . . "Judeo-Capitalist-Christian-Marxist West"[17]

Although the changes made in the 1967 version are subtly registered, they indicate Snyder's heightened sense of compassion, his growing sense of danger, and his greater awareness of geopolitical interconnectedness. Violent confrontation seems more likely: it is only "hopefully" to be avoided, or made "gentle," in a "totalistic" world where every false move has far-reaching consequences. Greed and aggressive behavior are seen to infiltrate all corners of this world, not just America. Witness Snyder's inclusion of Communists (not just Soviets) and Marxists (not just Judeo-Christians) on the list of perpetrators blocking humankind's potential for enlightenment and thus prohibiting the establishment of a "new kind of community." In 1967, Snyder regards political responsibility as collective, especially in a Pacific Rim region torn asunder by warfare and general distrust. What had been in 1961 an isolated call for individual "rebellion" in America has blossomed into a call for "social revolution" around the globe.

In 1967, Snyder's dream of a classless world of intercultural exchange no longer relied solely upon the example of "hip fellaheen peoples of Asia and Africa," but also upon the customs and behaviors prevalent in heterotopian cities like San Francisco, where young people were seeking alternative ways of belonging. Again, it seems crucial to inquire whether neotribal visionaries in the American counterculture avoided real contact with "traditional cultures" around the globe, making those cultures part of a meditative program, but otherwise rendering them superfluous. One passage from "Buddhism and the Coming Revolution" seems to sanction this type of appropriative behavior. "The traditional cultures are in any case doomed, and rather than cling to their good aspects hopelessly it should be remembered that whatever is or ever was in any other culture can be reconstructed from the unconscious, through meditation," Snyder opines. "In fact, it is my own view that the coming revolution will close the circle and link us in many ways with the most creative aspects of our archaic past. If we are lucky we may eventually arrive at a totally integrated world culture with matrilineal descent, free-form marriage, natural-credit communist economy, less industry, far less population and lots more national parks" (EHH 92–93).

A few contradictions surface in Snyder's visionary analysis, not the least of which is the fact that the communist and national paradigms he had blasted earlier in the essay now seem to provide the best economic model and the best park system. With meditation, apparently, all things are possible. Patrick Murphy is perceptive when he says that Snyder's "excessively optimistic perception of the possibility of swift cultural change is very American and very non-Buddhist."[18] All the same, I find "Buddhism and the Coming Revolution" to be a classic piece of Rimspeak owing to Snyder's emphasis on "cognitive mapping," described by Fredric Jameson as "the practical reconquest of a sense of place and the construction or reconstruction of an articulated ensemble which can be retained in memory and which the individual subject can map and remap along the moments of mobile, alternative trajectories."[19]

In his talk about "closing the circle," Snyder builds upon the geometric metaphor used by boosters of the Pacific Rim idea, not in any effort to conquer a place, as Jameson might say, but instead to chart a circular realm where cultures from various times and places loop back and become relevant to diverse groups of global citizens. Optimally, Snyder's meditative discovery of an alternative public sphere will allow unconscious and heretofore repressed desires to find their proper geographic coordinates, places where the invocation of Pacific Rim community is granted free expression. From the time he began composing *Myths & Texts*, Snyder had attempted to steer clear of cultural co-optation by granting everyone in the Rim community (including wildlife) his or her own voice. But as we shall see, other members of the San Francisco counterculture confused an appreciation of foreign cultures with their own flights of fancy, thereby foreclosing the possibility of true partnership with the tribal communities they professed to emulate.

Be-in Indians

In January 1967, in the Polo Grounds of Golden Gate Park, thousands of young people convened for a "Human Be-in" less than two weeks after "Buddhism and the Coming Revolution" appeared in the *Oracle*. Considered today to be a watershed event in the annals of hippie culture, the Be-in reveals a great deal about the way tribal models were invoked in San Francisco at this time. Just two days before the event, a press statement was issued by the Print Mint, a shop in the center of the Haight-Ashbury community. Signed by Snyder, Jerry Rubin, and other counterculture luminaries, the statement announced that "Berkeley political activists and the love generation of the Haight-Ashbury will join together with members of the new nation who will be coming from every state in the nation, every tribe of the young (the emerging soul of the nation) to powwow, celebrate, and prophesy the epoch of liberation, love, peace, compassion, and unity of mankind. . . . Hang your fear at the door and join the future. If you do not believe, please wipe your eyes and see."[20]

The Human Be-in was a rather hastily organized assemblage, relying upon this press release, a few posters, underground newspaper blurbs, and word of mouth. Its call for consolidation was common in Bay Area circles ever since the Jefferson Airplane composed the anthem "Let's Get Together" (a song later made popular by the Youngbloods) in 1965. By 1967, though, the cry for unity sounded far more desperate, for a huge fissure had developed between Berkeley's political radicals and the Haight's cultural radicals. The politicos blamed the hippies for their apolitical languor, and the latter blamed the former for laying a bum trip on their mystical visions. The Be-in was the first large-scale attempt to bring the two "tribes" together for a "powwow." Most of the impetus for the Be-in came from the Haight community, whose underground paper, the *Oracle*, was the first to advertise the event, promising that a "union of love and activism previously separated by categorical dogma and label mongering will finally occur ecstatically when Berkeley's political activists and hip community and San Francisco's spiritual generation all over California meet for a gathering of the tribes."[21] The Berkeley community was more suspicious. As a result, the Be-in was not widely publicized in the East Bay. A tiny notice ran in the *Berkeley Barb*'s "Scenedrome" calendar a day before the event: "Happening: Human Be-in, w/ Leary, Rubin, Gregory, Kandel, Ginsberg, Weinberg. All Rock Bands, plus flowers, beads, incense, you & me; Polo Grounds GG Park, SF 1–5 pm free."[22]

Despite these shortcomings, the event caused quite a stir. While millions of Americans settled in front of their television sets to watch the first Super Bowl, somewhere between 10,000 (police estimate) and 30,000 (hippie estimate) folks assembled in Golden Gate Park to listen to music by the Grateful Dead, Quicksilver Messenger Service, and the Jefferson Airplane. From the same stage they heard the love poetry of Lenore Kandel, the acid philosophy of Timothy Leary, and the political rants of Jerry Rubin. Sometime in the afternoon, Snyder, Ginsberg, Maretta Greer (Ginsberg's girlfriend, who lived in India), and Michael McClure appeared on stage to lead chants to Shiva and Maitreya, the future Buddha, whose attendance had been guaranteed on one of the posters advertising the event. A famous photograph taken by Lisa Law shows Snyder and Ginsberg sitting in the lotus position, wearing beads and finger cymbals, while a brooding McClure, outfitted in fashionable sunglasses, strums what looks to be a zither. That these poets have assumed the aura and status of rock stars is hardly surprising when we note that the Beatles once paused on stage to salute Ginsberg during a 1965 concert.[23]

As the Be-in was winding down, a parachutist descended from an unheard and unseen airplane, provoking a loud "Ah" from the crowd and, according to Barry Miles, "causing many of the people to think that they had just seen God." Replicating a ceremonial rite he had learned from the Yamabushi Buddhists a decade before, Snyder blew a long note on a conch shell to signal an end to the proceedings. While Ginsberg stayed behind to lead a cleanup session he called "kitchen yoga," Snyder joined the thousands of other participants who marched westward through Golden Gate Park to watch the sun set over the Pacific horizon, which from a hippie perspective was looking more and more like a Rim.[24]

According to most reports, the celebrants preferred the music above all else. They tuned out Leary and even Kandel, whose erotic *Love Book* was a best-seller in counterculture circles. The political rhetoric of Rubin also failed to go over with the largely hippie crowd. *Berkeley Barb* publisher Max Scherr, Rubin's sponsor, was furious over the Haight community's apathetic response, and in future issues of the *Barb* he expressed his disgust with the powwow. The *San Francisco Chronicle*, the mainstream daily, described the Be-in as a "staring match, eyeball to eyeball," between "Berkeley political activists and the farther out love hippies of the San Francisco Haight-Ashbury district."[25] As might be expected, the response in the Haight was much more positive. The *Oracle* was less concerned with confronting the problems that arose (including police harassment) than it was with nurturing the event's peaceful vibe. However much the Berkeley radicals complained about their apathy, and however much the establishment press derided them for their sunny idealism, people in the Haight believed that the Be-in had served notice of a new tribal collectivity.

Important in this context is the role assigned the Indian, the predominant image around which the Bay Area counterculture sought to solidify its ranks. In "Passage to More Than India," the second of six essays he published in 1967, Snyder recalls that there were two different posters used to advertise the "Gathering of the Tribes" in Golden Gate Park, "one based on a photograph of a Shaivite sadhu with his long matted hair, ashes and beard; the other based on an old etching of a Plains Indian approaching a powwow on his horse—the carbine that had been cradled in his left arm replaced by a guitar. The Indians, and the Indian" (EHH 103). According to Snyder, the two Be-in Indians, whose confused appellations attest to the arbitrary nature of the West's colonizing ventures, were held up as ideal images for several reasons. First, the Indians represent sources of ancient wisdom that the counterculture wants to tap into. Second, the appearance of Indians from different hemispheres suggests that an archaic East-West unity forsaken by cold war politicians might be restored. Third, both Indians represent peace and thus voice the counterculture's complaints against the Vietnam War. Fourth, the fact that the Plains Indian carries a guitar is symbolic of the strong tie between these contemporary noble savages and the raw emotions of rock music. This last connection would grow stronger once the spectacle of popular music festivals, in many ways the offspring of the tribal powwow in Golden Gate Park, gathered force in the years to come.

The hippie invocation of tribal cultures was made easy in an urban marketplace that catered to the production and consumption of primitive artifacts, which more often than not were just cheap simulacra. In the late 1960s, the primitive look, which for centuries ran counter to ideas of civic progress, could be purchased in San Francisco head shops, clothing boutiques, and record stores. Suddenly, primitive values no longer existed somewhere "out there," but had become through exploitative business practices consumable accessories purchased by bohemian types who wanted to announce that they were far-out. In time, it became clear that the hippies, who like the Beats before them had little face-to-face contact with Native Americans or Asian-Americans on the West Coast, were not only appropriating images of the Indian to sanctify their political agenda and facilitate their psychedelic voyaging, but also spending what little money they had in order to do so. Amidst its inventory of acidhead wares, the Psychedelic Shop, a bastion of "hip capitalism" located on Haight Street, displayed Indian paisley prints, brass bells, and bamboo flutes alongside a variety of dope pipes.[26]

During the "Trips Festival" held in the Longshoreman's Union Hall in the Tenderloin district, Ken Kesey and his Merry Pranksters enhanced the hallucinogenic atmosphere of their "Acid Test" by projecting slides of American Indians just as the paying customers began to feel the drugs take effect. A similar convergence of the hallucinogenic and the primitive occurred at the "Tribal Stomps" held at the Avalon Ballroom, which was festooned with beads, feathers, and mandalas, circular depictions of the Buddhist cosmos that, according to Carl Jung, "express the totality of the individual in his inner or outer experience of the world."[27] It was a short leap from there to the Monterey International Pop Festival, where Mickey Dolenz of the Monkees, along with other rock stars and fans, wore face paint, buckskin, and various Indian regalia (a feathered headdress in Dolenz's case) in an effort to articulate psychedelic tribal dreams. The festival's Indian-hippie vortex is captured beautifully in D. A. Pennebaker's colorful documentary film, *Monterey Pop*, no more so than when we see Jimi Hendrix (himself part Cherokee) and Dolenz (part Chickasaw) listening with rapture to the long raga played by Ravi Shankar, a sitar player from India.[28]

The counterculture's infatuation with tribal ideals was perhaps best expressed in the *San Francisco Oracle*'s advertisement for its "Indian Issue": "In the next issue of the *Oracle* we hope to tell the truth of the American Indian past, present and future. We invite all and everyone to make known their tribal visions."[29] Suffice it to say that, in the first half of 1967, Indian culture was routinely invoked to articulate a sense of communal belonging among America's (mostly white) internal émigrés. Ostensibly, the figure of the Indian was summoned to offer grace to a community seeking to redress the wrongs of the past. More often than not, what the hippies really wanted was an alter ego under whose guise they might announce personal feelings of estrangement from American society, or perhaps just another trippy costume to wear to the Haight's polyglot masquerade. Musical satirist Frank Zappa laughingly impugned Summer of Love tribalism when he had his drummer interrupt several songs on his anticoncept album, *We're Only in It for the Money*, to provide what had become by 1968 a requisite greeting: "Hi there boys and girls, I'm Jimmy Carl Black, the Indian of the group."[30]

Putting Zappa's caustic assessment aside, it is possible to see that some of the Haight "Indians" were conducting a complex sociological experiment. As archaic as the values of primitivism may seem, as distant as the decade of the 1960s now seems, the neotribal movement of 1967 resembles much of what can be found in theories of postmodern community offered by Michel Maffesoli, Gilles Deleuze and Felix Guattari, and James Clifford. Maffesoli, a self-proclaimed vagabond sociologist who writes about postmodernity's nostalgic longing for primitive cultural models, discerns in neotribal invocations a need for "emotional collectivity," a feeling of belonging that resists the rational forms of individuation promoted by modern society. In the words of Mike Featherstone, Maffesoli's concept of tribal belonging recognizes a "persistence of strong affectual bonds through which people come together in constellations with fluid boundaries to experience the multiple attractions, sensations, sensibilities and vitalism of extra-logical community, the embodied sense of being together, the common feeling generated by a common emotional adherence to a sign which is recognizable to others." Maffesoli himself describes his tribal vision as a "re-enchantment with the world," citing the work of Victor Turner to promote a "*communitas* [that] surpasses the utilitarian and functionalist aspect prevailing in the surrounding economic order."[31]

Although neotribal collectivities require places where they can convene and demonstrate shared desires, such places end up being malleable or provisional. Maffesoli takes as one example the Parisian neighborhood of Les Halles. People who travel to this urban space know that they will be joining a community of like-minded souls who hail from different spots around the world. Ultimately, the physical location of Les Halles is less important than the people who assemble there and regard the site as uniquely fluid, syncretic, and spiritual. Young Americans who traveled en masse to San Francisco in 1967 also believed that within a few special sites (Golden Gate Park, the Haight, the Fillmore and Avalon Ballrooms) they might dissolve the boundaries traditionally ascribed to place. As the Haight scene grew, San Francisco was conceived in the popular imagination not so much as a fixed place but instead as a space of transport, a launching pad into an otherworldly realm, a magical site where the term "locality" might be refined out of existence.

It was with these expectations that songs like Scott McKenzie's "San Francisco (Be Sure to Wear Flowers in Your Hair)" and Eric Burdon's "San Franciscan Nights" served as tourist advertisements for a countercultural heterotopia. Fittingly, neither of the singers hailed from San Francisco. McKenzie, in particular, was derided by long-standing members of the city's rock community for being an interloper: a clean-cut "Bel-Air hippie" handpicked by the songwriter, fellow Angeleno John Phillips, to make the Haight scene palatable to middle-class listening audiences. Some laughed at McKenzie's song and others were angry with it, but looking back there is no denying that it had a huge effect on migration patterns of American teenagers, who continued to flock to San Francisco in droves, even after fed-up members of the local counterculture declared "the death of the hippie" by dragging a coffin down Haight Street. Burdon was a British blues singer who was trying to reinvent himself as an American hippie. His comeback campaign, which was surprisingly successful, consisted of singing about the various West Coast scenes (Monterey Pop, the Haight) that he was in the process of discovering. When Burdon urged European citizens to "fly Trans-Love Airways to San Francisco, U.S.A.," he assured them that they would "not regret it," just as McKenzie, who asked "people in motion" to wear flowers in their hair in order to acclimate themselves to the "gentle people" they were sure to meet upon their arrival, promised a unique type of freedom offered in San Francisco, renamed "Psychedelphia" by some in the hip community.[32]

Maffesoli describes postmodern tribal ecstasy, or "ex-stasis," as both an "exit from the self" and a "being-together in motion."[33] In keeping with my geographic emphasis, I would like to add to his formulation the possibility of an "exit from place" or a "being-together in placelessness." For the wayward "tribes" who listened to ecstatic rock lyrics and made their way across the American continent to San Francisco, the magical city of their dreams promised all the comforts of a home space with none of its trappings, especially since the countercultural community awaiting them when they arrived, including the psychedelic bands they were listening to (Jefferson Airplane, Quicksilver Messenger Service), sought to transport them somewhere else. The effect resembles Deleuze and Guattari's concept of "the Natal." In *A Thousand Plateaus*, these two proponents of nomadism define the Natal as an "intense center," a place of raw aesthetic that anchors a territory but also marks "coefficients of deterritorialization" that point beyond that territory's boundaries, gesturing toward a heretofore unrecognized "interassemblage." The Natal represents an "unknown homeland"; it has the value of home but always exists elsewhere, beyond our cognitive grasp.[34] In the San Francisco counterculture, more often than not, that unknown homeland had a tribal cast and a Pacific Rim address.

In theory, as in culture, matters of human geography urge us to ask whether neotribal passions cause certain social groups to be marginalized or displaced from their own homelands. Caren Kaplan, for instance, asks why Deleuze and other "traveling theorists" (like James Clifford) rely so heavily upon Native Americans and other "primitives" as they try to articulate their own sense of drift. Kaplan suggests that the nostalgic romanticism prevalent in postmodern theory utilizes the example of primitive people while it conveniently overlooks, or distorts for its own profit, the violence done to those people.[35] Another cogent reproach comes from Marianna Torgovnick, who explains that when a group has "gone primitive," as the hippie community in San Francisco had surely done, it has signaled an uncanny desire to locate a "transcendental homelessness," an "oceanic" feeling of connection and unity that works through locality, only to dissolve the boundaries of that locality so that it may assume a more global sense of inclusiveness.[36]

As Torgovnick notes in a separate study on postmodern primitivism, "the primitive [has become] the sign of desires the West has sought to repress . . . [including] direct correspondences between experiences and language, direct correspondences between individual beings and the collective life force." All of this would be fine, she implies, were it not for the fact that, in most of these scenarios, the primitive stands as "a sign and symbol of desire for a full and sated sense of the universe" and little else.[37] San Francisco hippies may have gone primitive as a way to express their misgivings with a repressive cold war society, but most of them never fully assessed the pain and betrayal suffered by the primitive people whose examples they were invoking. The guitar-playing Indian and the bearded Shaivite sadhu on Human Be-in posters may have aided the hippies in their search for an unknown homeland, but very few Indians were actually on hand at counterculture events.

As Philip Deloria has argued in his book *Playing Indian*, there was a tricky dynamic at work in the neotribalism that emerged in postwar America. During the powwows attended by so-called hobby Indians in the 1950s, he explains, "non-Indians in effect ceded a degree of cultural power to Indians." According to Deloria, "that cession stemmed from a complex and contradictory set of ideas about assimilation, equality, and consensus on the one hand, and, on the other, a racial difference that was both desirable and frightening. Even as they ceded power, however, white hobbyists maintained—in a classic formulation of cold war liberalism—control over the ability to give it away."[38] To my way of thinking, something similar happened in San Francisco during the 1960s. Consider the performance of Ravi Shankar at the Monterey Pop Festival. A concert review published in the *Berkeley Barb* stated that "Shankar . . . was probably the outstanding event of the festival. It was more than his music. He got a reception that exceeded anything given any of the other performers, and the love and respect seemed mutual." We should notice that the emphasis the *Barb* reviewer places on Shankar's gracious and mutually amorous response toward white San Franciscan hippies is in keeping with the basic tenets of Orientalist exchange, in which the white Westerner gains a better understanding of himself through the eyes of the Easterner, who in turn views the Westerner with respect and love. The self-satisfaction one sees on the faces of blissed-out Monterey concertgoers during Shankar's performance is attributable, at least in part, to the approval these people thought they were receiving from an Indian musician. As Deloria underscores in his example of hobby Indians, white Westerners retain the power to give away their love and respect to marginalized people and expect to be repaid in kind.[39]

Even during the Summer of Love, the co-optation of Indian culture had its critics. In a scathing commentary published in the *Berkeley Barb* in July 1967, just after the Monterey Pop Festival had taken place, Native American folk singer Buffy Sainte-Marie excoriated the Haight's excessive romanticism and consumption of tribal culture. In an interview entitled "Buffy on Hippies—They'll Never Be Indians," Sainte-Marie took aim at a trendy and insidious variety of cultural violence. "It's the weirdest vampire idea. It's very perverted. It has something to do with the idea that people are always trying to identify with the race they've conquered. . . . I mean they won't even let the Indians have a soul."[40] Presumably, she failed to find much solace in the final line of Eric Burdon's "San Franciscan Nights," which celebrated the city's countercultural crescendo as "an American dream (includes Indians, too)." As it happened, Sainte-Marie's complaints preceded by several years similar accusations made by Leslie Marmon Silko and Geary Hobson against Snyder and other "white shamans" when Snyder won the Pulitzer Prize for poetry in 1975. In each case, Indians feared that the co-optation of tribal ways by middle-class whites heralded a new wave of cultural genocide. According to the real Indians, the white bohemians who wandered westward to San Francisco in the late 1960s perpetuated on the symbolic level the same kind of frontier violence their forebears meted out to native peoples a century beforehand.[41]

Compared to his compatriots in the Haight community, Snyder had a far more complex understanding and appreciation for the tribal models he invoked. He had studied indigenous cultures for years and had made contact with tribal communities on both sides of the Pacific. His writings from the late 1960s indicate that he was more interested in the political possibilities of the tribal movement than he was with facile modes of escapism. Indeed, he was particularly sensitive to the dangers of repressed history. In "Passage to

More Than India," another essay from 1967, he depicts the American Indian as "the vengeful ghost lurking in the back of the troubled American mind." Specifically, Snyder argues that America's repressed guilt over the harm it has inflicted on its indigenous peoples over the years "is why we lash out with such ferocity and passion, so muddied a heart, at the black-haired young peasants and soldiers who are the 'Viet Cong'" (EHH 112). Anticipating similar pronouncements made by Tom Hayden and Richard Drinnon in the 1970s, Snyder describes the war in Vietnam as an extension of American frontier violence, a negative transference of cultural baggage onto a new group of darker-skinned people who stand in the way of white imperialists.[42] The only way to bring an end to such violence, he argues in this essay, is to eradicate hierarchical paradigms. Once Americans see themselves as linked with all peoples of the Pacific Rim, including those they have displaced or ignored within their own country, they will no longer prolong a bitter legacy of violence, but will instead seek to reestablish the unifying and peaceful ideals that tribalism has to offer.

Although he was well aware of their excesses, Snyder knew that San Francisco hippies possessed the potential to affirm Pacific Rim communitarianism. In his opinion, the tribes who gathered in Golden Gate Park represented a "surfacing (in a specifically 'American' incarnation) of the Great Subculture which goes back as far perhaps as the late Paleolithic." Like the members of primitive tribes, he explains, the "ab/original" youth who traveled to San Francisco found a network of "house-holds" already in place. Contrary to popular belief, these neotribal nomads did not drop out of society so much as they dropped into an alternative society offering kindness and support (EHH 104). Snyder bolsters his case in an essay entitled "Why Tribe," suggesting that, unlike contemporary nation-state paradigms, the Great Subculture "has been attached in part to the official religions but is different in that it transmits a community style of life, with an ecstatically positive vision of spiritual and physical love; and is opposed for very fundamental reasons to the Civilization Establishment" (EHH 115). In this latest manifestation of global subculture, Snyder wants us to believe, "the Revolution has ceased to be an ideological concern," since it follows "the timeless path of love and wisdom, in affectionate company with the sky, winds, clouds, trees, waters, animals and grasses" (EHH 116). Reading such language, we notice that Snyder occasionally falls prey to the nonideological rhetoric perpetuated by those who made Pacific Rim discourse and Rimspeak recognizable quantities in the later years of the cold war. Clearly, though, Snyder differs in motivation, and in practice, from politicians like Nixon or global corporations like Nike.

Owing to the responsibilities inherent in any ideological agenda, San Francisco hippies eventually had to shift from satisfying their rebellious desires to thinking about practical action. The question of leadership was of vital concern in this context. During a "Houseboat Summit" meeting of Snyder, Ginsberg, Leary, and Alan Watts, held on Watts's houseboat in San Francisco Bay and published in typescript in a February 1967 issue of the *Oracle*, four recognizable spokesmen for a generation debated various courses of action. Not surprisingly, the Human Be-in and tribalism were hot topics. According to Ginsberg, who had the closest ties to the East Bay, Berkeley radicals feared that the Be-in, with its legion of apolitical followers, had sown the seeds of a neofascist movement. Leary and Watts disagreed with this analysis. Watts proclaimed that the genius of the underground is that it has no leadership. Leary preferred to call the organizers of the Be-in "foci of energy."[43] Snyder, for his part, turned to anthropological examples to promote tribal models with decentralized leadership. In particular, he recalled seeing at the Be-in a banner for *Maha-lila*, a "clan structure" of about three families that is able to share resources without any direction from an authoritative figurehead.

Snyder's thinking about tribal leadership dates back to the "Poetry and the Primitive" talk he delivered at UC–Berkeley, when he praised primitive societies for having a "communal pattern of leadership which is very fluid." In these types of societies or clans, Snyder explains, "there isn't just one chief, there are age group chiefs, there are fishing chiefs, there are war chiefs, there are getting drunk chiefs—almost everyone at some point in his life within the primitive society in which he was born is going to be a boss of something or other—& he knows it. . . . It's very fluid, & this, of course, is something which always disturbed the early white western contacts with primitive peoples—because they say, 'take me to your leader,' and then they thought they had the leader, but they didn't."[44]

After Snyder's discourse on leaderless tribes, the other participants of the Houseboat Summit plucked him out as the best example of a leader who did not act like a leader. Snyder was quick to blame his reputation on the press, but he did admit to being a model for the drop out generation owing to the fact that he had "never been in."[45] Neither Snyder nor the other countercultural leaders at the Houseboat Summit became a fascist dictator, as the Berkeley radicals had feared. But as David Perkins and Helen Vendler have argued, Snyder and Ginsberg did emerge as gurus for a hippie community seeking alternative visions.[46] Snyder no doubt wished to avoid the excessive adulation he had received in *The Dharma Bums* and other yellowface portraits of the 1950s, but his iconographic image was deeply ingrained on countercultural consciousness, and a decade down the line people were still eager to hear what he had to say. Lew Welch predicted as much in a 1962 letter to Snyder: "It will be as you say: those idiots will erect a cult about you. . . . What is to be feared . . . is that they may become fanatic; attributing such power to your person that you may be compelled to remain among them."[47]

Nanao Knows

Alas, Snyder did not remain among the San Francisco hippies in 1967, but returned to Japan, where he lived for the next year and a half. During this time, he established close ties with a Japanese group known as *Buzoku* (which was the name of its newspaper) and also as *Harijan* or "Bum Academy" (which is what its members called it). This bohemian tribe was led by a charismatic poet named Nanao Sakaki, a World War II veteran who dropped out of Japanese society to become, in Snyder's words, "a wandering scholar and itinerant artist, and, like Thoreau, the unofficial examiner of the mountains and rivers of all Japan. For fifteen years he walked up and down the land, penetrating backcountry fastness and the laborers' ghettos of Osaka. . . . His early experimental poems were published in the little magazines of the lively Shinjuku community of semioutlaw intellectuals" (PS 122). Sakaki's followers, Katsunori Yamazato tells us, were known to carry signs that read, "We are primitives of an unknown culture."[48] Snyder met Sakaki for the first time in Kyoto in 1963, after having heard of him from Neale Hunter, a young Australian he met aboard the *Cambodge* during his trip to India. "Allen Ginsberg was in Kyoto visiting at the time," Snyder recalled years later, "so ours became a transpacific friendship." Snyder and Ginsberg told Sakaki what was going on in Western literary circles, and "these stories were reciprocated by Nanao's warm and detailed accounts of the amazing number of quietly working, passionate, impoverished, proudly independent writers and thinkers he had met across Japan in his wanderings" (PS 123).

Before he returned to California to teach at Berkeley in 1964, Snyder enlisted Ginsberg to help him procure a creative writing post for Sakaki at an American university. Ginsberg wrote back with bad news: "It's a square scene & requires college degrees."[49] Snyder was more successful in introducing Sakaki's name and tribal vision to American radio listeners during his panel discussion with Welch and Whalen on KPFA. "There's a group now of writers around that follow Sakaki that are wandering the countryside and managing somehow to have some kind of international view of life and the world," he explained, "instead of just being hung up on what it is to be a Japanese."[50] As Snyder's comment suggests, *Harijan*'s cohesiveness resulted from tribal affiliations, a shared sense of being together, and not from any national identity. According to Kaiya Yamada, a member of the Bum Academy also known as "Pon," their program was influenced equally by bohemian strains of "cosmopolitanism" and "anti-modernism."[51]

By the time he returned permanently to America in 1968, Snyder seemed to have learned from their example. "The idea of 'nation' or 'country' is so solidly established in most people's consciousness now that there's no intelligent questioning of it," Snyder told an interviewer from the *Berkeley Barb*. "It's taken for granted as some kind of a necessity. The sense of tribal social structure is one of the ways of breaking out of that nation-state bag, another way of seeing how large groups of people can relate to and organize each other without having a 'social contract.' Part of our failure in understanding Africa, Southeast Asia—and India, for that matter—is our inability to deal with groups of people who see themselves tribally rather than in terms of a nation" (TRW 10). Sakaki's Bum Academy was exemplary, Snyder went on to say, for unlike American hippies, its members were not hung up on getting publicity. Neither were they supported by their middle-class parents. They knew what it was like to subsist on the bottom rungs of society. The *Harijan* tribe, Snyder insisted, was "a group of people who have literally dropped out so thoroughly that they have to learn to make it together. . . . They don't cheat each other. They're reliable with each other. It's because of this real level of necessity and total commitment to this role that they have a kind of strength and courage and a kind of group unity that is very exciting to see" (TRW 11).

Snyder's high estimation of Sakaki and his tribe was apparent early on. In conjunction with the "Freeway Reading" held at San Francisco's Long-shoreman's Hall in 1964, Snyder published a broadside he titled "Nanao Knows." In this poem, images float by in a surrealistic swirl, and the Pacific Rim becomes a pleasurably dizzy domain:

Mountains, cities, all so
    light, so loose.   blankets
Buckets—throw away—
Work left to do.
    it doesn't last.

Each girl is real
    her nipples harden, each has damp,
    her smell, her hair—
—What am I to be saying.
There they all go
Over the edge, dissolving.

Rivetters bind up
Steel rod bundles
For wet concrete.
In and out of forests, cities, families
    like a fish. (BC 98)

What Nanao knows is an easy style of movement, likened in this poem to the movement of fish, whose cohesion in schools provides a useful model for those wishing to live cooperatively or tribally. There is work to do in this communal atmosphere, to be sure, but it is completed soon enough, and pleasure is near at hand in the form of girls. Through it all, Nanao moves through Japanese bohemia in an austere yet stylized way, writing about his everyday experiences as though they hold spiritual significance. Like Snyder, he holds the attention of his community by traveling an unconventional route to salvation.

In the epigraph Snyder placed at the beginning of *The Back Country*, Basho writes, "So—when was it—I, drawn like a blown cloud, couldn't stop dreaming of roaming, roving the coast up and down." While Basho's peri-patetic energies are indicative of Snyder's own travels along the coastal

Pacific, they also describe the wanderings of Nanao Sakaki, who had been at it even longer. In a prefatory note appended to a 1966 edition of Sakaki's poetry, Snyder echoes Basho's language as he praises Japan's latest wandering poet: "There's almost no place he hasn't been, on foot. Without home or money, he has somehow become a gentle breeze-like force for the footloose generation."[52] Together, Snyder and Sakaki indicate that leadership in the Pacific Rim counterculture does not center around a single person so much as it depends on the fundamental movements that link people and places together. For both men, the best way to know things is to release oneself into the company of others, and to move freely in an effort to explore collective relationships that thrive in tribal cultures. By the time Snyder left San Francisco in early 1967, he was ready to realize Pacific Rim communion in Sakaki's Banyan Ashram, on Japan's Suwa-no-se Island. *Regarding Wave* is the lyrical record of that discovery.

Regarding Wave:
Pacific Rim Communion

In *Regarding Wave*, Snyder shifts from considering tribalism as the basis for anthropological study and hippie activism to considering it as the basis for daily family practice. Crucial in this context is the appearance of Masa Uehara, the young graduate student Snyder met in Tokyo in 1966 and married on Suwa-no-se Island in 1967. With Masa as his muse, the poet of *Regarding Wave* is able to "close the circle" on his long Pacific Rim sojourn and return to California accompanied by an intercultural family unit.

As Karen Kelsky has convincingly argued, unions between Western men and Asian women in the postwar period had many difficulties. Will Petersen spoke honestly about the pitfalls of Pacific Rim intermarriage in the 1950s when he told Snyder, "Being married to a Japanese gal shifts things a bit, one is always a little more in this society, and also further out. Get tired of Ami being called *pom-pom*, get tired of stereotypes et al—get tired of being *gaijin*."[53] The Japanese society that Petersen and other bohemian expatriates found so attractive on so many levels was restrictive when it came to gender relations and often prohibitive when it came to sanctioning interracial partnerships, hence the initial refusal of Ami's parents to approve her marriage to Petersen. During their courtship, Petersen delighted in Ami's intellectual independence and her love for Western arts such as jazz, personal qualities he knew were hardly common in the current cultural climate. In a 1957 letter to Snyder, Petersen says he once "wondered why there aren't more like her, but now wonder[s] how she managed to be what she is with these incredible pressures of society, this idiotic school system, this!!!"[54]

Although Snyder encountered a slightly different set of problems a decade down the line, he too encountered suspicious Japanese parents. According to Professor Hisao Kanaseki, Mr. Uehara got "very upset" upon learning of his daughter's romance with a Westerner. "He asked me what kind of poetry you write," Masa explains to Snyder in a letter from the summer of 1966. "He thinks artists often need to have many different women to give their art consistently new life. He is afraid that I might be just one of those women for you. . . . This is very like [the] Japanese. I suppose this idea will not occur in American parents of [your] circle." In a follow-up letter, Masa attributes her father's uneasiness to Japan's "shame complex," the societal belief that if one family member goes astray, the reputation of the entire family necessarily suffers.[55]

Fortunately, Snyder was able to avoid societal pressures by virtue of his acceptance in Sakaki's *Buzoku* tribe, which had established a spiritually based satellite, the Banyan Ashram, on Suwa-no-se Island, located south of Kagoshima. A letter that Nanao Sakaki sent to Snyder in June 1967, just prior to Snyder's arrival, describes Suwa-no-se as a natural paradise full of "birds, fish, turtle, firefly, clouds, wind, bush, coral, [and] stars."[56] His curiosity piqued by Sakaki's account of exotic flora and fauna, Snyder wrote to his mother to tell her about his plans to visit Suwa-no-se with Masa. "I'll be leaving in about a month, to spend some time on a small sub-tropical island in the southerly reaches of Japan, close to Okinawa," he writes. "A number of the comrades from Tokyo are down there already planting vegetables. . . . Masa (my girl friend) is going along with me. . . . I'll be out of contact with the world until I come back from the island."[57] Snyder was not dropping out of the world so much as he was dropping in on a whole new scene. "I'm hardly able to write because where I am is so far from writing and reading," Snyder tells Lew Welch in a letter he sent from Suwa-no-se in early August. Yet he proceeds to give his friend a detailed account of his daily routine at the ashram, which included fieldwork, fishing, and meditating. Most important, he divulges his intention to marry Masa in three days, along with plans to have other tribe members join in the festivities.[58]

Snyder's marriage to Masa on Suwa-no-se on 6 August 1967 is arguably the crowning moment of his Pacific Rim pilgrimage. In "Suwa-no-se Island and the Banyan Ashram," a euphoric essay he published in the *San Francisco Oracle* in the autumn of 1967 and eventually placed at the end of *Earth House Hold*, Snyder describes an event in which the couple bonded with the earth and the tribe as well as with each other:

> Masa UEHARA and I were married on the island on August 6, the new moon. The whole ashram stayed up late the night before, packing a breakfast for the morrow—and broiling a splendid pink tai that was a present from the village. (No marriage is complete if you don't eat tai afterwards, the noble, calm AUSPICIOUS FISH of Japan.) We got up at 4:30 and started up the brush trail in the dark. First dipping into a ravine and then winding up a jungly knife-edge ridge. By five we were out of the jungle and onto a bare lava slope. Following the long ridge to an older, extinct crater, and on to the crest of the main crater and the summit shortly after sunrise. The lip of the crater drops off into cloud; and out of the cloud comes a roaring like an airport full of jets: a billowing stream upwards. The cloud and the mist broke, and we could see 800 feet or so down into the crater—at least a mile across—and fumaroles and steam-jets; at the very center red molten lava in a little bubbly pond. The noise, according to the switch of the wind, sometimes deafening.
>
> Standing on the edge of the crater, blowing the conch horn and chanting a mantra; offering shochu to the gods of the volcano, the ocean, and the sky; then Masa and I exchanged the traditional three sips—Pon and Nanao said a few words; Masa and I spoke; we recited the Four Vows together, and ended with three blasts on the conch. Got out of the wind and opened the rucksacks to eat the food made the night before, and drink the rest of the shochu. We descended from the summit and were down to the Banyan tree by eleven—went direct on out to the ocean and into the water; so that within one morning we passed from the windy volcanic summit to the warm coral waters. At four in the afternoon all the villagers came to the Ashram—we served sake and shochu—pretty soon everyone was singing Amami folksongs and doing traditional dances. (EHH 141–42)

The ceremony is a sensuous affair, with physical actions (hiking up the crater, looking down into the mouth of the volcano, and being deafened by the molten roar) serving as a prelude to traditional rituals (blowing the conch, sipping shochu, and reciting Buddhist vows). Given my thematic focus, I find it significant that one of the couple's first acts as newlyweds is to baptize themselves in the waters of the Pacific. Also salient is the fact that their union takes place on the twenty-second anniversary of the Hiroshima bombing. In striking contrast to the craters produced by American bombers in World War II, the volcanic void that opens up on Suwa-no-se Island is of nature's own making and stands forth as a marker of the Pacific Rim's topographical origins. Throughout this ceremony, Snyder and Masa invoke the Pacific region as a place of peace, casting aside memories of modern military atrocities in their quest for primitive communion.

Not until *Regarding Wave*, though, do we see the full extent to which Masa Uehara shaped Snyder's Pacific Rim consciousness. Snyder's return to poetry, and his newfound appreciation for the psychical effects of song, gives him greater latitude to explore in bodily terms the communal commitments he had been advocating in public appearances and in the essays he published in the underground press. *Regarding Wave* was initially published in a small press edition in 1969 by Iowa City's Windhover Press. This shorter version contained a song cycle entitled "Regarding Wave, Parts I–III," most of which made its way into the 1970 New Directions edition. The inspirational "wave" referred to in this sequence is Masa, who in all of her elegant manifestations (the name Masa translates into English as "elegant") serves as the poet's muse. According to the etymological lesson provided in "Wave," the first poem of "Regarding Wave I," the word "wave" is an archaic name for "wife":

Wave wife.
   woman—wyfman—
"veiled;   vibrating; vague" (RW 3)

Snyder had in fact already extolled the virtues of a vibrating or wavelike muse in the revised version of "Poetry and the Primitive" included in *Earth House Hold*. In a section from that essay entitled "The Voice as a Girl," Snyder claims that "breath is the outer world coming into one's body. With pulse— the two always harmonizing—the source of our inward sense of rhythm. Breath is spirit, 'inspiration.' Expiration, 'voiced,' makes the signals by which the species connects. Certain emotions or states occasionally seize the body, one becomes a whole tube of air vibrating; all voice" (EHH 123). In this literal rendering of poetic "inspiration," Snyder suggests that the vibrating muse is a kindred spirit whose creativity breaks through the poet's "ego barrier." Vak, the wife of Brahma, is held up as one example: "As Vak is wife to Brahma ('wife' means 'wave' means 'vibrator' in Indo-European etymology), so the voice, in everyone, is a mirror of his own deepest self." Snyder proceeds by citing the example of Nayika, "the essence of *Ali*, the vowel series," or the "Queen of the Vajra-realm" in Tantric Buddhism: "She is known as the Lady, as Suchness, as Void, as Perfection of Wisdom, as limit of reality, as Absence of Self" (EHH 125).

These dynamic female presences seem to be conjoined in "Wave," for in this poem Snyder suggests that his voice derives from an Asian wife who lends not only inspiration but also a "limit of reality" to his endeavors: "Ah, trembling spreading radiating wyf / racing zebra / catch me and fling me wide / To the dancing grain of things / of my mind!" (RW 3). For all the love exuded in this poem, some readers might want to ask whether Masa suffers a fate similar to the one Rey Chow says native women are forced to endure in postmodern theory—whether, that is, she exists in this poem as "the total sign, the Other, the entire function of which is to contest the limits of the conventional (arbitrary) sign itself."[59] As an inspirational gift and swimming "limit of reality," Masa functions as Snyder's muse, his "Wave," the "total sign" by which his Pacific Rim communion becomes flesh. But just how far does her own agency extend?

Song as Orientation

The earliest poems in *Regarding Wave* appeared as a series entitled "Eight Songs of Clouds and Water," first published in *Poetry* in March 1968. Six of these eight songs make their way into the "Regarding Wave II" section in the 1970 volume. In these poems we come to hear the collaboratively voiced erotic sounds that guide the poet back here, to America, an unknown homeland made all the more uncanny by song's homophonic layering. Once we hear (rather than merely read) the poems of *Regarding Wave*, we find that song aids the poet who wants to orient himself to various far-flung places in the Pacific Rim region. In poetry, as in nature, the sounds of song are able to transcend or otherwise elude physical barriers that prevent us from realizing our visionary ideals.

Deleuze and Guattari, the French theorists whose discussion of an imaginary home space called "The Natal" I referenced in an earlier part of this chapter, discuss song's efficacy in matters of cognitive mapping in "Of the Refrain," a chapter from *A Thousand Plateaus*. With their creaturely emphasis, they are particularly astute in describing how birds use song to mark a territory. They explain that humans use song in the same way. According to their thesis, there are three aspects of song: an aspect of orientation, an aspect of domestication, and an aspect of improvisation in which we join the world. Early on, they argue, a child uses song to make his way in the world, to construct spaces of security, and to make himself at home. In this, the first aspect of song, "a child in the dark, gripped with fear, comforts himself by singing under his breath. He walks and halts to his song. Lost, he takes shelter, or orients himself with his little song as best he can. The song is like a rough sketch of a calming and stabilizing, calm and stable, center in the heart of darkness."[60] Interestingly, in a 1977 interview, Snyder likewise explained that "one of the things that little children do first is to sing and chant to themselves. People spontaneously sing out of themselves—a different use of voice. By 'song' we don't have to limit ourselves to the idea of lyric and melody, but should understand it as a joyous, rhythmic, outpouring voice, the voice *as* voice which is the Sanskrit goddess Vak—goddess of speech, music, language, and intelligence. Voice itself is a manifestation of our inner being" (TRW 121).

Although Snyder claims that song is a "manifestation of our inner being," I find it interesting that his description of song relies upon the invocation of an external being—the goddess Vak, the wife of Brahma. Analogous in some respects to the psychoanalytic theory of the gaze, song is a fundamental part of ourselves that is projected outward and (mis)recognized in the other, who in such cases is heard as an echo rather than seen as a reflection. In *Regarding Wave*, Snyder finds his own version of the goddess Vak in the presence of Masa, who functions as the embodiment of pure song, or "voice *as* voice." As the mantra that can be invoked again and again as a means to enlightenment, Masa draws out Snyder's inner being and brings it to a point of sonorous resonance that is external to the body and abstract in its form, yet surprisingly intimate and undeniably natural. In the process, she allows the poet and his readers to get a better sense of where they are in the world. "A scary chaos fills the heart as 'spir'itual breath—in'spir'ation; and is breathed out into the thing-world as a poem," Snyder explains in a statement he published in an Open Form anthology, *Naked Poetry*, in 1969. "From there it must jump to the hearer's under'stand'ing. The wider the gap the more difficult; and the greater delight when it crosses."[61] To the degree that the songs dedicated to Masa helped Snyder negotiate the rather wide gap of the Pacific Ocean, his delight must have been great indeed.

According to Deleuze and Guattari, song aids us most when it domesticates the chaos that surrounds us. In their second aspect of song, they point to a scenario not unlike the one Snyder faced when he composed *Regarding Wave* in the midst of his return home to America with Masa in December 1968: "Now we are at home. But home does not preexist; it was necessary to draw a circle around that uncertain and fragile center, to organize a limited space. . . . The forces of chaos are kept outside as much as possible, and the interior space protects the germinal forces of a task to fulfill or a deed to do. This involves an activity of selection, elimination, and extraction, in order to prevent the interior forces of the earth from being submerged, to enable them to resist, or even to take something from chaos across the filter or sieve of the space that has been drawn."[62]

Elsewhere in their discussion, Deleuze and Guattari liken this circumscribed space to a "wall of sound" in a child's circular dance, which combines "rhythmic vowels and consonants that correspond to the interior forces of creation as to the differentiated parts of an organism."[63] The child's dance, in their formulation, is an interior expression that sonorously constructs a secure home space by picking out and domesticating certain "chaotic" elements in a rhythmic landscape. That these domesticated elements correspond to "differentiated parts of an organism" would seem to bode well for a *blason* poet who has already equated female bodies with landscapes and seascapes during his Pacific Rim odyssey. If, as the French theorists assert, the second aspect of song urges the singer "to take something from chaos across the filter or sieve of the space that has been drawn," we might speculate that the American poet singing to his Asian "Wave" wants to transport across the circumscribed space of the Pacific Rim a domestic partner who is able to help him sort out the meaning of his travels and adventures in this region.

As I have asserted previously, it is crucial to ask whether whatever gets sung (women, landscape, or seascape) also gets trapped within the lyric economy marked out by the singer. Fortunately, Deleuze and Guattari suggest that this need not be the case, since every circumscribed space remains open to new variations called "reterritorializations," which are introduced sometimes by other songs and sometimes by that space's own internal energies. In order to move forward, a circular wall of sound must be permeable enough to join the larger world knocking at its door. The third aspect of song arrives when that door opens, when "one opens the circle a crack, opens it all the way, lets someone in, calls someone, or else goes out oneself, launches forth. One opens the circle not on the side where the old forces of chaos press against it but in another region, one created by the circle itself. As though the circle tended on its own to open onto a future, as a function of the working forces it shelters."[64]

Indeed, if it is to become the gesture whereby we call someone into our home space as well as the presence that accompanies us as we move outside that circumscribed area, a song must be able to travel across real and imagined boundaries that it is, in fact, already in the process of transforming. Only by acceding imaginatively to this kind of fluidity, Deleuze and Guattari maintain, will the singer be able to leave his domestic space and align himself with "cosmic forces," and from that point forward "begin to bud 'lines of drift' with different loops, knots, speeds, movements, gestures, and sonorities."[65] By the time we enter the third aspect of song, we discover that certain circumscribed localities (like Golden Gate Park, where acid rock anthems transported hippies to another realm) are permeable enough to welcome global or even "cosmic" forces into their particular domain.

As the "voice" of the song Snyder sings, Masa Uehara emerges as the external force that, very much like an ocean wave, crosses the Pacific and helps to determine the Rim's geographic contours. This is especially true in "Regarding Wave II," which unlike the first section focuses on sound instead of sight. Once Snyder's lyrical sensibility is supplemented by this new sensory mode, the *blason* form that initially aided his reorientation to America in *The Back Country* takes on a whole new aspect. Consider "Song of the Tangle," a poem, set in Japan, in which a female body and a landscape blend into one another:

> Two thigh hills hold us at the fork
>   round mount center
>
>   we sit all folded
> on the dusty planed planks of a shrine

drinking top class sake that was left
  for the god.

   calm tree halls
   the sun past the summit
   heat sunk through the vines,
      twisted sasa

   cicada singing,
      swirling in the tangle

the tangle of the thigh

   the brush
   through which we push (RW 14)

An obstruction stands at the fork of the path the poet wants to travel. He is
held by "two thigh hills," between which rises "mount center," a real mountain perhaps, but alternatively a woman's mons veneris, which rises at the
convergence of her thighs. Folded together, probably in the *yabyum* posture,
the lovers enjoy as gods the fruits of a mountain shrine.[66] The middle of the
poem puts me in mind of John Donne's "The Sunne Rising," since we see two
lovers whose microcosmic union renders the passage of time, marked in both
poems by the retreating sun, largely irrelevant. The final five lines help us
gauge Snyder's understanding of song's ordering powers. Deleuze and Guattari would probably say that the cicada singing in the tangle marks or "territo-
rializes" that spot as its domain. Through the example of this scratchy-voiced
insect, Snyder recognizes the tangled frontier through which he too must
push. The tangle represents a blockage temporarily preventing him from
achieving a desired (w)holeness, which will remain inaccessible without a
penetrating thrust. In "Wave," the opening poem in this volume, Snyder had
confessed, "sometimes I get stuck in thickets" (RW 3). In "Song of the Tangle,"
though, he appears to have learned how to break through entanglements
without losing the teasing pleasure provided by momentary blockages.

What I find most intriguing in "Song of the Tangle," however, is the way
in which the "brush / through which we push" emerges as the locus for community building. The "we" refers perhaps to the two lovers: the "us" in the first

line. But by the end of the poem, it is unclear as to whether the "thigh" that is being negotiated is still being used as a metaphor for the brush on the mountain, or whether it refers instead to a part of the woman's body. I wonder, therefore, whether the poet is representing woman and land as limits that need to be penetrated if a home space is to become available for communion of another sort, and if so, whether this (male) bonding is interdependent and equitable, or hierarchical and unfair. Tim Dean speaks to these issues in *Gary Snyder and the American Unconscious*, claiming that "in opposition to models of linearity and indebtedness, Snyder offers the model of the cycle (in *Myths and Texts*), the model of the wave (in *Regarding Wave*), and the model of the loop (in *Axe Handles*). All three figures—cycle, wave, loop—are ecologically derived metaphors which emphasize process (over product), interdependence (or 'interpenetration' . . .), reciprocity (over originality and independence), and influence as a two-way flow in which no element is privileged as primary over others. It is thus never a question of isolating cause and consequence, but rather of developing networks of connections which can only artificially be atomized and whose only primary term is the earth in which relationships are grounded and of which in fact they consist."[67]

According to Dean, the networks we find in Snyder's work are plentiful and decidedly nonhierarchical. The only primary term for Dean is the earth itself, the open space within which he believes shared connections are properly "grounded." What Dean fails to mention, however, is that Snyder's evocations of open spaces almost always get coded as feminine. As a primary term, the woman, like the earth (or Earth Goddess), is the site at which a community of penetrating male thrusters seeks reciprocal interdependence (tellingly equated with "interpenetration" by Dean) and erotic sharing. That the penetration of the tangle is accomplished by a plural "we" suggests that the real union may be between the thrusters themselves or between the singers of the song (the poet and the cicada), and not between the poet and the land or between the poet and the lover, now viewed as a commonly held third term. To the extent that woman and land are recognized in these types of relationships, it is as a surface barrier blocking off the desired nothingness they are seen to house or envelop, and only rarely as a subjective presence taking part in a truly reciprocal partnership.

Snyder's penetration motif shifts from land to sea in "Song of the Slip." Curiously, no primary agent (no "I" or "we") is named in what is surely an erotic scenario:

```
          SLEPT
        folded in girls
    feeling their folds; whorls;
        the lips, leafs,
    of the curling soft-sliding
        serpent-sleep dream.

        roaring and faring
    to beach high on the dark shoal
        seed-prow

    moves in and makes home in the whole. (RW 15)
```

The first word in the poem, "SLEPT," arrives without an attendant subject. All we know at first is that the sleeper lies in the midst of feminine "folds" and "whorls." The second verb, "feeling," could refer to another action undertaken by the sleeper, in which case this poem would hearken back to "Beneath My Hand and Eye," a poem whose protagonist was able to feel, but not to know, "what 'is' within" (BC 123). Alternatively, "feeling" could refer to an action undertaken by the girls themselves, in which case an enjambment would exist between the second and third lines. In this scenario, the sleeper has happened upon a same-sex or autoerotic encounter in which a male presence is rendered superfluous. This possibility is short-circuited, however, if we regard the "seed-prow" as the active agent of this poem: the head of an inseminating vessel come into its port of call. In erotic terms, the "dark shoal," like the "tangle" in Snyder's previous song, becomes a terrestrial representation of the female pubic region. The poetic bark that makes landfall here finds a "home in the whole," a somewhat clumsy pun linking the discovery of a vaginal "hole" with the Buddhist concept of the void, which finds a hole to be emblematic of the Whole.

Read through a second time, the poem reveals more about poetics than it does about sex. In "Song of the Tangle," Snyder seemed to require a forceful push through the "brush" of land and body. In "Song of the Slip," by contrast, he needs a different kind of movement, one that will allow him to join the vertiginous "whorl" of a mysterious space. In a way, Snyder appears to partake in an opening-out-toward-chaos similar to the kind described in Deleuze and Guattari's third aspect of song. This connection makes even more sense when we hear Snyder talk about "whorls" in a 1973 interview with the *New York Quarterly*. On this occasion, he links the dynamics in Japanese song forms to the tensions between whirling energies and the "knots" they sometimes form, especially since "the Japanese term for song, *bushi* or *fushi* . . . means a whorl in the grain. It means in English what we call a knot, like a knot in a board. It's a very interesting sense of song—like the grain flows along and then there's a turbulence that whorls, and that's what they call a song. It's an intensification of the flow at a certain point that creates a turbulence of its own which then as now sends out an energy of its own, but then the flow continues again" (TRW 44). By describing song's nodal points as "intensifications of flow," Snyder uses the same terminology Deleuze and Guattari employ to explain song's territorializing powers. Evidently, "whorls" are not merely open regions needing to be filled; rather, they are sonorous intensities creating the musical refrains we hear and want to join. Taking his cue not only from Japanese traditions but also from the "Plains Indian view of physical nature" as communicated by Black Elk, Snyder wants us to recognize that these "turbulence patterns . . . manifest themselves temporarily as discrete items, playing specific roles and then flowing back again." What looks to be "formless" is really just matter in its transitional state, matter as it exists somewhere between the vertiginous "recurrences" that get established by metrical periodicity (TRW 44–45).

Tom Lavazzi has referred to this reenactment of the natural world's swirling energies as Snyder's attempt to achieve "torsion form," a process by which "the spiral"—be it in the form of a seashell, animal horn, tree trunk, nebula, wave, or sex organ—"functions as energy graph, mapping forces both in the external world and the unconscious." As Lavazzi sees it, "the symbol-making hand of the poet is kept in the background, allowing free play of the archetypal motion to find its own forms in any given situation."[68] Robert Kern makes a similar point, arguing that if the goal in Snyder's Buddhist poetry is "the apprehension of the 'form beyond forms,' then the poet must literally risk formlessness (from a conventional perspective) in order to reach it. He must seem to do as little as possible of a traditionally formal nature in writing the poem so as to prevent it from getting in the way of such apprehension."[69] In "Song of the Slip," for instance, Snyder takes a hands-off approach in an attempt to join the spiraling, "whorling" forces of nature, within which distinctions between subject and object are prone to collapse. "Each poem grows from an energy-mind-field-dance, and has its own inner grain," Snyder explains in his *Naked Poetry* statement. "To let it grow, to let it speak for itself, is a large part of the work of the poet."[70]

In "Song of the View," the next poem in the "Regarding Wave II" sequence, Snyder appears to backtrack a bit from this equitable position. We will recall that the issue of letting the Earth Goddess speak for herself was of prime importance in "To Hell with Your Fertility Cult," one of the scariest poems in *The Back Country*. In "Song of the View," Snyder reverses the equation. Instead of offering a ventriloquized response from a female Asian deity tired of the way in which her land and body have been used like a train terminal, "Song of the View" opens with a direct apostrophe to a female erogenous zone eliciting the poet's desire:

O!   cunt
that which you suck in-
        to yourself, that you
                hold
            there,
hover over,
excellent emptiness your
    whole flesh is wrappt around,
        the

hollow you bear
        to
    bear,
shows its power and place
in the grace of your glance. (RW 16)

Snyder's graphic worship of Pacific Rim women reaches its peak here as he "regards" his wave/wife. Again, we see his fascination with an "empty" female space promising transcendent freedom. Be this as it may, many of the lines contain ambiguous language, suggesting that the woman's offer of her body is conditional. We will notice, for instance, that the relative clause following the apostrophe is separated by a line break, just as its directional word, "into," was about to provide some clarification. Our first tendency might be to regard the cunt as that which the female sucks "into" herself, thereby keeping it for herself only. Such a reading would render the penetrating male superfluous, in the same way he was made to feel obsolete in a variant reading of "Song of the Slip." In "Song of the View," the secret space that the woman is wont to "hold / there, / [and] hover over" is an "excellent emptiness" the poet fears will remain closed off from the male imagination. But what sight cannot grant him, even in a poem whose title suggests a sustained gaze, sound surely can, since two homophonic puns help him recover some of the lost ground. The "whole flesh" that wraps around or seals off the female's desired nothingness can also be heard as "hole flesh," or that which is easily penetrated. In the same way, the phrase "bear / to / bear" can be heard as "bear to bare" (whereupon we find the woman, presumably Masa, struggling to overcome her modesty as she unveils herself), "bare to bare" (whereupon she bares herself purely for the sake of being nude), or conceivably even "bare to bear" (whereupon she bares herself in order to become inseminated and eventually bear Snyder's child).

Any of these homophonic readings will make listeners conscious of song's ability to expand our interpretive scope. In this case, the interchangeability of "bear" and "bare" causes listeners to concentrate more closely on the "showing" mentioned in the poem's penultimate line. Because this denuding or unveiling is intimately linked with the woman's offering of "grace," the scenario is quite different from the one at the end of "To Hell with Your Fertility Cult." No steely stare is returned from a Medusa-like goddess. No egg-hurling hysteric speaks back to spoil a Western man's appreciation of an Asian woman's body. Instead, the power accorded to female sexuality is mediated by the "grace" of a native woman willing to bare her body and show her love, thereby consummating her partner's desire.

Once we read "Song of the View" in this way, it is possible to regard the female gaze to which the male speaker in "Fertility Cult" subjugated himself as the first step in a two-part Orientalist fantasy. In a second step, the Western male returns the gaze, asking an Asian woman to lend him "grace," both as proof of her humanity (think of Will Petersen's identification of his wife Ami as "human" rather than "Japanese") and as proof that he actually exists (since, according to the logic of Orientalist discourse, there is no Occident without an Orient). Rey Chow addresses similar dynamics when she insists that Western contacts with the East, especially those including Asian women, have been shaped by passive-aggressive behavior on the part of the (male) colonizer. "Contrary to the model of Western hegemony in which the colonizer is seen as a primary, active gaze subjugating the native as passive 'object,'" Chow argues, "it is actually the colonizer who feels looked at by the native's gaze. This gaze, which is neither a threat nor a retaliation, makes the colonizer 'conscious' of himself, leading to his need to turn this gaze around and look at himself, henceforth 'reflected' in the native-object. It is the self-reflection of the colonizer that produces the colonizer as subject (potent gaze, source of meaning and action) and the native as image, with all the pejorative meanings of 'lack' attached to the word 'image.'"[71]

As I have sought to demonstrate throughout this book, Snyder's advocacy of Pacific Rim community during the 1950s and 1960s, though occasionally complicit with the politics of "lack" mentioned by Chow, was designed precisely to counteract the imperial policies implemented by Manifest Destiny types in cold war America. I cite Chow, though, because I too believe, despite the idealism promoted in various strains of Pacific Rim discourse, that basic structural inequalities continue to affect relationships between Western men and Asian woman. To the extent that I accept Chow's theory, I want to offer the possibility that Snyder, acting out his own version of ex nihilo creationism in "Fertility Cult" and "Song of the View," initially codes native women of the Pacific Rim as the primordial nothingness (or "void") staring back at him in anger or mystery, only to put them in the position of offering him "grace" whenever he comes to warrant their recognition and love. Through her act of lending grace, the Asian woman summoned by the poet in "Song of the View" gets marked and enjoyed as the symptom of the Western male's quest for self-knowledge.[72] Snyder unwittingly implicates himself here in colonial discourse, Chow might say, insofar as he profits poetically and spiritually from his special relationship with Masa, the Asian "native."

Although my decision to situate analysis of *The Back Country* and *Regarding Wave* within such contexts might not sit well with some admirers of Snyder's work, I believe it has important implications for ongoing debates about multicultural politics and interracial partnerships, especially those proliferating in the Pacific Rim region. Anthropologist Karen Kelsky has concluded that even when romance between two distinct racial populations appears to be consensual, or when women of color assume the role of sexual aggressor (as happened during the "yellow cab" phenomenon in Japan during the late 1980s and early 1990s), the result is sometimes "old racism in a new guise." Following an argument advanced by African-American intellectual bell hooks, Kelsky seeks to expose as fallacious and insidiously exploitative any argument celebrating "the titillating possibilities of an interracial, transnational erotic partnership," possibilities that loom large in the "Bennetonesque multicultural carnival of the contemporary United States."[73]

According to Kelsky, "White America's eagerness to appropriate 'lovers of color' simultaneously enacts and masks efforts to employ them as signifiers within a self-serving agenda of white liberalism and/or postmodern chic." It is in this context that she quotes hooks. "Getting a bit of the Other, in this case engaging in sexual encounters with non-white females, [is now] considered a ritual of transcendence," hooks asserts in her 1992 book, *Black Looks: Race and Representation*. "White males claim the body of the colored Other instrumentally, as unexplored terrain, a symbolic frontier. . . . They see their willingness to openly name their sexual desire for the Other as affirmation of cultural plurality." Along with hooks, Kelsky wants us to recognize that "we have entered a new era of race relations, in which sexual contact is often constructed as a 'progressive change in white attitudes toward non-whites.'"[74] Informed by the writings of Ruth Frankenberg and Abou Farman, Kelsky asserts on another occasion that, although "love (as well as desire, affection, and intimacy) is never (or rarely) reducible simply to race," the "insistent refusal to countenance race as an element of attraction is a form of denial that inevitably accompanies desire." Consequently, she says, "there is a gap . . . between the real mechanisms of racism and their almost total denial in the space of interracial relationships."[75]

Like Chow and Kelsky, Asian-American historian David Palumbo-Liu prefers a structural model over an individual choice model when it comes to examining interracial relationships in the Pacific Rim region. On American shores, he is apt to remind us, intermarriage became in the twentieth century a means by which Asian immigrants sought to assimilate themselves. In the end, many of these immigrants adopted "whiteness" as their new identity. As Albert Palmer discovered in his 1934 study, their intermittently successful attempts to erase discernible racial difference involved self-imposed changes in bodily habits and physical deportment, with some of those changes directly attributable to their intimate relationships with white partners.[76] Backed by such evidence, Palumbo-Liu grows particularly petulant whenever he encounters communitarian arguments in favor of interracial unions advanced by liberal humanists, including Arthur Schlesinger Jr., who in a 1997 issue of *Foreign Affairs* (of all places) claimed that "sex—and love—between people of different creeds and colors can probably be counted on to arrest the disuniting of America." According to Palumbo-Liu, Schlesinger's Bennetonesque argument "discloses a particular notion of the interfaces, positive and negative, between the 'foreign' and the domestic" while simultaneously revealing "the problem that has plagued America since its modern incarnation—the accommodation of migrancy, race, and ethnicity." In sum, Schlesinger's appeal represents little more than a "downhearted liberal mode of reconciling America with its disunified self."[77]

The key question that arises is whether Snyder's lyrical paean to Masa Uehara falls prey to the same pitfalls—the same varieties of structural racism and abstract blindness espied by Chow, Kelsky, and Palumbo-Liu— or instead whether it points to new communitarian possibilities. We should also try to account for the ways in which Snyder's liberal celebrations of Pacific community have been received differently by the white American counterculture than they have by less privileged communities populating the Rim, paying particularly close attention to the way the women of this region enter into this discourse. The stakes of human geography being what they are, it is not surprising that theoretically engaged critics have begun in recent years to scrutinize the gendered coordinates of Snyder's countercultural dreamscape.

Richard Candida Smith, who analyzes Snyder's representations of women in the context of Buddhist cosmology (focusing on the "dark mother" simultaneously symbolizing the womb and the tomb), seems to share some of Rey Chow's suspicions about the way native women have been represented in the solipsistic Western imagination, lamenting that the fact that "Snyder presents 'intimacy' but seldom personalities, an apparent contradiction that is a recurrent stylistic feature contributing to the 'Buddhist' overtones of his poems." In Candida Smith's estimation, "to describe women also as individuals would explode the schematic, formalistic quality of a view that finds support for a sense of relationship with the cosmos in the most intimate of human relations. At the same time abstraction respected difference because Snyder assumed he had no knowledge of the interior states of women. He did not speak for them, but only of the role women and the feminine principle played in *his* interior life."[78]

My own view on Snyder and intermarriage is decidedly mixed. Even as I cite the work of Candida Smith and other cultural critics, I find that their work (and possibly some of my own) fails to account for the "true love" that is the basis for Snyder's marriage, which in turn becomes the basis for the

Regarding Wave sequence, a lyric representation that both reveals and obscures facts about human relationships. I do not wish to succumb to sentimentalism or to take back what I have said about structural inequalities affecting the Pacific Rim's human geography. Rather, I want to suggest that theorists who constantly cast aspersions upon love between "different" types of people often take "hermeneutics of suspicion" to a dangerous extreme (Karen Kelsky, with her evenhanded analysis, should be applauded for eluding such traps). Not only does such an approach delimit the agency of partners who mutually and lovingly consent to interracial marriage, it also threatens to denigrate the hybrid identities of their offspring: the millions of Americans whose family trees contain branches of different colors. As Palumbo-Liu himself points out, this type of rhetoric was employed throughout the twentieth century by white racists who "feared that miscegenation would bring about the dilution of American blood and lead to the eventual demise of the nation."[79]

Indeed, to assert that the peoples of the East and West can never find true communion is, at some fundamental level, to perpetuate stereotypes and remain chained to the same Manichaean worldview adopted by America's most ardent cold warriors. Ironically, it is also to revert to the categorical thinking that Chow and Candida Smith claim to deplore. As a scholar working in the field of cultural studies, I recommend the texts cited above as a good check for those tempted to read Snyder's love poetry too simplistically or outside of its larger cultural context of trans-Pacific exchange. Increasingly, however, I am forced to wonder whether some theoretical "tactics of intervention" (as Chow calls them) end up distorting our perceptions of real people and their everyday relationships, which, in light of their own private mysteries, remain unknown to us.

Notwithstanding a few reservations, I have found it best to propose as a counterweight the quirky arguments put forth by Deleuze and Guattari, who rarely write about East Asia, and not at all about Snyder, but provide some of the most astute descriptions of the way diverse beings seek pluralistic unions across space. Armed with the terminology used by these French neopragmatists, I am apt to regard Masa as an "assemblage converter" or "relay component," for she is the one who allows Snyder to convert his Pacific Rim idea into a companionable and distinctly mobile form. As Deleuze and Guattari might say, Masa shows Snyder the way toward "an innovative opening of the territory" by deterritorializing an oceanic hemisphere carved up by competing nations.[80] As is evident in the poems of *Regarding Wave*, Masa is a variable and dynamic muse attuned to nuances of sight and sound. As an oceanic "wave," she moves easily between continents and is praised accordingly by a male poet who worships the "swimming limits" of her body. As a sound "wave," known alternatively as "the voice of the Dharma" (RW 35), she fulfills Deleuze and Guattari's three aspects of song: she orients Snyder to Pacific Rim geography; she domesticates the sublimity and mysteriousness of the East; and she opens out toward the world by traveling across the Pacific as part of an Amerasian family unit. In each of her manifestations, she allows Snyder to celebrate the culminating experience of his overseas odyssey. Unfortunately, we have no documentation from Masa to indicate how she regarded this Pacific Rim communion, nothing from her own hand to suggest how her journey differed from the great trans-Pacific jump made by Japanese war brides two decades earlier.[81]

Paying heed to the cogent assessments Caren Kaplan includes throughout *Questions of Travel*, her important study in cultural geography, we should continue to examine the roles native women are forced to play in the "cosmopolitan diaspora" popularized by "traveling theorists" such as Gilles Deleuze and James Clifford. All the same, we should try to grant to all traveling writers, Snyder included, the opportunity to extol the joys of consensual love between different types of people, free from the categorical prejudices that postmodern theoretical discourse strives to expose and eradicate, but occasionally appears to perpetuate. The exception, of course, would be when such writers fall victim to the "romantic nostalgia" that Kaplan espies in "postmodern discourses of displacement," or when they succumb to the "pieties of American multiculturalism and diversity" that Kelsky believes are distorting the truth about trans-Pacific cultural exchange, issues that loom large in any discussion of Snyder and the San Francisco Renaissance.[82] In his college thesis, Snyder discovered that "mixed marriages" among traveling peoples had for centuries accommodated a "diffusion of culture" along the Rim (HWHB 36). In the late 1960s, he experienced for himself the wavelike motion of Pacific cultures coming into loving contact. Regarded from other vantage points, though, the symbolic frontier Snyder marks out in *Regarding Wave* remains problematic, situated as it is in a contact zone where relationships between Western men and Asian women are often less than equitable.

Eventually, theoretical debates about interracial unions should try to address the practicalities affecting any domestic partnership. Daily practices are on full display in "Regarding Wave III," where Snyder chronicles the communal atmosphere that he and Masa enjoyed on Suwa-no-se Island. In "Burning Island" (RW 23–24), the romantic poem which inaugurates this section, Snyder asks a variety of righteous beings—the Wave God, the Volcano Belly Keeper, the Sky Gods, and the Earth Mother, along with the people of the Banyan Ashram—to bless the couple as they prepare to marry. In other poems, like "Roots" (RW 25), "Shark Meat" (RW 29), and "Everybody Lying on Their Stomachs, Head toward the Candle, Reading, Sleeping, Drawing" (RW 28), he pays homage to the work and leisure activities that take place in the Banyan Ashram's remote island habitat. Later in the sequence, Snyder introduces his first child, Kai, a mixed-race son born to him and Masa in Japan in 1968. Four consecutive poems in "Regarding Wave III" describe the conception, gestation, birth, and nursing of this boy. I call these "Kai poems." From the early chronicles of the boy in "Regarding Wave III" up through poems in *Turtle Island* (1974) and *Axe Handles* (1983), Snyder celebrates his son's hybrid presence and thereby consecrates a Pacific Rim "communionism" (RW 39) made transubstantial flesh.

The first of the Kai poems, "It Was When" (RW 31), revisits the evening Snyder's "sprout / took grip" in Masa's womb. The following poem, "The Bed in the Sky," depicts Kai as a fetus and marks a point at which the poet forsakes grand metaphysical musings to concentrate on intimate mysteries closer to home. "I ought to stay outside alone / and watch the moon all night," he thinks. "But the bed is full and spread and dark / I hug you and sink in the warm / my stomach against your big belly / feels our baby turn" (RW 32). In this scenario, the student of Pacific Rim religions, who "ought" to stay up all night contemplating the constellations (he once referred to "moon-watching" as one of the "arts of the Japanese" in a journal entry composed on Crater Mountain Lookout), finds a richer realm of mystery in the swirling, kicking energies within his wife's body. According to Katsunori Yamazato, this poem marks "the crucial moment in which the poet emerges out of the world of *The Back Country*, a world permeated, as in Snyder's quotation from Basho on the dedication page, with wandering spirit."[83] I concur with this judgment. Unlike "An autumn morning in Shokoku-ji" (BC 48), one of the "Four Poems for Robin," in which Snyder's flight from commitment results in his sleeping alone under the stars, "The Bed in the Sky" portrays a moment in which domestic life provides him with a sense of grounding. Just as Snyder's "sprout / took grip" in Masa, so too does the couple's mutual creation, Kai, take hold of the maturing poet to stop him from drifting.

"Kai, Today" (RW 33) reports on the child's birth from his mother's "sea," a fecund realm that nonetheless suggests a sublime void. Indeed, Kai's birth seems to awaken in Snyder a condition that Christopher Connery, drawing upon Freudian theory, refers to as the "oceanic feeling of limitlessness and boundlessness." Connery explains that some strands of Pacific Rim discourse invoke the ocean as a "maternal sublime, a horizon that is also a source." By so doing, they hearken back to a gendered description of the sea offered by Jules Michelet, who once referred to it as "the globe's great female, whose tireless desire, ceaseless procreation, and childbirthing never end." According to Michelet's utopian understanding of the maternal sublime, the sea emerges as a long-lost original site within which all current differences are subject to dissolution.[84] A child born out of that sea would seemingly embody all of its roiling sublimity and would therefore stand as a key representative for those wanting to promote original forms of Pacific Rim community while resisting the arbitrary divisions drawn by modern civilizations. Interestingly, the name Snyder has chosen for his son hints at these primordial possibilities, since "Kai" is the Sino-Japanese word meaning "open," "beginning," or "founding."[85] It is hardly surprising, then, to come across the rhetorical question and answer that Snyder includes in the middle of "Kai, Today": "What's your from-the-beginning face? / Kai."

In "Not Leaving the House," the fourth consecutive Kai poem in *Regarding Wave*, Snyder admits, "When Kai is born, I quit going out." Instead, he hangs around the kitchen, bakes cornbread, drinks green tea, and along with the couple's Suwa-no-se friend, Non, watches Masa nurse his son. The inclusion of a Banyan Ashram member implies that the presence of a child helps bring people together:

Masa, Kai,
And Non, our friend
In the green garden light reflected in
Not leaving the house.

> From dawn til late at night
> > making a new world of ourselves
> > around this life. (RW 34)

As is so often the case, Snyder's use of enjambment helps us understand his subtext. To read "the green garden light reflected in / Not leaving the house" in fluid fashion, as though there were no line break, is to hear the word "in" change from a directional (marking something reflected "into" the house through a window) to a preposition (giving way to the object of inquiry: the poet's decision not to leave the house). This enjambment makes us realize that "Not leaving the house" is neither an isolated line nor an isolated action, but is instead something that reflects forth a "green garden light," a paradise of the family's own making. Far from being restrictive, "not leaving the house" can spur us to cultivate our own garden and invite friends into it, "making a new world of ourselves" in the process.

Above all, Snyder praises Kai for bridging the physical distance between East and West. In "First Landfall on Turtle Island," a poem he wrote to commemorate his family's journey back to America in December 1968, Snyder marvels at his son's innate ability to navigate the waters of the Pacific. I find this to be one of Snyder's finest poems, even though he declined to include it in *Regarding Wave* or to reprint it in selected editions of his work:

> Crossing eastward the Pacific on the Washington Bear
> The high route, just under the Aleutians
> Twelve days storms and heavy seas
> Kai laughs in his playpen hanging on
> Rough or gentle weather, it's all one to him—
> Masa seasick, naps in the daytime,
> Last morning early: blue and smooth.
> Watch for Gray Whales from the flying deck
> A whale blows over by the lightship
> > brisk winds, Ah, Ah,
> Masa in her yellow parka, "the SKIN
> > of the California hills!"
> Seagull sails in, hangs there, a yard off my eye
> Past the port side the flash of the Point Reyes lighthouse—
> A whale rolls up, doesn't blow, just by the ship.

The long dawn chilly curve blue-purple.
    that's Bolinas, that's the oak in the
meadow on the ridge under Tam
I sat with Lew at—

A long land, a smooth land, clear sky,
    a whale
    a gull,
To say hello. (LOITR 115)

This family journey traces the route taken by the first voyagers to America, who came across the Pacific Ocean (not the Atlantic) thousands (not hundreds) of years ago. Once aboard the *Washington Bear,* a ship whose arcing route brings it close to the northern periphery of the Rim, "just under the Aleutians," Kai reveals his proclivity for Asian-American unity. "Hanging on" in rough or gentle weather, he traverses the Pacific like a pro. As the offspring of a Pacific Rim marriage, "it's all one to him." Just as the migrating family is about to make landfall on the American continent (renamed "Turtle Island" by Snyder, who borrows the geographic appellation from Native American creation stories), the birds and beasts of the eastern Rim pass by the boat in order to greet them, and Snyder takes the opportunity to point out Mount Tamalpais, where he and Lew Welch once shared a friendly moment. Still, I get the sense that it is Kai—more than the mediating presence of Masa, the sea animals, or old San Francisco friends—who best represents the syncretic mindset required to cognitively map the Pacific Rim and rename the land on its eastern periphery. If Snyder's poetry is notable for its incarnation of spiritual and communal values, as Michael Davidson convincingly argues, I think it is also right to say that Snyder finds in Kai an incarnate version of the Pacific Rim community he had been searching for all along.[86]

I want to close this section with a pair of poems that, taken together, indicate the instinctual ease with which Kai, once landed on Turtle Island, communes with its natural forms. In the 1950s, we will recall, Snyder's effortless communion with rugged West Coast landscapes elicited the wonderment of Lew Welch, Jack Kerouac, and others in San Francisco's Beat community. In "Water," a poem from *Riprap,* we are given a good reminder of the creaturely way the young poet moved through space:

Pressure of sun on the rockslide
Whirled me in a dizzy-hop-and-step descent,
Pool of pebbles buzzed in a Juniper shadow,
Tiny tongue of a this-year rattlesnake flicked,
I leaped, laughing for little boulder-color coil—
Pounded by heat raced down the slabs to the creek
Deep tumbling under arching walls and stuck
Whole head and shoulders in the water:
Stretched full on cobble—ears roaring
Eyes open aching from the cold and faced a trout. (RRCM 12)

Such face-to-face meetings with nature became the stuff of Beat legend and fodder for stories shared in the meeting places of the San Francisco counterculture. Years later, though, the creaturely poet appears to have met his match in the form of his one-year-old son, who practices nearly the same ritual at Sawmill Lake. Snyder records Kai's natural communion in "Meeting the Mountains":

He crawls to the edge of the foaming creek
He backs up the slab ledge
He puts a finger in the water
He turns to a trapped pool
Puts both hands in the water
Puts one foot in the pool
Drops pebbles in the pool
He slaps the water surface with both hands
He cries out, rises up and stands
Facing toward the torrent and the mountain
Raises up both hands and shouts three times! (RW 60)

Kai's gradual immersion in the mountain pool ends, much like his father's head-dunking some years before, with a face-to-face communion with the forces of nature. For good measure, the boy adds a ritualistic shout to signal his triumphant arrival in a new homeland. Importantly, Snyder does not feel the need to lend his son any guidance. Neither does he feel obliged to make this lyric seem "poetic." Instead, he registers the event in tentative and repetitive language, staying true to the thought processes Kai must have employed at the time. In the end, Kai figures things out for himself. In a manner I find rather touching, Snyder sees that the practical and unself-conscious behavior he had exhibited as a young man has been reborn in his son, whose "meeting the mountains" becomes his greatest lesson to date.

Culture Honors the Man Who Has Visited Other Realms

The concept of an Asia-Pacific culture region became increasingly Asia-specific for Snyder as he composed the poems of *Regarding Wave*. Having traced the contours of the Pacific Rim's human geography in *The Back Country*, the poet communes more directly and intimately with the people of that region and returns to Turtle Island with Amerasian family members in tow. "The pull to Asia had begun with an artificial element to it," Richard Candida Smith admits (after arguing that Snyder's children helped him turn his rupture with European-American traditions into a legacy), "but once accomplished in a way that created responsibilities and ties, there was nothing particularly out of the ordinary or exotic about seeking a synthesis of what had been distinct cultures." In making this claim, Candida Smith implies that Snyder may have been following the lead of Wallace Berman, an assemblage artist who was among the first members of the California counterculture to put his family members in the public arena as part of an avant-garde stance.[87]

Snyder himself would probably disagree with such speculations, preferring to say that the family is a "natural unit of practice" able to exist in any variety of shapes, sizes, and "constellations," and that a true *sangha* (or community) is open to all sentient beings in search of enlightenment (TRW 136–37). There is nothing special that sets him apart from other Americans, who are capable of the same kind of tribal communion, provided they are willing to open themselves up to new experiences. Still, as Candida Smith points out, there is no denying that Snyder's decision to include photographs of his attractive Amerasian family on the covers of his paperback editions in the 1970s solidified his standing as a spokesman in Pacific Rim matters and provided him with a good deal of (counter)cultural capital over the years.[88]

To highlight his accomplishments during his long residence in Asia, the *Berkeley Barb* ran an interview with Snyder immediately after his return to

America in 1968. The interview included pictures of Snyder, Masa, and Kai and was titled "The Return of Japhy Ryder," announcing to all that a famous figure from the Beat era had just completed his lengthy quest romance. In the interview, Snyder talks about the tribal models he would like to see take root in America, using the opportunity to praise the methods employed by Sakaki and his Bum Academy tribe in Japan. In due course, Snyder began to attract attention in the mainstream media as well. In "Poke Hole Fishing after the March," a late addition to *Regarding Wave*, Snyder speaks of being recognized by a roofing contractor, who in the aftermath of the People's Park confrontation in Berkeley turned to Snyder and said, "Yeah I saw you guys on TV" (RW 57). A few months later, in a photography layout entitled "Land Lovers," *Look* magazine featured a cast of American celebrities (Judy Collins, Arthur Godfrey) expressing their desire to live in harmony with the earth. Most prominent among the photographs was a two-page spread of the Snyder family enjoying a dip in a mountain creek. Snyder is naked, sitting on a rock with his back to the camera but turning around to smile. In his uplifted hands he holds Kai, who is also naked and squealing with delight, probably anticipating the dunk he is about to receive in the crystal-clear mountain pool shimmering in the background. On an adjacent rock sits Masa, her back arched, laughing heartily as her family frolics in front of her. It is a beautiful picture, one that is emblematic of the euphoria Snyder must have felt after having closed the circle on his Pacific Rim journey.[89]

By the end of the 1960s, the bohemian community in San Francisco had sufficient proof that their most famous Dharma Bum knew the distant lands and peoples of which he spoke. Snyder's reputation as a countercultural ambassador was enhanced by a glowing review of *Regarding Wave* in *Rolling Stone* magazine, a review that ended with an authenticating phrase: "Snyder's been there." Snyder himself could not have been blind to the admiration he had earned in the 1950s and 1960s, for as he put it in "Passage to More Than India," in the midst of explaining the elevated status accorded American Indians returning from their vision quests, "culture honors the man who has visited other realms" (EHH 107). As I describe the completion of Snyder's cultural return and continue to think about his ongoing quest for Pacific Rim community, lines from Whitman's "Passage to India" come to mind. Snyder declined to include these lines in "Passage to More Than India," his 1967 essay, but like his larger body of work they suggest that Americans will continue to expand their cultural horizons so long as they are willing to commune with regions and peoples that are never quite as distant, or as foreign, as they seem:

> Lo, soul, seest thou not God's purpose from the first?
> The races, neighbors, to marry and be given in marriage,
> The oceans to be cross'd, the distant brought near,
> The lands to be welded together.[90]

DIGGING IN

The Reinhabitation of Turtle Island

Throughout this study in cultural geography, I have sought to highlight the importance of mobility and diffusion in Snyder's life and work. As a boy, Snyder was struck by the trans-Pacific exchange epitomized by cargo ships in Puget Sound and *sumi* paintings in the Seattle Art Museum. As a student at Reed College, he learned about the routes of various Pacific Rim mythologies, many of which followed the coastal paths initially taken by the animals that inspired such stories. A few years later, as a fire lookout and logger in the Pacific Northwest, he was granted a panoramic view of his region and responded with a fluid verse technique, which allowed him to accommodate a diverse array of traveling cultures and wildlife migrations. As a traveler across Pacific Rim space in the late 1950s and 1960s, Snyder acted as a countercultural ambassador, providing members of the San Francisco Renaissance with a set of geographical coordinates by which to chart their far-flung desires, which ranged from a fascination with Zen Buddhism to the adoption of neotribal practices. At mid-century, Snyder traversed Pacific Rim space both imaginatively and physically, consistently shifting his vantage points to redraw the borders of an extensive cultural frontier. Countering cold war political rhetoric, he urged others to disrupt their fixed ideas about national citizenship, offering as an alternative a cultural identity that was more flexible, more inclusive, and more representative of America's first patterns of settlement, which were routed across the

Pacific, not the Atlantic. Advocating a transformative ethnopoetics, Snyder proved that a place-based identity did not mean a place-bound identity.

When he returned to California in December 1968, this indefatigable cultural voyager made the decision to stay put, thereby announcing a new phase of his life and career. Settling into an apartment on Pine Street, in San Francisco's Japantown, Snyder readied *Regarding Wave* for publication and made plans to build a rustic homestead in the Sierra Nevada foothills on a hundred-acre parcel of land that he had purchased along with Allen Ginsberg and Richard Baker (the future abbot of San Francisco Zen Center) back in 1966. On this site, Snyder and a group of backcountry friends spent much of the next two years constructing a farmhouse. According to plans first hatched in the early 1960s, Snyder followed a design inspired by Japanese and Mandan Indian architecture.[1] He named his rural compound Kitkitdizze, after the aromatic tarweed that, along with native species of pine and oak, covered the surrounding slopes. Over time, Kitkitdizze has become associated with Snyder in the same way that Tor House is associated with Robinson Jeffers, or Rowan Oak with William Faulkner.

With his Pacific Rim journeys of the 1950s and 1960s complete, Snyder devoted attention to his Amerasian family (a second son, Gen, was born in 1969) and to the nurturing of local community on San Juan Ridge. Working alongside his neighbors, Snyder built a schoolhouse and established a Buddhist meditation hall named after a line in a Lew Welch poem. Ring of Bone Zendo was formally dedicated in 1982, on the eleventh anniversary of Welch's mysterious disappearance into the woods near Kitkitdizze on 23 May 1971. Though most historians of the Beat movement assume that Welch died soon afterward, either from the shotgun he was carrying or from exposure to the elements, letters Snyder exchanged with his mother and his friend Howard McCord indicate that Welch was found alive in San Francisco shortly thereafter.[2] Whatever the true outcome, Welch's disappearance was just the latest in a series of events signaling the end of the San Francisco Renaissance. In 1969, Jack Kerouac, who had been absent from the scene for more than a decade, died at his mother's house in Florida. That same year, Phil Whalen departed for Kyoto to study Buddhism. Meanwhile, Allen Ginsberg was spending much of his time on a farm he had purchased in Cherry Valley, New York.

With the Beat community dispersed and the hippie community still shaken by the disastrous rock concert at Altamont and Ronald Reagan's crackdown on Berkeley demonstrators at People's Park, Snyder's decision to leave the Bay Area for a rustic retreat in the Sierras does not seem so surprising. At Kitkitdizze, he directed his attention toward homesteading practices. In doing so, he edged closer to Japhy Ryder's stated intention in *The Dharma Bums*, which was to assemble a "fine free-wheeling tribe in these California hills." At the same time, Snyder adopted a more grounded approach, using his extensive knowledge of the natural world and his recent experience as a member of the Banyan Ashram tribe to nurture the Buddhist concept of *sangha*, or a community of all beings, appropriate to his new locality.

In essays and interviews, Snyder has described his return to America in the late 1960s as a process of reinhabitation. Accordingly, the Pacific Rim emphasis in his work sometimes takes a backseat to local issues such as school district policies and watershed maintenance. Snyder seemed to revel in a newfound freedom that came with living in the interior. "I'm developing a sense of the Continent and don't like the coast as much as I did," Snyder confessed in a 1970 letter to Phil Whalen. In another letter sent that year, he told his Reed classmate, now stationed in Kyoto, "Lots of room here if you want to live in the country when you come back (if you come back!). USA actually not so bad."[3] In his professional writing, Snyder echoed such sentiments. In "Four Changes," a politically charged prose piece written just a few months after his return from Japan, Snyder inspired American environmentalists with the following mantra: "Find your place on the planet, dig in, and take responsibility from there" (TI 101). Only by taking a local approach, he argued, would citizens of this continent come to appreciate the natural boundaries (watersheds, drainages, wildlife habitats) sustaining their daily life and conditioning their psychological well-being. "One of the key problems in American society right now," Snyder told Peter Barry Chowka in a 1977 interview, "is people's lack of commitment to any given place—which again, is totally unnatural and outside of history" (TRW 117). From Kitkitdizze, his chosen place, Snyder has spent the past three decades redressing this imbalance.

Over the years, Snyder's environmental advocacy has become increasingly pronounced and intellectually complex. This second phase of his career—which to date includes four volumes of poetry (*Turtle Island* [1974], *Axe Handles* [1983], *Mountains and Rivers without End* [1996], and *Dangers on Peaks* [2004]), three volumes of prose (*The Old Ways* [1977], *The Practice of the Wild* [1990], and *A Place in Space* [1995]), a volume of interviews and talks

(*The Real Work* [1980]), and two substantial selected editions (*No Nature* [1992] and *The Gary Snyder Reader* [1999])—deserves deep and thoughtful analysis. In this epilogue, I will try to provide a transition to such a project, which will rely upon letters and private papers that are just now being catalogued at UC–Davis. To begin this transition, and to bring my present discussion of Snyder's early career to a close, I have chosen to address two trends emerging in his work during the early 1970s. The first is his identification with the native peoples of America. The second is his recognition of interconnected ecological zones, or "bioregions," which provide the natural basis for all geographic constructs. In the first instance, Snyder draws closer to the North American continent. In the second, he finds new reasons for claiming citizenship within a larger Pacific Rim community.

Becoming Native

In the late 1960s, it seemed like everyone in the American counterculture was getting "back to the land." A musical fusion called "country rock"— spearheaded by the Band, the Byrds, and Bob Dylan—began appearing in record store bins. Popular acid rock bands on the Haight-Ashbury scene, including the Grateful Dead and Quicksilver Messenger Service, began to spend more time at their rural ranches. The leaders of San Francisco Zen Center, founded in 1962, also made tracks for the hinterlands, opening the doors to their new mountain monastery at Tassajara Springs, ten miles inland from Big Sur, in 1969. Three years later, Zen Center established another rural outpost at Green Gulch, a "teaching farm" located near Muir Beach in Marin County.[4] Even those remaining in San Francisco found a way to incorporate rural values into their urban lifestyle. Readers of Ed Brown's *Tassajara Bread Book* and Stewart Brand's *Whole Earth Catalogue* adopted macrobiotic diets and set up cooperative food stores. Taking a more political approach, Peter Berg and other members of San Francisco's most visible anarchist group, the Diggers, began distributing the "Planetedge Papers" to promote their "Green City" program.[5] Meanwhile, thousands of middle-class citizens from across the country who picked up magazines such as *Life* and *Look* and saw features about "The Great Woodstock Rock Trip" and "Land Lovers" decided that they too wanted to join the back-to-the-land movement, leading Yale law professor Charles Reich, in a controversial best-seller entitled *The Greening of America*, to surmise that America was becoming a nation of hippies.[6]

The initial phase of the back-to-the-land movement reached its climax in the spring of 1970, when America celebrated its first Earth Day. On this occasion, Snyder delivered a speech at Colorado State College. Repeating Chief Seattle's famous (and probably apocryphal) warning to Anglo invaders who took possession of Indian lands, Snyder nonetheless expressed his hopes for the countercultural youth of America, who he predicted will "meet the spirits of the dead Indians and will themselves, in their hearts, become Indians, not white men, and will become natives of this place, not invaders."[7] Unfortunately, in the years to come, the back-to-the-land movement, like most utopian experiments, was plagued by naive rhetoric and misguided assumptions about rural living. Woodstock may have temporarily provided hippies with a muddy baptism equal to their capacity for self-righteousness, but a film like *Easy Rider*, with its devastating portrayal of a dysfunctional New Mexico commune, clearly exposed the limitations of their pastoral project.

In his attempt to counter this trend, Snyder spent much of the 1970s stressing the idea of "becoming native" to North America, by which he meant cultivating a familiarity with, and deep respect for, one's natural surroundings. Not surprisingly, American Indians provided Snyder with his core of knowledge on this subject. In January 1969, just a month after his return from Japan, he attended a pantribal conference of Indian activists in southern California, where he became increasingly aware of a "native-inspired cultural and ecological renaissance for all of North America," the land mass that one of the Navajos in attendance intriguingly referred to as "Turtle Island." Snyder remembers that this alternative name for America was "instantly illuminating," for it allowed him to accept the natural and mythical relationships conditioning his geographical identity. Digging deeper into the indigenous mythologies he had studied as a young man, Snyder once again realized that "the landscape was intimately known" to most Indian cultures, and that their "very idea of community and kinship embraced and included the huge populations of wild beings" (PS 241–42). In an era when ecological devastation and geopolitical warfare between aggressive nation-states had become the norm, he argued, Americans would do well to follow the example set by the Indians, who for years had nurtured a sense of community being by being and place by place.

Inspired by the lesson handed down by the Navajo man and informed by his own immersion in ecological discourses, Snyder chose *Turtle Island* as the title for his Pulitzer Prize–winning volume of verse. Upon its publication in 1974, *Turtle Island* became an essential guidebook for the environmental wing of the American counterculture. In an introductory note to this volume, Snyder repeats what he learned at the tribal conference back in 1969, namely that Turtle Island refers to "the old/new name for the continent, based on many creation myths of the people who have been living here for millennia, and reapplied by some of them to 'North America.'" In effect, *Turtle Island* offered an invitation for American readers to leave the United States behind and enter an alternative realm, which curiously enough happened to be situated right under their feet.

Just as Haight-Ashbury hippies appropriated certain tribal motifs, many counterculture environmentalists tended to view the ancestral homelands of American Indians as something to share. Snyder himself has called the Turtle Island continent a "commons," a shareable space available to anyone fully dedicated to the process of "becoming native." Accordingly, the name "Turtle Island" usually appears whenever Snyder claims indigenous status. For example, in an essay from the 1980s entitled "The Place, The Region, and the Commons," Snyder writes, "There are tens of millions of people in North America who were physically born here but who are not actually living here intellectually, imaginatively, or morally. Native Americans to be sure have a prior claim to the term native. But as they love this land they will welcome the conversion of the millions of immigrant psyches into fellow 'Native Americans.' For the non-Native American to become at home on this continent, he or she must be *born again* in this hemisphere, on this continent, properly called Turtle Island" (PW 43).

In 1992, speaking to an audience at the 92nd Street Y in New York City, Snyder reiterated his belief that non-Native Americans could become indigenous to Turtle Island:

> I don't know if I'm an Indian or not. However, I do know that I'm a Native American. Here again is a Turtle Island bioregional point. Anyone is, metaphorically speaking, a Native American who is 'born again on Turtle Island.' Anyone is a Native American who chooses, consciously and deliberately, to live on this continent, this North American continent, with a full spirit for the future, and for how to live on it right, with the consciousness

that says, 'Yeah, my great-great-grandchildren and all will be here for thousands of years to come. We're not going on to some new frontier, we're here now.' In that spirit, African-Americans, Euro-Americans, Asian-Americans, come together as Native Americans. And then you know that those continents that your ancestors came from are great places to visit, but they're not home. Home is here. (GSR 336)

A year later, during a lecture at UC–Davis, Snyder once again gave his approval to native conversion experiences, asserting that "ultimately we can all lay claim to the term *native* and the songs and dances, the beads and feathers, and the profound responsibilities that go with it. We are all indigenous to this planet, this mosaic of wild gardens we are being called by nature and history to reinhabit in good spirit" (PS 250).

After *Turtle Island* won the Pulitzer Prize in 1975, Native Americans began to raise serious questions about Snyder's "born again" indigeneity. For writers such as Geary Hobson, Leslie Marmon Silko, and Wendy Rose, the ecological reasoning that lay behind Snyder's use of the term "native" was as groundless as the familial reasoning offered in support of the Haight community's neotribal paradigms in the late 1960s. In particular, Silko blamed Snyder for tapping into Indian history while ignoring the history of his own ancestors, who had moved to the West Coast from Texas, joining a long line of Anglo settlers "occupying stolen property" in this region.[8] Even more disturbing to Native Americans (and to native activists of the interior Pacific, including Haunani-Kay Trask, who in a 1984 talk reminded Hawaiian settlers that "'local' does not translate into 'indigenous'") was a growing tendency on the part of white writers to "steal" their cultural stories. The "white shamanism" initiated "inadvertently" by Snyder and practiced by "the bastard children . . . who began to imitate him" was nothing less than a "new version of cultural imperialism," Hobson argued in the late 1970s. Following up on Hobson's thesis fifteen years later, Rose suggested that Snyder was the one who "set the entire whiteshaman phenomenon in motion with his 'shaman songs' included in his *Myths and Texts*."[9]

Although Snyder had long ago sought to justify his role in the San Francisco Renaissance by linking the "ancient function of the shaman" with that of the community-minded poet, or he who "articulates the semi-known for the tribe" (TRW 5), Hobson and Rose lamented the fact that members of the white counterculture continued to ignore original Native

American mythologies, insofar as they preferred to hear about "the work of being together on Turtle Island" (TI, "Introductory Note") from the mouth of a white spokesperson. As Silko pointed out, at least Snyder admitted to "borrowing" his volume title and poems like "Prayer for the Great Family" from indigenous myths, thus avoiding the bogus posturing of Carlos Castenada, Lynn Andrews, Sun Bear, and other New Age writers, who either falsified or obscured Native American source material in their popular books.[10] Ultimately, however, Silko found that Snyder "intellectualizes his complicity in the land theft by enthusiastically quoting the pre-columbian notion that 'the land belongs to itself.'" Along with other Native Americans who were "very much aware of the occupancy and use rights of land," she voiced her concern that Snyder's "rediscovery" of Turtle Island, despite his good intentions, avoided the responsibilities handed down by history and thus missed an opportunity to locate a "genuine American identity."[11]

Seemingly undaunted by such criticism and bolstered by the support offered by other Native American writers such as Scott Momaday and Vine Deloria Jr., Snyder pressed forward with his agenda for becoming native. "In poetry we all know we are free to lovingly use anything that's available," Snyder told Michael Helm in a 1979 interview, when asked to respond to Hobson's charges of white shamanism. "I'm speaking from a lot of sources, from what I've learned. But it's like the air. It's free and there for all of us. Just as Coyote is free for all of us. Coyote doesn't belong to anybody. Coyote is a trickster. The trickster is an archetype in all of us. There's no cultural monopoly on any of this. What I have done is draw from what I perceive to be certain constituencies that led in the direction of a certain kind of health and sanity, of a certain kind of vision, wherever I found them" (TRW 155, 156).

Although Snyder's statement hints at the appropriative strategies Silko and Hobson angrily dismiss, it dovetails nicely with a defense offered recently by Tim Dean. According to Dean, Snyder's predilection for including Native American stories in his poetry should not be confused with any strategy on his part to appropriate or steal Native American culture. Instead, we should notice that the poet's pluralistic approach has "departed from a long tradition of figuring North American landscape and its native inhabitants in distinctly insidious ways." Countering Silko, who at one point claims that whites in America have adopted Indian ways because "they have failed to create a satisfactory identity for themselves," Dean asserts that Snyder "is not remotely interested in identity" and has therefore successfully steered clear of aesthetic discourses "incorporating, romanticizing, or otherwise appropriating otherness in order to constitute the self." Snyder is far more interested in nurturing "forms of continuity among living beings" and locating "a web of interdependence that connects human beings to nonhuman nature," Dean postulates, than he is in claiming other cultures as his own.[12]

In this context, it is important to mention that Snyder has taken care not to intrude upon the most intimate and sacred aspects of Native American life. In a discussion with Jonathan White that took place twenty years after the white shamanism controversy first erupted, Snyder opined, "I long ago learned to control my desire to go to certain Indian ceremonies—out of respect for them, actually. I felt it was better that they happened without me intruding, and that I could enjoy them from afar. I feel that way about grizzly bears, that their space should be their own. And yet I would love to hang out with them, ideally. But maybe one of the ways we hang out with them is in stories, since it's not a good idea to try to do it too literally."[13]

To hear Snyder tell it, his ideas about indigenous identification in the 1970s did not stem from any naive quest for exotica, but rather from his belief that twentieth-century Americans shared collective responsibility for living peacefully in a "post-frontier" environment where old divisions between cowboys and Indians, white men and red men, were fast disappearing. Speaking to Peter Barry Chowka in 1977, Snyder expressed his hope that people in the postfrontier West would discard the outdated ideal of rugged individualism and edge closer to ecological and anthropological models of sustainability and reciprocity (TRW 129–30). The seeds of Snyder's postfrontier thesis were already evident in the statement he provided for the "Land Lovers" feature in *Look* magazine back in 1969: "The old idea of taming the Wild West is a cheap chamber of commerce idea. But *who was* that frontiersman, that cowboy? Not a very pleasant human being—irresponsible, violent, drunken, brutal. We've got to leave the cowboys behind. We've got to become natives of this land, join the Indians and recapture America."[14] It therefore seems a bit incongruous to hear Snyder, in an interview with Ann Charters conducted that same year, celebrate Neal Cassady as a "cowboy," an archetypal "frontier type" not unlike Jedediah Smith, "the first white man to go through Utah."[15]

Regardless of whether Snyder deserves the charges of cultural appropriation levied against him by certain Native American writers (and this remains a highly debatable issue), he clearly meant *Turtle Island* to serve as a wake-up call, not only for the millions of Americans out of touch with their native environment but also for a generation of San Francisco hippies susceptible to pie-in-the-sky idealism. In particular, he cautioned his peers in the counterculture against rushing into rural areas without sufficient knowledge of the various biotic communities such moves were bound to affect. Of course, the process of peaceful reinhabitation had become second nature for Snyder after decades of traveling through various wilderness areas. Consider "Night Herons," a poem Snyder cherishes for its ability to break down city/country "dualisms" (TRW 91). In this poem, the Pacific Rim voyager equates his return to American shores with a migratory bird's return to San Francisco Bay:

> How could the
> night herons ever come back?
> to this noisy place on the bay.
> like me. . . .
>
> We pick our way
> through the edge of the city
> early
> subtly spreading changing sky;
> ever-fresh and lovely dawn. (TI 36)

Unfortunately, not everyone in the back-to-the-land movement was able to locate a creaturely path to natural communion. In due time, Snyder felt forced to divulge his frustration with neophyte homesteaders in a poem entitled "Call of the Wild":

> The ex acid-heads from the cities
> Converted to Guru or Swami,
> Do penance with shiny
> Dopey eyes, and quit eating meat.
> In the forests of North America,
> The land of Coyote and Eagle,
> They dream of India, of
>   forever blissful sexless highs.
> And sleep in oil-heated

Geodesic domes, that
Were stuck like warts
In the woods.
And the Coyote singing
    is shut away
    for they fear
    the call
    of the wild. (TI 21–22)

By placing short, choppy lines at the end of this passage, Snyder re-creates the huffy breathing patterns of shaky San Francisco acidheads, who try in vain to keep the wilderness at bay, even though their initial mission supposedly involved communion with the earth and its creatures. Along with the other guilty parties called to task in this poem—an elderly man who intends to ask a "Government Trapper" to kill the singing coyote interrupting his nighttime sleep and U.S. bomber pilots dropping munitions on the jungles of Southeast Asia—these hippie vagabonds need to realize that they are also participating in a "war against the earth." In Snyder's opinion, they have wavered in their commitment to the land in the same way that other "dopey-eyed" spiritualists changing swamis and gurus on a whim have been less than steadfast in their commitment to Eastern religious practices. As a result, they have forsaken the cooperative vision necessary for a sustainable life in the postfrontier West. "Long haired or not long haired, there is a streak of selfish individualism that the Chinese, for example, see as America's downfall," Snyder told Ekbert Faas, when asked to reflect upon the failure of counterculture communes in the late 1960s. "The survivors were the ones who became practical, so to speak, realized their limits and realized that they would have to do a lot of hard work and realized that they would have to get along with their neighbors."[16] In "Call of the Wild," as in so many of Snyder's creaturely texts, we learn that those "neighbors" include more than just human beings.

To a certain extent, the cautionary language employed in "Call of the Wild" represents the direction Snyder was taking his verse in the 1970s, which is to say closer to the style of argumentative prose. *Turtle Island* was Snyder's big statement, his recommendation of "how to be" in a time of political and environmental crisis.[17] In an effort to get his message across, he found himself relying less on nuance and more on invective. One can trace the advent of Snyder's harder-edged and plainspoken style back to 1967, when Digger activist Emmett Grogan interrupted a meeting of Students for a Democratic Society (SDS) to read "A Curse on the Men in Washington, Pentagon," a broadside that Snyder had composed during his brief stay in San Francisco that year. In this poem, Snyder expresses his desire to "kill the white man, / the 'American' / in me," so that "my children may flourish / And yours won't live." To a degree, Snyder's broadside anticipated the incendiary antiwhite language used in Weather Underground manifestos, one of which famously claimed, "We are against everything that's 'good and decent' in honky America." So vituperative was Snyder's "Curse," in fact, that the *San Francisco Oracle*, an important venue for the poet during the Summer of Love, hesitated to publish the poem in its Indian issue, and actually ended up pulling it from the second printing.[18]

In 1973, as the Vietnam War was winding down, Snyder was more concerned with people doing harm to the environment than he was with members of the Defense Department. Even so, his poetry retained the political bite he had demonstrated in "Curse" six years previously. Catching wind of this change in his writing, a group of Snyder's friends gathered in Berkeley to hear him read early versions of the *Turtle Island* manuscript. On this occasion, he pointedly asked whether his new poems, many of which railed against politicians and polluters, could "succeed as poetry."[19] Although his peers reportedly refused to pass judgment at this gathering, a number of literary critics—most notably Charles Altieri, David Carpenter, and Michael Davidson—have come down hard on Snyder, dismissing his poetry of the 1970s as sloganeering, misanthropic, and "hectoring" in its tone. Davidson quotes from "Tomorrow's Song," a poem in *Turtle Island*, to illustrate his point:

> The USA slowly lost its mandate
> in the middle and later twentieth century
> it never gave the mountains and rivers,
> > trees and animals,
> > a vote.
> all the people turned away from it
> > myths die; even continents are impermanent
>
> > Turtle Island returned.
> > my friend broke open a dried coyote-scat

removed a ground squirrel tooth
pierced it, hung it
from the gold ring
in his ear.

We look to the future with pleasure
we need no fossil fuel
get power within
grow strong on less. (TI 77)

"Instead of his haiku-like spareness," Davidson argues in his response to this poem, "Snyder permits himself a degree of discursiveness that limits playfulness in language and diminishes acoustic richness." Drawing a distinction between "the poet who regards his lyric skills as a dimension of an ecological, natural order and the poet who places those skills in the service of an ethical system beyond those orders," Davidson suggests that Snyder's transition from seer to prophet—which is to say his transition from the poet who simply presents to the poet who merely instructs—essentially undermines the Buddhist sensibility that made his early nature writing so successful.[20] To his credit, Snyder has accepted criticism of this kind rather openly and good-naturedly. "I allowed myself to be didactic," he confessed to a pair of interviewers in the 1990s, "and with varying results!"[21] Despite his modesty, there is no denying that *Turtle Island*'s dedication to the environmental issues of its day thrust Snyder into the national spotlight. Readers who were less inclined to engage his early experimental poetry or his anecdotes about Zen training in Japan discovered that they were quite willing to encounter essays that addressed water and air pollution simply because these problems hit closer to home. "*Stay together / learn the flowers / go light*," the closing lines of "For the Children" (TI 86), may come across as pedantic, but these instructions were easily grasped and appreciated by mainstream Americans eager to find their way back to the land.

Interestingly, it was Snyder's humor, not simply his pedantry or sanctimoniousness, which accounted for *Turtle Island*'s success. With a sense of detachment, the poet discovered that he could address heated issues in an even-keeled and slightly ironic fashion. Taking multiple points of view into account, he promoted the idea of inclusiveness, and thereby pushed closer to his goal of establishing *sangha* on Turtle Island soil, while managing to avoid excessive rhetorical posturing. In poems such as "Why Log Truck Drivers Get Up Earlier Than Students of Zen" and "I Went into the Maverick Bar," for example, we see Snyder reaching out to establish friendly contact with constituencies that most Bay Area radicals tended to dismiss out of hand. In the first poem, Snyder wonders aloud about the thoughts of a truck driver traveling the "thirty miles of dust" up the Tyler Road grade, just beyond the Kitkitdizze homestead, out near Tahoe National Forest. Eventually, he surmises that this blue-collar worker lives his life fully, moment by moment. For the truck driver in the "before-dawn dark," as for the serious student of Buddhism just beginning his morning *zazen* practice, "there is no other life" (TI 63). With one simple and pithy phrase, Snyder simultaneously deflates religious piety and pays homage to the everyday mysteries that cause him, and anyone else trying to attain Buddhist mindfulness, to stop and chuckle.

In "I Went into the Maverick Bar," Snyder once again takes a break from pressing concerns, in this case an ecological advocacy program in New Mexico, and enters a space of leisure where double shots of bourbon and Merle Haggard, not LSD and the Jefferson Airplane, are the drugs and music of choice. Tucking his long hair under a cap and leaving his earring in the car, he arrives at a scene of "short-haired joy and roughness": American "stupidity" he calls it later in the poem. He then recalls the good times he spent with woodsmen in Madras, in this case a town in Oregon, not the city in India. The irony of a San Francisco bohemian listening to Haggard belt out lines like "We don't smoke Marijuana in Muskokie" is undeniable, and yet there is little here that seems awkward or insincere. By poem's end, Snyder leaves the bar and becomes a countercultural leader once more: "I came back to myself, / To the real work, to / 'What is to be done'" (TI 9). He cannot quite bring himself to love America in this instance, but he nonetheless appears to hold an abiding affection for the various groups populating this continent, rednecks included.

Snyder's sense of humor is also on display in "Smokey the Bear Sutra." Like Allen Ginsberg's "Wichita Vortex Sutra," this poem fuses Asian religion and American landscape to offer a prophetic commentary on modern man's destructive tendencies, but does so in a more playful fashion. The idea for "Smokey the Bear Sutra" was born in February 1969, when Snyder picked up a copy of the *San Francisco Chronicle* and saw an advertisement for a Sierra Club Wilderness Conference scheduled at UC–Berkeley the following day.

Working quickly, he composed and printed a broadside that night and distributed it at the conference, noting at the bottom of the sheet that it "may be reproduced free forever." Based in part on Fudo iconography that Snyder had learned from Japan's Yamabushi Buddhists, "Smokey the Bear Sutra" shows the National Forest Service's ursine representative using his "vajra shovel" to "crush [the] butts" of those doing ecological harm. Presumably, Smokey's list of offenders would include National Guard troops, who at the time were occupying the Berkeley campus and forcefully preventing citizens from restoring the ragtag parcel of city land known as People's Park.[22]

The irony of a Buddhist peacenik bear brandishing a weapon will prompt some readers to recall the "gentle violence" Snyder mentioned in his "Buddhism and the Coming Revolution" essay. To my mind, though, the browbeating tone of "Smokey the Bear Sutra" is too over-the-top to be dismissed simply as heavy-handed rhetoric. With his fusion of Eastern and Western symbolism, Snyder satirizes National Guardsmen, technocrats, and environmental activists (including himself) in one fell swoop, poking fun at America's most famous environmental icon but loving him all the same. The result is a poem that mobilizes environmentally conscious readers to take serious political action with a smile on their faces. A big hit with Sierra Club members, "Smokey the Bear Sutra" was reprinted in the *Berkeley Barb* and distributed nationwide by the Underground News Service. Even the *New Yorker* expressed interest in publishing the sutra but apparently refused on the grounds that the poem was both free and anonymous (PS 30–31).

Judging by the tone of these poems, the "real work" of the Dharma, with its emphasis on detachment and equitable behavior, helped diverse groups of people recognize a common good while gently censuring counterculture radicals, who were apt to take themselves and their activism too seriously. Dedicating himself to Buddhism's fundamental precepts of mindfulness, loving-kindness, and nonviolent action, Snyder was able to launch a new phase of his career without betraying the spiritual vision he had helped to nurture in the 1950s and 1960s. As Katsunori Yamazato and Julia Martin have pointed out on separate occasions, the poems Snyder wrote upon his return to America emphasized a cross-fertilization of ancient Buddhist tradition and current ecological strategies in a playful effort to guarantee the well-being of the greatest number of sentient beings.[23] Such serious playfulness served him well as he challenged long-standing regional paradigms in ensuing years.

Catapulted by the popularity of *Turtle Island*, Snyder saw his readership increase dramatically in the 1970s and 1980s, during which time he became one of the few American poets able to support his family solely through his writing. Tellingly, this writing included fewer poems and an increasing number of prose pieces, interviews, and public speeches, many of them on the topic of environmentalism. By the 1990s, Helen Vendler felt justified in saying that "Gary Snyder is more widely known as an ecological activist than as a poet."[24] As it happens, Snyder has continued to garner praise for his poetry. *No Nature*, his 1992 book of selected poems, was short-listed for a National Book Award, and *Mountains and Rivers without End*, published complete in 1996, won the prestigious Bollingen Prize. All the same, I agree with Vendler that in recent years Snyder has utilized prose writing to great effect as he has sought to shape thinking about Pacific Rim environmentalism.

Most of Snyder's post-1970 essays are concerned with bioregionalism, a paradigm that scholars working in environmental studies often link with flexible notions of reinhabitation and indigeneity.[25] In a 1992 essay entitled "The Rediscovery of Turtle Island," Snyder explains that "bioregionalism calls for commitment to this continent place by place, in terms of biogeographical regions and watersheds. It calls us to see our country in terms of its landforms, plant life, weather patterns, and seasonal changes—its whole natural history before the net of political jurisdiction was cast over it" (PS 246–47). As noted in the first part of this epilogue, Snyder had been advocating this commitment to the continent years before bioregionalism became a popular buzzword. In his Earth Day speech of 1970, for instance, we find Snyder declaring his citizenship on Turtle Island in strictly bioregional terms: "I am, supposedly, an American, because I was born on this continent, which happens at this time to be classified by the arbitrary notions of politics as something called the United States of America. Something to which I hold no particular loyalty to at all, because it's an arbitrary distinction. There is no line between here and Canada on the ground, and there is no line between here and Mexico on the ground. The boundaries are oceans and the Arctic and the Antarctic, and I won't accept any other boundaries. The boundaries within that are the natural boundaries of watersheds, mountain ridges, and climactic zones—biomes, life zones—which are reflected humanly in the lives of the American Indians."[26]

In an interview with Richard Grossinger conducted the following year, Snyder said he was seeking to transform his relationship with his state and nation, insofar as he hoped to "correlate the overlap between ranges of certain types of flora, between certain types of biomes, and climatological areas, and cultural areas, and get a sense of that region, and then look at more or less physical maps and study the drainages, and get a clearer sense of what drainage terms are and correlate those also. All these are exercises toward breaking our minds out of the molds of political boundaries or any kind of habituated or received notions of regional distinctions" (TRW 24).

Snyder's bioregional/antinational message was certainly not lost on the girl who showed up at his Earth Day speech wearing a T-shirt that read, "I am an Enemy of the State" (PS 57), nor was it lost on thousands of others who came into contact with him during the latter stages of the counterculture era. Allen Ginsberg might not have known it at the time, but he too was receiving a lesson in bioregionalism when he looked out upon a magnificent panorama from atop Glacier Peak during a 1965 hike, turned to Snyder, and asked incredulously, "You mean, there is a senator for all this?" There is not a senator for all that, Snyder remembers telling Ginsberg at the time, simply because the United States has so far failed to establish a democratic forum for all living beings (TI 106–8). It thus fell to Snyder, and other environmental activists seeking the "profound citizenship" that bioregionalism offers (PS 235), to propose new models of belonging. In a 1998 interview, Snyder remembered that he and other budding bioregionalists "were looking for any language that would help us clarify that there was a distinction between finding your membership in a natural place and locating your identity in terms of a social or political group. The landscape was my natural nation, and I could see that as having a validity and a permanence that would outlast the changing political structures. It enabled me to be critical of the United States without feeling that I wasn't at home in North America."[27]

Eventually, Snyder's belief in the primacy of bioregions and the fleetingness of nation-states led him, in a poem from *Axe Handles* entitled "For All," to revise one of America's most compulsory recitations:

I pledge allegiance to the soil
    of Turtle Island,
and to the beings who thereon dwell
    one ecosystem

> in diversity
>> under the sun
> With joyful interpenetration for all. (AH 114)

Ironically, the U.S. government had been promoting the idea of bioregionalism for years, at least since 1803, when Thomas Jefferson directed Meriwether
Lewis and William Clark to draw maps and collect specimens as they explored
the upper reaches of the Missouri River. In 1890, John Wesley Powell, recently
returned from a journey in the American Southwest, presented Congress with
a colored map of the region that outlined 24 "natural provinces" and desig-
nated 140 sites as "commonwealths" based on drainage and topographical
cohesion.[28] Bioregional mapping was still on the government agenda in 1996,
when the U.S. Department of Agriculture sponsored a revised version of *Ecore-
gions of the United States*, a work that differentiated various natural zones or
domains. As his own writings suggest, Snyder would have appreciated the scientific findings in these government projects, but not the expansionist motivations that lay behind some of them, for he would want to eschew the
sanctioning body of the nation-state altogether and pledge allegiance instead
to the natural provinces listed on Powell's map.

While Snyder's bioregional writings in the early 1970s chiefly concerned
his reinhabitation of California—"the only area I'm capable of talking about
really right now," he told Grossinger (TRW 24)—global issues attracted his
attention with increasing frequency. In 1972, he joined Stewart Brand, Arne
Naess, Michael McClure, and American Indian tribal leaders at the United
Nations Environmental Conference in Stockholm, Sweden. Here, on the
summer solstice, Snyder composed "Mother Earth: Her Whales," a poem
showing the deep suspicion with which he and his fellow activists regarded
the nations assembled in Sweden to discuss global environmental policies.
As it calls attention to the plight of the world's largest animals, "Mother
Earth: Her Whales" argues that all living beings ("Standing Tree People! / Flying Bird People! / Swimming Sea People! / Four-legged, two legged, people!")
must stand in solidarity to protest the spoliation of our oceans, a realm
Lawrence Buell has convincingly referred to as our "global commons."[29] Not
surprisingly, Snyder takes this opportunity to blame the human "invaders"
of Turtle Island for the ecological devastation they have inflicted upon
oceans over the centuries. Significantly, though, he also lashes out at "once-

great Buddhist nations" across the Pacific for their role in the endangerment of the whales' natural habitat:

> . . . Japan quibbles for words on
>   what kinds of whales they can kill?
> A once-great Buddhist nation
>   dribbles methyl mercury
>   like gonorrhea
>   in the sea.

> Pere David's Deer, the Elaphure,
> Lived in the tule marshes of the Yellow River
> Two thousand years ago—and lost its home to rice—
> The forests of Lo-yang were logged and all the silt &
> Sand flowed down, and gone, by 1200 AD—
> Wild Geese hatched out in Siberia
>   head south over basins of the Yang, the Huang,
>   what we call "China"
> On flyways they have used a million years.
> Ah China, where are the tigers, the wild boars,
>   the monkeys,
>   like the snows of yesteryear
> Gone in a mist, a flash, and the dry hard ground
> Is parking space for fifty thousand trucks.
> IS man the most precious of all things?
> —then let us love him, and his brothers, all those
> Fading living beings—(TI 47–48)

In earlier poems such as "Migration of Birds" and "First Landfall on Turtle Island," Snyder spoke affectingly of Pacific Rim creatures that travel ocean currents and coastal flyways with little regard for national boundaries. He offered his opinion rather more bluntly when he told an interviewer that "salmon don't give a fuck" about the border between Canada and the United States, "nor does the air pollution or the water pollution."[30] In "Mother Earth: Her Whales," as in "Night Herons," Snyder comes to the same conclusion as he details the damage done by the "robot nations" that drew those borders. Of course, he seems decidedly more pessimistic about the fate of the whales than he does about the night herons, which he regards as his fellow survivors in the Bay Area.

Snyder's commitment to Pacific Rim environmentalism intensified during the mid-1970s, when he embarked on two ambitious scholarly projects. In July 1972, just a month after "Mother Earth: Her Whales" appeared as an editorial piece in the *New York Times*, Snyder traveled to Japan for the first time since his 1968 return to Turtle Island, heading north to Hokkaido Island to study the Ainu people indigenous to that region. In a preface he wrote for a collection of Ainu epics translated by Donald Philippi, Snyder claims that the Ainu people once stood "at the center of an archaic internationalism," for Hokkaido was once "a meeting place of circumpolar hunting culture pathways with Pacific seacoast cultures" (PS 95–96). Ultimately, Snyder's investigation of Hokkaido culture helps him see that the local and the bioregional (or in this case, the "circumpolar") are deeply intertwined concepts, both on the map and in the mind. Seizing upon the Ainu term *iworu*, Snyder explains that this culture's "field of force" not only refers to a watershed, biome, or territory, "but has spirit-world implications as well" (PS 96). This is simply another of way of saying that planetary responsibility starts in one's own backyard. "The Ainu suggest to us with great clarity that this life-support system is not just a mutual food factory, it is mysteriously *beautiful*. It is what we are. We now see the Ainu not as a fading remnant, but as elders and teachers whose playful sense of their own bioregion points a way to see and live on our planet as a whole" (PS 97).

Later in the 1970s, Snyder turned his attention to China, beginning work on "The Great Clod," a manuscript detailing that ancient land's shift from a wilderness state to an agricultural society during the T'ang and Sung Dynasties. Influenced no doubt by what he saw happening in America's back-to-the-land movement, Snyder took note of the ways in which China's high-ranking government officials sought to commune with nature, despite the fact that their policies were abetting the destruction of their nation's wetlands and forests. "Nature and its landscapes were seen as realms of purity and selfless beauty and order, in vivid contrast to the corrupt and often brutal entanglements of politics that no active Chinese official could avoid," Snyder explains in "The Brush," a chapter of "The Great Clod" manuscript he included in *The Gary Snyder Reader*. "The mountain horizons were a reminder of the vivid world of clear water, patient rocks, intensely focused trees, lively coiling clouds and mists—all the spontaneous processes that seemed to soar above human fickleness" (GSR 313).

As Snyder states in another section of the manuscript, "the Chinese and Japanese traditions carry within them the most sensitive, mind-deepening poetry of the natural world ever written by civilized people. Because these poets were men and women who dealt with budgets, taxes, penal systems, and the overthrow of governments, they had a heart-wrenching grasp of the contradictions that confront those who love the natural world and are yet tied to the civilized. This must be one reason why Chinese poetry is so widely appreciated by contemporary Occidentals."[31] Fittingly, Snyder provides an ancient context for contemporary studies offered by Charles Reich, Theodore Roszak, and other writers who set out to expose middle America's growing uneasiness with technocratic thinking in the late 1960s and early 1970s. For centuries, it seems, powerful citizens in the Pacific region have paradoxically sought to assuage their feelings of guilt by seeking refuge in the dwindling natural environments they have had a hand in spoiling.

Although Snyder never completed "The Hokkaido Book" or "The Great Clod," his research on these projects apparently deepened his appreciation of local/global dialectics around the Rim. Speaking to an interviewer in the 1970s, he predicted that his ongoing study of Hokkaido Island would allow him to "come back and look at North America with a really fine eye," and that living among the Ainu would provide another way of "getting my geological understanding of place and history in North America, the North Pacific and Pacific Basin."[32] Given the geographical specificity of Snyder's statement, it seems altogether fitting that he published a portion of his Hokkaido research in a 1974 *Planet/Drum* issue entitled "North Pacific Rim Alive." Increasingly, Snyder used the term "North Pacific Rim" whenever he wanted to indicate the larger bioregional community that he and his friends in the Yuba Watershed, along with millions of others on America's West Coast, share with their peers across the Pacific. In his 1977 interview with Peter Chowka, for example, Snyder invokes this geographic construct after explaining that local place is naturally connected to hemispheric space:

> What I realistically aspire to do is keep up with and stimulate what I think is really strong and creative in my own viable region, my actual nation: northern California/southern Oregon, which we might call Kuksu country, a subdivision of Turtle Island continent. . . . We also have our own way of keeping in

touch in terms of our local drainage (which is the North Pacific) across the North Pacific Rim, with the companion poets of Japan, like Nanao Sakaki and his circle—great Japanese bioregional poets who, analogously to calling North America "Turtle Island," call Japan "Jomonia" and have an island-Pacific-bioregion sense of it. I don't see anything parochial in it because it implies a stimulus to others to locate themselves equally well. Having done so, we will see a mosaic of natural regions which can then talk across the boundaries and share specifics with each other. (TRW 125)

According to Snyder, any place along the Rim, be it San Francisco or Hokkaido Island—where Nanao Sakaki urged prospective Bum Academy members to travel in order to get a sense of walked-in landscapes (TRW 12)—is always situated within, and conditioned by, a larger geography of subsistence, exchange, and cooperation. Viewed in this light, localities are hardly fixed or circumscribed entities. Taking instruction from the aptly titled "Surre(gion)alist Manifesto" authored by Max Cafard, Snyder chooses to regard regions as "interpenetrating bodies in semi-simultaneous spaces" (PW 40–41). At other times, he has adopted a slightly different spatial model, preferring to envision his Kitkitdizze compound as a "node" in the larger "net" of natural homesteads and camps (PS 252). This particular image calls to mind the glimmering jewels in Indra's Net, which reflect off each other so as to provide a composite view of the universe. In either case, Snyder has evidently found a way to stay connected with Pacific Rim community even after "digging in" to a local domain in the California backcountry. "Living in the country for me is not a retreat," he explained in a 1973 interview. "It's simply placing myself at a different point in the net, a different place in the network, which does not mean that I'm any less interested in the totality of the network, it's simply that's where I center myself" (TRW 37). Even when he acts locally, Snyder is always thinking globally.

Tracing the global/local dialectic in his environmentalist writing, we find that Snyder's statements about natural communities along the Rim align closely with current definitions of bioregional cosmopolitanism, a movement that environmental scholar Mitchell Thomashow regards as more progressive than literary regionalism insofar as it emphasizes "the connections between place-based knowledge and global environmental change, the interdependence of local ecology and global economies, and the matrix of affiliations and networks that constitute ecological biodiversity and multicultural and multispecies tolerance—allowing different people to understand all the different places that may be considered home." In their quest to provide a big picture, Thomashow says, bioregional cosmopolitans are quite willing to erase and redraw political boundaries and to stress the need for "'mind regions' that cut through bioregional distinctions" in order to provide "broader symbolic meaning."[33]

Jonathan Bate sounds much the same call in *The Dream of the Earth* when he says that "the dream of deep ecology will never be realized upon the earth, but our survival as a species may be dependent upon our capacity to dream it in the work of our imagination."[34] Not surprisingly, this imaginative approach to global environmentalism has encountered resistance from empiricists like Dana Phillips, who blames John Elder's *Imagining the Earth* for conflating an "organistic" idea of ecological community with the "mechanistic" ecosystem originally defined by A. G. Tansley in 1935. Basically, Phillips finds Elder and other bioregional cosmopolitans to be misguided in their assumptions about "the inextricable wholeness of the world." What Elder and his peers do not seem to realize, Phillips asserts, is that "the science of ecology has not been able to confirm 'the indivisibility of natural process.' Since the 1960s, ecology has had to divest itself, one after another, of vague concepts of this sort, of which the classic example is 'everything is connected to everything else.' Such concepts have not proved amenable to scientific confirmation, however ripe they may be for poetic affirmation."[35]

Although Snyder would seem to share Bate's aesthetic sensibility and Elder's holistic worldview, and although he too has advocated moving "toward a style of planetary and ecological cosmopolitanism" (PS vii), it is difficult to say whether Phillips would similarly impugn his invocation of a North Pacific Rim bioregion. On one hand, Snyder's descriptions of Pacific Rim localities as jewels in Indra's Net and his equation of ecosystems with Buddhist mandalas (PS 73, 76) suggest the abstract or vague model of global interconnectedness that Phillips so clearly despises. On the other hand, Snyder's bioregional cosmopolitanism is almost always based on firsthand reports from specific locations, not simply on flights of the imagination, a tendency that holds true for his recent writings about Asia as well as his writings about Turtle Island.

Since 1970, Snyder's travels along the Rim have not been as frequent as they once were, but they have certainly been extensive. "Starting from when I returned to the Pacific coast, I gradually extended my range of walked-in landscapes," he notes in the short essay he appended to *Mountains and Rivers without End*: "North to Alaska, as far as the Brooks Range and the Arctic Sea; south to the Southwestern U.S. and the length of Baja California. Overseas I spent time in the Central Australian Desert; traveled in the Himalayan nation of Ladakh; visited China; and made another brief visit to the wilder parts of Taiwan" (MR 157). Inspired equally by these travels and by the cosmopolitan imagination shaping his Pacific Rim consciousness, Snyder's recent writing has presented aesthetic value, ethical purpose, and empirical reasoning as fundamentally inseparable concerns, thereby complicating Phillips's attack on bioregional cosmopolitanism and lending credence to Neil Evernden's pronouncement that "environmentalism without aesthetics is merely regional planning."[36]

Although Snyder does not write as much poetry as he once did, his environmentalist prose writings have increasingly displayed the kind of luminous articulation routinely reserved for lyric forms. His imaginative talents are on full display in "Coming into the Watershed," a 1992 essay that has been reprinted in many environmental magazines and newsletters over the years. With its softly musical tone and existential sensibility, "Coming into the Watershed" closely resembles James Clifford's "Fort Ross Meditation," the essay I cited at the beginning of Chapter 1 to frame my discussion of Snyder's early writings. Like Clifford, Snyder opens his Pacific Rim meditation with an indication of what he is searching for: "I had been too long in the calm of the Sierra pine groves and wanted to hear the surf and the cries of seabirds" (PS 219). He proceeds to describe a trip that he and his younger son Gen make to the California coast, near Trinidad Head.

From his vantage point on the shore, Snyder finds all forms and identities to be fluid, so that California, Mexico, Alaska, and the North Pacific—all of them arbitrarily fixed zones—become something more "porous, permeable, [and] arguable." In fact, the drive from Kitkitdizze to Trinidad Head had already shown father and son that ecosystem borders—such as those separating the dry interior range, the majestic redwood forests, and the maritime Pacific Northwest—are rarely "hard and clear," simply because they have changed so gradually and subtly over the millennia. "A thin line drawn on the map would not do them justice," Snyder explains. "Yet these are the real markers of the natural nations of our planet, and they establish real territories with real differences to which our economies and our clothing must adapt" (PS 220).

As a fitting example of the bioregional knowledge he has gained and the creaturely behavior he wants to emulate, not just on this journey or in this essay, but in so much of his life and work, Snyder ends "Coming into the Watershed" by mentioning the puffins that fly across the northern Pacific, simply because these migratory birds accept bioregional porosity rather instinctively. As is the case with the poems of *Myths & Texts*, Snyder discovers that identity and habitat are at some deeper level connected to real and imagined movements across space. This is the lesson he and Gen take away as they stand on the shore at Trinidad Head, where the puffins nest every April: "At this spot, Trinidad, we could not help but feel that we touched on the life realm of the whole North Pacific and Alaska. We spent that whole day enjoying 'liminality,' dancing on the brink of the continent" (PS 221).

It is quite appropriate that the fluid aspects of geographic identity outlined in Snyder's Pacific Rim writings should inform his masterwork, *Mountains and Rivers without End*, at nearly every stage. Although I have decided to reserve my analysis of this long poetic sequence for another time, I would like to bring my present study to a close with an excerpt that illustrates this poet's deep-seated commitment to Pacific Rim community.[37] The following passage is taken from "We Wash Our Bowls in This Water," one of the last sections of *Mountains and Rivers* to be composed before the sequence was published complete in 1996. In this passage, Snyder incorporates an old Zen training hall riddle about dreamlike transformations of identity and habitat:

Su Tung-p'o sat out one whole night   by a creek   on the slopes of
Mt. Lu. Next morning he showed this poem to his teacher:

    The stream with its sounds   is a long broad tongue
    The looming mountain   is a wide-awake body
    Throughout the night   song after song
    How can I   speak at dawn.

Old Master Chang-tsung approved him. Two centuries later
Dogen said,
    "Sounds of streams and shapes of mountains.
    The sounds never stop and the shapes never cease.
    Was it Su who woke
    or was it the mountains and streams?

Billions of beings see the morning star
and all become Buddhas!
If *you*, who are valley streams and looming
mountains,
can't throw some light on the nature of ridges and rivers,

who can?" (MR 138–39)

Like many of Snyder's writings, this poem suggests that Pacific Rim culture is as mysterious as it is enduring. In this instance, a dreamtime epiphany
about Buddhist compassion is not only the subject of a poem a Sung Dynasty
disciple shows his Ch'an Master but also a koan mystery contemplated by a
Zen monk in Japan in the thirteenth century as well as an environmental
challenge Snyder issues to American readers at the end of the twentieth
century. Like Su Tung-p'o, postmodern Americans who seek communion with
an "emergent Pacific culture" (NN v) might have a hard time distinguishing
reality from fantasy. Perhaps we will never know. What Snyder wants us to
realize, however, is that the Pacific Rim has been the stuff of dreams for
centuries. Ancient visions of collective cultural identity and natural harmony
refuse to vanish in a realm where space and time are collapsible categories.
Along with Snyder, we are obliged to look to the past, even as we continue to
scan the oceanic horizon for new and better forms of imagined community.

NOTES

The Pacific Rim and the San Francisco Renaissance

1. See Eric Hobsbawm, *The Age of Extremes: A History of the World, 1914–1991* (New York: Pantheon, 1994).

2. Henry R. Luce, "The American Century," *Life*, 17 February 1941, pp. 61–65.

3. Robert A. Manning and Paula Stern, "The Myth of Pacific Community," *Foreign Affairs* 73, no. 6 (November/December 1994): 81.

4. See Staffan Burenstam Linder, *The Pacific Century: Economic and Political Consequences of Asian-Pacific Dynamism* (Stanford, CA: Stanford University Press, 1986). See also Robert Elegant, *Pacific Destiny: Inside Asia Today* (London: Hamish Hamilton, 1990).

5. See David Rieff, *Los Angeles: Capital of the Third World* (New York: Simon and Schuster, 1991). For discussion of the 1990 Los Angeles festival, see Peter Plangens and Lynda Wright, "Multiculturalism or Bust, Gang," *Newsweek*, 24 September 1990, pp. 68–69. For discussion of Shonen Knife's impact on American indie bands, including those on the Seattle scene (Beat Happening, Nirvana), see Michael Azerrad, *Our Band Could Be Your Life: Scenes from the American Indie Underground, 1981–1991* (2001; Boston: Back Bay Books, 2002), pp. 465–66, as well as the tribute album *Every Band Has a Shonen Knife That Loves Them* (Various Artists) (Positive Records, 1989).

6. See William Gibson, *Neuromancer* (New York: Ace, 1984), and Alejandro Morales, *The Rag Doll Plagues* (Houston: Arte Público, 1992). Whereas Gibson's

novel explores a postmodern corporate structure that bridges distances but shatters lives, Morales's novel zeroes in on the ecological destruction resulting from centuries of unchecked imperial aggression and corporate greed. For more on Ridley Scott's *Blade Runner* (1982), a film that transformed sunny Los Angeles into a dystopian Rim city replete with neon-lit sushi stands, mutant humans, and acid rain, see Paul Sammon, *Future Noir: The Making of "Blade Runner"* (New York: HarperPrism, 1996). Also see Mike Davis, *The Ecology of Fear: Los Angeles and the Imagination of Disaster* (1998; New York: Vintage, 1999), pp. 359–63. For a look at how "techno-orientalism" has infused the political arena, see David Morley and Kevin Robbins, "Techno-Orientalism: Futures, Foreigners and Phobias," *New Formations* 16 (Spring 1992): 136–56.

7. See John Berger, quoted in Edward Soja, *Postmodern Geographies: The Reassertion of Space in Critical Social Theory* (London: Verso, 1989), p. 93.

8. For a brief but trenchant synopsis of this trend, see Michael Davidson, *Guys Like Us: Citing Masculinity in Cold War Politics* (Chicago: University of Chicago Press, 2004), chap. 3, "The Lady from Shanghai: California Orientalism and 'Guys Like Us.'" In addition to Snyder and the members of the San Francisco Renaissance but rather unlike those bohemian writers, a handful of other cold war Orientalists aspired to a more middlebrow evocation of Asian-American unity during these years. This trend, which came to a head in the South Pacific novels of Joseph Michener and the musicals of Richard Rodgers and Oscar Hammerstein, emphasized sentimental attachments between Easterners and Westerners. As Christina Klein notes in her marvelous study, *Cold War Orientalism: Asia in the Middlebrow Imagination, 1945–1961* (Berkeley: University of California Press, 2003), Westerners in this type of discourse continued to adopt paternalistic roles. Klein cites as one example "Getting to Know You," a showstopping song from the 1951 production of *The King and I*, which Anna Leonowens sings to Siamese children and wives in front of a global map redrawn to emphasize Siam's small stature in an interconnected postmodern world.

9. Cogent discussion of the writers and activists at work in the "New Oceania" can be found throughout Rob Wilson's comprehensive study, *Reimagining the American Pacific: From "South Pacific" to Bamboo Ridge and Beyond* (Durham, NC: Duke University Press, 2000). For an example of the exclusionary Western attitude inspiring their bitter response, see "The Pacific Idea," *Economist*, 16 March 1991, pp. 15–18. See also John Naisbitt and Patricia Aburdene, *Megatrends 2000: Ten New Directions for the 1990s* (New York: Avon, 1990), chap. 6, "The Rise of the Pacific Rim." Over the past decade or so, many writers and activists have begun to use the more inclusive term "Asia-Pacific" primarily as a means of avoiding the hollowed-out nature of Pacific Rim discourse.

10. See Christopher L. Connery, "Pacific Rim Discourse: The U.S. Global Imaginary in the Late Cold War Years." *Boundary 2* 20, no. 1 (Spring 1994): 30. See also Connery's "The Oceanic Feeling and the Regional Imaginary," in *Global/Local:*

Cultural Production and the Transnational Imaginary, ed. Rob Wilson and Wimal Dissanayake (Durham, NC: Duke University Press, 1996), especially pp. 284–87.

11. Rob Wilson and Wimal Dissanayake, "Introduction: Tracking the Global/Local," in *Global/Local,* p. 6.

12. Bruce Cumings, "Rimspeak: Or, the Discourse of the 'Pacific Rim,'" in *What Is in a Rim? Critical Perspectives on the Pacific Region Idea,* ed. Arif Dirlik (Lanham, MD: Rowman and Littlefield, 1993), pp. 29–47.

13. Connery, "Pacific Rim Discourse," p. 30.

14. For more on the frontier spirit of the California expositions, see Carolyn Peter, "California Welcomes the World: International Expositions, 1894–1940, and the Selling of a State," in *Reading California: Art, Image, and Identity, 1900–2000,* ed. Stephanie Barron, Sheri Bernstein, and Ilene Susan Fort (Berkeley: Los Angeles County Museum of Art/University of California Press, 2000), pp. 68–83. For more on the "thirteenth labor of Hercules" in the isthmus of Panama, see Bill Brown, "Science Fiction, the World's Fair, and the Prosthetics of Empire, 1910–1915," in *Cultures of United States Imperialism,* ed. Amy Kaplan and Donald E. Pease (Durham, NC: Duke University Press, 1993), especially pp. 140–47.

15. John Dower, *War without Mercy: Race and Power in the Pacific War* (New York: Pantheon, 1986), p. 162.

16. Allen Ginsberg's statement about cold war barriers is quoted in Robert von Hallberg, "Poetry, Politics, and Intellectuals," in *The Cambridge History of American Literature, Volume Eight: Poetry and Criticism, 1940–1995,* ed. Sacvan Bercovitch (New York: Cambridge University Press, 1996), p. 124. Kevin Starr praises McWilliams's *California: The Great Exception* (1949) for showing that "California was the one state of the Union that constituted a regional culture unto itself, with its own distinctive geography, climate, and history, along with its own way of being American. . . . [McWilliams] also—elusively, in the conclusion of the book—suggests that California must consider itself a Pacific commonwealth as well as a member of the American union" ("Carey McWilliams's California: The Light and the Dark," in Barron, Bernstein, and Fort, eds., *Reading California,* p. 17).

17. Harvey Klehr and Ronald Radosh, *The "Amerasia" Spy Case: Prelude to McCarthysim* (Chapel Hill: University of North Carolina Press, 1996), p. 38. For more on the IPR's relationship with *Amerasia* and its difficulties during the McCarthy probes, see Paul F. Hooper, "The Institute of Pacific Relations and the Origins of Asian and Pacific Studies," *Pacific Affairs* 61, no. 1 (Spring 1988): 98–121. For more on the IPR's spiritual mission, see Henry Yu, "Orientalizing the Pacific Rim: The Production of Exotic Knowledge by American Missionaries and Sociologists in the 1920s," *Journal of American/East Asian Relations* 5, nos. 3–4 (Fall/Winter 1996): 331–59.

18. William T. Stone, "Topics in Brief," *Amerasia* 1, no. 1 (March 1937): 2.

19. Cyrus H. Peake, "Topics in Brief," *Amerasia* 1, no. 2 (March 1937): 50.

20. See the discussion of Olson in Connery, "Pacific Rim Discourse," pp. 35–36, as well as the discussion of the 1939 East-West Philosophers' Conference in David Palumbo-Liu, *Asian/American: Historical Crossings of a Racial Frontier* (Stanford, CA: Stanford University Press, 1999), p. 43.

21. See Walter Lippmann, *The Cold War: A Study in U.S. Foreign Policy* (New York: Harper and Brothers, 1947). See also "Exporting Capitalism," *Fortune*, June 1947, pp. 81–85, 187–92.

22. *Amerasia* 11, no. 7 (July 1947), table of contents page.

23. Philip Jaffe, "America: The Uneasy Victor," *Amerasia* 11, no. 7 (July 1947): 201–2. Many of the pronouncements and warnings in this article can also be found in the book Jaffe had just completed, *New Frontiers in Asia: A Challenge to the West* (New York: Knopf, 1946).

24. For the speeches by Acheson and MacArthur, see Walter A. McDougall, *Let the Sea Make a Noise: A History of the North Pacific from Magellan to MacArthur* (New York: Basic Books, 1993), pp. 680–81. For Eisenhower's attack on the "Asia-last" policy put forth by the Democrats during the 1952 campaign, see Stephen E. Ambrose, *Rise to Globalism: American Foreign Policy since 1938*, 7th rev. ed. (New York: Penguin, 1993), p. 128.

25. James Clifford, *Routes: Travel and Translation in the Late Twentieth Century* (Cambridge, MA: Harvard University Press, 1997), p. 345.

26. Thomas J. McCormick, *America's Half-Century: United States Foreign Policy in the Cold War and After*, 2d ed. (Baltimore: Johns Hopkins University Press, 1995), pp. 99–100, 111.

27. Gerald L. Houseman, *America and the Pacific Rim: Coming to Terms with New Realities* (Lanham, MD: Rowman and Littlefield, 1995), p. 222.

28. William P. Bundy, "New Tides in Southeast Asia," *Foreign Affairs* 49, no. 2 (January 1971): 196. The original ASEAN partnership included Malaysia, Thailand, Indonesia, Singapore, and the Philippines.

29. Mike Mansfield, "The Rim of Asia: Report of Senator Mike Mansfield to the Committee on Foreign Relations, United States Senate, on a Study Mission to the Western Pacific, September 1967" (Washington, DC: U.S. Government Printing Office, 1967), pp. 1, 14.

30. Richard M. Nixon, "Asia after Vietnam," *Foreign Affairs* 46, no. 1 (October 1967): 111.

31. "14 Experts Look at U.S. Future in Asia," *U.S. News and World Report*, 1 January 1968, pp. 25–31. The political scientists and historians on this panel included Robert Scalopino, Oscar Handlin, and E. O. Reischauer.

32. Tad Szulc, *The Illusion of Peace: Foreign Policy in the Nixon Years* (New York: Viking, 1978), p. 124.

33. Richard Nixon, quoted in ibid., p. 126.

34. Gerald Ford, "Presidential Remarks, USS Arizona Memorial, Pearl Harbor, Hawaii, Sunday, December 7, 1975," quoted in John J. Casserly, *The Ford White*

House: The Diary of a Speechwriter (Boulder: Colorado Associated University Press, 1977), p. 354.

35. George Shultz, speech to the Association of Indonesian Economists, 11 July 1988, quoted in David I. Hitchcock Sr., "The United States in a Changing Pacific Rim," *Washington Quarterly* 12, no. 4 (1989): 131. Additionally, Christopher Connery notes that, in an address to a Pacific Rim conference in California, Shultz ecstatically referred to the Pacific as "the twentieth century's economic fountain of youth" ("Pacific Rim Discourse," p. 47).

36. Rudolph Peterson, quoted in Palumbo-Liu, *Asian/American*, p. 273.

37. See Alvin Toffler, *The Third Wave* (London: Pan, 1981); Willam Ouchi, *Theory Z: How American Business Can Meet the Japanese Challenge* (Reading, MA: Addison-Wesley, 1981); and Francis Fukuyama, *The End of History and the Last Man* (New York: Free Press, 1991). In the context of the Ouchi book, it is important to remember that, during the years of the Asian miracle, several nations were quick to attribute their success to Asian values, which they believed the West could never fully share. This position was spelled out most consistently by longtime Singaporean president Lee Kuan Yew. A good synopsis of this issue can be found in Frank Gibney, *The Pacific Century: America and Asia in a Changing World* (New York: Scribners, 1992). Nicholas D. Kristof and Sheryl WuDunn, *Thunder from the East: Portrait of a Rising Asia* (New York: Vintage, 2001), pp. 155, 169–70, provide a strikingly different perspective, arguing that Lee and Indonesia's General Suharto, along with other authoritarians who expounded Asian values in the cold war years, were not much different from the "highly educated philosopher kings" who ruled European society for centuries. Supporting this view but taking a different angle, David Palumbo-Liu explains that Western educational principles had by the late twentieth century already made substantial inroads in large East Asian cities. As a result, the new strain of Confucianism, which on the surface appears to be "a product of the ancient 'Orient,'" has become "a social form eerily like 'our own'" (*Asian/American*, pp. 197–98, 202, 362–65).

38. Carolyn See, *Golden Days* (New York: Fawcett, 1987), p. 29.

39. For President Bush's remarks, see Elisabeth Bumiller, "Bush Affirms U.S. Role in Asia in New 'Pacific Century,'" *New York Times*, 19 February 2002, A8. Similar strains of Pacific Rim boosterism can be found in Naisbitt and Aburdene, *Megatrends 2000*, pp. 184–217. On the other hand, a pointed critique of IMF and U.S. Treasury Department policy in the region is offered by Joseph E. Stiglitz, *Globalization and Its Discontents* (New York: Norton, 2002).

40. Bruce Cumings, "What Is a Pacific Century—and How Will We Know When It Begins?" *Current History* 3, no. 587 (December 1994): 402. For more on the specifically American character of the Rim construct, see Arif Dirlik, "The Asia-Pacific Idea: Reality and Representation in the Invention of a Regional Structure," *Journal of World History* 3 (Spring 1992): 55–79.

41. "The Pacific Idea," p. 16.

42. Arif Dirlik, *The Postcolonial Aura* (Boulder, CO: Westview, 1997), p. 129.

43. Arif Dirlik, "The Asia-Pacific in Asian-American Perspective," in *What Is in a Rim?* p. 310.

44. See Connery, "Pacific Rim Discourse," p. 41, and Doreen Massey, *Space, Place, and Gender* (Minneapolis: University of Minnesota Press, 1994), p. 150. The "time-space compression" to which Massey alludes is outlined most thoroughly in David Harvey, *The Condition of Postmodernity* (Oxford: Basil Blackwell, 1989).

45. Palumbo-Liu, *Asian/American*, p. 370. For an excellent analysis of global capitalist flows and their effect on the Pacific Rim's "ethnoscapes," "finanscapes," "technoscapes," "mediascapes," and "ideoscapes," see Arjun Appadurai, "Disjuncture and Difference in the Global Cultural Economy," *Public Culture* 2, no. 2 (Spring 1990): 1–24.

46. Wilson, *Reimagining the American Pacific*, p. 14.

47. Ibid., pp. 112, 130. Haunani-Kay Trask, *From a Native Daughter: Colonialism and Sovereignty in Hawaii* (Monroe, ME: Common Courage Press, 1993), has also weighed in forcefully on this issue, offering a stinging critique of U.S. imperialism in Hawaii from 1893 up to the present day, targeting in particular a Western tourist industry that "prostitutes" native island culture with fanciful constructions of Edenic paradise. More recently, Trask has extended her criticism to East Asian immigrants and tourists, especially the Japanese, in "Settlers of Color and 'Immigrant' Hegemony: 'Locals' in Hawaii," *Amerasia Journal* 26, no. 2 (2000): 1–24.

48. Wilson, *Reimagining the American Pacific*, p. 8.

49. Ibid., p. 274.

50. According to Edward Said, *Orientalism* (1978; New York: Vintage, 1979), in traditional Orientalist discourse the East served primarily to orient the West, which came to see itself as the pinnacle of civilization and Asia as an exotic but ultimately empty vessel in need of European direction and domination. And yet, at other times, the invocation of Asia could bring forth some pleasurably disorienting effects, especially on the temporal register. Indeed, for many Europeans, "the Orient . . . alternated in the mind's geography between being an Old World to which one returned, as to Eden or Paradise, there to set up a new version of the old, and being a wholly new place to which one came as Columbus came to America, in order to set up a New World" (p. 58).

51. Dirlik, "The Asia-Pacific Idea," p. 55.

52. Mary Louise Pratt, *Imperial Eyes: Travel Writing and Transculturation* (London: Routledge, 1992), p. 6.

53. For an analysis of how the abstract activity of "taking place" derives from Martin Heidegger's ideas about "presencing" and "spacing through difference," see Derek Gregory, *Geographical Imaginations* (Cambridge, MA: Basil Blackwell, 1994), pp. 104, 112–14. In *Asian/American*, David Palumbo-Liu likewise examines the way in which certain populations have "taken place" in the Pacific Rim region, solidifying his promise to treat spatialization "not only symbolically but also literally" (p. 7).

54. Jack Kerouac, *The Dharma Bums* (1958; New York: Penguin, 1986), pp. 13–14.

55. Gary Snyder, quoted in *On Bread and Poetry: A Panel Discussion with Gary Snyder, Lew Welch & Philip Whalen*, ed. Donald Allen (Bolinas, CA: Grey Fox, 1977), p. vii.

56. Jack Goodman, letter to John Allen Ryan, November 1955, quoted in Richard Candida Smith, *Utopia and Dissent: Art, Poetry, and Politics in California* (Berkeley: University of California Press, 1995), p. 163.

57. There is some confusion as to whom Rexroth contacted first. According to biographer Linda Hamalian, Rexroth himself was tapped by painter Wally Hedrick to put on a reading at the Six Gallery, since Robert Duncan's reading of *Faust Foutu* had set a precedent. Most accounts agree that Rexroth then contacted Ginsberg and suggested that he in turn contact Snyder, who had just returned to San Francisco after a summer of trail crew work in Yosemite. Snyder subsequently invited his college friend Philip Whalen, who at the time was living in Oregon, to participate in this "poetickall bombshell" (undated letter, Philip Whalen Papers, Special Collections and Archives, Eric V. Hauser Memorial Library, Reed College, Portland, Oregon), while Ginsberg rounded up McClure and Lamantia. But Barry Miles insists that it was McClure who first contacted Ginsberg, and that Ginsberg became the de facto organizer of the event only because McClure did not have the time to do so. Even more curious is the fact that these differing accounts derive from interviews with Ginsberg conducted just months apart in 1985 (Miles's in March, Hamalian's in July). See Linda Hamalian, *A Life of Kenneth Rexroth* (New York: Norton, 1991), pp. 242–43, 409n, and Barry Miles, *Ginsberg: A Biography* (1989; New York: HarperPerennial, 1990), p. 194. See also the anthology of articles on the Six Gallery reading included in Allen Ginsberg, *Howl: Original Draft Facsimile, Transcript and Variant Versions*, ed. Barry Miles (New York: Harper and Row, 1986). McClure, for his part, hazily (mis)remembers that the reading took place in December 1955, two months after the actual event. See Michael McClure, *Scratching the Beat Surface* (San Francisco: North Point, 1982), p. 12. For more on the boredom and disappointment McClure and Ginsberg suffered before Rexroth introduced them to fellow travelers in San Francisco, see Thomas Albright, *Art in the San Francisco Bay Area* (Berkeley: University of California Press, 1985), pp. 85–86.

58. William Everson, interview with David Meltzer, Jack Shoemaker, and Tina Meltzer (1969), in *San Francisco Beat: Talking with the Poets*, ed. David Meltzer (San Francisco: City Lights, 2001), pp. 29–30.

59. Robert Hass, "Some Notes on the San Francisco Bay Area as a Culture Region: A Memoir," in *Twentieth Century Pleasures: Essays on Poetry* (New York: Ecco, 1984), p. 224.

60. See William Everson, "Rexroth: Shaker and Maker" (1980), in *The Portable Beat Reader*, ed. Ann Charters (New York: Penguin, 1992), p. 243.

61. See Rick Fields, *How the Swans Came to the Lake: A Narrative History of Buddhism in America*, 3d rev. ed. (Boston: Shambhala, 1992), p. 145. See also Ilene Susan Fort, "Altered States: California Art and the Inner World," in Barron, Bernstein, and Fort, eds., *Reading California*, pp. 39–40.

62. Philip Whalen, *Off the Wall: Interviews with Philip Whalen* (San Francisco: Four Seasons Foundation, 1978), p. 57.

63. For the naming of "Saffroncisco," see Philip Whalen, letter to Gary Snyder, 7 March 1952, Gary Snyder Papers, Department of Special Collections, University of California Library, Davis.

64. Shunryu Suzuki, quoted in David Chadwick, *Crooked Cucumber: The Life and Zen Teaching of Shunryu Suzuki* (New York: Broadway Books, 1999), p. 253. For more information about Western practitioners at Soko-ji and the establishment of the East-West and Hyphen Houses, see pp. 173, 195; for Suzuki's opinion about San Francisco's freewheeling Buddhists, see p. 227. For evidence of the syncretic variety of Buddhism that has flourished most recently in America, see *Blue Jean Buddha: Voices of Young Buddhists*, ed. Sumi D. Loudon (Boston: Wisdom Publications, 2001).

65. See Theodore Roszak, *The Making of a Counterculture: Reflections on the Technocratic Society and Its Youthful Opposition* (Garden City, NY: Anchor/Doubleday, 1969), p. 134.

66. Allen Ginsberg, letter to Neal Cassady, 14 May 1953, in *Big Sky Mind: Buddhism and the Beat Generation*, ed. Carole Tonkinson (New York: Tricycle/Riverhead, 1995), p. 92.

67. Ibid., p. 93.

68. See Kenneth Rexroth, interview with David Meltzer (1969), in Meltzer, ed., *San Francisco Beat*, p. 247, and Gary Snyder, interview with David Meltzer and Marina Lazzara (1999), in ibid., p. 291.

69. Alan Watts, *The Way of Zen* (1957; New York: Vintage, 1989), p. xiv.

70. Allen Ginsberg, biographical note, in *The New American Poetry 1945–1960*, ed. Donald Allen (1960; Berkeley: University of California Press, 1999), p. 438.

71. See Kenneth Rexroth, "Disengagement: The Art of the Beat Generation" (1957), in *World Outside the Window: The Selected Essays of Kenneth Rexroth*, ed. Bradford Morrow (New York: New Directions, 1987), pp. 41–56.

72. Rexroth, interview with Meltzer, in Meltzer, ed., *San Francisco Beat*, p. 247.

73. Alan Watts, "Beat Zen, Square Zen, and Zen" (revised 1959), in Charters, ed., *The Portable Beat Reader*, pp. 606–14.

74. See Jack Kerouac, letter to Gary Snyder, 14 February 1956, in *Jack Kerouac: Selected Letters 1940–1956*, ed. Ann Charters (New York: Viking, 1995), p. 558. See also Jack Kerouac, letter to Gary Snyder, 14 July 1958, in *Jack Kerouac: Selected Letters 1957–1969*, ed. Ann Charters (New York: Viking, 1999), p. 139.

75. Kerouac, *The Dharma Bums*, p. 16.

76. Everson, interview with D. Meltzer, Shoemaker, and T. Meltzer, in Meltzer, ed., *San Francisco Beat*, p. 44.

77. See Paul O'Neil, "The Only Rebellion Around" (1959), in *A Casebook on the Beat*, ed. Thomas Parkinson (New York: Crowell, 1961), p. 232; in ibid., see Norman Podheretz, "The Know-Nothing Bohemians" (1958), pp. 201–12.

78. Richard Eberhart, "West Coast Rhythms," *New York Times Book Review*, 2 September 1956, p. 18.

79. Herbert Gold, "The Beat Mystique" (1958), in Parkinson, ed., *A Casebook on the Beat*, p. 253.

80. See *I Want to Take You Higher: The Psychedelic Era 1965–1968*, ed. James Henke and Parke Puterbaugh for the Rock and Roll Hall of Fame and Museum, with essays by Charles Perry and Barry Miles (San Francisco: Chronicle Books, 1997), p. 82.

81. Michael Downing, *Shoes Outside the Door: Desire, Devotion, and Excess at San Francisco Zen Center* (Washington, DC: Counterpoint, 2001), pp. 31–32.

82. Poet Don Bogen, a graduate student at UC–Berkeley in the 1970s, shared his recollection of Brown's appearance on stage in a 21 January 2003 phone conversation.

83. Michael Davidson, *The San Francisco Renaissance: Poetics and Community at Mid-century* (New York: Cambridge University Press, 1989), pp. 16, 20.

84. Geoff Ward, "Literary San Francisco and the Poetry of the Excitements," *Critical Quarterly* 36, no. 3 (Autumn 1994): 81.

85. "For years the Poetry Center was in fact the poetry readings and seminars at my house," Rexroth explained in one letter. "When this activity became unmanageable, Robert Duncan, Madeleine Gleason and I set up the Poetry Center and got Ruth Witt Diamint to sponsor the readings at S.F. State College" (Hamalian, *A Life of Kenneth Roxroth*, pp. 111–12n). Diamint left to take a teaching post in Japan in 1961.

86. For an excellent chronology of these readings, see Stephen Vincent, "Poetry Readings/Reading Poetry: San Francisco Bay Area, 1958–1980," in *The Poetry Reading: A Contemporary Compendium on Language and Performance*, ed. Stephen Vincent and Ellen Zweig (San Francisco: Momo's Press, 1981), pp. 19–54.

87. See Steven Watson, *The Birth of the Beat Generation: Visionaries, Rebels, and Hipsters, 1944–1960* (1995; New York: Pantheon, 1998), pp. 189–91. This map is illustrated by Eric Hanson. For more on the barroom antics of Spicer, whose rough-and-tumble version of Pacific community (or "Pacific Nation") excluded Zen and concentrated solely on the West Coast of America, see Davidson's discussion in *The San Francisco Renaissance*, pp. 150–71, as well as the exhaustive biography written by Lewis Ellingham and Kevin Killian, *Poet Be Like God: Jack Spicer and the San Francisco Renaissance* (Hanover, NH: Wesleyan University Press/University Press of New England, 1998).

88. Roland Barthes, "Semiology and Urbanism" (1967), in *The Semiotic Challenge*, trans. Richard Howard (New York: Hill and Wang, 1988), p. 200.

89. Soja, *Postmodern Geographies*, p. 246n.

90. Michel Foucault, "Of Other Spaces," trans. Jay Miskowiec, *Diacritics* 16, no. 1 (Spring 1986): 24. An important psychoanalytic critique of specular identity formation in human individuals can be found in Jacques Lacan, "The Mirror Stage as Formative of the Function of the I as Revealed in Psychoanalytic Experience" (1949), in *Ecrits: A Selection*, trans. Alan Sheridan (New York: Norton, 1977), pp. 1–7.

91. Julia Kristeva, *Strangers to Ourselves*, trans. Leon S. Roudiez (New York: Columbia University Press, 1991), p. 11.

92. Davidson, *The San Francisco Renaissance*, p. 7.

93. Kenneth Rexroth, "The Visionary Painting of Morris Graves" (1955), in Morrow, ed., *World Outside the Window*, p. 27. For more on Graves, see my next chapter, "Migrating."

94. Lawrence Ferlinghetti, "Genesis of *After the Cries of Birds*," in *Poetics of the New American Poetry*, ed. Donald M. Allen and Warren Tallman (New York: Grove, 1973), pp. 446–47.

95. Hamalian, *A Life of Kenneth Rexroth*, p. 234.

96. Allen Ginsberg, letter to John Allen Ryan, 9 September 1955, in *Beat Down to Your Soul: What Was the Beat Generation?* ed. Ann Charters (New York: Penguin, 2001), p. 207.

97. Gary Snyder, statement on poetics, in Allen, ed., *The New American Poetry 1945–1960*, p. 421.

98. Patrick Murphy has reminded me several times in the past few years about Snyder's decision not to reprint overtly sexist material in his two volumes of selected works, *No Nature* (1992) and *The Gary Snyder Reader* (1999), and about his exposure to feminist thought during his teaching career at UC–Davis (1986–2001). For brief hints about feminist influences on Snyder's thinking during this time, particularly in the field of ecology, see Jack Hicks, "The Poet in the University," in *Gary Snyder: Dimensions of a Life*, ed. Jon Halper (San Francisco: Sierra Club Books, 1991), p. 280.

99. William Everson, *Archetype West: The Pacific Coast as a Literary Region* (Berkeley, CA: Oyez, 1976), p. 141.

1. Migrating

1. James Clifford, *Routes: Travel and Translation in the Late Twentieth Century* (Cambridge, MA: Harvard University Press, 1997), pp. 2–3.

2. Ibid., pp. 301–2.

3. Ibid., pp. 303, 341.

4. See Thomas J. Lyon, "The Ecological Vision of Gary Snyder," in *Critical Essays on Gary Snyder*, ed. Patrick D. Murphy (Boston: G. K. Hall, 1991), p. 42.

5. Gary Snyder, quoted in Nicholas O'Connell, *At the Field's End: Interviews with Twenty Pacific Northwest Writers* (Seattle: Madrona Publishers, 1987), p. 311.

For a list of the western writers young Snyder read, see John P. O'Grady, "Living Landscape: An Interview with Gary Snyder," *Western American Literature* 33, no. 3 (Fall 1998): 279–80.

6. Gary Snyder, interview with David Meltzer and Marina Lazzara (1999), in *San Francisco Beat: Talking with the Poets*, ed. David Meltzer (San Francisco: City Lights, 2001), p. 278.

7. Gary Snyder, interview with Bill Moyers, in *The Language of Life: A Festival of Poets*, ed. James Haba (New York: Doubleday, 1995), p. 367.

8. O'Grady, "Living Landscape," pp. 276–77.

9. Snyder, quoted in O'Connell, *At the Field's End*, p. 312. The Indian names for the peaks of the Pacific Northwest are provided in O'Grady, "Living Landscape," p. 275. For more on Snyder's first adventures in the mountains, see Jerry Crandall, "Mountaineers Are Always Free," in *Gary Snyder: Dimensions of a Life*, ed. Jon Halper (San Francisco: Sierra Club Books, 1991), pp. 3–7.

10. Gary Snyder, "The San Francisco Renaissance: A Reappraisal," conference talk delivered at the University of California, San Diego, 10 February 1982, quoted in Michael Davidson, *The San Francisco Renaissance: Poetics and Community at Mid-century* (New York: Cambridge University Press, 1989), p. 13.

11. Gary Snyder, correspondence with the author, 9 December 1996.

12. Gary Snyder, quoted in Dan Mcleod, "Asia and the Poetic Discovery of America," in *Discovering the Other: Humanities East and West*, ed. Robert S. Ellwood (Malibu, CA: Udena, 1984), p. 177.

13. According to Ann Charters, *The Portable Jack Kerouac* (1995; New York: Penguin, 1996), William Burroughs passed along a copy of *Decline of the West* to Jack Kerouac soon after meeting him in New York in 1944 with the instruction to "edify your mind, me boy, with the grand actuality of fact" (p. 552).

14. Philip Whalen, "Liberal Shepherds," in Halper, ed., *Gary Snyder*, p. 207.

15. Lew Welch, letter to Dorothy Brownfield, 16 May 1949, in *I Remain: The Letters of Lew Welch & the Correspondence of His Friends, Volume One, 1949–1960*, ed. Donald M. Allen (Bolinas, CA: Grey Fox, 1980), p. 6.

16. Lew Welch, letter to Gary Snyder, 8 December 1951, *I Remain, Volume One*, p. 62.

17. Gary Snyder, letter to Philip Whalen, 2 February 1954. Philip Whalen Papers, Special Collections and Archives, Eric V. Hauser Memorial Library, Reed College, Portland, Oregon.

18. Henry David Thoreau, "Conclusion" to *Walden*, in *The Portable Thoreau*, rev. ed., ed. Carl Bove (1964; New York: Penguin, 1982), p. 571.

19. Carol Baker, "1414 SE Lambert Street," in Halper, ed., *Gary Snyder*, p. 24.

20. David Perkins, *A History of Modern Poetry, Volume Two: Modernism and After* (Cambridge, MA: Harvard University Press, 1987), p. 542.

21. J. Michael Mahar, "Scenes from the Sidelines," in Halper, ed., *Gary Snyder*, p. 10.

22. Snyder, correspondence with the author, 9 December 1996.

23. Daniel DuBois et al., *Morris Graves: Reconciling Inner and Outer Realities, 1932–1983* (New York: Schmidt Bingham Gallery, 1992), n.p.

24. Morris Graves, quoted in *Pacific West Art: The Haseltine Collection* (Eugene: Museum of Art, University of Oregon, 1963). For a description of the nocturnal migration patterns of sandpipers, see Frederick C. Lincoln, *Migration of Birds* (Garden City, NY: Doubleday, 1952), pp. 15–18. As my next chapter will show, Snyder was familiar with Lincoln's book and used its title for one of his own poems.

25. Kenneth Rexroth, "The Visionary Painting of Morris Graves," in *World outside the Window: The Selected Essays of Kenneth Rexroth*, ed. Bradford Morrow (New York: New Directions, 1987), p. 31.

26. Graves, quoted in *Pacific West Art*, n.p.

27. Steven Watson, *The Birth of the Beat Generation: Visionaries, Rebels, and Hipsters, 1944–1960* (1995; New York: Pantheon, 1998).

28. See Lawrence Ferlinghetti, "A Coney Island of the Mind" (section 11), in *The New American Poetry 1945–1960*, ed. Donald Allen (1960; Berkeley: University of California Press, 1999), p. 131. See also Brother Antoninus, "A Canticle to the Waterbirds," ibid., p. 121.

29. See Geoffrey Chaucer, *The Canterbury Tales*, "General Prologue," I, 1–18; "The Reeve's Tale," I, 4064–66; "The Squire's Tale," V, 499–650. The characterization of "wehee" as a "whinny of sexual desire" in "The Reeve's Tale" is taken from Jack A.W. Bennett, *Chaucer at Oxford and Cambridge* (1974), cited in *The Riverside Chaucer*, 3d ed., ed. Larry D. Benson (Boston: Houghton Mifflin, 1987), p. 851n.

30. Walter Benjamin, "Franz Kafka," in *Illuminations*, ed. Hannah Arendt, trans. Harry Zohn (New York: Schocken, 1968), p. 132.

31. Walter Benjamin, *The Origin of German Tragic Drama*, trans. John Osborne (London: Verso, 1977), pp. 86–87.

32. See Gilles Deleuze and Felix Guattari, *A Thousand Plateaus: Capitalism and Schizophrenia*, trans. Brian Massumi (Minneapolis: University of Minnesota Press, 1987).

33. David H. French, "Gary Snyder and Reed College," in Halper, ed., *Gary Snyder*, p. 17. The only tribute higher than having one's thesis copied, Reed graduate Alan Sun once told me, is having it stolen.

34. Gary Snyder, quoted in David Kherdian, *Six Poets of the San Francisco Renaissance: Portraits and Checklists* (Fresno, CA: Giligia Press, 1967), p. 48.

35. Throughout this book, I shall use quotation marks to refer to the original "He Who Hunted Birds" myth, as it was told to McGregor, and italics (*He Who Hunted Birds*) or an abbreviation (HWHB) to refer to the thesis that Snyder wrote at Reed and eventually published as a book.

36. For more on the identification of the hunter with the hunted in this myth, see Sherman Paul, *In Search of the Primitive: Rereading David Antin, Jerome Rothenberg, and Gary Snyder* (Baton Rouge: Louisiana State University Press, 1986), p. 208.

37. Joseph Campbell, *The Masks of God: Primitive Mythology* (1959; New York: Penguin, 1976), pp. 15, 205.

38. Ibid., pp. viii, 137–38, 207–8.

39. Keith Penner, "Aboriginal Peoples in Canada and the Pacific Rim," *Plural Societies* 18, no. 1 (July 1988): 56. Similar findings are noted by Campbell, *The Masks of God: Primitive Mythology*, pp. 362–63.

40. Gary Snyder, quoted in Katsunori Yamazato, "Seeking a Fulcrum: Gary Snyder in Japan, 1956–1975" (Ph.D. diss., University of California, Davis, 1987), p. 10.

41. Ibid., p. 36n.

42. Snyder, quoted in Kherdian, *Six Poets*, p. 49.

43. See Patrick D. Murphy, *A Place for Wayfaring: The Poetry and Prose of Gary Snyder* (Corvallis: Oregon State University Press, 2000), pp. 5–6. See also Kherdian, *Six Poets*, pp. 49–50. In 1954, Phil Whalen was working as a lookout on Sourdough Mountain, where Snyder had been stationed the previous summer. In February of that year, Snyder wrote a letter to Whalen containing the text of the document banning him from lookout work. After hearing about his friend's blacklisting debacle, Whalen wrote back describing how the FBI traveled to Sourdough to dig up evidence from his coworkers and supervisors. "FBI plagued Blackie, who said hell, he'd hire you again & 6 more like you if they'd let him. He don't believe you are a communist & wouldn't care if you was on account you did your job so good" (Philip Whalen, letter to Gary Snyder, 18 July 1954, Gary Snyder Papers, Department of Special Collections, University of California Library, Davis). See also Gary Snyder, letter to Philip Whalen, 16 February 1954, Philip Whalen Papers, Reed College.

44. For more on the monomythic readings of *Myths & Texts*, see Lee Bartlett, *The Sun Is But a Morning Star: Studies in West Coast Poetry and Poetics* (Albuquerque: University of New Mexico Press, 1989), pp. 92–105. Tim Dean, *Gary Snyder and the American Unconscious: Inhabiting the Ground* (New York: St. Martin's Press, 1990), pp. 126–38, raises the stakes of this discussion by comparing Snyder's first volume of verse to the modern Grail quest in *The Waste Land*. My reservations about these monomythic readings echo those already rehearsed by Patrick D. Murphy, "Alternation and Interpenetration: Gary Snyder's *Myths & Texts*," in *Critical Essays on Gary Snyder*, who argues that the "linear conceptions of the sequence's development . . . describe only its outer skeleton. While one may say that *Myths & Texts* loosely follows a quest motif based on the monomyth, such a statement does not emphasize how the sequence is internally structured" (pp. 210–29). Accordingly, Murphy is apt to praise studies of the sequence's internal dynamics (which he finds in the linguistic analyses of Bert Almon and Wai-Lim Yip) and to rely upon detailed exegeses of the poem's multifarious cultural references (which he locates in the work of Howard McCord and William Jungels). For the critical studies Murphy considers in this important article, see Bert Almon, *Gary Snyder*, Western American Writers Series 37 (Boise, ID: Boise State University, 1979);

Wai-Lim Yip, "Classical Chinese and Modern Anglo-American Poetry: Convergences and Languages of Poetry," *Comparative Literature Studies* 11 (March 1974): 21–47, an article that was subsequently revised and reprinted in his *Diffusion of Distances: Dialogues between Chinese and Western Poetics* (Berkeley: University of California Press, 1993); Howard McCord, *Some Notes to Gary Snyder's "Myths & Texts"* (Berkeley, CA: Sand Dollar, 1971); and William Jungels, "The Use of Native-American Mythologies in the Poetry of Gary Snyder" (Ph.D. diss., State University of New York at Buffalo, 1973). My own praise for these studies is not offered on the same level as Murphy's, since I find little in Almon or Yip that addresses cultural influences and little in McCord or Jungels that addresses the cohesive and specifically geographical attempts by which Snyder brings those cultural influences into play. This last qualification notwithstanding, I join other Snyder scholars in acknowledging the achievement of the Jungels dissertation, which although it is still unpublished after thirty years remains one of the most useful and fascinating documents in Snyder criticism. Its discoveries of the poet's oral and textual sources are unsurpassed, and anyone who studies *Myths & Texts* is certainly indebted to it.

45. See Richard Howard, *Alone with America: Essays on the Art of Poetry in the United States since 1950* (New York: Atheneum, 1969). According to a 1953 journal entry, Snyder carried the 1942 Signet edition of *Walden* with him to Sourdough Mountain. Gary Snyder Papers, University of California, Davis.

46. For more on this connection, see Jungels, "The Use of Native-American Mythologies," p. 15.

47. Murphy, *A Place for Wayfaring*, p. 24.

48. Jungels, "The Use of Native-American Mythologies," p. 38. By providing this reference, Jungels makes it clear that he is correcting McCord, who in *Some Notes* had claimed that the Drinkswater quotation came from Joseph Epes Brown, ed., *The Sacred Pipe: Black Elk's Account of the Seven Rites of the Oglala Sioux* (Norman: University of Oklahoma Press, 1953).

49. Jungels, "The Use of Native-American Mythologies," pp. 38–39.

50. Matthew Arnold, "Dover Beach," in *Matthew Arnold*, the Oxford Authors, ed. Miriam Allot and Robert H. Super (Oxford: Oxford University Press, 1986), p. 136.

51. Murphy, "Alternation and Interpenetration," in *Critical Essays on Gary Snyder*, p. 216.

52. In the estimation of John Muir, the California naturalist Snyder had been reading from a very young age, "more than seventy-five per cent of all the rain this [winter] season came from the northwest, down the coast over southeastern Alaska, British Columbia, Washington and Oregon" (*The Mountains of California* [1894; New York: Penguin Nature Library, 1985], p. 238). Today, deviations from this weather pattern are usually given colorful nicknames, as evidenced by the "Pineapple Express" (a warm storm track that shoots directly overseas from

Hawaii toward the California coast) and the much discussed "El Niño" phenomenon.

53. A first mention of Vaux's swifts can be found in Snyder's journal entry from Crater Mountain Lookout, dated 10 August 1952: "Vaux Swifts: in great numbers, flying before the storm, arcing so close that the sharp wing-whistle is heard" (EHH 8).

54. In tracking down McCord's sources, Jungels finds that the Berbeau reference "does not exist," but he identifies the A. Irving Hallowell article as "Bear Ceremonialism in the Northern Hemisphere," *American Anthropologist* 28, no. 1 (new series) (1926): 87ff. See Jungels, "The Use of Native-American Mythologies," p. 83. In a letter dated 9 December 1954, Snyder tells Phil Whalen about the Hallowell article, explaining that it is part of his research for a "new huge odd poem, the Bear Mother" (Philip Whalen Papers, Reed College).

55. Campbell, *The Masks of God: Primitive Mythology*, pp. 334–35, 339.

56. Like the passage on the arcing Vaux's swifts, the depiction of the jumping deer is first recorded in Snyder's journal in an entry dated 25 July 1953 (EHH 18).

57. Almon, *Gary Snyder*, p. 18.

58. Jungels, "The Use of Native-American Mythologies," p. 130.

59. Ralph Waldo Emerson, in *Emerson in His Journals*, ed. Joel Porte (Cambridge, MA: Harvard University Press, 1982), pp. 481–82.

60. In his primer on Zen practice, Shunryu Suzuki, *Zen Mind, Beginner's Mind*, rev. ed., ed. Trudy Dixon (1970; New York: Weatherhill, 1999), offers an alternative analysis of such insouciant attitudes, thereby complicating our reading of "Burning 1." According to Suzuki, "When you say, 'Whatever I do is Buddha nature, so it doesn't matter what I do, and there is no need to practice zazen,' that is already a dualistic understanding of our everyday life. If it really does not matter, there is no need for you to even say so. . . . If you say, 'It doesn't matter,' it means you are making some excuse to do something in your own way with your small mind. It means you are attached to some particular thing or way" (p. 42).

61. Lawrence Buell, *The Environmental Imagination: Thoreau, Nature Writing, and the Formation of American Culture* (Cambridge, MA: Belknap/Harvard University Press, 1995), p. 167.

62. Paul, *In Search of the Primitive*, p. 242.

63. See Joseph Campbell, *The Masks of God: Oriental Mythology* (1962; New York: Penguin, 1976), p. 281.

64. For more on Prajna's role in the Mahayana pantheon, see *Astasahasrika Prajnaparamita*, VII, 170–71, and XXII, 403, in *Sources of the Indian Tradition, Volume One: From the Beginning to 1800*, 2d ed., ed. Ainsle T. Embree (New York: Columbia University Press, 1988). In 1971, Snyder told McCord that the naked image of Prajna in his poem derives from a picture he saw in a book entitled *Buddhist Texts through the Ages*, published in 1954. This picture must have confirmed an image Snyder already had in mind or had seen elsewhere, since in a 1953 journal entry composed at the Sourdough Mountain Lookout station he envisions

and pays homage to this female deity: "True insight a love-making hovering between the void & the immense worlds of creation. To symbolically represent Prajna as female is right. The Prajna girl statue from Java" (EHH 22).

65. Muir, *The Mountains of California*, p. 44.

66. Murphy, "Alternation and Interpenetration," in *Critical Essays on Gary Snyder*, p. 224.

67. Lao Tzu, *Tao Te Ching*, trans. D. C. Lau (Harmondsworth: Penguin, 1963), p. 104.

68. Jack Kerouac, *The Dharma Bums* (1958: New York: Penguin, 1986), p. 85.

69. Huston Smith, *The Religions of Man* (1958; New York: Harper Perennial, 1965), p. 204.

70. See Murphy, "Alternation and Interpenetration," in *Critical Essays on Gary Snyder*, p. 226.

71. As Joanne Kyger, *The Japan & India Journals 1960–1964* (Bolinas, CA: Tombouctou, 1981), would note in her journal a few years later, the Beat community's tendency to equate women with the void lent a sense of disparity to heterosexual relationships, especially in the course of metaphysically charged activities like *yabyum* (a form of sitting coitus resembling *zazen*). Kyger's disgust is reflected in the facetious epithets she assigns *yabyum* partners: "Mr. Fullness of Soul and Miss Vacant Nothingness" (p. 40). In *The Dharma Bums*, Japhy Ryder demonstrates the *yabyum* position with a young woman named Princess, telling Ray Smith, "I'm the thunderbolt and Princess is the dark void, you see" (p. 29).

72. Evan Eisenberg, *The Ecology of Eden: An Inquiry into the Dream of Paradise and a New Vision of Our Role in Nature* (1998; New York: Vintage, 1999), p. 71, points out that Sumeru, "a vast pyramidal mountain rising from the cosmic ocean," was initially worshiped by Buddhist Kalmucks in Siberia but derives from Meru, the mountainous "world-pole" referred to in Indian Hindu texts.

73. See Aldo Leopold, *A Sand County Almanac, with Essays on Conservation from Round River* (1966; New York: Ballantine, 1970), pp. 137–41.

74. For the array of beasts who scurry away from the cruel fox, Daun Russel, in "The Nun's Priest's Tale," see *The Canterbury Tales*, VII, 3375–401. In keeping with the spirit of mock epic, Chaucer puffs up the fear felt by the scrambling geese, ducks, and chickens to apocalyptic proportions: "And therewithal they shriked and they howped / It semed as that hevene sholde falle" (ll. 3400–3401). In "Burning 17," Snyder does much the same thing, albeit without Chaucer's satirical tone. Snyder attests to reading Chaucer while working on Crater Mountain Lookout station. See the journal entry dated 3 August 1952 (EHH 6).

75. See "Dharma Rain" (excerpt from the *Lotus Sutra*), trans. Burton Watson, in *Dharma Rain: Sources of Buddhist Environmentalism*, ed. Stephanie Kaza and Kenneth Kraft (Boston: Shambhala, 2000), pp. 43–48.

76. Henry David Thoreau, journal entry dated 5 January 1850, quoted in Laura Dassow Walls, *Seeing New Worlds: Henry David Thoreau and Nineteenth-Century Natural Science* (Madison: University of Wisconsin Press, 1995), p. 138.

77. Yamazato, "Seeking a Fulcrum," p. 71.

78. For more detail on Snyder's plans for "bhikku hostels," which included the Marin-an hermitage, see John Suiter, *Poets on the Peaks: Gary Snyder, Philip Whalen & Jack Kerouac in the North Cascades* (Washington, DC: Counterpoint, 2002), p. 186.

79. Gary Snyder, quoted in Katherine McNeill, *Gary Snyder: A Bibliography* (New York: Phoenix Bookshop, 1983), pp. 8–9.

80. See Charles Olson, statement on poetics, in Allen, ed., *The New American Poetry 1945–1960*, p. 387.

81. Clifford, *Routes*, p. 327.

2. Translating

1. See Gary Snyder, letter to Philip Whalen, 12 December 1956, Philip Whalen Papers, Special Collections and Archives, Eric V. Hauser Memorial Library, Reed College, Portland, Oregon. For the time frame of publication, see Katherine McNeill, *Gary Snyder: A Bibliography* (New York: Phoenix Bookshop, 1983), pp. 7, 9.

2. McNeill, *Gary Snyder*, p. 6.

3. Gary Snyder, letter to Philip Whalen, 16 June 1955, Philip Whalen Papers, Reed College.

4. Walter Benjamin, "The Task of the Translator," in *Illuminations*, ed. Hannah Arendt, trans. Harry Zohn (New York: Schocken, 1968), p. 80.

5. Gary Snyder, quoted in Jonathan White, "Hanging Out with Raven" (interview with Gary Snyder), in *Talking on the Water: Conversations about Nature and Creativity* (San Francisco: Sierra Club Books, 1994), p. 153.

6. For more on Po-chang and his establishment of the "first purely Zen community of monks," see Alan Watts, *The Way of Zen* (1957; New York: Vintage, 1989), pp. 98–99.

7. Gary Snyder, statement on poetics, in *The New American Poetry 1945–1960*, ed. Donald Allen (1960; Berkeley: University of California Press, 1999), p. 420.

8. Joseph Campbell, *The Masks of God: Oriental Mythology* (1962; New York: Penguin, 1976), p. 273.

9. John Suiter, *Poets on the Peaks: Gary Snyder, Philip Whalen & Jack Kerouac in the North Cascades* (Washington, DC: Counterpoint, 2002), p. 65, explains that Sourdough Mountain Lookout is two thousand feet lower than Crater Mountain Lookout but has much better sight lines. On Sourdough, Snyder was able to see all six major drainages in the Upper Skagit region as well as the abandoned Crater Mountain post he had occupied the summer before.

10. Robert Kern, "Silence in Prosody: The Poem as Silent Form," in *Critical Essays on Gary Snyder*, ed. Patrick D. Murphy (Boston: G. K. Hall, 1991), pp. 111, 114–15.

11. Laszlo Géfin, "[Ellipsis and Riprap: Gary Snyder]," in ibid., p. 127.

12. Gary Snyder, correspondence with the author, 9 August 1997.

13. See Matsuo Basho, "The Records of a Travel-Worn Satchel," in *The Narrow Road to the Deep North and Other Travel Sketches*, trans. Nobuyuki Yuasa (Harmondsworth: Penguin, 1966), p. 87. The Tao Yuan-ming poem is quoted in Beongcheon Yu, *The Great Circle: American Writers and the Orient* (Detroit: Wayne State University Press, 1983), p. 220.

14. Gary Snyder, quoted in David Kherdian, *Six Poets of the San Francisco Renaissance: Portraits and Checklists* (Fresno, CA: Giligia Press, 1967), p. 48.

15. See Jack Kerouac, *Desolation Angels* (New York: Coward-McCann, 1965); Philip Whalen, "Sourdough Mountain Lookout," in *Overtime: Selected Poems* (New York: Penguin, 1999); and William Stafford, *West of Your City* (San Jose, CA: Talisman, 1960).

16. Patrick D. Murphy, *A Place for Wayfaring: The Poetry and Prose of Gary Snyder* (Corvallis: Oregon State University Press, 2000), p. 45.

17. D. T. Suzuki, *An Introduction to Zen Buddhism* (1934; New York: Grove/Evergreen Black Cat, 1964), p. 88.

18. Gary Snyder, letters to Philip Whalen, 9 June and 25 July 1955, Philip Whalen Papers, Reed College.

19. Gary Snyder, quoted in David Robertson, "Gary Snyder Riprapping in Yosemite, 1955," *American Poetry* 2, no. 1 (1984): 52–53.

20. John Muir, *My First Summer in the Sierra* (1911; New York: Penguin Nature Classics, 1997), p. 235.

21. See Tim Dean, *Gary Snyder and the American Unconscious: Inhabiting the Ground* (New York: St. Martin's Press, 1990), p. 93. In critiquing Snyder's poetry, Dean makes reference to the "inescapable grounding of any American aesthetic." Stanley Kunitz, by contrast, is more likely to attribute such grounding to Chinese poetry and not to American poetry, which he thinks is often excessive. Kunitz does see fit to praise Snyder and Deep Image poet Robert Bly, however, since he believes that their "sensing and grounding" or their "physical response to a poem" lends a reticence and decorum missing in most American verse. Kunitz's thoughts are taken from a 1977 symposium of the Academy of American Poets in New York, the proceedings of which were subsequently published in "Chinese Poetry and the American Imagination," ed. Gregory Orr, *Ironwood* 9, no. 1 (1981): 42–43.

22. Gary Snyder, correspondence with the author, 18 May 1997.

23. See Annette Kolodny, *The Lay of the Land: Metaphor as Experience and History in American Life and Letters* (Chapel Hill: University of North Carolina Press, 1975).

24. Gary Snyder, letter to Philip Whalen, 14 August 1955, Philip Whalen Papers, Reed College.

25. Snyder, quoted in Kherdian, *Six Poets*, p. 51.

26. Robertson, "Gary Snyder Riprapping in Yosemite," p. 56.

27. Snyder, statement on poetics, in Allen, ed., *The New American Poetry 1945–1960*, pp. 420–21.

28. Snyder, quoted in Robertson, "Gary Snyder Riprapping in Yosemite," p. 53.

29. Gary Snyder, quoted in Julia Martin, "Coyote Mind: An Interview with Gary Snyder," *TriQuarterly* 79 (Fall 1990): 166. Ezra Pound, for his part, tended to translate *tao* as "the process" rather than "the way," influenced as he was by Confucian doctrines of strict classical thinking, summed up by the aphorism he took from the *Analects* and reprinted on the final page of his *Confucian Odes*: "Have no twisty thoughts" (Yu, *The Great Circle*, p. 196). Snyder and his cohorts in the San Francisco Renaissance were obviously much more willing to explore unconventional pathways.

30. Snyder, quoted in Martin, "Coyote Mind," p. 166.

31. Snyder, correspondence with the author, 18 May 1997.

32. Dean, *Gary Snyder and the American Unconscious*, p. 168.

33. For a brilliant description of the Kantian/Freudian scenario known as the Romantic Sublime, in which a moment of blockage or bewilderment is followed by a series of compensatory actions taken by an imaginative mind able to circumvent that blockage, see Thomas Weiskel, *The Romantic Sublime: Studies in the Structure and Psychology of Transcendence* (Baltimore: Johns Hopkins University Press, 1976). See also Neil Hertz, "The Notion of Blockage in the Literature of the Sublime," in *The End of the Line: Essays on Psychoanalysis and the Sublime* (New York: Columbia University Press, 1985).

34. See T. S. Eliot, *The Waste Land*, in *Collected Poems 1909–1962* (San Diego: Harcourt, Brace, Jovanovich, 1963). Interestingly, in a journal entry dated 23 July 1952, Snyder records a revelatory moment on Crater Mountain that sounds uncannily like the one he describes in "Piute Creek": "Even here, cold foggy rocky place, there's life" (EHH 3). The main difference, as Snyder's comments to David Robertson bear out, derives from the fact that coastal fog often shrouds the Cascades, whereas the Sierra Nevada mountains, an inland range situated a hundred miles or so from the California coast, are notable for their dry conditions and their unfiltered sunlight.

35. For the comparison of the Unconscious to a fading neon light at dawn, see Jacques Lacan, "Of Structure as an Inmixing of an Otherness Prerequisite to Any Subject Whatever," in *The Structuralist Controversy: The Languages of Criticism and the Sciences of Man*, 2d ed., ed. Richard Macksey and Eugenio Donato (Baltimore: Johns Hopkins University Press, 1972), p. 189. For a concise description of the Lacanian Unconscious as a trajectory, see Samuel Weber, *Return to Freud: Jacques Lacan's Displacement of Psychoanalysis* (Cambridge: Cambridge University Press, 1992), p. 5.

36. For Snyder's use of this phrase, see James McKenzie, "Moving the World a Millionth of an Inch: An Interview with Gary Snyder," *The Beat Diary: The Unspeakable Visions of the Individual* 5 (1977): 149.

37. Dean, *Gary Snyder and the American Unconscious*, p. 170.

38. Watts, *The Way of Zen*, p. 15.

39. Gary Snyder, introduction to *Beneath a Single Moon: Buddhism in Contemporary American Poetry*, ed. Kent Johnson and Craig Paulenich (Boston: Shambhala, 1991), p. 4.

40. Snyder, quoted in Robertson, "Gary Snyder Riprapping in Yosemite," pp. 56–57.

41. See Muir, *My First Summer*, pp. 102, 229.

42. Gary Snyder, correspondence with the author, 19 April 1997. Also see the discussion in Suiter, *Poets on the Peaks*, pp. 181–85. Jack Kerouac alludes to Snyder's trip to Nooksack Valley, but makes no mention of Ginsberg, in *The Dharma Bums* (1958; New York: Penguin, 1986), p. 151.

43. Henry David Thoreau, *Cape Cod* (1865; New York: Penguin Nature Library, 1987), p. 319.

44. Frederick C. Lincoln, *Migration of Birds* (Garden City, NY: Doubleday, 1952), pp. 66–67.

45. Curator Frederick S. Wight offers an assessment of Graves's *Flight of the Plover* that is quite in keeping with the spirit of Snyder's Pacific Rim communitarianism, describing the painting as "a fluid pattern of living motion, in control of that instinct which makes a spiritual harmony out of many living things" (Frederick S. Wight, John I. H. Baur, and Duncan Phillips, eds., *Morris Graves* [Berkeley: University of California Press, 1956], p. 56). Zen poet Matsuo Basho included a number of references to plovers as he walked the beaches of Japan; see "Records of a Weather-Exposed Skeleton" (pp. 51–64) and "Records of a Travel-Worn Satchel" (pp. 71–90) in *The Narrow Road to the Deep North and Other Travel Sketches*. Additionally, Albert Saijo, a Japanese-American poet who had some contact with members of the San Francisco Renaissance (he is best known in Beat circles for having composed collaborative haiku with Jack Kerouac and Lew Welch during a cross-country road trip), cites the example of the plover to describe his own disjointed travels in the Pacific region. Pacific Rim scholar Rob Wilson explains that, for Saijo, "the plover is an admirable figure of 'ANIMAL CIVILITY' living on edges and borders, embodying nomadic movement, improvisation and risk, jazzy flights between solitary foraging and communal roosting: anarchic and poetic existence on a small budget." Similarly, in traditional hula *mele*, Wilson tells us, Hawaiian dancers mime the plover's bobbing head motions, emphasizing the spontaneous bird's role as "flighty lovemaker and heroic wayfarer whose sea journey is linked . . . to a brave flight from Kahiki, land of mythic origins and bounty from heaven, and thus serves as a metaphor for the Hawaiian quest for beauty, royal protection, and love." Native Hawaiian activist Haunani-Kay Trask, by contrast, views the plover as a symbol of haole colonization, a land-grabbing settler "thickened by the fat / of our land." For a consideration of these competing views, see Rob Wilson, *Reimagining the American Pacific: From "South Pacific" to Bamboo Ridge and Beyond* (Durham, NC: Duke University Press, 2000), pp. 191–92, and the original sources he cites: Albert Saijo, *Outspeaks: A Rhapsody* (Honolulu:

Bamboo Ridge Press, 1996); Nathaniel B. Emerson, *Unwritten Literature of Hawaii: The Sacred Songs of the Hula* (Rutland, VT: Tuttle, 1982); and Haunani-Kay Trask, *Light in the Crevice Never Seen* (Portland, OR: Calyx Books, 1994).

46. Murphy, *A Place for Wayfaring*, p. 6.

47. See Snyder's recollections in McNeill, *Gary Snyder*, pp. 9–12. Snyder sent *The Wooden Fish* to Philip Whalen in a letter dated 9 April 1961, Philip Whalen Papers, Reed College.

48. See Paul Rossiter and John Evans, "Interview: Gary Snyder," *Studies in the Humanities* 26, nos. 1–2 (June and December 1999): 13.

49. Sanehide Kodama, *American Poetry and Japanese Culture* (Hamden, CT: Archon, 1984), pp. 183, 237n.

50. See J. Michael Mahar, "Scenes from the Sidelines," in *Gary Snyder: Dimensions of a Life*, ed. Jon Halper (San Francisco: Sierra Club Books, 1991), p. 14, and David H. French, "Gary Snyder and Reed College," in ibid., p. 17.

51. Gary Snyder, interview with David Meltzer and Marina Lazzara (1999), in *San Francisco Beat: Talking with the Poets*, ed. David Meltzer (San Francisco: City Lights, 2001), p. 280.

52. Gary Snyder, quoted in Orr, ed., "Chinese Poetry and the American Imagination," p. 41.

53. Gary Snyder, letter to Philip Whalen, 2 November 1953, Philip Whalen Papers, Reed College.

54. Gary Snyder, letter to Philip Whalen, 12 November 1953, Philip Whalen Papers, Reed College.

55. Gary Snyder, "Cold Mountain Poems," *Evergreen Review* 2, no. 6 (Autumn 1958): 69. The prefatory note in the book version of *Riprap & Cold Mountain Poems* omits the first sentence. In *Poets on the Peaks*, John Suiter claims that, while he was stationed on Sourdough Mountain in the summer of 1953, Snyder received a postcard from an ex-girlfriend telling him about the Han-shan exhibition, which had recently come to Portland (pp. 75–76).

56. Campbell, *The Masks of God: Oriental Mythology*, p. 136.

57. Snyder, quoted in Orr, ed., "Chinese Poetry and the American Imagination," p. 41.

58. Ibid.

59. Gary Snyder, quoted in Dell Hymes, "Some North Pacific Coast Poems: A Problem in Anthropological Philology," *American Anthropologist* 67, no. 2 (1965): 335–36.

60. Gary Snyder, quoted in Lee Bartlett, "Gary Snyder's Han-Shan," *Sagetrieb* 2, no. 1 (Spring 1983): 107. Also useful is Bartlett's discussion of "Cold Mountain Poems" in *The Sun Is But a Morning Star: Studies in West Coast Poetry and Poetics* (Albuquerque: University of New Mexico Press, 1989), pp. 82–92.

61. See Gary Snyder, letter to Philip Whalen, 2 January 1955, Philip Whalen Papers, Reed College. See also Philip Whalen, letter to Gary Snyder, 30 October

1953, Gary Snyder Papers, Department of Special Collections, University of California Library, Davis.

62. See Kenneth Rexroth, *One Hundred Poems from the Japanese* (New York: New Directions, 1955), and *One Hundred Poems from the Chinese* (New York: New Directions, 1956). Rexroth's publisher at New Directions, James Laughlin, recalls his belated discovery that the translations in these books owed a debt to previous translations: "I was poking around [Rexroth's] library one day and I came on some French translations of the oriental poems done in the 1890s, which seemed very familiar. I read them against Kenneth's translations and discovered that he had drawn them from the French of Judith Gautier. Nothing wrong with that. Later he taught himself many Chinese and Japanese characters and worked directly" (Laughlin's reminiscence is quoted in Bartlett, *The Sun Is But a Morning Star*, p. 80). Notwithstanding his publisher's forgiveness, I find it rather ironic in light of this evidence that Rexroth took such delight in chastising Kerouac for not knowing Asian languages. Interestingly, in a piece he published a few years after his popular translations, Rexroth was already hedging his bets, claiming that "the greatest translators of Chinese—Judith Gautier, Klabund, Pound—knew less than nothing of Chinese when they did their best translations. In fact, Judith Gautier's lover and informant was a Thai, and he himself had only the foggiest notions of the meanings of the Chinese texts" ("The Poet as Translator" [1960], in *World outside the Window: The Selected Essays of Kenneth Rexroth*, ed. Bradford Morrow [New York: New Directions, 1987], p. 187). Assuming Rexroth really did translate from the Gautier version, we can see just how many steps removed he was from the original Chinese.

63. Philip Whalen, letter to Gary Snyder, 14 November 1958, Gary Snyder Papers, University of California Library, Davis.

64. Richard Bernstein, *Ultimate Journey: Retracing the Path of an Ancient Buddhist Monk Who Crossed Asia in Search of Enlightenment* (2001; New York: Vintage Departures, 2002), pp. 28–29.

65. Consider the editorial decisions made by Stephen Owen, one of today's most esteemed anthologists of Chinese literature. In the *Norton Anthology of Chinese Literature: Beginnings to 1911* (New York: Norton, 1996), Owen makes room for only five of Han-shan's poems, which fit compactly onto two of the anthology's more than twelve hundred pages. Actually, this paltry inclusion can be taken as a sign of progress, since Han-shan had been excluded entirely by Owen on previous occasions. In *The Poetry of the Early T'ang* (New Haven, CT: Yale University Press, 1977), Owen remarked, "The omission [of Han-shan] is unfortunate but necessary; [his] poems stand so far outside the mainstream of the poetic tradition and present so many problems of dating and attribution that consideration of them would distract from the real literary and historical problems of the period." In another of his collections, *The Great Age of Chinese Poetry: The High T'ang* (New Haven, CT: Yale University Press, 1981), Owen rationalizes another omission of

Han-shan on the grounds that the poet was not only "casual and colloquial" but also "unpoetic."

66. For a list of the earliest editions of Han-shan's work, see Wu Chi-Yu, "A Study of Han Shan," *T'oung Pao Archives* 45, nos. 4–5 (1957): 445–50. In his brief monograph, *Han Shan in English* (Buffalo: White Pine Press, 1989), Paul Khan claims that the earliest extant edition is dated 1189. In addition to his research on various editions, Wu translates fifty of Han-shan's poems into English, leaving open the possibility that one of them was written by the poet's sidekick, Shih-te.

67. John Blofeld, introduction to *The Collected Songs of Cold Mountain*, trans. Red Pine (Bill Porter), rev. edition (Port Townsend, WA: Copper Canyon Press, 2000), p. 21.

68. Red Pine (Bill Porter), translator's preface to *The Collected Songs of Cold Mountain*, p. 9.

69. Wu Chi-Yu, "A Study of Han Shan," pp. 394–411.

70. Robert G. Henricks, *The Poetry of Han Shan: A Complete, Annotated Translation of "Cold Mountain"* (Albany: State University of New York Press, 1990), p. 4.

71. Red Pine, translator's preface, p. 10.

72. See Iriya Yoshitaka, *Kanzan* (Tokyo: Iwanami Shoten, 1958), pp. 11, 15–17. Also see the discussion about collective authorship in Henricks, *The Poetry of Han Shan*, pp. 6–7, 23n.

73. See E. G. Pulleybank, "Linguistic Evidence for the Date of Han-shan," in *Studies in Chinese Poetry and Politics, Volume One*, ed. Ronald C. Miao (San Francisco: CMC, 1978), pp. 163–85. Of the twenty-four poems Snyder translates, seven are classified by Pulleybank as "Han-shan II" poems: 7, 11, 16, 17, 18, 20, and 24.

74. See Arthur Waley, "27 Poems by Han-shan," *Encounter* 3, no. 3 (1954): 3–8.

75. Snyder, correspondence with the author, 9 August 1997. For information on the "Cold Mountain Poems" manuscript housed at Kent State, see Jacob Leed, "Gary Snyder, Han Shan, and Jack Kerouac," *Journal of Modern Literature* 11 (1984): 185–93.

76. Snyder, quoted in Orr, ed., "Chinese Poetry and the American Imagination," pp. 50–51.

77. See Sherman Paul, *In Search of the Primitive: Rereading David Antin, Jerome Rothenberg, and Gary Snyder* (Baton Rouge: Louisiana State University Press, 1986), p. 189.

78. Henricks, *The Poetry of Han Shan*, p. 12.

79. The sources for translations by Henricks, Owen (*Norton Anthology of Chinese Literature*), and Red Pine are cited above. The Burton Watson translations can be found in the reprint of his 1962 volume, *100 Poems by the T'ang Poet Han-shan* (1962; New York: Columbia University Press, 1970). From this point forward, sources already cited are included parenthetically in the text. Each group of translations is arranged according to its own numbering system, but for the sake of clarity, I have chosen to reference only Snyder's translations by number. For

those interested, a concordance to English language translations of Han-shan is included in Red Pine, *The Collected Songs of Cold Mountain*, pp. 301–6.

80. See Gary Snyder, *Riprap and Cold Mountain Poems* (San Francisco: Four Seasons Foundation, 1969), p. 32.

81. Edward H. Schafer, "Han Shan," in *Sunflower Splendor: Three Thousand Years of Chinese Poetry*, ed. Wu-chi Liu and Irving Lo (Bloomington: Indiana University Press, 1975), p. 549.

82. Gary Snyder, letters to Philip Whalen, 14 November 1959 and 13 January 1960, Philip Whalen Papers, Reed College.

83. Kerouac, *The Dharma Bums*, p. 22.

84. See the letters from Snyder quoted in Ling Chung, "Whose Mountain Is This?—Gary Snyder's Translations of Han Shan," *Renditions* 7 (Spring 1977): 100, 102. In correspondence dated 9 August 1997, Snyder reiterated to me his belief that his translations of "Cold Mountain Poems" are more Western than Eastern in their topographical register.

85. Ling Chung, "Whose Mountain Is This?" pp. 99–100.

86. Leed, "Gary Snyder, Han Shan, and Jack Kerouac," pp. 185–93.

87. *The View from Cold Mountain: Poems of Han-shan and Shih-te*, trans. Arthur Tobias, James Sanford, and J. P. Seaton (Buffalo, NY: White Pine Press, 1982). Subsequent citations are included parenthetically in the text.

88. Geoff Ward, "Literary San Francisco and the Poetry of the Excitements," *Critical Quarterly* 36, no. 3 (Autumn 1994): 68.

3. Embodying

1. David Palumbo-Liu, *Asian/American: Historical Crossings of a Racial Frontier* (Stanford, CA: Stanford University Press, 1999), p. 138.

2. See Allen Ginsberg, "Afternoon Seattle," in *Collected Poems 1947–1980* (New York: Harper and Row, 1984), p. 150. Ginsberg composed this poem during his 1956 hitchhiking trip with Snyder.

3. Philip Whalen, letter to Gary Snyder, 29 November 1953, Gary Snyder Papers, Department of Special Collections, University of California Library, Davis.

4. Lew Welch, letter to Philip Whalen, 7 July 1957, in *I Remain: The Letters of Lew Welch & the Correspondence of His Friends, Volume One, 1949–1960*, ed. Donald M. Allen (Bolinas, CA: Grey Fox Press, 1980), p. 107.

5. Lew Welch, letter to Gary Snyder, 27 January 1952, in ibid., p. 67.

6. Lew Welch, letter to Gary Snyder, 14 June 1955, in ibid., p. 79.

7. Lew Welch, letter to Philip Whalen, 2 September 1957, in ibid., pp. 111–12.

8. For this description of Melville's cultural gaze, see Charles Olson, *Call Me Ishmael* (1947; San Francisco: City Lights, n.d.), pp. 12–13.

9. Jack Kerouac, *The Dharma Bums* (1958; New York: Penguin, 1986), pp. 10, 11.

10. Ibid., pp. 18, 19.

11. Ibid., pp. 79, 25, 165, 201, 229.

12. Ginsberg, "Howl," in *Collected Poems 1947–1980*, p. 128.

13. Gary Snyder, quoted in Ann Charters, *Kerouac: A Biography* (San Francisco: Straight Arrow Books, 1973), p. 287.

14. Jack Kerouac, *On the Road* (1957; Harmondsworth: Penguin, 1972), p. 170.

15. Jack Kerouac, "October in the Railroad Earth," *Evergreen Review* 1, no. 2 (1957): 120.

16. Jack Kerouac, letter to Gary Snyder, 14 February 1956, in *Jack Kerouac: Selected Letters 1940–1956*, ed. Ann Charters (New York: Viking, 1995), p. 558. A *bhikku* is a Buddhist wanderer. In the reply Charters includes, Snyder holds open the possibility of establishing "bhikku hostels" across America, every five hundred miles or so, "a day's hitchhike" (p. 560). Kerouac has Japhy Ryder speak about this network for Zen hitchhikers in *The Dharma Bums*, pp. 97–98.

17. Kerouac, *The Dharma Bums*, p. 208.

18. Jack Kerouac, letter to Gary Snyder, May 1956, in *Jack Kerouac: Selected Letters 1940–1956*, p. 584.

19. Kerouac, *The Dharma Bums*, p. 216.

20. Ibid., pp. 243–44.

21. Jack Kerouac, letter to Gary Snyder, 14 July 1958, in *Jack Kerouac: Selected Letters 1957–1969*, ed. Ann Charters (New York: Viking, 1999), p. 138. To assuage Snyder's anxiety, Kerouac tells him that Ginsberg signed a similar release form before *On the Road* was published.

22. Gary Snyder, letters to Philip Whalen, undated [1958] and 9 October 1958, Philip Whalen Papers, Special Collections and Archives, Eric V. Hauser Memorial Library, Reed College, Portland, Oregon. See also Philip Whalen, letter to Gary Snyder, 30 September 1958, Gary Snyder Papers, University of California Library, Davis.

23. Gary Snyder, correspondence with the author, 19 April 1997. The contents of Snyder's letter to Kerouac, which I have not seen, are paraphrased in Douglas Brinkley, "The American Journey of Jack Kerouac," in *The Rolling Stone Book of the Beats: The Beat Generation and American Culture*, ed. Holly George-Warren (New York: Hyperion, 1999), p. 118.

24. John Suiter, *Poets on the Peaks: Gary Snyder, Philip Whalen & Jack Kerouac in the North Cascades* (Washington, DC: Counterpoint, 2002), pp. 23–24. Suiter records a similar recollection of Snyder in an interview with Tommy Buller, another Forest Service worker who met the poet that summer: "He wouldn't set in a chair like you or me, he would set cross-legged. He was really working on being able to be a monk. From here he was supposed to go into a monastery, and he told us it was going to be a tough show, and he was training himself. Everything he did pointed in that direction. . . . He knew that he was going to have to

live on rice and he might as well make up his mind to do it. And me, I'm about eighteen years old and I see all this, and I said, 'Is that boy in this world or some other world?'" (p. 24).

25. See Alexander Saxton, *The Indispensable Enemy* (Berkeley: University of California Press, 1971); Ronald Takaki, *Strangers from a Different Shore: A History of Asian Americans* (1989; New York: Penguin, 1990); Maxine Hong Kingston, *China Men* (1980; New York: Vintage International, 1989); and Lisa Lowe, *Immigrant Acts: On Asian American Cultural Politics* (Durham, NC: Duke University Press, 1996).

26. Gary Snyder, letter to Lew Welch, 13 May 1957, in *I Remain, Volume One*, p. 102.

27. Kerouac, *The Dharma Bums*, p. 203.

28. For references to the items Snyder sent, see his letters to Philip Whalen dated 16 February, 8 March, 21 April, and 5 June 1957, Philip Whalen Papers, Reed College. Whalen's response comes from a letter to Snyder dated 23 July 1957, Gary Snyder Papers, University of California Library, Davis.

29. For instructions on "how to have a Tibetan style robe," see Gary Snyder, letter to Lew Welch, 11 October 1962, in *I Remain: The Letters of Lew Welch & the Correspondence of His Friends, Volume Two, 1960–1971*, ed. Donald M. Allen (Bolinas, CA: Grey Fox Press, 1980), p. 68.

30. See Rich Lowry, "Selling Out? China Syndrome," *National Review*, 24 March 1997, along with the corresponding analysis offered in Palumbo-Liu, *Asian/American*, pp. 288–90. For a discussion of Jonathan Pryce's "yellowface" role on Broadway, see Frank H. Wu, *Yellow: Race in America beyond Black and White* (New York: Basic Books, 2002), pp. 280–81. In an ironic development, Pryce resurfaced as a television pitchman for a line of Japanese luxury cars soon after his departure from the cast of *Miss Saigon*. For a historical look at yellowface traditions in nineteenth-century America, see John Kuo Wei Tchen, *New York before Chinatown: Orientalism and the Shaping of American Culture 1776–1882* (Baltimore: Johns Hopkins University Press, 1999).

31. Eric Lott, "White Like Me: Racial Cross-Dressing and the Construction of American Whiteness," in *Cultures of United States Imperialism*, ed. Amy Kaplan and Donald E. Pease (Durham, NC: Duke University Press, 1993), p. 482.

32. For an assessment of Saijo as an Asian-American hipster, see Jack Kerouac, *Big Sur* (New York: Farrar, Straus and Cudahy, 1962). See also Lew Welch, letter to Philip Whalen, 15 October 1958, in *I Remain, Volume One*, pp. 149–50. Welch, Kerouac, and Saijo later embarked on a cross-country tour from San Francisco to Long Island during which time they collectively composed a haiku travelogue. See Jack Kerouac, Albert Saijo, and Lew Welch, *Trip-Trap: Haiku on the Road*, rev. ed. (San Francisco: Grey Fox Press, 1998). Along with Ferlinghetti, Shig Murao was arrested on obscenity charges for selling Allen Ginsberg's *Howl and Other Poems* (which contains the poem "America") at City Lights Bookstore. In October 1957, he and Ferlinghetti were found not guilty by Judge Clayton W. Horn. For a dis-

cussion of this trial, see Steven Watson, *The Birth of the Beat Generation: Visionaries, Rebels, and Hipsters, 1944–1960* (1995; New York: Pantheon, 1998), pp. 251–53. For more on Murao's "cool" persona and his reputation as a playful con artist (he was known to tell naive tourists that he was an Eskimo, and that the wooden egg beaters he purchased cheaply in Chinatown and displayed in the bookstore were rare Zen prayer wheels), see "City Lights Bookstore 50th Anniversary: The Birth of Cool: 1953–1960," *San Francisco Chronicle*, 8 June 2003, D6, and "City Lights Bookstore 50th Anniversary: City Lights Enters the Modern Age: 1975–2003," *San Francisco Chronicle*, 10 June 2003, D4.

33. Kerouac provides a fictionalized account of the farewell party in *The Dharma Bums*, pp. 192–99. According to Steven Watson, *The Birth of the Beat Generation*, pp. 236–37, Snyder banged a frying pan like a gong and chanted the Gocchami chant to announce the serving of pancakes to a weary bunch of revelers on the second morning.

34. Philip Whalen, letter to Gary Snyder, 12 January 1957, Gary Snyder Papers, University of California Library, Davis. The Basho haiku to which Whalen refers reads "*Faru-ike ya kawazu tobi-komu mizu-no-oto,*" which Harold G. Henderson translates as "Old pond / frog jumps in / water-sound" (*Masterpieces of the Orient*, expanded ed., ed. G. L. Anderson [New York: Norton, 1977], p. 747).

35. See Katsunori Yamazato, "Snyder, Sakaki, and the Tribe," in *Gary Snyder: Dimensions of a Life*, ed. Jon Halper (San Francisco: Sierra Club Books, 1991), p. 102. See also the discussion of Yamabushi influences that Patrick D. Murphy includes in *A Place for Wayfaring: The Poetry and Prose of Gary Snyder* (Corvallis: Oregon State University Press, 2000), p. 211. For an early account of Snyder's interest in these Mountain Buddhists, see Gary Snyder, "Anyone with Yamabushi Tendencies," *Zen Notes* 1, no. 11 (November 1954): 3. In 1961, Snyder told Phil Whalen that he planned to bring Yamabushi practice back home to America: "I climbed Mt. Omine (sacred) and was initiated a Yamabushi and got to do magic on mountaintops (branch of Shingon) look out look out! I'll sacredize Tamalpais" (Gary Snyder, letter to Philip Whalen, 17 June 1961, Philip Whalen Papers, Reed College). Snyder reflects on the evolution of his Buddhist thought during his time in Asia in an interview with Ekbert Faas, *Towards a New American Poetics: Essays & Interviews* (Santa Barbara, CA: Black Sparrow Press, 1978), p. 114.

36. "Spring Sesshin at Shokoku-ji," first published in *Chicago Review* 12, no. 2 (Summer 1958): 41–49, is reprinted in *Earth House Hold* (EHH 44–53). *Chicago Review*'s Zen issue also includes an excerpt from *The Dharma Bums* entitled "Meditation in the Woods" (pp. 17–22). At one point in this excerpt, Kerouac slips and refers to Gary Snyder instead of Japhy Ryder. As a result, Snyder appears twice in the Zen issue, once as a serious student in religious training and once as Kerouac's archetypal Orientalist hero.

37. For a thorough examination of the *kyodatsu* condition, see John Dower, *Embracing Defeat: Japan in the Wake of World War II* (1999; New York: Norton/New Press, 2000), pp. 87–120.

38. Burton Watson, "Kyoto in the Fifties," in Halper, ed., *Gary Snyder*, p. 54.

39. Philip Yampolsky, "Kyoto, Zen, Snyder," in ibid., p. 61.

40. There are several good studies on the sex trade in Japan and the advent of antiprostitution legislation. See, for instance, Sheldon Garon, "The World's Oldest Debate? Prostitution and the State in Imperial Japan, 1900–1945," *American Historical Review* 98, no. 2 (June 1993): 710–32. See also Vera Mackie, "Division of Labour: Multinational Sex in Asia," in *The Japanese Trajectory: Modernization and Beyond*, ed. Gavin McCormick and Yoshio Sugimoto (Cambridge: Cambridge University Press, 1988), pp. 218–32, and Sumiko Iwao, *The Japanese Woman: Traditional Image and Changing Reality* (Cambridge, MA: Harvard University Press, 1994), pp. 106, 108. In a letter Snyder received shortly after his arrival in Kyoto, Jack Kerouac asks and answers his own question about the recent crackdown on the sex trade by the Japanese government: "Who the hell outlawed prostitution in Japan it must be the U.S. authorities" (Kerouac, letter to Gary Snyder, May 1956, in *Jack Kerouac: Selected Letters 1940–1956*, p. 582). As Karen Kelsky, *Women on the Verge: Japanese Women, Western Dreams* (Durham, NC: Duke University Press, 2001), pp. 53–54, points out, Japanese historians continue to debate the extent to which occupation forces, rather than Japanese feminists, were responsible for such reforms.

41. See Dower, *Embracing Defeat*, pp. 123–32.

42. Daniel Ellsberg, "The First Two Times We Met," in Halper, ed., *Gary Snyder*, p. 332.

43. Ibid., p. 333.

44. Clayton Eshelman, "Imagination's Body and Comradely Display," in ibid., pp. 235–36.

45. Snyder lists members of Kyoto's "beat set" in a letter to Whalen dated 13 January 1960, Philip Whalen Papers, Reed College. Described by Alan Golding as "one of recent American poetry's great networkers," Cid Corman did not arrive in Japan until the summer of 1959, but he quickly became a fixture on the Kyoto scene, publishing Snyder's *Riprap* (with funds provided by Lawrence Ferlinghetti) at Genichi-do that same year. While in Kyoto, Corman also put out the second series of his influential little magazine *Origin*, which published several early sections from Snyder's *Mountains and Rivers without End*. Along the way, Corman urged others on the scene to start their own magazines. Clayton Eshelman's *Caterpillar* was one such publication. For more on Corman's role in the New American Poetry movement, see Alan Golding, *From Outlaw to Classic: Canons in American Poetry* (Madison: University of Wisconsin Press, 1995), chap. 4, "Little Magazines and Alternative Canons: The Example of *Origin*."

46. Will Petersen, letters to Gary Snyder, 17 November 1957 and 8 November 1958, Gary Snyder Papers, University of California Library, Davis. For the classic account of the Westerner's feeling of semiotic suspension in postmodern Japan, see Roland Barthes, *Empire of Signs*, trans. Richard Howard (1970; New York: Hill and Wang, 1982). Barthes's intention in this book, Iain Chambers, *Migrancy,*

Culture, Identity (London: Routledge, 1994), explains, was "to use his encounter with the [Asian] Other not to explain that alterity, but rather to go beyond himself, his own language and sign culture, and thereby disturb and question the presumed stability of the symbolic order of which he is a part" (pp. 100–101). Christopher L. Connery, "Pacific Rim Discourse: The U.S. Global Imaginary in the Late Cold War Years," *Boundary 2* 21, no. 1 (Spring 1994), espies a similar destabilization of East-West symbolism in the 1980s *wanderjahre* novels set in Japan, including Jay McInerny's *Ransom*, Brad Leithauser's *Equal Distance*, and John David Morley's *Pictures from the Water Trade* (all published in 1985). In a typical plot, Connery says, "young American men go to Japan for a year or two and either find themselves or muse on the confusion of life reflected in the odd juxtapositions that surround them (such as Coke machines in Buddhist temples)." Eventually, Connery argues, these Coke machines become, "in the paradoxical workings of Pacific Rim discourse, more exotic than the Buddha images" (pp. 49–50). I would add to the list of books Connery mentions two collections of travel essays from the same era: Pico Iyer's *Video Night in Katmandu* (New York: Vintage Departures, 1989), and Ian Baruma's *God's Dust: A Modern Asian Journey* (New York: Farrar, Straus, Giroux, 1989). Both books contain humorous and pithy anecdotes, the majority of which serve forth a feast of ironic juxtapositions while dismissing naive conceptions about "exotic" Asian culture. More recently, writer and director Sofia Coppola has scored critical raves for *Lost in Translation* (Focus Features, 2003), a moody romance about American business travelers similarly bemused by the cultural contradictions of postmodern Tokyo.

47. See Gary Snyder, "Letter from Kyoto," *Evergreen Review* 1, no. 3 (1957): 132. Rick Fields, *How the Swans Came to the Lake: A Narrative History of Buddhism in America*, 3d rev. ed. (Boston: Shambhala, 1992), explains that Ernest Fenollosa went through much the same disillusionment while visiting Japan in the 1880s. In a lecture delivered at a Japanese club in 1882, this famous Orientalist lamented that "the Japanese despise their classical paintings, and with adoration for Western civilization admire its artistically worthless modern paintings and imitate them for nothing. What a sad sight it is!" (p. 149). As Beongcheon Yu, *The Great Circle: American Writers and the Orient* (Detroit: Wayne State University Press, 1983), has noted, Lafcadio Hearn expressed similar misgivings about the "New Japan" at the turn of the twentieth century, for he too had become "painfully aware of the shallowness of the young generation fast drifting away from their cultural roots" (p. 113). Also see the evaluation put forth by Will Petersen in a letter to Snyder dated 17 August 1956: "I do hope the West gains enough from the Orient before the Orient goes completely Western. But you may be right—they may have to become Occidental before they find Buddhism's meanings" (Gary Snyder Papers, University of California Library, Davis).

48. Snyder, "Letter from Kyoto," p. 134.

49. Kerouac, *The Dharma Bums*, p. 203. Kerouac's Orientalist assessment provides Michael Davidson with the title of his incisive study of American

homosociality, *Guys Like Us: Citing Masculinity in Cold War Poetics* (Chicago: University of Chicago Press, 2004).

50. Snyder, "Letter from Kyoto," pp. 132–33. Will Petersen sounds a similar note when he gushes about his Japanese girlfriend (and future wife), Ami, who instinctively takes to the hip American culture (jazz clubs, for instance) that Petersen introduces her to. "She's not Japanese, she's human," Petersen tells Snyder in an undated letter. "She can dig any scene anywhere, and is a fish to all waters—most of what we've done has been first time for her, yet no one would guess it" (Gary Snyder Papers, University of California Library, Davis). Regarding Petersen's choice of words, it is interesting to hear Japanese writer Ebisaka Takeshi comment that in today's Japan "the word *human being* crops up frequently in the speech of . . . unhappy wives" (Kelsky, *Women on the Verge*, p. 88) complaining about their domineering husbands.

51. Gary Snyder, letter to Philip Whalen, 25 May 1956, Philip Whalen Papers, Reed College.

52. Gary Snyder, letter to Philip Whalen, 12 December 1956, Philip Whalen Papers, Reed College.

53. See Doreen Massey, *Space, Place and Gender* (Minneapolis: University of Minnesota Press, 1994), pp. 23, 254. Other studies in human geography influencing my analysis of gender dynamics in Snyder's work include Linda McDowell, *Gender, Identity & Place: Understanding Feminist Geographies* (Minneapolis: University of Minnesota Press, 1999), Gillian Rose, *Feminism & Geography: The Limits of Geographical Knowledge* (Minneapolis: University of Minnesota Press, 1993), and Caren Kaplan, *Questions of Travel: Postmodern Discourses of Displacement* (Durham, NC: Duke University Press, 1996). Given my interests in the Pacific Rim, I find it interesting that the classic study of race in human geography is one that takes another oceanic region as its topic; see Paul Gilroy, *The Black Atlantic: Modernity and Double Consciousness* (Cambridge, MA: Harvard University Press, 1993).

54. Gary Snyder, quoted in Katherine McNeill, *Gary Snyder: A Bibliography* (New York: Phoenix Bookshop, 1983), p. xi.

55. Ibid., p. 35.

56. See Peter Matthiessen, *The Snow Leopard* (1978: New York: Penguin Nature Classics, 1996), and Richard Bernstein, *Ultimate Journey: Retracing the Path of an Ancient Buddhist Monk Who Crossed Asia in Search of Enlightenment* (2001; New York: Vintage Departures, 2002).

57. See James McKenzie, "Moving the World a Millionth of an Inch: An Interview with Gary Snyder," *The Beat Diary: The Unspeakable Visions of the Individual* 5 (1977): 149.

58. See Joseph Campbell, *The Masks of God: Oriental Mythology* (1962; New York: Penguin, 1976), p. 3. See also Thomas J. Lyon, "A Taxonomy of Nature Writing," in *The Ecocriticism Reader: Landmarks in Literary Ecology*, ed. Cheryll Glotfelty and Harold Fromm (Athens: University of Georgia Press, 1996), pp. 279–80.

In *A Place for Wayfaring*, Patrick D. Murphy makes a nice point about the ecological aspect of Snyder's return when he notices that *The Back Country* begins with "A Berry Feast" and ends with "Oysters," both of which "speak of feasts through immersion and gathering in wild nature" (p. 67). Murphy's point is well taken, but I continue to believe that Snyder's immersion in human populations was more pertinent to this book's exploration of the Pacific Rim.

59. In *A Place for Wayfaring*, Patrick Murphy makes it clear that he disagrees with my readings of these poems, putting forth the contrary argument that, "whereas in the later *Riprap* poems Snyder has the speaker being explicit about plans to travel to Japan, no such foreshadowing has so far appeared in 'Far West'" (p. 73).

60. For more on the significance of the Marin-an hermitage, see Suiter, *Poets on the Peaks*, pp. 186–88.

61. See Thomas Frank, *The Conquest of Cool: Business Culture, Counterculture, and the Rise of Hip Capitalism* (Chicago: University of Chicago Press, 1997). For a philosophical analysis of the middle-class alienation that gave way to hip consumer culture in the 1950s and 1960s, see Herbert Marcuse, *Eros and Civilization* (Boston: Beacon Press, 1955), and *One Dimensional Man: Studies in the Ideology of Advanced Industrial Society* (Boston: Beacon Press, 1964). For a topical account of masculine consumption patterns in this era, see Barbara Ehrenreich, *The Hearts of Men: American Dreams and the Flight from Commitment* (Garden City, NY: Anchor/Doubleday, 1983).

62. See Maria Damon, "Victors of Catastrophe: Beat Occlusions," in *Beat Culture and the New America, 1950–1965*, ed. Lisa Phillips (New York: Whitney Museum of Art/Flammarion, 1995), p. 146. See also Michael Davidson, *The San Francisco Renaissance: Poetics and Community at Mid-century* (New York: Cambridge University Press, 1989), chap. 6, "Appropriations: Women and the San Francisco Renaissance." Regarding the proliferation of personal accounts published by Beat women (Joyce Johnson, Carolyn Cassady, Hettie Jones) in the 1980s and 1990s decrying the subservient roles they were forced to play decades earlier in a male-dominated subculture, see the stories and memoirs excerpted in *Women of the Beat Generation: Writers, Artists, and Muses at the Heart of a Revolution*, ed. Brenda Knight (Berkeley, CA: Conari Press, 1996).

63. David Wyatt, *The Fall into Eden: Landscape and Imagination in California* (New York: Cambridge University Press, 1986), pp. 196–99. Wyatt argues that *The Back Country*'s circular route of return is sexually coded, and that in his memories of lovers and landscapes he has left behind, Snyder "initiates and completes a process of mourning." Accordingly, the poet's account of his Pacific Rim journey gets "acted out through many figures of regret." Wyatt is astute in mentioning Alison Gass and Masa Uehara as "figures of regret," but I think that Robin Collins (Snyder's college girlfriend) and Joanne Kyger (his third wife) are other candidates for this distinction, as are the multitude of Asian women Snyder met overseas. By extending my analysis of *The Back Country* to include these women, I

hope to give fuller consideration to the sexual dynamics at play in Snyder's cultural return.

64. Gary Snyder, quoted in Nicholas O'Connell, *At the Field's End: Interviews with Twenty Pacific Northwest Writers* (Seattle: Madrona Publishers, 1987), p. 315.

65. Gary Snyder, letter to Philip Whalen, 3 November 1962, Philip Whalen Papers, Reed College.

66. Hisao Kanaseki, "An Easy Rider at Yase," in Halper, ed., *Gary Snyder*, p. 71.

67. Gary Snyder, letter to Philip Whalen, 21 March 1960, Philip Whalen Papers, Reed College. Just six months before this letter was written, Snyder had expressed his uneasiness about Japan's raging interest in Beat culture, telling Joanne Kyger, "I don't want no damned Jap literati hanging around my cabin door asking 'What pot mean?' 'What dig mean?'" (Gary Snyder, letter to Joanne Kyger, 12 September 1959, Gary Snyder Papers, University of California Library, Davis). Today, Snyder takes a rather different view on his reception by the Japanese public. Asked by Paul Rossiter and John Evans whether he would do anything differently were he to live in Japan again, Snyder responded, "I would not be so intent on keeping my own style and would blend in more. And in blending in more, as I know only too well now, I would have been far more acceptable, far less off-putting to [the] Japanese and could have seen much more of the culture from the inside" ("Interview: Gary Snyder," *Studies in the Humanities* 26, nos. 1 and 2 [June and December 1999]: 16). Snyder makes the same case in an interview with David Meltzer, *San Francisco Beat: Talking with the Poets* (San Francisco: City Lights Books, 2001), admitting that he would "dress better" and give up his "West Coast blue-jeans style" (p. 282) if he were to go back and meet the Japanese for the first time.

68. Anne Allison, *Nightwork: Sexuality, Pleasure, and Corporate Masculinity in a Tokyo Hostess Club* (Chicago: University of Chicago Press, 1994), p. 8.

69. Gary Snyder, letters to Philip Whalen, 8 April 1957, 15 February 1958, and an undated letter from 1958, Philip Whalen Papers, Reed College.

70. See Gary Snyder, journal entries dated 4 April 1957, 17 August 1957, and 3 February 1958, as well as his letter to Joanne Kyger dated 3 July 1959, Gary Snyder Papers, University of California Library, Davis.

71. Gary Snyder, journal entry dated 22 June 1959, Gary Snyder Papers, University of California Library, Davis. The reading of "March" that Yamazato includes in his unpublished manuscript expands upon an earlier reading he published in "Snyder, Sakaki, and the Tribe," in Halper, ed., *Gary Snyder*, pp. 93–94.

72. Joanne Kyger, quoted in Knight, ed., *Women of the Beat Generation*, p. 198.

73. See Gary Snyder, journal entries dated 3 November and 16 December 1958, Gary Snyder Papers, University of California Library, Davis.

74. See Gary Snyder, letters to Joanne Kyger, 9 April and 31 October 1959, and also Joanne Kyger, letter to Gary Snyder, 27 February 1959, Gary Snyder Papers, University of California Library, Davis.

75. Joanne Kyger, *The Japan and India Journals 1960–1964* (Bolinas, CA: Tombouctou, 1981), pp. 6–7, 10.

76. See Gary Snyder, letters to Joanne Kyger, 6 and 14 August 1959, Gary Snyder Papers, University of California Library, Davis.

77. Yampolsky, "Kyoto, Zen, Snyder," in Halper, ed., *Gary Snyder*, p. 66.

78. Kyger, *The Japan and India Journals*, p. 45.

79. Gary Snyder, letter to Philip Whalen, 21 March 1960, Philip Whalen Papers, Reed College.

80. For more on Kyger's attitude toward expatriate women in Japan, see Linda Russo, "To Deal with Parts and Particulars: Joanne Kyger's Early Epic Poetics," in *Girls Who Wore Black: Women Writing the Beat Generation,* ed. Ronna C. Johnson and Nancy M. Grace (New Brunswick, NJ: Rutgers University Press, 2002), pp. 188–90.

81. Kyger, *The Japan and India Journals*, p. 280.

82. J. Michael Mahar, "Scenes from the Sidelines," in Halper, ed., *Gary Snyder*, pp. 10–11.

83. Wyatt, *The Fall into Eden*, p. 196.

84. Joanne Kyger, "October 29, Wednesday," in *Going On: Selected Poems 1958–1980* (New York: Dutton, 1983), p. 34. Kyger's other recollections of the star treatment accorded Snyder and Ginsberg can be found in *The Japan and India Journals*, pp. 186, 195, 198. The India trip was not the first occasion she complained about playing second fiddle within Beat circles. During a 1959 poetry reading in San Francisco, Kyger once told Snyder, she "heard someone whisper that I was G. Snyder's girlfriend and this made me feel incompletely identified" (Kyger, letter to Gary Snyder, 11 March 1959, Gary Snyder Papers, University of California Library, Davis).

85. Philip Whalen, letter to Gary Snyder, 31 March 1962, Gary Snyder Papers, University of California Library, Davis.

86. Lawrence Ferlinghetti, undated letter to Allen Ginsberg, quoted in Kyger, *The Japan and India Journals*, p. 190.

87. Alice Glaser, "Back on the Open Road for Boys," *Esquire*, July 1963, p. 48. Kyger, as the odd woman out on this male bohemian odyssey, came to identify herself with Penelope, who in Homeric texts remained faithful to the adventurous Odysseus but also might have had some tricks up her sleeve. According to Linda Russo, "Parts and Particulars," in Johnson and Grace, eds., *Girls Who Wore Black*, Kyger's feminist take on the Penelope legend emerges most forcefully in *The Tapestry and the Web* (1965), a revisionist poetic project in which Kyger "saw it as her task to be 'the instigator' and 'propagator' of her own definition of female—one that could encompass the contraries of being herself the muse to her circle of male poets and her life the medium of her own poetry" (p. 189). Like many Beat texts authored by women, Russo suggests, Kyger's first volume offers a needed counterweight to the freewheeling quests recorded and published by better-known male Beats.

88. Gary Snyder, correspondence with the author, 9 December 1996. Ginsberg's analysis of *The Back Country* is included in a letter dated 13 January 1968, Gary Snyder Papers, University of California Library, Davis.

89. Campbell, *The Masks of God: Oriental Mythology*, p. 5.

90. See Huston Smith, *The Religions of Man* (1958; New York: Harper Perennial, 1965), pp. 18–19, 22, 52–53. The passage from the *Syama Rahasya* is quoted in Campbell, *The Masks of God: Oriental Mythology*, p. 359.

91. For more on the plight of imported leisure industry workers in Japan, see Neferti Xina Tadiar, "Sexual Economies in the Asia-Pacific Community," in *What Is in a Rim? Critical Perspectives on the Pacific Region Idea*, ed. Arif Dirlik (Lanham, MD: Rowman and Littlefield, 1993), pp. 183–210. See also Yayori Matsui, "The Plight of Asian Migrant Women Working in Japan's Sex Industry," in *Japanese Women: New Feminist Perspectives on the Past, Present, and Future*, ed. Kumiko Fujimora-Fanselow and Atsuko Kameda (New York: Feminist Press, 1995), pp. 309–19. In addition, I have found it interesting to consider the awkward goodbye in "Kyoto Footnote" alongside two contemporary articles published in the American mainstream press. The first article, published in the 15 July 1946 issue of *Time*, cites a series of instructions included in a phrase book handed out to American occupation troops in Japan: "Since U.S. occupation forces are unalterably determined to fraternize, the military authorities began helping them out last week by issuing a phrase book. Sample utility phrases: 'You're very pretty' . . . 'How about a date?' . . . 'Where will I meet you?' And since the sweet sorrow of parting always comes, the book lists no less than 14 ways to say goodbye" (Cynthia Enloe, "It Takes Two," in *Let the Good Times Roll: Prostitution and the U.S. Military in Asia,* ed. Saundra Pollock Sturdevant and Brenda Stoltzfus [New York: New Press, 1992], p. 22). The second article, which bore the ignominious title "What the Jap Is Thinking Now," appeared in the 11 May 1946 issue of the *Saturday Evening Post*. In it, author Edgar Snow spoke of American servicemen who were "husbanding" the freedom of Japanese women at odds with their patriarchal society. As Caroline Chung Simpson, "'Out of an Obscure Place': Japanese War Brides and Cultural Pluralism in the 1950s," *Differences: A Journal of Feminist Cultural Studies* 10, no. 3 (Fall 1998): 47–81, shows in her response to Snow's article, many occupation troops who could not bear to say goodbye to the women circulating near their compounds ended up marrying them and bringing these war brides back to the States.

92. For Campbell's discussion of the Earth Goddess and the Cannibal Mother, see *The Masks of God: Oriental Mythology*, pp. 161–63, 179, and *The Masks of God: Primitive Mythology* (1959; New York: Penguin, 1976), pp. 62–71.

93. Philip Whalen, "Souffle" (Take X), in *Overtime: Selected Poems* (New York: Penguin, 1999), p. 24.

94. See the excerpts of these novels included in *The Portable Jack Kerouac*, ed. Ann Charters (1995; New York: Penguin, 1996), pp. 137, 275.

95. See Allen Ginsberg, *Indian Journals March 1962–May 1963* (San Francisco: City Lights, 1970), pp. 80, 128.

96. Snyder, correspondence with the author, 9 December 1996. Alternatively, in a 1990 interview with Julia Martin, "Coyote-Mind: An Interview with Gary Snyder," *TriQuarterly* 79 (Fall 1990), Snyder says that gender does, in fact, enter into the equation, explaining that many schools of Hinduism and Buddhism actually switch genders back and forth. "I'm not much interested in the *gender-ization* of those things," he tells Martin. "But I see the *use* of gender imagery in India in its poetic mythology and Tibet in its poetic mythology as charming—and sometimes useful. You might say that in a bhakti tradition, a devotional tradition, they tend to concretize their imagery into gender and have goddesses and gods. And in a Gnostic tradition, a jnana tradition, a wisdom tradition, they would prefer not to see it as a gender-tied imagery" (p. 153).

97. According to Julia Kristeva's reading of "The Uncanny," Freud's famous essay of 1919, "the death and the feminine, the end and the beginning that engross and compose us only to frighten us when they break through," represent a "weaving together of the symbolic and organic—perhaps *drive* itself, on the border of the psyche and biology" (*Strangers to Ourselves*, trans. Leon S. Roudiez [New York: Columbia University Press, 1991], p. 185).

98. Gary Snyder, letter to Philip Whalen, 12 January 1954, Philip Whalen Papers, Reed College.

99. Gary Snyder, journal entry dated 13 January 1957, Gary Snyder Papers, University of California, Davis. Jacques Lacan, *The Seminar of Jacques Lacan, Book VII, The Ethics of Psychoanalysis 1959–1960*, ed. Jacques-Alain Miller, trans. Dennis Potter (New York: Norton, 1992), makes a vivid connection between nuclear destruction and the unconscious desire to return to an original receptacle of being, also known as "the Real." Our death drive ultimately breaks through any economy of goods, Lacan explains, especially when that drive is manifested by some "cut" or break that reminds us of our role as bearers of language, or that which creates phenomena ex nihilo. In the late 1950s, he goes on to assert, signification, desire, death, and the return of the Real came together most pressingly in the form of the atomic bomb. Lacan argues that modern physics, in its quest for impossible knowledge, is to blame: "Science is animated by some mysterious desire, but it doesn't know, anymore than anything in the unconscious itself, what that desire means" (pp. 223, 236, 325).

100. See Lacan, *The Seminar*, pp. 191–203. Recounting a similar situation in a March 1958 journal entry, Snyder describes his shipmates' sexual encounters with the women of Oceania during his oil tanker's stopover in Pago Pago, Samoa; see "Tanker Notes" (EHH 64–67).

101. See Haunani-Kay Trask, *From a Native Daughter: Colonialism and Sovereignty in Hawaii* (Monroe, ME: Common Courage Press, 1993), as well as the other writings from Oceania cited in my "Introduction." See also Christopher L. Connery, "The Oceanic Feeling and the Transnational Imaginary," in *Global/Local: Cultural*

Production and the Transnational Imaginary, ed. Rob Wilson and Wimal Dissanayake (Durham, NC: Duke University Press, 1996), p. 285, and Hortense J. Spillers, "Who Cuts the Border? Some Readings on 'America,'" in *Comparative American Identities: Race, Sex and Nationality in the Modern Text*, ed. Hortense J. Spillers (New York: Routledge, 1991), pp. 1–25.

102. Gary Snyder, journal entry dated 23 January 1959, Gary Snyder Papers, University of California Library, Davis.

103. See Joanne Kyger, *The Tapestry and the Web* (San Francisco: Four Seasons Foundation, 1965), p. 53, as well as the corresponding commentary in Russo, "Parts and Particulars," in Johnson and Grace, eds., *Girls Who Wore Black*, pp. 198–99.

104. Lee Swenson, "Swimming in a Sea of Friends," in Halper, ed., *Gary Snyder*, recalls that one of the first industrial eyesores to transform the Berkeley wetlands in the 1940s was "the huge Williams Paint Factory, with its global neon symbol: Williams paint flowing down over half the world" (p. 352).

105. For more on Snyder's journal entries, see Suiter, *Poets on the Peaks*, p. 31.

106. For a good overview of the *blason* tradition's equation of female bodies with landscapes, see Jonathan Sawday, *The Body Emblazoned: Dissection and the Human Body in Renaissance Culture* (London: Routledge, 1995).

107. Kyger, *The Japan and India Journals*, p. 34.

108. Wyatt, *The Fall into Eden*, p. 199.

4. Communing

1. Michael Davidson, *The San Francisco Renaissance: Poetics and Community at Mid-century* (New York: Cambridge University Press, 1989), p. 32.

2. Gary Snyder, "Poetry and the Primitive," typescript of a lecture given at the Berkeley Poetry Conference, 16 July 1965, Gary Snyder Papers, Department of Special Collections, University of California Library, Davis.

3. This quote is Welch's paraphrase of Nessel's on-the-air comment. See *On Bread and Poetry: A Panel Discussion with Gary Snyder, Lew Welch & Philip Whalen*, ed. Donald Allen (Bolinas, CA: Grey Fox, 1977), p. vii.

4. Snyder, "Poetry and the Primitive" (lecture version).

5. Gary Snyder, quoted in David Robertson, *Real Matter* (Salt Lake City: University of Utah Press, 1997), pp. 132–33.

6. Ibid., p. 101.

7. Ibid., p. 131.

8. Ibid., p. 124.

9. Ibid., pp. 128–29. Phil Whalen disputes the inclusion of some of these items, claiming that he did not carry them until he performed another circumambulation in April 1968.

10. Gary Snyder, "The Circumambulation of Mt. Tamalpais/Coast Miwok: Bay Mountain" (early version), quoted in David Robertson, "The Circumambulation of Mt. Tamalpais," *Western American Literature* 30, no. 1 (Spring 1995): 25–26.

11. Snyder, quoted in Robertson, *Real Matter*, p. 127; for a discussion of the three goals of the 1965 circumambulation, see pp. 132–34.

12. Snyder, quoted in Robertson, "The Circumambulation of Mt. Tamalpais," p. 20.

13. Gary Snyder, journal entry dated 9 May 1957, Gary Snyder Papers, University of California Library, Davis.

14. Jack Kerouac, *The Dharma Bums* (1958; New York: Penguin, 1986), p. 201.

15. See Benedict Anderson, *Imagined Communities: Reflections on the Origin and Spread of Nationalism*, rev. ed. (London: Verso, 1991), and Jürgen Habermas, *The Structural Transformation of the Public Sphere* (Cambridge, MA: MIT Press, 1989).

16. Kerouac, *The Dharma Bums*, p. 203.

17. The 1961 citations are taken from Gary Snyder, "Buddhist Anarchism," *Journal for the Protection of All Beings* 1 (San Francisco: City Lights, 1961), pp. 10–12. The 1967 citations are taken from Gary Snyder, "Buddhism and the Coming Revolution," *San Francisco Oracle* 3 (January 1967), reprinted in EHH 90–93.

18. Patrick D. Murphy, *A Place for Wayfaring: The Poetry and Prose of Gary Snyder* (Corvallis: Oregon State University Press, 2000), p. 93.

19. Fredric Jameson, *Postmodernism, or, the Cultural Logic of Late Capitalism* (Durham, NC: Duke University Press, 1991), p. 51.

20. The Print Mint statement is quoted in Ben Fong-Torres, *The Rice Room: Growing Up Chinese-American—From Number Two Son to Rock 'n' Roll* (New York: Plume, 1994), pp. 145–46.

21. *San Francisco Oracle* editorial, quoted in Laurence Leamer, *The Paper Revolutionaries: The Rise of the Underground Press* (New York: Simon and Schuster, 1972), p. 43.

22. "Scenedrome," *Berkeley Barb*, 13 January 1967.

23. Harvey R. Kubernik, "Innerview (Interview with Allen Ginsberg)," in *The Rolling Stone Book of the Beats: The Beat Generation and American Culture*, ed. Holly George-Warren (New York: Hyperion, 1999), p. 265. For photographs of Snyder, Ginsberg, Greer, and McClure at the Be-in, see Lisa Law, *Flashing on the Sixties: Photographs by Lisa Law* (1987; San Francisco: Chronicle Books, 1997).

24. See Barry Miles, *Ginsberg: A Biography* (1989; New York: HarperPerennial, 1990), pp. 394–95. Also see the discussions of the Be-in included in *I Want to Take You Higher: The Psychedelic Era 1965–1969*, ed. James Henke and Parke Puterbaugh for the Rock and Roll Hall of Fame and Museum, with essays by Charles Perry and Barry Miles (San Francisco: Chronicle Books, 1997), and in Lawrence Ferlinghetti and Nancy Peters, *Literary San Francisco* (San Francisco: City Lights/Harper and Row, 1980).

25. "Hippies' Love and Activism: They Came . . . Saw . . . Stared," *San Francisco Chronicle*, 15 January 1967.

26. See David Farber, "The Intoxicated State/Illegal Nation: Drugs in the Sixties Counterculture," in *Imagine Nation: The American Counterculture of the 1960s and '70s*, ed. Peter Braunstein and Michael William Doyle (New York: Routledge, 2002), p. 29.

27. Carl Jung, quoted in Ilene Susan Fort, "Altered State(s): California Art and the Inner World," in *Reading California: Art, Image, and Identity, 1900–2000*, ed. Stephanie Barron, Sheri Bernstein, and Ilene Susan Fort (Berkeley: Los Angeles County Museum of Art/University of California Press, 2000), p. 45. Fort explains that the mandalas projected at the Trips Festival "derived from emulsions floating in water." For more on the psychedelic atmosphere of the Trips Festival and the Avalon Ballroom scene, see Henke and Puterbaugh, eds., *I Want to Take You Higher*, pp. 68–69, 91–96.

28. See D. A. Pennebaker, *Monterey Pop* (The Foundation, January 1969), 79 minutes, 35 mm film. For photographs of hippie Indians at Monterey, see Law, *Flashing on the Sixties*, and Joel Selvin, *Monterey Pop: The Concert That Rocked a Generation* (San Francisco: Chronicle Books, 1992).

29. *San Francisco Oracle* 7 (February 1967): 31.

30. See Frank Zappa and the Mothers of Invention, *We're Only in It for the Money* (1968) (Rykodisc 10503, 1995).

31. Michel Maffesoli, *The Time of the Tribes*, trans. Don Smith (London: Sage, 1996), pp. 28, 79. See also Mike Featherstone, *Undoing Culture: Globalization, Postmodernism and Identity* (London: Sage, 1995), pp. 42, 46–47. The distinction between *communitas* and *societas*, as theorized by Victor Turner in the late 1960s and picked up by Maffesoli and Featherstone decades later, has been crucial to the ideological programs of leftist collectives since the nineteenth century, according to Raymond Williams, *Keywords: A Vocabulary of Culture and Society*, rev. ed. (New York: Oxford University Press, 1983), who contrasts "the more direct, more total and therefore more significant relationships of *community* and the more formal, more abstract and more instrumental relationships of the *state*, or of *society* in its modern sense" (p. 76).

32. For the original hit singles, both of which made the *Billboard* Top Ten during the Summer of Love, see Scott McKenzie, "San Francisco (Be Sure to Wear Flowers in Your Hair)" (Ode 103, 1967), and Eric Burdon and the Animals, "San Franciscan Nights" (MGM 13769, 1967). In a recent essay, Jeff A. Hale, "The White Panthers' 'Total Assault on the Culture,'" in Braunstein and Doyle, eds., *Imagine Nation*, p. 130, reveals that British folk singer Donovan may have tipped off Burdon, since he urged listeners to "Fly Translove Airways, get you there on time," in his 1966 song "The Fat Angel." What is more, the Jefferson Airplane subsequently covered Donovan's song in live Bay Area performances in 1966 and 1967. Michael William Doyle tracks the emergence of the name "Psychedelphia" in "Staging the Revolution: Guerilla Theater as a Countercultural Practice, 1965–1968," *Imagine Nation*, p. 83.

33. Maffesoli, *The Time of the Tribes*, pp. 19, 53.

34. See Gilles Deleuze and Felix Guattari, *A Thousand Plateaus: Capitalism and Schizophrenia*, trans. Brian Massumi (Minneapolis: University of Minnesota Press, 1987), pp. 321, 325–26.

35. Caren Kaplan, *Questions of Travel: Postmodern Discourses of Displacement* (Durham, NC: Duke University Press, 1996), chap. 3, "Traveling Theorists: Cosmopolitan Diasporas."

36. Marianna Torgovnick, *Gone Primitive* (Chicago: University of Chicago Press, 1990), pp. 205, 223. For an example of how the oceanic ideal functioned in hippie consciousness, see the Thalassa theory as reworked by Norman O. Brown, *Love's Body* (1966; Berkeley: University of California Press, 1990). The Thalassa theory, which derives from Freud's *Beyond the Pleasure Principle* and Sandor Ferenczi's *Thalassa: A Theory of Genitality*, emphasizes an uncanny human desire, prevalent in each act of coitus, to return to an "oceanic" intrauterine existence. In the 1960s, Brown used this theory as the basis for healing and community building in an erotic "mass psychology." According to Brown, Thalassa was "not a mob psychology, but the psychology of mankind as a whole, as one mass, or one body . . . a collective unconscious" (pp. 85–86). For oceanic themes in recent Pacific Rim discourse, see Christopher L. Connery, "The Oceanic Feeling and the Regional Imaginary," in *Global/Local: Cultural Production and the Transnational Imaginary*, ed. Rob Wilson and Wimal Dissanayake (Durham, NC: Duke University Press, 1996), pp. 284–311.

37. Marianna Torgovnick, *Primitive Passions: Men, Women, and the Quest for Ecstasy* (New York: Knopf, 1997), p. 8.

38. Philip J. Deloria, *Playing Indian* (New Haven, CT: Yale University Press, 1998), pp. 144–45.

39. For the review of Shankar at Monterey, see the *Berkeley Barb*, 29 June 1967. Arguably, the same patronizing attitude colored perceptions of performances by Otis Redding and Jimi Hendrix, two African-American performers on the festival bill. In a concert review appearing in *Esquire*, rock critic Robert Christgau, "Anatomy of a Love Festival," in *Any Old Way You Choose It: Rock and Other Pop Music, 1967–1973* (Baltimore: Penguin, 1973), pp. 12–34, ignominiously called the outlandishly dressed Hendrix a "psychedelic Uncle Tom," suggesting that Hendrix was not just playing (and burning) his guitar during his memorable performance but also playing to the desires of his white audience. Similarly, it is not so much the music of Redding that has been remembered over the years but rather his gracious gesture of naming the Monterey audience the "Love Crowd." "This is the 'Love Crowd,' right?" the southern soul singer asked the hippies during a break between songs. "We all love each other, don't we?" I cannot help but think that some portion of the audience took this bestowal of good feelings as an assurance that all was right with race relations in the United States in the late 1960s, when clearly it was not.

40. Buffy Sainte-Marie, "Buffy on Hippies—They'll Never Be Indians" (interview), *Berkeley Barb*, 6 July 1967.

41. See Leslie Marmon Silko, "An Old-Time Indian Attack Conducted in Two Parts," *Shantih* 4, no. 2 (Summer–Fall 1979): 3–5. See also Geary Hobson, "The Rise of White Shamanism as a New Version of Cultural Imperialism," in *The Remembered Earth: An Anthology of Contemporary Native American Literature*, ed. Geary Hobson (1979; Albuquerque: University of New Mexico Press, 1981), pp. 100–108. I discuss these texts in more detail in the epilogue.

42. See Richard Drinnon, *Facing West: The Metaphysics of Indian-Hating and Empire-Building* (Minneapolis: University of Minnesota Press, 1980). Also see Michael Castro, *Interpreting the Indian: Twentieth-Century Poets and the Native American* (Albuquerque: University of New Mexico Press, 1983). Castro states that Tom Hayden's *The Love of Possessions Is a Disease with Them* (1972) illustrates a common transference of liberal sympathies from the Vietnamese to Native Americans, a people "similarly wronged" (p. 156). In *Playing Indian*, Philip Deloria quotes Tuscarora activist Wallace Mad Bear Anderson as saying, "When I walk down the streets of Saigon, those people look like my brothers and sisters" (p. 163). Similarly, in one of Louise Erdrich's most affecting stories, "A Bridge," in *Love Medicine* (1993; New York: Perennial, 2001), pp. 167–80, a Vietnam War veteran has flashbacks when he sees the "Asian, folded eyes" of the young Indian girl with whom he is about to have sex.

43. Allen Ginsberg, Timothy Leary, and Allen Watts, quoted in "Changes" (Houseboat Summit transcript), *San Francisco Oracle* 7 (February 1967): 3, 6.

44. Snyder, "Poetry and the Primitive" (lecture version).

45. Gary Snyder, quoted in "Changes," p. 34.

46. See David Perkins, *A History of Modern Poetry, Volume Two: Modernism and After* (Cambridge, MA: Harvard University Press, 1987), p. 542. See also Helen Vendler, "American Zen: Gary Snyder's *No Nature*," in *Soul Says: On Recent Poetry* (Cambridge, MA: Harvard University Press, 1995), p. 117.

47. Lew Welch, letter to Gary Snyder, 6 May 1962, in *I Remain: The Letters of Lew Welch & the Correspondence of His Friends, Volume Two, 1960–1971*, ed. Donald M. Allen (Bolinas, CA: Grey Fox, 1980), pp. 68–69.

48. Katsunori Yamazato, "Snyder, Sakaki, and the Tribe," in *Gary Snyder: Dimensions of a Life*, ed. Jon Halper (San Francisco: Sierra Club Books, 1991), pp. 99–100. The seedy atmosphere of the Shinjuku district during the 1960s is captured brilliantly (if also scarily) in photographs by Daido Moriyama, *Daido Moriyama: Stray Dog*, ed. Sandra S. Phillips and Alexandra Monroe (San Francisco: San Francisco Museum of Modern Art, 1999).

49. Allen Ginsberg, letter to Gary Snyder, 15 March 1964, Gary Snyder Papers, University of California Library, Davis.

50. Snyder, quoted in Allen, ed., *On Bread and Poetry*, p. 44.

51. See Kaiya Yamada ("Pon"), *Towairaito Furiikusu: Kokon Hankobunkajin-tachi* (Twilight of the Counterculture "Freaks") (Osaka: Bireji Presu, 2002). I refer here to a portion of the unpublished English translation done by Sachiko Tamura and provided to me by Gary Snyder.

52. Gary Snyder, note included in Nanao Sakaki, *Bellyfulls*, trans. Neale Hunter (Eugene, OR: Toad Press, 1966), n.p.

53. Will Petersen, letter to Gary Snyder, 22 January 1958, Gary Snyder Papers, University of California Library, Davis.

54. Will Petersen, letter to Gary Snyder, 2 December 1957, Gary Snyder Papers, University of California Library, Davis.

55. See Masa Uehara, letters to Gary Snyder, 14 and 17 July 1966, Gary Snyder Papers, University of California Library, Davis. Hisao Kanaseki's memory of Mr. Uehara appears in "An Easy Rider at Yase," in Halper, ed., *Gary Snyder*, p. 75.

56. Nanao Sakaki, letter to Gary Snyder, 30 June 1967, Gary Snyder Papers, University of California Library, Davis.

57. Gary Snyder, letter to Lois Snyder Hennessy, 3 July 1967, Lois Snyder Hennessy Papers, Special Collections and Archives, Eric V. Hauser Memorial Library, Reed College, Portland, Oregon.

58. See Gary Snyder, letter to Lew Welch, 3 August 1967, in *I Remain, Volume Two*, pp. 143–44.

59. Rey Chow, *Writing Diaspora: Tactics of Intervention in Contemporary Cultural Studies* (Bloomington: University of Indiana Press, 1993), p. 50.

60. Deleuze and Guattari, *A Thousand Plateaus*, p. 311.

61. Gary Snyder, "Some Yips & Barks in the Dark," in *Naked Poetry*, ed. Stephen Berg and Robert Mezey (Indianapolis: Bobbs-Merrill, 1969), p. 357.

62. Deleuze and Guattari, *A Thousand Plateaus*, p. 311.

63. Ibid.

64. Ibid.

65. Ibid., pp. 311–12.

66. For evidence of *yabyum* (or sitting coitus meditation) in this poem, see Murphy, *A Place for Wayfaring*, p. 96.

67. Tim Dean, *Gary Snyder and the American Unconscious: Inhabiting the Ground* (New York: St. Martin's Press, 1990), p. 145.

68. Tom Lavazzi, "Pattern of Flux: The 'Torsion Form' in Gary Snyder's Poetry," *American Poetry Review* 18, no. 4 (July/August 1989): 41.

69. Robert Kern, "Recipes, Catalogues, Open Form Poetics: Gary Snyder's Archetypal Voice," *Contemporary Literature* 18, no. 2 (Spring 1977): 183.

70. Snyder, "Some Yips & Barks in the Dark," in Berg and Mezey, eds., *Naked Poetry*, p. 357.

71. Chow, *Writing Diaspora*, p. 51.

72. The Asian woman's offering of grace in this instance is similar to the one Slavoj Zizek, *Tarrying with the Negative: Kant, Hegel, and the Critique of Ideology* (Durham, NC: Duke University Press, 1993), notices in Hegelian dialectics. According to Zizek, "when the subject, the human mortal, by way of his offer of self-sacrifice, surmounts his finitude and attains divine heights, the Master responds with the sublime gesture of Grace, the ultimate proof of his humanity. Yet this act of grace is at the same time branded by the irreducible mark of a

forced empty gesture: the Master ultimately makes a virtue out of necessity, in that he promotes as a free act what he is in any case compelled to do. . . . Is not the Master, insofar as he depends on the other's recognition, effectively his own servant's servant?" (p. 166).

73. Karen Kelsky, "Flirting with the Foreign: Interracial Sex in Japan's 'International' Age," in Wilson and Dissanayake, eds., *Global/Local*, pp. 187–88. In the late 1980s, "yellow cab" was the degrading epithet assigned by Japanese males to a single Japanese woman who actively sought sexual relations with Western men, usually during a freewheeling holiday from her boring office job.

74. Ibid., p. 188.

75. Karen Kelsky, *Women on the Verge: Japanese Women, Western Dreams* (Durham, NC: Duke University Press, 2001), pp. 147, 186–87.

76. See David Palumbo-Liu, *Asian/American: Historical Crossings of a Racial Frontier* (Stanford, CA: Stanford University Press, 1999), pp. 90–91. For a related discussion of how Japanese war brides attempted to acquire the " 'culturally superior' poise of whites" in postwar suburban America, see Caroline Chung Simpson, " 'Out of an Obscure Place': Japanese War Brides and Cultural Pluralism in the 1950s," *Differences: A Journal of Feminist Cultural Studies* 10, no. 3 (Fall 1998): 47–81.

77. Palumbo-Liu, *Asian/American*, pp. 385–86.

78. Richard Candida Smith, *Utopia and Dissent: Art, Poetry, and Politics in California* (Berkeley: University of California Press, 1995), p. 387.

79. Palumbo-Liu, *Asian/American*, p. 26. Of course, as Susan Koshy, "Morphing Race into Ethnicity: Asian Americans and Critical Transformations of Whiteness," *Boundary 2* 28, no. 1 (Spring 2001): 153–194, reminds us, it is crucial to recognize that miscegenation debates have been subject to various rhetorical triangulations over the years. In the American South, for example, Asian-American immigrants who have not yet mixed with whites have nonetheless been able to "prove their whiteness" by distinguishing themselves from African-Americans, with whom white southerners have a complex sexual history, one that is shrouded in secrecy and wrapped by denial.

80. See Deleuze and Guattari, *A Thousand Plateaus*, p. 325.

81. For the "great trans-Pacific jump" taken by Japanese war brides, see J. W. Smith and William L. Worden, "They're Bringing Home Japanese Wives," *Saturday Evening Post*, 19 January 1952, p. 24, along with the corresponding discussion in Chung Simpson, " 'Out of an Obscure Place,' " p. 52.

82. See Kaplan, *Questions of Travel*, 85–91, 131–39, and Kelsky, *Women on the Verge*, pp. 14, 32, 234–35.

83. Katsunori Yamazato, "Seeking a Fulcrum: Gary Snyder and Japan, 1956–1975" (Ph.D. diss., University of California, Davis, 1987), p. 103. Snyder describes the art of "moon-watching" in "Lookout's Journal" (EHH 2).

84. See Connery, "The Oceanic Feeling," in Wilson and Dissanayake, *Global/Local*, pp. 292–93. Earlier in his essay (p. 289), Connery explains that

Freud, who gave an account of his own "oceanic feelings" in *The Future of an Illusion*, later referred to them in *Civilization and Its Discontents* as the survival of an infantile stage that is usually sublimated in the adult ego's acceptance of civilization and all its attendant neuroses.

85. Gary Snyder, correspondence with the author, 23 March 1998. In an uncanny coincidence, "Kai" also happens to be the Polynesian word for the Pacific Ocean. See Arrell Morgan Gibson, *Yankees in Paradise: The Pacific Basin Frontier* (Albuquerque: University of New Mexico Press, 1993), p. 13.

86. Compare my take on incarnation with the argument put forward by Michael Davidson in *The San Francisco Renaissance*, chap. 3, "Spotting That Design: Incarnation and Interpretation in Gary Snyder and Philip Whalen."

87. Candida Smith, *Utopia and Dissent*, pp. 253, 377.

88. Ibid., pp. 394–95. Nanao Sakaki appears alongside Snyder, Masa, Kai, and Gen on the cover of the first edition of *The Real Work* (1980).

89. See "Land Lovers" (photographs by Phillip Harrington), *Look*, 4 November 1969, pp. 54–61.

90. Walt Whitman, "Passage to India," in *Leaves of Grass*, ed. Sculley Bradley and Harold W. Blodgett (New York: Norton Critical Editions, 1973), p. 412.

Digging In

1. Joanne Kyger speaks about Snyder's early plans to build a Japanese-style house back in America in *The Japan and India Journals 1960–1964* (Bolinas, CA: Tombouctou, 1981), p. 119.

2. Three weeks after Welch's disappearance, Snyder told his mother, "Lew was found alive—ok—guess he's in SF" (Gary Snyder, letter to Lois Snyder Hennessy, 11 June 1971, Lois Snyder Hennessy Papers, Special Collections and Archives, Eric V. Hauser Memorial Library, Reed College, Portland, Oregon). A week later, Howard McCord wrote to Snyder, confirming the news: "Heard about Lew Welch from Jack, then later, *revidivus*, the prodigal found. Bless him. Hope he's getting it all together" (Howard McCord, letter to Gary Snyder, 18 June 1971, Gary Snyder Papers, Department of Special Collections, University of California Library, Davis).

3. Gary Snyder, letters to Philip Whalen, 18 February and 5 October 1970, Philip Whalen Papers, Special Collections and Archives, Eric V. Hauser Memorial Library, Reed College, Portland, Oregon.

4. For information on San Francisco Zen Center's rural outposts at Tassajara and Green Gulch, including the fund-raising "zenefits" conducted by Snyder, Alan Watts, and San Francisco rock bands, see Michael Downing, *Shoes Outside the Door: Desire, Devotion, and Excess at San Francisco Zen Center* (Washington, DC: Counterpoint, 2001), especially p. 107. Also see David Chadwick, *Crooked Cucumber: The Life and Zen Teaching of Shunryu Suzuki* (New York: Broadway Books,

1999), especially p. 278, as well as Rick Fields, *How the Swans Came to the Lake: A Narrative History of Buddhism in America*, 3d rev. ed. (Boston: Shambhala, 1992), p. 259. Photographs of Tassajara and Green Gulch are set alongside illuminating Zen lessons in *Wind Bell: Teachings from the San Francisco Zen Center 1968–2001*, ed. Michael Wenger (Berkeley: North Atlantic Books, 2002).

5. For discussion of the Diggers' Green City program in the late 1960s, see Peter Berg, "Beating the Drum with Gary," in *Gary Snyder: Dimensions of a Life*, ed. Jon Halper (San Francisco: Sierra Club Books, 1991), p. 381. Snyder mentions the Green City idea in two essays about bioregionalism: "The Place, the Region, and the Commons" (PW 47) and "Coming into the Watershed" (PS 233).

6. See Charles A. Reich, *The Greening of America* (1970; New York: Bantam, 1971). For a similar evaluation, see Theodore Roszak, *Where the Wasteland Ends: Politics and Transcendence in Postindustrial Society* (Garden City, NY: Doubleday, 1972). The "Land Lovers" feature, with photographs by Phillip Harrington, was published in *Look*, 4 November 1969, pp. 54–61. "The Great Woodstock Rock Trip" was a special issue of *Life* published shortly after the music festival took place in the summer of 1969.

7. Gary Snyder, "The Poet Speaks Out: Earth Day Speech," Colorado State College, Greeley, Colorado, 22 April 1970, Gary Snyder Papers, University of California Library, Davis. Snyder's memory of this event is the subject of "Earth Day and the War against the Imagination" (PS 56–64). Philip Deloria, *Playing Indian* (New Haven, CT: Yale University Press, 1998), pp. 166–67, is one of a growing number of scholars who claim that "Seattle's wisdom" was actually the work of a white screenwriter in Texas, who published the speech as part of an obscure television script in 1972.

8. Leslie Marmon Silko, "An Old-Time Indian Attack Conducted in Two Parts," *Shantih* 4, no. 2 (Summer–Fall 1979): 4.

9. Wendy Rose, "The Great Pretenders: Further Reflections on Whiteshamanism," in *The State of Native America: Genocide, Colonization, and Resistance*, ed. Annette Jaimes (Boston: South End Press, 1992), p. 418n. See also Geary Hobson, "The Rise of White Shamanism as a New Version of Cultural Imperialism," in *The Remembered Earth: An Anthology of Contemporary Native American Literature*, ed. Geary Hobson (1979; Albuquerque: University of New Mexico Press, 1981), p. 105. For more on Haunani-Kay Trask's indictment of the "local" affiliations adopted by white settlers in Hawaii, see Rob Wilson, *Reimagining the American Pacific: From "South Pacific" to Bamboo Ridge and Beyond* (Durham, NC: Duke University Press, 2000), pp. 122, 149.

10. For discussion of Snyder's cultural "borrowing," see Silko, "An Old-Time Indian Attack," p. 5. For pointed critiques of New Age falsification of Native American sources, see Rose, "The Great Pretenders," in Jaimes, ed., *The State of Native America*, pp. 404, 412–15. See also Marianna Torgovnick, *Primitive Passions: Men, Women, and the Quest for Ecstasy* (New York: Knopf, 1997), chap. 8, "Medicine Wheels and Spirituality: Primitivism in the New Age."

11. See Silko, "An Old-Time Indian Attack," p. 5. In this context, it is interesting to note that "Prayer for the Great Family," a poem Snyder clearly indicated was borrowed from "a Mohawk prayer" (TI 25), appeared in *Look* magazine next to a photograph of an anonymous white couple cradling a newborn baby. See Gary Snyder, "Prayer for the Great Family," *Look*, 26 January 1971, pp. 54–59. The photograph was taken by Paul Fusco.

12. See Tim Dean, "The Other Voice: Cultural Imperialism and Poetic Impersonality in Gary Snyder's *Mountains and Rivers without End*," *Contemporary Literature* 41, no. 3 (Fall 2000): 462–94, especially pp. 486–91.

13. Gary Snyder, quoted in Jonathan White, "Hanging Out with Raven (interview with Gary Snyder)," in *Talking on the Water: Conversations about Nature and Creativity* (San Francisco: Sierra Club Books, 1994), p. 149.

14. Gary Snyder, quoted in "Land Lovers."

15. Gary Snyder, quoted in Ann Charters, *Kerouac: A Biography* (San Francisco: Straight Arrow Books, 1973), pp. 286, 287.

16. Gary Snyder, quoted in Ekbert Faas, *Towards a New American Poetics: Essays and Interviews* (Santa Barbara, CA: Black Sparrow Press, 1978), pp. 113, 114.

17. See Katsunori Yamazato, "How to Be in This Crisis: Gary Snyder's Cross-Cultural Vision in *Turtle Island*," in *Critical Essays on Gary Snyder*, ed. Patrick D. Murphy (Boston: G. K. Hall, 1991), pp. 230–46.

18. See Gary Snyder, "A Curse on the Men in Washington, Pentagon," *San Francisco Oracle* 8 (March 1967). A copy of this broadside, which Snyder has chosen not to include in any of his selected editions, is conveniently available at the Diggers Web site: http://www.diggers.org. For more on Emmett Grogan's impromptu recitation of "Curse" at a 1967 SDS meeting, the ethnic and racial sparring that followed, and the Weather Underground manifestos to which the poem bore an uncanny resemblance, see Todd Gitlin, *The Sixties: Days of Hope, Days of Rage* (New York: Bantam, 1987), pp. 227–28, 400. For discussion of the *Oracle*'s decision to pull Snyder's poem from the second printing of the "Indian Issue," see Allen Cohen, "The *San Francisco Oracle*: A Brief History," in *Voices from the Underground: Insider Histories of the Vietnam Era Underground Press, Volume One*, ed. Ken Wachsberger (Tempe, AZ: Mica Press, 1993), p. 151.

19. John Oliver Simon, "Sinking Deeper and Deeper into Earth (A Review of *Turtle Island*)," *Kuksu: Journal of Backcountry Writing* 4 (1975): 123.

20. Michael Davidson, *The San Francisco Renaissance: Poetics and Community at Mid-century* (New York: Cambridge University Press, 1989), pp. 109–12. For a similar appraisal of Snyder's political poetry in the early 1970s, see Charles Altieri, "Gary Snyder's *Turtle Island*: The Problem of Reconciling the Roles of Seer and Prophet," *Boundary 2* 4, no. 3 (Spring 1976): 761–77. David A. Carpenter extends the debate over Snyder's prophetic role in "Gary Snyder's Inhumanism, From *Riprap* to *Axe Handles*," *South Dakota Review* 26, no. 1 (Spring 1988): 110–38, as does Andrew Schelling in his negative review of *Axe Handles*, "How the Grinch Imitated Gary Snyder," *Sulfur* 13 (1985): 157–61.

21. See Paul Rossiter and John Evans, "Interview: Gary Snyder," *Studies in the Humanities* 26, nos. 1 and 2 (June and December 1999): 16.

22. For more on the shutdown of People's Park, see Gitlin, *The Sixties*, pp. 253–61. Like the San Francisco hippies at the Be-in, the Berkeley radicals saw fit to afix the image of an American Indian (in this case Geronimo) to their leaflets, which asked the rhetorical question, "Who Owns the Park?" Providing an answer to their own question, the leaflets tracked land ownership in Berkeley back to the Costanoan Indians, and thereby claimed that the university's land title was "covered with blood." As it happened, very few of the people fighting to take this land back in 1968 and 1969 were actually Native Americans.

23. See Yamazato, "How to Be in This Crisis," in Murphy, ed., *Critical Essays on Gary Snyder*, especially p. 233. See also Julia Martin, "Practicing Emptiness: Gary Snyder's Playful Ecological Work," *Western American Literature* 27, no. 1 (1992): 3–19.

24. Helen Vender, "American Zen: Gary Snyder's *No Nature*," in *Soul Says: On Recent Poetry* (Cambridge, MA: Harvard University Press, 1995), p. 117. Patrick D. Murphy, *A Place for Wayfaring: The Poetry and Prose of Gary Snyder* (Corvallis: Oregon State University Press, 2000), offers a rather different assessment, arguing that "while Snyder is gaining increasing recognition as a public intellectual, he nevertheless remains primarily a poet in most of his readers' eyes" (p. 213).

25. For the link between bioregionalism and reinhabitation, see Lawrence Buell, *The Environmental Imagination: Thoreau, Nature Writing, and the Formation of American Culture* (Cambridge, MA: Harvard University Press, 1995), p. 108. Also see Doug Aberley, "Interpreting Bioregionalism: A Story from Many Voices," in *Bioregionalism*, ed. Michael Vincent McGinnis (London: Routledge, 1999), p. 13. For suggestions that indigeneity "need not be based on aboriginal inhabitation," see Bruce Evan Goldstein, "Combining Science and Place-based Knowledge: Pragmatic and Visionary Approaches to Bioregional Understanding," in McGinnis, ed., *Bioregionalism*, p. 161.

26. Snyder, "The Poet Speaks Out."

27. Gary Snyder, quoted in John P. O'Grady, "Living Landscape: An Interview with Gary Snyder," *Western American Literature* 33, no. 3 (Fall 1998): 285.

28. Dan Flores, "Place: Thinking about Bioregional History," in McGinnis, ed., *Bioregionalism*, p. 47.

29. See Lawrence Buell, *Writing for an Endangered World: Literature, Culture, and Environment in the U.S. and Beyond* (Cambridge, MA: Harvard University Press, 2001), chap. 6, "Global Commons as Resource and Icon: Imagining Oceans and Whales."

30. Gary Snyder, quoted in Nicholas O'Connell, *At the Field's End: Interviews with Twenty Pacific Northwest Writers* (Seattle: Madrona Publishers, 1987), p. 318.

31. Gary Snyder, "'Wild' in China," *CoEvolution Quarterly* 19 (Fall 1978): 44.

32. See James McKenzie, "Moving the World a Millionth of an Inch: An Interview with Gary Snyder," *The Beat Diary: The Unspeakable Visions of the Individual* 5 (1977): 152.

33. Mitchell Thomashow, "Toward a Cosmopolitan Bioregionalism," in McGinnis, ed., *Bioregionalism*, pp. 121, 129, 131.

34. Jonathan Bate, *The Dream of the Earth* (Cambridge, MA: Harvard University Press, 2000), p. 38.

35. Dana Phillips, "Ecocriticism, Literary Theory, and the Truth of Ecology," *New Literary History* 30, no. 3 (Summer 1999): 581.

36. Neil Evernden, "Beyond Ecology: Self, Place, and the Pathetic Fallacy," in *The Ecocriticism Reader: Landmarks in Literary Ecology*, ed. Cheryll Glotfelty and Harold Fromm (Athens: University of Georgia Press, 1996), p. 103.

37. For the definitive account of this poetic sequence, see Anthony Hunt, *Genesis, Structure, and Meaning in Gary Snyder's "Mountains and Rivers without End"* (Reno: University of Nevada Press, 2004).

Coyote, Peter, 31
Crapsey, Adelaide, 50
Creeley, Robert, 27, 99
Cumings, Bruce, 6, 17–18, 19

Damon, Maria, 183–84
Davidson, Michael, 31–32, 36, 183, 216, 218, 263, 280–81
De Man, Paul, 106
Dean, Tim, 72, 109, 115, 119, 250, 276–77, 307n
Deleuze, Gilles, 19, 56, 231, 233, 246–49, 251–52, 258–59
Deloria, Philip, 217, 234–35, 338n
Deloria, Vine, 41, 276
Derrida, Jacques, 106
Di Prima, Diane, 31
Diggers, 272, 280
Dirlik, Arif, 18–20
Dissanayake, Wimal, 6
Dolenz, Mickey, 231
Donne, John, 249
Drinkswater, 73, 77
Drinnon, Richard, 236
Duncan, Robert, 23, 36, 190, 217, 219, 301n
Dylan, Bob, 272

Earth First!, 42
Eberhart, Richard, 29
Eisenberg, Evan, 310n
Eisenhower, Dwight, 12, 15
Elder, John, 291
Elegant, Robert, 3
Eliot, T. S., 88, 131; *The Waste Land*, 117
Ellsberg, Daniel, 171
Emerson, Ralph Waldo, 86
Enloe, Cynthia, 328n
Erdrich, Louise, 334n
Eshelman, Clayton, 171, 199
Everson, William (Brother Antoninus), 23, 24, 29, 37, 43; "A Canticle to the Waterbirds," 55

Faas, Ekbert, 279
Farman, Abou, 256
Faulkner, William, 270; "The Bear," 118
Feng-kan, 138
Feng Kuan, 174
Fenollosa, Ernest, 26, 323n
Ferlinghetti, Lawrence, 34, 36–37, 168, 197; "A Coney Island of the Mind," 55
First Zen Institute of America, 129, 140, 169–70, 174
Ford, Gerald, 15–16
Foucault, Michel, 35
Frank, Thomas, 181
Frankenberg, Ruth, 256
Frazer, James, 202
Freud, Sigmund, 58, 204
Frobenius, Leo, 60–63
Fukuyama, Francis, 17

Ganesh, 75
Gass, Alison, 93, 144, 184–85, 196, 200
Gautama Buddha, 69, 89
Géfin, Laszlo, 104–05
Gibson, William, 3
Ginsberg, Allen, 9, 12, 22–23, 25–27, 29–30, 33, 37, 38, 43, 52, 124, 126, 158–62, 173, 188, 196–97, 203, 217–20, 228–29, 237–39, 270, 285, 301n, 319n; "America," 168; "Howl," 22, 124, 160–61; *Howl and Other Poems*, 51; "Wichita Vortex Sutra," 282
global/local dialectics, 45–46, 48–49, 60
Goddard, P. E., 63
Godfrey, Arthur, 266
Gold, Herbert, 29–30
Gore, Al, 166
Grateful Dead, 228, 272
Graves, Morris, 36, 53–56, 128; *Bird Wearied by the Length of the Winter of 1944*, 54–56; *Consciousness Assuming the Form of a Crane*, 54; *Shorebirds*, 54

Rivera, Diego, 7
Rivet, Paul, 62
Robertson, David, 109, 111–12, 123, 220–21
Rolling Stone, 223, 266
Roosevelt, Franklin Delano, 9
Roosevelt, Theodore, 8
Rose, Wendy, 217, 275
Roszak, Theodore, 25, 289
Rubin, Jerry, 227–29
Russo, Linda, 327n

Said, Edward, 300n
Saijo, Albert, 128, 168
Sainte-Marie, Buffy, 235
Sakaki, Nanao, 189, 238–43, 290
San Francisco: Chinatown district, 28, 33, 167–68; City Lights Bookstore, 34, 100, 129, 168; Haight-Ashbury district, 30–31, 37, 216, 223, 227–38, 274; international expositions, 7–8, 49, 59; North Beach district, 33–34, 37, 168, 190; *San Francisco Oracle*, 223, 228–29, 231, 237, 280; San Francisco Renaissance, 21–37, 101, 216; San Francisco State Poetry Center, 33; San Francisco Zen Center, 24, 31, 272; Tenderloin district, 230
Sasaki, Ruth Fuller, 129, 169, 190
Sasaki Sokei-an, 129
Sauer, Carl, 61
Saxton, Alexander, 165
Schafer, Edward, 143
Scherr, Max, 223, 229
Schlesinger, Arthur, 256–57
Seami Motokiyo, 72
See, Carolyn, 17
Sellars, Peter, 3
Sesso, Oda, 169
Seton, Ernest Thompson, 48
Shaku, Soyen, 24
Shankar, Ravi, 30, 231, 234–35
Shelley, Percy, 173

Shih poetry, 104–05
Shih-te, 133, 138, 141, 143–44
Shiva, 75, 198, 228
Shonen Knife, 3
Shultz, George, 16
Sierra Nevada mountains, 100, 102, 108–24, 135, 146–48, 154, 180, 270
Silko, Leslie Marmon, 217, 235, 275–76
Simpson, Caroline Chung, 328n, 336n
Six Gallery Reading, 22–23, 28, 32–33, 38, 123, 160, 168
Smith, Huston, 91, 198
Smith, Jedediah, 277
Snyder, Anthea, 199
Snyder, Gary: and bioregionalism, 129, 272, 284–94; and blacklisting by FBI, 66, 108, 126, 128–29; boyhood of, 47–50, 269; creaturely sensibility of 54; departure for Japan, 157, 161, 163–64, 168, 180, 222; and gender relations, 41–42, 88, 92–93, 109–10, 157–58, 176, 179, 182–85, 187–213, 241–42, 247–51, 253–59, 329n; on Hokkaido Island, 288; at "Houseboat Summit," 237–38; in India, 196–200, 213, 216, 218; at Indiana University, 64–65, 132; at Kitkitdizze, 41, 270–71, 282, 290; in Kyoto, 157, 168–74, 187–88, 213, 220, 238; and National Park Service, 65–66, 100, 226; as off-shore ambassador of the San Francisco Renaissance, 156, 160, 162–63, 172, 199, 213, 216, 266, 269; on oil tankers, 131, 182; Pulitzer Prize recipient, 41, 235, 275; and "real work," 110–11, 122, 135, 222, 282–83; at Reed College, 50–53, 57, 64, 132, 159, 193–94, 269; return to Turtle Island, 222, 239, 241, 259, 262–63, 270–75, 278, 288; at Six Gallery Reading, 22–23, 28; on Suwa-no-se Island, 41, 241–44, 260–61, 266; at University of California—Berkeley, 66–67, 100–01,

Snyder, Gary (continued)
104, 112–13, 132–33, 135, 155, 158–60, 208, 215, 217–19, 239, 283; at University of California—Davis, 275, 304n; "yellowface" portraits of, 40, 157–68, 178

Snyder, Gary (published poetry): "Above Pate Valley," 153–54; "Across Lamarck Col," 212; "After Work," 182–84, 208; "Alysoun," 200; "At Five A.M. Off the North Coast of Sumatra," 131; "August on Sourdough, A Visit from Dick Brewer," 179–80; *Axe Handles*, 250, 260, 271; *The Back Country*, 40, 59, 107, 110, 155–58, 175–216, 240, 248, 255, 265; "The Bath," 193; "The Bed in the Sky," 260–61; "Beneath My Hand and Eye the Distant Hills, Your Body," 208, 210–12; "Burning," 85–96, 99, 111; "Burning Island," 260; "Call of the Wild," 278–79; "The Circumambulation of Mt. Tamalpais," 220; "Cold Mountain Poems," 101, 132–55, 157; "A Curse on the Men in Washington, Pentagon," 280; *Dangers on Peaks*, 271; "Dullness in February: Japan," 204; "Everybody Lying on Their Stomachs, Head toward the Candle, Reading, Sleeping, Drawing," 260; "Fire in the Hole," 182; "First Landfall on Turtle Island," 262–63, 287; "For All," 285–86; "For the Boy Who Was Dodger Point Lookout Fifteen Years Ago," 184–85, 196; "For the Children," 281; "For the West," 207–10, 222; "Four Poems for Robin," 193–96, 222, 260–61; *Fudo Trilogy*, 220; *The Gary Snyder Reader*, 272; "Go Round," 200; "Hay for the Horses," 71; "Home from the Sierra," 179–80; "How Many More Times," 200; "Hunting," 74, 77–85, 89, 92; "I Went into the Maverick Bar," 282; "It Was When," 260; "Kai, Today," 261; "Kyoto Footnote," 200–01; "Kyoto: March," 130; "Logging," 68–77, 81, 89, 93, 179, 183; "Lying in Bed on a Late Morning," 200; "The Manichaeans," 192, 200; "Marin-an," 181; "Maya," 200; "Meeting the Mountains," 264–65; "Mid-August at Sourdough Mountain Lookout," 104–08, 115, 117, 125; "Migration of Birds," 80, 126–28, 179, 287; "Milton by Firelight," 114, 119–22; "Mother Earth: Her Whales," 286–88; *Mountains and Rivers without End*, 50, 66, 169, 271, 284, 292–94; *Myths & Texts*, 39, 60, 66–100, 102–03, 111, 135, 146, 154, 156–57, 185, 190, 203, 227, 250, 275, 293; "Nanao Knows," 240; "Night," 200; "Night Herons," 80, 278, 287–88; *No Nature*, 272, 284; "Nooksack Valley," 124–26, 179; "North Beach Alba," 200; "Not Leaving the House," 261–62; "Oil," 181–82; "Piute Creek," 114–19; "The Plum Blossom Poem," 208; "Poke Hole Fishing after the March," 266; "Prayer for the Great Family," 276; "The Public Bath," 186–87; "The Rainy Season," 154; *Regarding Wave*, 40–41, 74, 110, 193, 203, 208, 213, 216, 241–67, 270; *Riprap*, 40, 100–31, 135, 146, 148, 154, 156–57, 171, 186; "Riprap," 122–24; "Robin," 200; "Rolling in at Twilight," 180; "Roots," 260; "The Sappa Creek," 131; "Shark Meat," 260; "Six Years," 188–89, 192–93, 207; "Smokey the Bear Sutra," 282–83; "Song of the Slip," 250–51; "Song of the Tangle," 248–51; "Song of the View," 253–55; "The Spring," 182; "A Stone Garden," 131; "T-2 Tanker Blues," 131; "This Tokyo," 131, 204–06; "Three Worlds,